Managing Decentralisation

A New Role for Labour Market Policy

OECD

ORGANISATION FOR ECONOMIC CO-OPERATION AND DEVELOPMENT

ORGANISATION FOR ECONOMIC CO-OPERATION AND DEVELOPMENT

Pursuant to Article 1 of the Convention signed in Paris on 14th December 1960, and which came into force on 30th September 1961, the Organisation for Economic Co-operation and Development (OECD) shall promote policies designed:
- to achieve the highest sustainable economic growth and employment and a rising standard of living in member countries, while maintaining financial stability, and thus to contribute to the development of the world economy;
- to contribute to sound economic expansion in member as well as non-member countries in the process of economic development; and
- to contribute to the expansion of world trade on a multilateral, non-discriminatory basis in accordance with international obligations.

The original member countries of the OECD are Austria, Belgium, Canada, Denmark, France, Germany, Greece, Iceland, Ireland, Italy, Luxembourg, the Netherlands, Norway, Portugal, Spain, Sweden, Switzerland, Turkey, the United Kingdom and the United States. The following countries became members subsequently through accession at the dates indicated hereafter: Japan (28th April 1964), Finland (28th January 1969), Australia (7th June 1971), New Zealand (29th May 1973), Mexico (18th May 1994), the Czech Republic (21st December 1995), Hungary (7th May 1996), Poland (22nd November 1996), Korea (12th December 1996) and the Slovak Republic (14th December 2000). The Commission of the European Communities takes part in the work of the OECD (Article 13 of the OECD Convention).

© OECD 2003

Permission to reproduce a portion of this work for non-commercial purposes or classroom use should be obtained through the Centre français d'exploitation du droit de copie (CFC), 20, rue des Grands-Augustins, 75006 Paris, France, tel. (33-1) 44 07 47 70, fax (33-1) 46 34 67 19, for every country except the United States. In the United States permission should be obtained through the Copyright Clearance Center, Customer Service, (508)750-8400, 222 Rosewood Drive, Danvers, MA 01923 USA, or CCC Online: www.copyright.com. All other applications for permission to reproduce or translate all or part of this book should be made to OECD Publications, 2, rue André-Pascal, 75775 Paris Cedex 16, France.

Foreword

Over the past few years, the OECD's Co-operative Action Programme on Local Economic and Employment Development (LEED) has been exploring the theme of local governance and employment. Back in 1998, it published a ground-breaking report on Local Management for More Effective Employment Policies and organised a high-level conference on Decentralisation of Employment Policy and Local Management in Venice, which revealed that institutional reforms in employment policy not only pursue the goal of policy effectiveness, but also that of improving local governance. This work also came up with a practical definition of the concept of local governance (in terms of policy co-ordination, adaptation to local needs and participation of civil society and business in the orientation of measures) and set an ambitious work agenda, leading to the OECD Study on Local Partnerships carried out in 14 countries and regions.

In March 2003, a conference was held in Warsaw on Decentralisation and New Forms of Governance to examine the lessons thus far and to look at critical issues such as the trade-off between administrative flexibility and public accountability. Not only did the conference identify ways to increase flexibility in policy management while guaranteeing public accountability, but it also put forward a new vision for labour market policy, identifying a key role for it in local and regional economic development strategies. This new vision needs to be articulated and concrete instruments must be developed, and this will be the subject of future work by the OECD, as recommended by the conference. This publication presents the results achieved in Warsaw.

Sylvain Giguère, Deputy Head of the LEED Programme, designed this project and prepared this publication. Mark Considine, of the University of Melbourne, Xavier Greffe, of the Université de Paris I (Sorbonne) and Hugh Mosley, of Social Science Research Centre Berlin (WZB), provided essential advice and assistance throughout the project. Sheelagh Delf, Jane Finlay, Jennah Huxley, Jakub Kotelecki, Corinne Nativel, Jonathan Potter, Ekaterina Travkina and Ewa Wróbel provided essential assistance with the organisation of the conference and/or the preparation of this publication.

This book is published on the responsibility of the Secretary-General of the OECD.

Table of Contents

Chapter 1. **Managing Decentralisation and New Forms of Governance**
by Sylvain Giguère   11
Driving institutional reform: local governance   12
Local governance and policy effectiveness.   13
Decentralisation and flexibility in policy management   15
The challenge of accountability   18
Accountability and cost efficiency.   19
Partnerships and their real contribution   20
Partnership flaws   22
Towards new forms of governance   24
Bibliography   26

Part I
Decentralisation: What Difference Does it Make?

Chapter 2. **Decentralisation: What Difference Does it Make?**
A Synthesis
by Xavier Greffe   31
The foundations, objectives and evaluation criteria
of decentralisation   33
Implementing decentralisation   40
The evaluation function   50
The difficulties and problems of decentralisation.   54
Conclusion: the three debates involving decentralisation   61
Bibliography   62

Chapter 3. **Denmark: Anchoring Labour Market Policies in the Regions**
by Jan Hendeliowitz   65
Unprecedented positive trend in the Danish labour market   66
Limits to the general economic capacity for growth.   67
Reduction in structural unemployment   68
Aim and effect   69
Regionalisation and central co-ordination   71
Challenges to future labour market policies   73
Bibliography   75

Chapter 4. **The US: Decentralisation from the Bottom Up**
by Robert Straits.   77
Shifting powers.   78

From de-categorisation to the one-stop concept................. 79
Funding constraints.. 81
Recommendations... 83

Chapter 5. Germany: The Challenge of Taking an Integrated Approach in a Centralised Framework
by Hartmut Siemon.. 87

The Hartz Commission and the German experience.............. 89
Leipzig's integrated approach of economic clustering
and promoting integration...................................... 92
Implementing the strategy: an example......................... 93

Chapter 6. Italy: Opening the Circuits
by Michele Dau... 97

Decentralisation of employment policy: the main results.......... 98
Better adaptation of local policies to local conditions and needs.... 100
Participation of civil society and private sector actors in decision
making.. 101
What are the limits to flexibility in decentralised frameworks?..... 101

Chapter 7. The Flemish Region of Belgium: Moving Decentralisation One Step Further
by Marion Vrijens... 103

The policy framework.. 104
Two cases of decentralisation of labour market policy............ 111
Some conclusions.. 115

Chapter 8. Poland: Opportunities, Mistakes and Challenges of Decentralisation
by Michał Boni.. 117

Setting up labour market policy................................. 118
Early results... 119
Raising governance issues 122
Challenges for the future 125

Part II
Reconciling Flexibility and Accountability

Chapter 9. Flexibility and Accountability in Labour Market Policy: A Synthesis
by Hugh Mosley... 131

Accountability and flexibility................................... 132
Managerial decentralisation.................................... 136
Political decentralisation: partnerships and accountability......... 141
Privatisation though contracting out............................. 148
Conclusions... 152

Notes 154

Bibliography 155

Chapter 10. **Spain: Modernisation through Regionalisation**
by *Dolores Ruiz* 157
The Spanish labour market. 158
The institutional instruments in employment policy. 158
How Spain is tackling the regionalisation of the public
employment services. 160
Management reform: an example 164
Reforming the PES further 165

Chapter 11. **Canada: Partnerships across Levels**
by *Don Rymes* 169
The labour market and the institutional context 170
Case study 1: the Labour Market Development Agreements. 172
Case study 2: Aboriginal Human Resources Development Strategy.. 175
Case study 3: National Homelessness Initiative 178

Annex. Performance Measurement under the Labour Market
Development Agreements 182

Chapter 12. **The US: Managing Different Levels of Accountability**
by *John Dorrer* 189
Key innovations advanced by WIA 191
The performance accountability framework 193
Performance accountability challenges: data systems and technology. 196
WIA reform proposals: responding to some of the early lessons 198
Conclusion. 200
Bibliography 201

Chapter 13. **The Netherlands: Tackling the Trade-off between Efficiency and Accountability**
by *Elsa Sol* 203
The transition from hierarchy to market 205
The market. What now? 209
Tendering and contracting in practice 211
Conclusions 214
Notes 215
Bibliography 216

Chapter 14. **France: Providing Greater Flexibility at Local Level**
by *Bernard Simonin* 219
A rigid, hierarchical model progressively made more flexible
and decentralised. 220
Uncertainty in the 1990s about which model to adopt. 221
A clarification of approach in 1998: strengthening the accountability .. 225
A limited number of strategic objectives well adapted to policy
priorities 226
The limits of flexibility 229
How to interpret these choices?. 229
Accountability is still insufficient 230

The dominant role of the central government and the creation
of partnerships 232
Two key reforms for the future: the new phase of decentralisation
and a new financial constitution 233
Notes 235
Annex. The Main Components of Employment Policy 236
Bibliography 236

Chapter 15. Poland: A New Accountability Framework for Human Resources Development Programmes
by Grażyna Gęsicka 239

The Polish Agency for Enterprise Development 240
Implementing European structural funds programmes 241
Accountability 242
Flexibility 243
Characteristics of the implementing tools in accordance
with the criteria of accountability and flexibility 244
Conclusions and future perspectives 247

Part III
New Forms of Governance in Practice

Chapter 16. Local Partnerships: Different Histories, Common Challenges – A Synthesis
by Mark Considine 253

The partnership movement 256
The partnership model and current practice 260
Conclusions 269
Bibliography 270

Chapter 17. Tackling the Challenge of Policy Integration
by Murray Stewart 273

From government to governance 274
Area-based initiatives 277
Partnerships 280
Conclusions 288
Bibliography 289

Chapter 18. Improving Governance: The Role of the European Union
by Xavier Prats-Monné 293

Policy orientations of the European Commission on governance 294
Decentralisation and the local dimension of the European
Employment Strategy 296
Conclusion : the role of the European Commission 299
Notes 300

Chapter 19. **The US: Leveraging Government Capacity through New Forms of Governance**
by Randall Eberts 301
US perspective on decentralising services 303
Revisiting the principal-agent theory of decentralisation 304
The role of Workforce Development Boards in partnerships 305
Requisites of effective partnerships at the local level 305
Guidelines 309
Conclusions 310
Bibliography 311

Chapter 20. **Ireland: Linking Public Services and the Local Community**
by Patrick O'Callaghan 313
Partnership in Ireland 314
The local partnership approach 315
Mainstreaming of partnership innovations 319
FÁS' particular experiences 320
Conclusion and perspectives for good governance in Ireland 321
Bibliography 323

Chapter 21. **Austria: Bridging Economic Development and Labour Market Policy**
by Michael Förschner 325
The beginning 326
Reasons for success 328
The future – New design, new relationships? 330

Chapter 22. **The UK: Co-ordinating Public Services through Local Partnerships**
by Michael Geddes 333
Local strategic partnerships 334
Local public service agreements 336
Challenges facing the partnership model of local governance 337
Local and strategic? 337
Inclusive, effective and accountable? 338
From strategy to action to outcomes 340
Performance management 340
Conclusions 341
Bibliography 342

Chapter 23. **Norway: Developing an Integrated Approach in the Regions**
by Petter Knutzen 343
Regional policy and regional reform 344
The background picture 344
Scale and scope of the regional policies 345
Accountability and partnerships 346
New role for the ministry and central government 348
Economic forecasts provide threats and possibilities 349

Chapter 24. **Sweden: New Pathways for Labour Market Policy**
by Leni Svenningsson... 351
The rise of the Swedish model... 352
The fall of the Swedish model... 353
A shift in favour of bipartite decision-making and negotiations... 354
Responsibility for labour market policy taken over
by the government... 354
Partial revival of tripartite co-operation in regional growth
agreements... 355
A long-term, nationwide model for overall national growth policy... 356
A compromise between market and democracy... 357
A process of learning has started... 358

Chapter 25. **Russia: Experimenting with Local Partnerships**
by Valery Popov... 359
A need for a cross-sector approach... 360
Introducing new ways to tackle labour market problems... 360
Applying the partnership concept... 361
Conclusions and perspectives... 362

Chapter 26. **The Impact of Partnerships on Public Governance**
by Paul Cullen... 363
Life cycle issues in partnership organisations... 364
The EU Employment Strategy and the local development dimension... 366
The positive contribution of central co-ordination and technical
assistance to partnership models at national level... 368
Lessons for the OECD and its LEED Programme... 369
Bibliography... 369

List of Boxes
1.1. National governments and partnerships... 21
1.2. Employment and local governance: the next steps... 25

List of Tables
6.1. Distribution of tasks before and after the reform in Italy... 99
8.1. Number of participants and efficiency measure for active labour
market programmes, Poland, 1999-2001... 122
15.1. Implementation of the Human Resource Development
Operational Programme in Poland: projects and beneficiaries... 242
15.2. Scope for accountability and flexibility per instrument
of programme implementation, Poland... 245
16.1. Partnership governance... 261
20.1. Participation of PES staff in Irish partnerships... 320

List of Figures
7.1. Overall employment rate (as a percentage of the population
aged 15 to 64 in Flanders... 105

ISBN 92-64-10470-4
Managing Decentralisation
A New Role for Labour Market Policy
© OECD 2003

Chapter 1

Managing Decentralisation and New Forms of Governance

by

Sylvain Giguère
Deputy Head of the LEED Programme, OECD

Driving institutional reform: local governance

Today, governments devote significant efforts to improve local governance. Local governance, or the ways society finds solutions to its problems and meets its needs, can also be defined using its three main components following OECD (2001a): co-ordination of policies, adaptation of policies to local conditions and participation of civil society and business in the orientation of measures. Through improving local governance, governments seek to make their actions more coherent locally and enhance their contribution to solving local problems in areas falling between individual policy fields. Decentralisation and partnership are tools that they use to reach this goal.

Labour market policy is often at the core of government initiatives to improve local governance. The main reason is the important interactions that labour market policy has with economic development and social inclusion, two key policy areas at local level. Indeed, *co-ordination* of labour market policy with social and economic policies is perhaps the most crucial aspect of local governance. The rationale for co-ordination with social policies is based on the need to improve the employability of disadvantaged workers through more effective active labour market policies (ALMPs) and on the evidence that re-integration into employment is effective in fighting social exclusion and poverty (OECD, 2001b). Basic facts also underpin the need to co-ordinate labour market policy with economic development: tailored labour market programmes and training services can support economic development activities promoting entrepreneurship, enterprise networking and inward investment.

Co-ordination as such is an empty word, however. To enforce co-ordination in practice and release concrete synergies in the local implementation of policies, the two other key elements of local governance need to be applied: adaptation and participation.

Adaptation. There are increasing calls for a better fit of labour market policy to local conditions and needs. Training programmes must meet business demands for skills that change rapidly and adjust to forthcoming local investments. The delivery of employment services must take account of existing (and gaps in) infrastructure, public transport and municipal services. Labour market programmes are more likely to be effective when they take into account the local characteristics of the target groups and seek to match them with local labour market needs (Martin and Grubb, 2001). To generate sustainable outcomes, placement and training services of disadvantaged groups sometimes need to be combined with psychological assistance and traineeship in intermediate labour market (ILM) initiatives or other organisations specialised in progressive re-integration in employment. Additional skills upgrading measures may be required to ensure employment sustainability and progression for the low-qualified re-integrating into the labour market after a long period of inactivity (OECD, 2002).

Participation. Successful policy co-ordination and adaptation require the participation not only of civil servants in neighbouring policy areas, but also of representatives of local civil society and business as both have helpful information on local conditions and needs (Greffe, 2002). For example, information provided by local employers and representatives of the target groups can help target labour market programmes better; in this way, they may contribute to reducing the substitution and displacement effects (respectively, non-subsidised workers and activities displaced by subsidised ones) and deadweight loss (jobs that would have been created anyway) associated with some ALMPs. Organisations of civil society, including employer organisations and trade unions, often provide services that complement those of the public employment service (PES), such as vocational training, placement and special re-integration services through ILMs, and joint steering is required to maximise complementarity while avoiding duplication (OECD, 1998).

Local governance and policy effectiveness

Though it has become a priority in many countries, improving local governance is not the sole driver for institutional reform. Another objective, which is perhaps cited most, is enhancing the effectiveness of policies. Yet the evidence to support the relationship between institutional reform and effectiveness is thin. From the available information, it is hard to draw any clear conclusions on the impact of changes in the institutional framework on the effectiveness of labour market policies (De Koning, 2001). For example, an econometric analysis of decentralisation of ALMPs in Sweden has merely identified an increase of local initiatives as a result of greater involvement of municipalities in decision-making (Lundin and Skedinger, 2000).

Nevertheless, improvements in local governance may have a positive impact on policy effectiveness. This is mainly due to a greater, and better, use of information – a central aspect of local governance. Adapting policies to local conditions implies a greater emphasis on the identification of target group characteristics, a key factor of effectiveness for job subsidies and training services. Information provided by local actors (employers, trade unions, municipalities, community-based organisations) help identify those characteristics and contribute to tailor policies to local labour market conditions and other relevant elements of the local context. The use of sophisticated information represents the main benefit from decentralisation following the principal-agent theory, which concerns the relationship between a principal (central government in this case) and an agent (for example, a lower level of government). But benefits rarely come without costs.

There are costs associated with decentralisation. According to the principal-agent theory, the main cost with decentralisation is the loss of control over the agent's actions. In a decentralised framework, the agent uses the greater flexibility granted to pursue his own interest, which may differ from that of the principal. The size of this cost is proportional to the degree of divergence between the objectives of the agent and those of the principal.

Yet the concept of local governance welcomes such divergence to some extent. Co-ordinating policies implies trying to reconcile different sets of objectives. Also, adapting policies to local conditions suggests that national concerns should be matched with local ones. And greater participation in the orientation of measures means taking account of more views in the conduct of policy. Clearly, a labour market policy implemented in a local governance perspective is likely to pursue a set of objectives broader than a dedicated, nationally-defined one.

Thus, despite better use of the information available, institutional reforms may hardly be led in the sole name of policy effectiveness since the concentration of efforts dedicated to meeting the main policy targets may in the end be weaker. (This does not concern reforms aimed specifically at improving cost-efficiency, as will be seen below.) As the 1998 Venice Conference on Decentralisation and Local Management concluded, "decentralisation is likely to lead to efficiency gains but also to some efficiency losses. In a proper cost-benefit assessment of decentralisation, these efficiency losses must be set against the gains in efficiency, gains in social equity and gains in direct democracy" (OECD, 1999). This explains why the objectives stated for institutional reforms often reflect a mix of governance and effectiveness considerations (see Greffe, Chapter 2 in this book). To reflect a joint concern for local governance and greater effectiveness, "appropriateness" is probably a better word to summarise the objective pursued by institutional reforms.

While co-ordination, adaptation and participation, together with effectiveness are the main principles that guide governments in their local governance reforms, flexibility in policy management is the common mechanism implemented in those reforms. Administrative flexibility is needed in order to design specific programmes or adapt the implementation of existing ones through modifying their terms, conditions and targets in function of the local conditions identified, the information made available by other actors, the development strategies pursued and the initiatives led by other instances. Various tools have been developed with the aim of achieving this.

Decentralisation and flexibility in policy management

The main tool developed by governments to improve local governance is decentralisation. In the 1990s, several countries embarked upon labour market policy decentralisation to ensure that it would be designed and implemented closer to where strategies for economic development are defined and social demands expressed. It has been widely agreed that decentralised decision-making promotes pragmatic solutions to local problems (OECD, 1996).

In principle, decentralisation gives more room for manoeuvre to area-based and integrated approaches. Programmes may be combined with efforts from local and regional governments, the private sector, trade unions and community groups to support better development strategies balancing concerns for economic development, social inclusion and the quality of life. Through greater flexibility in policy management, decentralisation is also expected to make it easier to respond to the growing concern with the inactive, i.e. lone parents, men in their 50s or people receiving disability benefits, who face complex issues and barriers that centralised employment services alone are unable to tackle. In practice, is it the case?

The various forms of decentralisation need to be explored to answer this question. Following OECD (1998), there are two main types of decentralised structure for the design and implementation of labour market policy. The first is when, within the framework of an integrated, country-wide PES, programmes are designed and implemented at regional level, following guidelines or within a policy framework established at national level. This is often the case when the PES is managed in a tripartite fashion, involving trade unions and employer organisations, under the jurisdiction of the Ministry of Labour. Austria and Denmark provide examples of this form of decentralisation.

The other form of decentralisation is when powers to design and implement policies are devolved to regional governments, which may then transfer the responsibility to their own regional PES. Elected assemblies at regional level ensure public accountability as does the national parliament in the case of centrally managed labour market policies. Some federal countries provide examples of this form of decentralisation – Belgium, Canada (in most of the provinces), Mexico and Switzerland – and so do unitary states, such as Italy and Spain. Some of these countries have recently devolved responsibilities in an asymmetric way, giving more powers to some of the regions according to their administrative capacity and willingness to endorse responsibility in the field of labour market policy.

At first glance, the second model, which involves a shift of responsibility, provides greater flexibility at regional level than the integrated PES. However, the central government often continues to play a strong role in the conduct of policy in this model. Apart from Belgium, where there is a clear-cut distribution of powers between the federal state and the three regions, Bruxelles-Capitale, Flanders and Wallonia, which are responsible for ALMPs, in all countries the central government remains responsible for the broad policy framework and its funding, and may also design specific programmes to be implemented by regional PES. In Canada, even in the five provinces where policy-making powers have been fully devolved to the regional government, the federal government remains responsible for the main source of funding for active labour market policy through the Employment Insurance (EI) account and continues to be responsible for youth, women, disabled and indigenous populations for which it designs and delivers specific programmes (see Chapter 11 by Rymes).

In Canada, the provinces and territories also fund social assistance and design ALMPs for its recipients. Regional employment services thus manage a series of programmes funded in different ways and following different accountability patterns. Some other countries also have a mix of policies from national and regional governments being implemented by different networks of offices at local level. This is the case of the United States, where measures and services are provided in a multi-level governance framework involving the federal, state and local levels. To reduce the complexity of this system on the user side, the federal government supports the development of Workforce Investment Boards (WIBs) to co-ordinate the delivery of programmes and operate one-stop agencies. Local offices of this sort exist in several other OECD countries. This does not reduce the administrative burden on the manager side, however, which must comply with different accountability criteria for the various labour market programmes. Programmes funded at various levels are often difficult to co-ordinate, let alone to co-ordinate them with programmes in other policy areas.

Another concern with flexibility in a devolved framework is related to the frequent mismatch between the official and actual degree of decentralisation. There is always some extent of uncertainty with regard to how the new responsibilities will be assumed and managed once powers are granted from one government level to another. Decision-making power that lies with the local offices when labour market policy is under the jurisdiction of the central government may be re-centralised after powers are transferred to regional governments (OECD, 1998). There may also be a mismatch between the responsibilities and the funding transferred ("unfunded mandates"), and the quantity and quality of professional skills may be insufficient at local level with regard to the new responsibilities transferred (see Chapter 8 by Boni). These problems, encountered in several OECD countries, suggest that, even in the case of devolution, decentralisation may in certain circumstances result in a loss of actual flexibility in the local management of policies.

In the integrated PES model of decentralisation, the main determinant of flexibility in policy management lies within the performance management system and more particularly with the targeting mechanism. While broad policy orientations and funding are provided at the national level, local officers are free to vary the use of the different measures available in response to the local conditions and requests, and in some cases to initiate new ones. The flexibility granted is matched by performance monitoring to ensure that progress is made with respect to targets set for a series of outputs (*e.g.* placements into jobs, referrals to various programmes, number of people trained), broken down by categories of users (unemployed, long-term unemployed, social assistance recipients, women, young, ethnic minorities, etc.) following management by objectives.

This sort of flexibility may appear unsatisfactory to local development stakeholders. Performance management systems are often designed to maximise the output-based performance of the PES, which can conflict with local development preoccupations (*e.g.* fostering endogenous development, retaining young people and skilled workers in depressed areas, promoting the social inclusion of disadvantaged groups). For example, monitoring and evaluation of performance sometimes generate screening effects, privileging short-term unemployed over individuals with less skills and work experience, which may not be an acceptable outcome for local actors involved in social inclusion or economic development activities (Finn and Blackmore, 2001).

The actual degree of flexibility in a decentralised framework depends largely on how these targets are fixed and by whom. Are targets set unilaterally at national level? Are they negotiated with the regional and local offices? Is there any role for other government departments, social partners and other local stakeholders in establishing the targets to be pursued by public service offices?

The methods for targeting measures vary significantly across countries. In centralised PES, such as in France, Sweden and the United Kingdom, targets are allocated to the regional level in a top-down fashion. In others, however, such as in Austria, Denmark and, to some extent, Germany, they are agreed in a decentralised procedure (see Mosley *et al.*, 2001; and Mosley, Chapter 9 in this book), though the targeting process does not always involve local actors. In some countries, adjustments have been made to the targeting system to ensure that policies are suited to the local and regional context. In Denmark, the traditional tripartite system has evolved to make room for local and regional authorities in the regional labour market councils, and all take part in a complex negotiation process to reconcile local and national objectives and to reach an agreement regarding the annual targets for the ALMPs (see Hendeliowitz, Chapter 3 in this book). The local community at large is consulted on the main local priorities as part of this process.

The challenge of accountability

Guaranteeing public accountability represents a challenge in a decentralised framework. Decentralisation implies a sharing of responsibility for decision-making among a number of actors, yet the main funding usually comes from the same source, *i.e.* central government. Thus, for public accountability to be maintained in full, policy outcomes still need to be reported to the central government (and ultimately to parliament) with the same rigour as under a centralised framework. There are many obstacles to this.

In the case of devolution, it sometimes proves difficult to agree on an accountability framework politically acceptable to the various government levels concerned. Elected regional governments may pursue policy objectives different from those of the national government and may not consider the accountability framework as binding if not accompanied by financial penalties. The above-mentioned Swedish study identified significant divergences between local and national objectives for labour market policy. Sub-national governments can also transfer responsibilities to an agency and involve social partners and other organisations in the management of programmes, leading to a multiplication of intermediaries which may blur the lines of responsibility (OECD, 1999). All this may weaken the management of performance, and performance itself.

Greater difficulty arises when two government levels are each responsible for funding one of two complementary financial assistance regimes, such as in Canada where the federal government finances the EI account through contributions from employers and employees and the provinces provide the budget for social assistance. This system gives provinces incentives to place social assistance beneficiaries into ALMP programme slots which can serve to requalify them for EI, thereby lowering the burden on provincial budget (a so-called "fiscal displacement" effect).

Managing measures in a multi-level governance framework also increases the administrative burden associated with fulfilling accountability requirements, as illustrated above. In several countries, the PES is responsible for implementing programmes designed at various levels, including national, regional and local. In the US the Workforce Investment Boards implement up to 27 labour market programmes administered at various levels. Each programme has its own accountability line, its own set of terms and conditions and its own timeframe for monitoring and reporting. Being accountable to various administrative layers on a plethora of measures may reduce the local capacity to take a strategic approach to policy implementation in a local governance perspective (OECD, 2001a).

The Warsaw conference identified ways to overcome some of these problems and meet the need to increase flexibility in policy management while guaranteeing accountability. In cases where powers are devolved, service providers should be made accountable to the local authorities for the quality and quantity of services provided and, in turn, local authorities must be accountable to the funding sources. This could reduce the administrative burden on employment services facing multiple accountability lines (see Chapter 4 by Straits). There is also a general consensus that targets for active labour market policies should be subject to negotiations between the central and regional/local levels, as in the Danish case, already mentioned, the Irish (see O'Callaghan, Chapter 20, and below) or the French one (Simonin, Chapter 14 in this book). Such mechanisms can be applied to both models of devolved powers and integrated PES.

Accountability and cost efficiency

Not all models of decentralisation are concerned to the same extent by the challenge of accountability. Decentralisation reforms pursuing cost-efficiency as the main goal are less likely to meet difficulties in guaranteeing public accountability. Yet the outcomes of these reforms in terms of local governance are uncertain.

Reforms pursuing the goal of cost-efficiency usually decentralise the part of policy implementation processes which concerns service delivery. Decentralisation in this case means a transfer of responsibility to private or non-profit service providers. There are many examples of such reforms. The Netherlands progressively privatised the PES in the 1990s. The PES has been split up into a public provider of basic employment services (placement and processing benefit claims) and a privatised company to compete with private service providers for contracts to promote return to work (see Struyven and Steurs, 2002). Placement and part of vocational training services are being transferred to the private sector in several countries, including Belgium and Denmark. In Australia, ALMPs are now delivered through the Job Network, a network of private/community partnerships under contract with the federal government. The Network has been operating in Australia now for five years and contracts have been signed for a further three years. Organisations are contracted through a competitive tender process, and many providers are not-for-profit organisations from the community sector. They are held accountable by local offices of the Department of Employment and Workplace Relations (DEWR) (see OECD, 2001c, for a descriptive evaluation of the Job Network).

Clearly, decentralisation within this type of framework does not encounter the same problems of accountability as those reforms concentrating on improving governance and concerned with co-ordination, adaptation and participation. Private and non-profit providers focus on well-specified targets and report on the results obtained in a format agreed by both parties. Hence, the main benefits from these reforms are likely to be in terms of greater efficiency and effectiveness rather than in improved local governance. In the Australian case, it has been argued that competition and poor linkages within a federal system prevent effective co-ordination with economic development and social inclusion initiatives. Increased reliance on contestability and privatisation may reduce costs and increase efficiency in service delivery, but also create greater problems of fragmentation, with an emphasis on competition rather than co-operation (Considine, 2001). Similar observations have been made at the Warsaw conference on the Dutch experience, emphasising the fact that successful re-integration into the labour market necessitates co-operation between actors involved in the re-integration chain (see Sol, Chapter 16 in this book).

Yet the Australian case suggests that the dichotomy between efficiency and governance may be less clear than it appears. As the Australian market has matured the emphasis on cost competitiveness has been replaced by performance and quality measures. Job Network is now forming partnerships with other government agencies through memoranda of understanding, which identify opportunities to co-ordinate services and invest in regional economic development. For example, remote indigenous communities are being asked to identify their priorities and all levels of governments are being mobilised to share responsibility with communities so that their priorities are met. Service providers have been required to form close partnerships with employers and have demonstrated strong community support at the local level. Many deliver services for other government agencies and are registered training organisations.

Partnerships and their real contribution

Decentralisation reforms transfer decision-making powers to the regional level mainly. Recipients of powers through decentralisation of the PES are regional governments (in the case of devolution) and tripartite labour market councils (in the case of decentralisation within integrated PES), often at regional level too. Yet economic development and social exclusion are clearly issues that must be tackled at local level. Therefore, decentralisation alone does not guarantee better co-ordination between labour market policies managed at regional level and economic development and social initiatives led at the local level. Partner relationships between labour market authorities and local actors involved in economic and social development are required to complete the process successfully and improve local governance, as the Venice conference concluded (OECD, 1999).

The most solid and established forms of partner relationships are commonly found within area-based partnerships. They involve government services, local authorities, employers, trade unions and community-based organisations working together to design area-based strategies, adapt policies to local conditions and take initiatives consistent with shared priorities. From

> **Box 1.1. National governments and partnerships**
>
> National governments have created, or supported, most of the networks of partnerships that exist in OECD countries today. Through these networks, governments seek the co-operation of partners from the private sector and civil society in the pursuit of various objectives, from stimulating economic development to promoting social cohesion.
>
> Ireland provides good illustrations of such initiatives, which have served as a model in several European countries. Through successive steps, in 1991 and 1994, the government launched a network of 38 partnerships aimed at improving social inclusion. It repeated the experience in 2000, establishing development boards in all counties and cities of the country, tasked with the design of economic, social and cultural development strategies. Another country where partnerships have become a significant element of the institutional framework is Austria. In each of the nine *Länder*, a partnership supported by the federal government now co-ordinates employment measures and provides a platform for co-operation between the main actors in this field, particularly the regional governments, the public employment service, the social partners and non-governmental organisations (NGOs).
>
> The development councils of the *pays* (historic areas) promoted by the legislation in France, the regional growth agreements in Sweden and the local strategic partnerships in the United Kingdom are all a part of this trend. Partnerships also flourish in Canada and the United States, where they have long been involved in diverse tasks ranging from co-ordinating government policies in the labour market to pooling resources for economic development. In the US, the Workforce Investment Act of 1998 has led to the creation of partnerships in charge of co-ordinating a broad range of policies, from employment and social assistance to education, including those measures targeted on youth. In Norway, a reform proposing the creation of regional partnerships responsible for co-ordinating the implementation of policies, including those issued at national level, is being debated by parliament.
>
> *Source:* OECD (2001a).

the 1980s and the first half of the 1990s when those partnerships were mainly the result of isolated local initiatives in distressed areas, governments started to use them as a tool to improve governance and addressed more systematically issues of economic development, employment, social cohesion and the quality of life throughout the country (see Box 1.1).

The OECD Study on Local Partnerships (2001a) has identified the main mechanisms through which partnerships impact on local governance. Partnerships: i) stimulate the take-up of government programmes that are consistent with priorities shared locally; ii) identify local synergies and combine government programmes with local initiatives to enhance their impact; and iii) assist government officers in targeting national programmes to match local conditions. In doing so, partnerships often manage to fill policy gaps and help communities meet their needs.

The study also highlighted that improving local governance should be considered as the main outcome of area-based partnerships. While in some countries, partnership networks are better known for the services they deliver directly to the community, evidence shows that this aspect of their work remains fairly limited in practice. Analysis of the budget of partnerships in Ireland, a country where partnerships are particularly active, shows that the measures directly implemented by partnerships amount to only 3% of the total budget for ALMPs annually. Similar ratios have been obtained for other countries. Clearly, the Irish partnerships play a more significant role in terms of stimulating the take-up of government programmes that are compatible with the priorities defined locally and adapting them to local needs. For example, the Community Employment (CE) framework agreement requires local PES offices to agree with the partnerships on the terms and conditions and targets to be given to the implementation of the CE job subsidy, which is one of the main ALMP in Ireland in terms of budget allocation (40 million EUR in 2000). The PES remains fully in charge of the delivery of the programme.

Partnership flaws

Partnerships bring a useful contribution to local governance, yet their work raises challenges for accountability and policy effectiveness. First, partnerships seek to raise their profile as direct providers of services to the community, taking advantage of the sluggish capacity of the public sector to respond to changing local situations. Legitimate though it may be, the resulting distribution of responsibilities may not be optimal since public services are endowed with greater financial resources and better skills to provide the services required efficiently. An additional difficulty arises when a partnership-based organisation gets involved in the implementation of a programme managed by a public service partner, since both have incentives to report on positive outcomes while ignoring failures. Double reporting on job creation involving both the PES and a partnership has been signalled in several countries.

The weak response from national ministries represents another challenge for partnerships. The limit to what partnerships can achieve in terms of policy co-ordination at the local level is provided by the degree of coherence at national level. Government departments should make their missions and goals consistent and compatible with the goal assigned to the network of local partnerships if the latter are to generate any significant and sustainable outcomes. Partnerships are often supervised by a single ministry or agency, and other departments face little incentive to get involved. Instead each ministry is tempted to set up its own network of partnerships, which may then be used to legitimise new government action.

Another difficulty with partnership lies with the evaluation of performance. If their main outcome is to improve local governance, then partnerships must be evaluated against changes in governance as a result from working in partnership. Performance management should seek to monitor and assess the added value from working in partnership. What is the result of a better policy co-ordination, adaptation to local conditions, and participation of civil society and business? Consistently, their performance should not be assessed in terms of policy impacts (*e.g.* number of jobs created, business start-ups), which are actually the result of the actions of the individual members of the partnership (unless the partnerships' staff themselves or a partnership-based organisation deliver the services). This calls for the challenging task of identifying governance indicators, which can be meaningful and give partners incentives to sustain participation (Giguère, 2002). The issue of evaluating partnerships properly should be clearly distinguished from that of evaluating local development initiatives and programmes. As a recent OECD conference on evaluation of local development programmes (Vienna, 2002) showed, good quality evaluation is essential in appraising the merits of different policy approaches, and this obviously applies to measures to promote economic development and social inclusion at local level. In creating the conditions for identifying new opportunities and areas for synergies, partnerships may originate from these initiatives. But partnership is essentially a way of working, not a substitute for the public service or the private sector. In the absence of explicit delegations of powers, the partners remain responsible for the respective programmes and initiatives they manage and fund.

The uneven capacity of the partners is another weakness of partnership as a form of governance. For a partnership to generate fruitful and effective co-operation, its main partners must share a similar degree of legitimacy. Yet the means of the three main sectors of society that are normally represented in partnerships – public, private and civil society – differ significantly: the largely unstructured civil society is often represented on a volunteer basis and on the leisure time of its members. The NGOs that often volunteer to represent civil society indeed represent the interest of their respective members and not that of the wider local community, generating conflicts of interest and undermining the accountability of partnerships as a whole. In various circumstances, business, and in particular small and medium-size enterprises (SMEs), also finds it difficult to be represented appropriately. As a result, partnership may set objectives for local development and labour market policies that do not portray representative priorities, as they would be expressed and addressed in a wider and more balanced partnership. For the various sectors to be in a position to play a significant and comparable role in partnerships, mechanisms enabling broad representation, the definition of mandates and reporting structures need to be designed and implemented. The stronger partners (i.e. the government) may have a role to play to help build the capacity of the weakest parties.

These challenges explain the general difficulty of involving civil servants in area-based partnerships: civil servants report to central agencies on policy objectives which may not be consistent with those pursued by partnerships; they lack the flexibility in policy management that would enable them to play a significant role in area-based strategic planning and implementation of locally-specific projects; they resent competition from partnership-based organisations raising funds and developing new services to deliver to the population; they fear that the delegates appointed may not be representative of the wider local community and business circles and that they may promote their own interest; and they realise that the assessment of their professional performances by their employers is not likely to take account of the efforts they devote in a cross-sector dimension as part of partnership mechanisms. This is particularly true of the situation faced by local PES officers.

Towards new forms of governance

Yet government agencies and public services, especially in the area of labour market policy, have a crucial role to play in initiatives to improve governance. This is reflected by current reforms, which are placing civil servants at the centre of new governance arrangements.

Good examples are provided by Ireland, with its Community Employment framework, which requests local public employment service offices to agree with the representatives of the local community (involving local government, employers and civil society) on the terms and conditions to be applied to the implementation of certain active labour market programmes, as seen above; by the Norwegian reform of co-ordination of national and regional policies by regional partnerships involving local governments, community-based organisations, trade unions and employer associations (see Knutzen, Chapter 23 in this book); by the public service agreements in the UK, instruments for a better co-ordination of public policies and services which take orientations from local strategic partnerships involving other local stakeholders (see Geddes, Chapter 22); and by Flanders where sub-regional co-ordinating bodies chaired by both the employment service and the local government seek to reconcile labour market objectives with those of economic development and social inclusion (see Vrijens, Chapter 7).

Box 1.2. **Employment and local governance: the next steps**

The Warsaw conference requested that the OECD and its LEED Programme undertake more work on the relationship between employment and local governance. What are the right incentives to encourage the employment services to form effective partnerships with other stakeholders from the public sector, business circles and civil society, and to promote a better *integration between labour market policy and economic development at local and regional levels?* This activity would build on the lessons learnt from the OECD Study on Local Partnerships led in 14 countries and regions and on synergies between the LEED and ELSA Committees.

The conference identified a number of issues that would need to be addressed as part of such investigations:

1. *Vertical co-operation.* What are the best mechanisms for agreeing on local targets? What "carrots" and "sticks" should accompany them? Who should be the participants in this process?

2. *Horizontal co-ordination.* What are the best mechanisms for taking a cross-sector approach among government agencies and public service offices? How to solve the dichotomy between employment policy and economic development? What are the implications for co-ordination at national level? How to involve representatives of civil society, business circles and local authorities in an effective way?

3. *Financing.* What financing mechanisms would support these co-operative relationships best? This relates to the budgetary aspects of performance management systems, such as management by objective and management by programme, and to fiscal federalism in the case of devolution of powers.

4. *Capacity building and the supply of professional skills at the local level.* How best to develop the capacity of civil servants and local actors to support local development, to work effectively in networks, and to foster innovation? This raises the issue of both training of local officers and capacity building of civil society and local business circles.

5. *Trust and social capital.* What are the best mechanisms for building and maintaining social capital, especially in those countries where it appears to be relatively lacking at regional and local levels?

6. *Monitoring and evaluation.* How best to assess the impact of decentralisation and partnership mechanisms? How can improvements in local governance be monitored and evaluated? What should be the appropriate indicators?

These models leave the responsibility for programme implementation and service delivery to those who have most resources and skills for assuming it, i.e. the public services (and the private sector for those services for which responsibility is delegated). On the other hand, they emphasise the duty for civil servants to co-operate with other stakeholders, be they from the public service, civil society or business circles. In these models, public services are welcome by other stakeholders to seek improved efficiency as the policy targets they pursue reflect broader preoccupations. This probably represents the best way to reduce the trade-off between flexibility and accountability, and it deserves to be explored further (see Box 1.2).

What emerges from the study of decentralisation and new forms of governance in the OECD is that, while it can be helpful to create new local partnership organisations in some situations [see the fruitful experience of Austria, Ireland and Russia in this book (Chapters 20, 21 and 25), as examples among many others], more important is to embed local governance principles in the decision-making processes of existing organisations. It is important to stimulate co-ordination between labour market policy, local and regional economic development, social inclusion, as well as education; to foster the adaptation of policies to local needs; and to encourage the participation of employers, trade unions and civil society in the design and implementation of measures. This is a key condition for improving labour market, social and economic outcomes.

No unique governance model can be applicable to all countries to achieve this. Yet inserting the right consultation, negotiation and partnership mechanisms in policy management frameworks will build the effective forms of governance required.

Bibliography

CONSIDINE, Mark (2001), *Enterprising States: The Public Management of Welfare to Work*, Chapter 6: "Australia: Governance as Competition", Cambridge University Press, London.

DE KONING, Jan (2001), "How Can We Make Active Labour Market Policies More Effective? The Role of Organisations, Implementation and Optimal Allocation in Active Labour Market Policy", in OECD (2001d), *Labour Market Policies and the Public Employment Service*, Paris.

FINN, D. and BLACKMORE, M. (2001), "Activation: the Point of View of Clients and 'Front Line' Staff", in OECD (2001d), *Labour Market Policies and the Public Employment Service*, Paris.

GIGUÈRE, Sylvain (2002), "Enhancing Governance through Partnerships", in T. Bovaird, E. Löffler and S. Parrado Díez (eds.), *Developing Local Governance Networks in Europe*, Nomos Publishers, Baden-Baden.

GREFFE, Xavier (2002), *Le développement local*, Éditions de l'Aube, Paris.

LUNDIN, Martin and SKEDINGER, Per (2000), "Decentralisation of Active Labour Market Policy: the Case of Swedish Local Employment Committees", Working Paper 2000:6, IFAU (Office of Labour Market Policy Evaluation), Stockholm.

MARTIN, John P. and GRUBB, David (2001), "What Works and for Whom: a Review of OECD Countries' Experience with Active Labour Market Policies", Working Paper 2001:14, IFAU (Office of Labour Market Policy Evaluation), Stockholm.

MOSLEY, Hugh, SCHUTZ, Holger and BREYER, Nicole (2001), "Management by Objectives in European Public Employment Services", Discussion Paper FSI01-203, Social Science Research Centre (WZB), Berlin.

OECD (2002), "Skills Upgrading for the Low-qualified: a New Local Policy Agenda?", Official Document, DT/LEED/DC(2002)5, Paris.

OECD (2001a), *Local Partnerships for Better Governance*, Paris.

OECD (2001b), *Employment Outlook*, Paris.

OECD (2001c), *Innovations in Labour Market Policy: the Australian Way*, Paris.

OECD (2001d), *Labour Market Policies and the Public Employment Service*, Paris.

OECD (1999), *Decentralising Employment Policy: New Trends and Challenges*, Paris.

OECD (1998), *Local Management for More Effective Employment Policies*, Paris.

OECD (1996), *Enhancing the Effectiveness of Active Labour Market Policies*, The OECD Jobs Strategy, Paris.

STRUYVEN, Ludo and STEURS, Geert (2002), "The Competitive Market for Employment Services in the Netherlands", Official document DEELSA/ELSA/WD(2002)10, OECD, Paris.

PART I

Decentralisation: What Difference Does it Make?

> *The main tool used by governments to improve local governance is decentralisation. In principle, decentralisation gives more room for manoeuvre to area-based and integrated approaches. Programmes may be combined with efforts of local and regional governments, the private sector, trade unions and community groups to support better development strategies balancing concerns of economic development, social inclusion and the quality of life. Through greater flexibility in policy management, decentralisation is also expected to make it easier to respond to unmet needs. However, there are some obstacles to this.*

PART I
Chapter 2

Decentralisation:
What Difference Does it Make? A Synthesis

by

Xavier Greffe
Université de Paris I (Sorbonne)

For over thirty years, decentralisation has been a key component of the institutional design adopted in many OECD countries and the European Union alike, and the trend has intensified continuously. Australia, Belgium, France, Italy, the Netherlands, Spain and Sweden have introduced major decentralisation policies, not to mention countries that have extended their own federal structures, such as Mexico, Germany, Canada, etc. A few years ago, the United Kingdom also embarked upon an original process of devolution.

These decentralisation movements are all based on one simple idea – that our societies can be governed more effectively and more democratically if decisions are taken at a level that is as close as possible to the needs of the populations and the communities they affect, and if the resources deployed are flexible enough to adjust to those needs. When this is the case, decisions are based on better information and a clearer understanding of the issues, they are more responsive to needs, they can tap synergies with local agents often neglected by national power centres, and they create clearer and more sharply focused systems of accountability.

Such a trend might seem like an anachronism at a time when globalisation is highlighting the importance of trans-national connections and widespread mobility of capital and also, in a way, labour mobility. It must be remembered, however, that the competitiveness of businesses in a global economy hinges fundamentally on the particular characteristics of the local environments in which they operate, and that in many cases neither capital nor business activities are as mobile as is commonly thought. Consequently, decentralisation can be seen as an instrument for smoother entry into the global economy and not as a weakening factor. Moreover, studies of territorial convergence show that the territories that progress most successfully are in fact those that are able to combine a variety of educational, technical, social and productive capital.

Today, it is difficult to speak of decentralisation without evoking external effects or subsidiarity, and at this juncture two introductory remarks are necessary:

- A redistribution of powers does not prevent the effects of any given power from being felt at levels other than the one to which it is assigned. The presence of external effects to be felt at other levels prevents decentralisation from being considered a hierarchical partitioning of powers, even if a particular level emerges as the desirable centre of gravity for the exercise of a given power.

- Subsidiarity does not mean that the levels not constituting the centres of gravity for a given power have no responsibility for the exercise of the said power. What it means is that those other levels should remain prepared to assist the level to which the power has been delegated, either because that level might lack the required resources or because it might use the power to the detriment of other entities at the same level. This takes us back to the etymology of the term: for the Romans, the subsidium was the force held in reserve and deployed when the front-line battalions started to weaken.

The decentralisation trend has entrusted local authorities with new powers in highly varied areas outside the sovereign prerogatives of the State. Above all, it has given them a growing role in economic and social development, with respect to employment in particular. The instruments of such responsibility vary from one country to another, as will be seen below, and a number of different tracks have been explored. In some countries, decentralisation has chiefly been applied to the public employment service, and local partners have not been concerned directly. Here, it has been through a process of "contagion" that local partners have been associated with and integrated into decentralisation. In other countries, responsibilities in the realm of employment and social inclusion have been decentralised directly to local agents, generally local authorities but in some cases private entities or community-sector organisations. Whether directly or indirectly, territorial authorities and local partners have become fully fledged players in the realm of employment governance.

Analysing the outcomes resulting from a decentralisation of employment-related responsibilities and powers involves more than just identifying mechanisms that have altered traditional approaches to employment policies. Such an assessment must be based on good employment governance criteria, which fundamentally entails an explicit linkage tie-in between the economic and social dimensions, and a better co-ordination of public and private agents, both vertically and horizontally. It is thus from this standpoint that the positive effects of decentralisation of powers in the area of employment, the problems it raises, and the solutions it requires should be explored.

The foundations, objectives and evaluation criteria of decentralisation

Employment policies have long been centralised. In the context of the welfare state, the State's role was to ensure labour market transparency and oversee the protection of rights for the unemployed. The main differences between countries involved the role that States accorded to the social partners: in some countries, the social partners virtually administered such policies, by delegation of the State, and in others they were working alongside the State within a tripartite structure, in which case they were consulted, at best.

But a whole series of reasons prompted States to shift the centre of gravity of employment policies to local partners. These reasons can in turn be cited as criteria for a successful decentralisation.

The first reason, and probably the least relevant, was the fact that States could no longer afford costly protection schemes with reduced tax revenues and budgetary scope. Moreover, this reaction was not unique to the area of employment, since the reasons behind it applied to all government action. The shift also reflected a new approach to public management, in response to the distortion induced by an overly centralised administration (see Chapter 24 by Svenningsson). The initial reaction here was to make a clearer separation between decision-making and implementation, by considering that implementation could be delegated without major problems, whereas decision-making entailed centralised thinking tied in with the principles of the welfare state. This approach appeared at first glance to have the positive effects of instituting management by objectives and defining responsibilities more clearly. But this new style of public management raised problems of moral hazard: implementing bodies had access to information not available to the central government. Moreover, it created major grassroots co-ordination problems insofar as public services had to act independently of each other, whereas the results of such initiatives had to be reported in a uniform manner.

States thus came to formulate more pragmatic administrative approaches, with local authorities able to plan their actions more freely and collaborate amongst themselves, with the State continuing to lay down guidelines, mitigate resource inequalities and, if needed, formulate systems to evaluate such localised programmes (Sabel and O'Donnell, 2001). This trend is often captured by the term "deconcentration" rather than "decentralisation". Even if such reforms are aimed primarily at State services, they prompt easier dialogue with local partners, and even the institution of partnerships.

The second reason is related to the particularities of certain territories (see Dau, Chapter 6 and Boni, Chapter 8). Here, islands or mountainous areas are generally cited as examples, because the severity of their problems precludes reliance on spontaneous labour market mechanisms, or on policies formulated far afield as they do not take local particularities into account. This is for example the case of Greece and Italy. From the outset, consideration must be given to initiatives involving the various agents – local or central – based on an exploration of the types of activities that can be undertaken or maintained. Moreover, here the term "decentralisation" must be interpreted broadly, because it encompasses the need for both horizontal grassroots co-ordination and vertical co-ordination between the central, regional and local levels. The European Union's Leader Programme has in fact turned this aspect into a real laboratory for local development. In this connection, it has harnessed decentralisation in a number of ways in order to help create or preserve jobs: better co-ordination amongst authorities, initiation of dialogue between the authorities and the social partners, linkages between economic and social developments, incorporation of environmental problems into the formulation of an economic strategy, etc.

The third reason involves the multifaceted nature of employment problems. Today, many problems of employment involve more than a mismatch between labour supply and demand, even if that is how they appear (see Boni, Chapter 8 and Förschner, Chapter 21).

Labour demand is increasingly emerging as predetermined by aspects involving training, housing or mobility, health care, minimum wage constraints, etc. The existence of a supply of labour *per se* is therefore no longer sufficient to mobilise this demand if one of those factors has a negative impact, thus complicating a strategy based on labour market transparency alone. These factors can in fact be identified and managed only in a precise manner and in proximity to the people involved, meaning that initiatives must be planned, carried out and co-ordinated at the local level. It is not illogical that the first experiments and the first decentralisation mechanisms dealt in many cases with young people, who are a group combining often unfavourable factors in terms of housing, training and so on (see Simonin, Chapter 14).

Labour supply is in most cases a potentiality, which materialises only if other problems are solved – obtaining land or a loan, acknowledgement of intellectual property rights, etc. Problems of adjustment and co-ordination must therefore be resolved if the supply of labour is to materialise – problems which to a large extent can only be solved locally. With regard to solutions that must come from the central level, an interface must be set up between potential employers and the various financial, urban planning and logistical entities involved, which once again involves setting up a favourable local environment.

These elements therefore necessitate a local approach to employment issues. This does not mean that solutions will always be found at the local level alone, but that the way problems are posed and solutions formulated should begin at the local level, which is defined here as the environment of the people involved.*

---

* An illustration of the multifaceted nature of employment problems leading to local initiatives can be found in the strategy of the European Social Fund. No programme of integration through employment can succeed if other mechanisms of exclusion, such as those involving housing, are not dealt with simultaneously. The ESF considers that such initiatives must mobilise existing capacities at the local level in order to qualify for financing (*European Governance: A White Paper*, report by Working Group 3b on "Decentralisation: Better Involvement of National, Regional and Local Actors", June 2001, p. 13).

A good illustration of the potentials and the limitations held out of the social environment can be found in relation to training (Greffe, 2001). In many countries, the existence of agreements between local agents (*e.g.*, compacts in the United States, or locally initiated training programmes in France) has made it possible to meet training challenges and to institute and fine-tuning balance between labour supply and demand. Bringing together businesses, private and public training institutes, labour market administration and associations that help people find jobs can help businesses find the skilled workers they need to carry out their plans for production, and help job-seekers find the work they have been trained to do. But adjustments like these have to be made on a level close to the people involved. Yet training also underscores the limitations of a local initiative: businesses squeezed by their profit margins may seek expedients, and workers who have lost their jobs, and even their professional identities, may hesitate to get involved in new training schemes if they do not feel that those schemes will help them (see Eberts, Chapter 19 and Straits, Chapter 4).

The fourth reason stems from another characteristic of the labour market. The duration of jobs shortens and labour market adjustments become more and more frequent, as illustrated by the predominance of fixed-term and temporary employment contracts. Transitional adjustments also occur through training leaves as exemplified by job rotations (Netherlands, Denmark), etc. People are required to change jobs – and even qualifications – frequently, and must thus assume ever-higher costs of job-seeking, adaptation, mobility and so on. The challenge is no less substantial for businesses – except that it is generally believed that, apart from certain skills, businesses will more readily find workers with the desired qualifications than workers will find the jobs they are seeking. This situation is even pushed to extremes in the case of adhocratic labour markets, *i.e.* markets in which employment lasts for the duration of a single project for which a person has initially been hired (Greffe, 1999). Such is the case, for example, of artistic markets in which artists are recruited for a given product, and in which the production structure is created for a single product only, another product entailing another structure and other employment contracts. In this specific context, buyers and sellers are prompted to come closer together and even to live in the same geographical space – hence the expression "cultural district".

The "volatility" of employment prompts labour market agents to seek the shortest channels of information and training, which bestows great importance on the way in which labour markets are organised at the local level. This organisation involves not only information and transparency – challenges that can be met to a great extent thanks to the new information technologies – but the prospects of the choices to be made, both by job-seekers and by potential employers. In French-speaking Belgium, the example of the *Maisons de l'emploi* that match training and trades illustrates the need to supplement information with personalised advice, with respect to employers and job-seekers alike. This forward-looking function is organised differently, depending on the specificity of the skills involved and on the level of demand within the relevant markets (see Chapter 3 by Hendeliowitz).

A fifth reason stems from the desire to make employment policies active. On the national level, a distinction is traditionally made between so-called "passive" measures and "active" ones. Passive measures deal essentially with the labour market environment and with mechanisms to compensate for the loss of income. Active measures seek to make a more direct impact on the behaviour of market agents and thus to restore a greater reactive capacity. Examples include training schemes, the organisation of rotating or shared employment, direct job creation, measures for start-ups, measures to assist disadvantaged groups, etc.

Over time, it became clear that employment policies did not have the right mix of these two types of measures – active and passive. When they encounter employment problems, countries tend to start out with policies that feature mainly passive measures, more or less relying on prospects for spontaneous economic recovery. In contrast, transforming markets and employment systems requires intervention that, on the contrary, is more and more proactive – hence the recommendation to increase the relative weight of active measures. Nobody challenges the existence of a rather negative correlation between the preponderance of active measures and the jobless rate. Accordingly, some countries have given a high priority to active measures, as have Sweden (56% of outlays) and the Netherlands (38%) (see *OECD Employment Outlook*).

There are two prerequisites for the institution of such measures: their provisions must be diversified in line with the actual circumstances of a market, an industry or a company; and the groups that the measures are to target must be identified. In either case, decentralisation is the environment that active measures require, even if some of their principles must obviously still be laid down centrally, if only to justify budgetary choices and assess effectiveness. It was on this basis that Denmark redefined the role of its regional labour councils in 1995 (see Chapter 3 by Hendeliowitz).

Furthermore, we may consider that effective implementation of such measures requires the participation of a large number of local agents. A measure such as job rotation (or the organisation of transitional markets) as practiced in Denmark or the Netherlands entails the mobilisation of entire groups of the population and institutions that are bypassed by traditional employment policies. But this is possible only if discussions, stock-taking and problem-solving are carried out in the territory concerned. Likewise,

Germany's implementation of "alliances for jobs" at the regional level makes possible a far more systematic co-ordination of stakeholders to promote employment and job creation (European Union, 2001a).

Lastly, implementing active policies does not mean that those targeted by such policies will benefit from them. More often than not they are vulnerable persons or groups, far removed from the information mechanisms concerning such policies and the places where they are put in place. So decentralisation is doubly justified as it is a matter not only of implementing active policies, but also of drawing closer to those who are supposed actually to benefit from them – and this is what the Belgian experiments have shown.

A sixth reason concerns today's more and more frequent time-lag between employment and activity. In many countries, a considerable proportion of those disadvantaged and of long-term unemployed people will not find jobs quickly and, when they do, it will often be through family service employment, neighbourhood services and the like. Hence the approach has to be very meticulous, with the characteristics of the people concerned being matched with work opportunities at local level, without any direct link with the jobs available or likely to be available on the labour market; and this type of approach is by nature decentralised.

France provides a good illustration of this. For nearly ten years, the *régies de quartiers* (local district authorities), managed within a municipal or sub-municipal framework, have been seeking to develop such activities, with the objective of facilitating labour market reintegration. Moreover, the current reform of the RMI (social minimum income), to which is to be added a RMA (activity minimum income), is a move in the same direction inasmuch as the integration being sought will take the form of neighbourhood services and not just a return to normal employment. The reform will completely decentralise the way things are being done by making departmental councils (*conseils généraux des départements*) responsible for managing both the financial and the occupational aspects, *i.e.* for allocating an income and making it possible to develop an activity.

A seventh reason stems from the desire to find innovative solutions. In Flanders, for example, the desire to create new jobs and open up the corresponding markets was envisaged at local level because it seemed that this innovation was feasible at a level involving all the required partnerships. It needs to be emphasised that innovation usually involves contacts between the social partners who will be responsible for carrying it through. This dialogue must take place in the closest possible proximity to the problems to be solved.

An eighth, more specific reason stems from the desire to revive forms of social dialogue and partnership that had finally lost their meaning at national level. This case is illustrated by the changes that have taken place in Sweden, where the government decided in 1998 to introduce regional development policies based on the principle of regional growth agreements. The said agreements, which benefit from structural funds, are signed between local government authorities, firms and their local representatives, social partners, the regional employment council, universities, etc. The procedure is viewed empirically, the object being to launch a collective learning process, and is supposed to be part of a long-term development process rather than just offering short-term solutions.

The last reason incorporates the all the others, and goes farther. It arises from the need to adopt a strategic approach to employment. Traditionally, the primary aim of initiatives to promote employment had been to create the greatest possible transparency, and to help ensure that disadvantaged groups were taken into consideration, which was predicated on a certain stability of jobs and skills. But in a global, knowledge-based economy in which skills and jobs are constantly evolving as a result of a myriad of variables, it is impossible to adhere to this first approach. A greater understanding of the labour market, and of the governance of employment can only be spurred by a strategic vision of economic development – one that anticipates transformations and can link economic development with social development. The sanctions for the failure to make this linkage are well-known: on the one hand, we find two-track growth; on the other, labour market inclusion but without satisfying prospects. Yet while this vision must clearly reflect a global outlook, it must also necessarily begin with an outlining of the opportunities and possibilities of a given territory by the agents of that territory themselves.

The decentralisation of job promotion mechanisms is a means of putting initiatives back into a context where economic development is strongly linked to employment and social inclusion. It gives people the margin of freedom and flexibility they need to grasp, and to cope with, the various dimensions of their territory. It enables the government agencies responsible for such issues to be more effective at solving common problems, and it lets all partners in employment operate at an appropriate level with respect to information, analysis, resource-gathering and accountability. As a result, top-down sectoral approaches are transcended, and microeconomic policies that are tailored more closely to the needs of local people can be implemented. Likewise, horizontal co-ordination, which involves co-ordinating initiatives and adapting them to local conditions, and which fosters the participation of local people, in no way precludes the need to strengthen vertical co-ordination between local partners and partners in the centre.

This has three implications:

- The term "local" must be used very carefully, as here there can be some confusion between an employment approach that is conducive to decentralisation, and the forms of local territories, which are necessarily restricted from an institutional standpoint. An employment approach entails seeking to enhance coherence between participants in the employment system, at a level that is as close as possible to the sources of their information and their projects. The local focus must be regarded here as a method rather than an end in itself, because very few employment trends are shaped by territorial factors alone. While that may be the case for certain neighbourhood services, it would be better to consider that an exception rather than the rule. When speaking of local employment or local employment policy, the approach taken will be to stress the extent to which local factors shape employment problems in contrast to the popular idea that jobs depend exclusively on decisions that are taken locally.

- "Local" in an employment management context does not necessarily correspond to the meaning "local" in a context of decentralisation or devolution reforms. This is fairly logical, insofar as it would be difficult for any State to map out geographical entities having unique properties from the standpoint of economics, employment, social welfare, training, etc. Moreover, horizontal co-ordination does not preclude the need for vertical co-ordination between all levels. For both these reasons, it is necessary to accept a wide variety of institutional designs. In this context, employment contracts or pacts can play at least as important a role as the division of powers, since they can make it possible to tailor the necessarily highly formal division of powers to the reality of external effects or overlap.

- In a global economy, a local approach is justified because it allows for greater synergy between the economic and social foundations of employment, and for better allocation of jobs. Any initiative to promote employment at the local level must be economically relevant and, in particular, contribute to the competitiveness of a region or city. Breaking such a balance would soon cause local initiatives to turn into make-work programmes without a future or result in two-track economic development, leaving a substantial part of the population by the wayside.

Implementing decentralisation

Decentralisation is intended to institute ways to formulate and carry out employment policies that are more open and more participatory; mechanisms that are more flexible and more differentiated, in many cases involving contractual agreements between horizontal and vertical partners; and greater accountability of local authorities and their partners in the realm of employment. To accomplish this, four processes are used and in practice are often combined:

- decentralisation of public employment services, generally beginning with central government agencies involved directly or indirectly in labour market regulation;

- a new division of powers in the realm of employment and training, to the benefit of local authorities;
- contractualisation of certain aspects of employment policy;
- increased mobilisation of social economy institutions to promote employment.

Decentralisation of public employment services

Welfare-state systems have instituted central government agencies that are in charge of labour and unemployment problems. Together, the government departments, services or agencies that help with job placement, the administration of unemployment and the corresponding benefit schemes, and the implementation of active measures to promote employment, constitute what is traditionally called the "public employment service" (PES) (OECD, 1996a, 1997). It will be noted, however, that in recent years, and following Conventions adopted by the ILO, the placement role of public agencies has been regressing significantly and in some countries has even been abolished.

This variety of PES missions has often resulted in a lack of co-ordination, with top-down sectoral approaches generating a multitude of organisations, creating not only classic organisational problems such as overlap and duplication of effort, but also inefficiency resulting from the lack of coherence. This lack of coherence was reinforced over time by the creation of different administrative cultures, and it had such a major impact at the local level that certain initiatives were frozen. A possible solution would have been to reform all of the agencies simultaneously, but such reforms would have run up against exceedingly complex problems of structures and technical powers. An alternative (and radical) solution would have been to decentralise these agencies while attempting to consolidate them in a single mould at local level and to have them run by a local authority. Apart from the obstacles mentioned above, there was reluctance to pursue this direction because these centralised agencies, consolidated under the banner of the public employment service, were considered to warrant equal treatment of workers regardless of their industry or the territory in which they lived. Any dissolution of this system was thus viewed as a threat to the preservation of such rights. But in the face of a deteriorating job situation, this argument became harder and harder to cite as a reason for not reforming the PES.

Thus decentralisation initially took the form of a reshuffling of responsibilities within the public employment service, which was considered the prerequisite for restoring a minimum of coherence at the local level. To accomplish this, four steps were commonly taken: to establish a location from which the respective strategies and initiatives could be made coherent; to expand discretionary powers in this connection; to set up a "one-stop shop" for delivering services; and – in a measure that went still farther – to accept the principle of regionalised benefits (see Chapter 3 by Hendeliowitz):

- A first instrument of PES decentralisation is to institute coherency between the various departments. Generally, this is done in two ways. Services are placed under the direction of a representative of the State at the local level (a prefect, director of the local employment agency, etc.). Nonetheless, this responsibility is not conferred on a local authority, since to do so would amount to embarking on another form of decentralisation, namely that of the powers of the State. Services are prompted to make their strategies and initiatives part of a local employment scheme. This is the solution taken by France, which has adopted departmental employment plans formulated by departmental employment and labour directorates, which all State administrations (employment agencies, adult further training agencies, national education services, health services, etc.) are asked to help carry out.

- A second instrument of decentralisation is to increase the discretionary powers of the administrations constituting the public employment service. Introducing coherence locally would be virtually meaningless if it involved no more than shifting choices made at the top without prompting exchanges of information at the local level. Here, the discretion in question concerns mainly the forms of initiatives, *e.g.*, in the realm of disseminating information and training.

- A third instrument of decentralisation is to set up "one-stop shops". It is striking that virtually all countries go about reforming their public employment services by first reshaping their local services along the lines of a single services centre (Denmark, Flanders, Germany, the Walloon Region, etc). If the effect of these shops is to simplify considerably the formalities imposed on the unemployed and job-seekers, it also makes government agencies work together, harmonise their terminology, and achieve economies of scale and scope in service delivery. It is therefore not surprising that many countries endeavour to fulfil such an objective. Austria, for instance, is planning to institute a network of one-stop shops in 2003. For its part, Germany is setting up a new model for local agencies. But in this area, other authorities, such as Belgium's Walloon Region, maintain the principle of institutional diversity – for reasons involving federalism, but also in order not to integrate services for the unemployed too closely with services for job-seekers (see Förschner, Chapter 21 and Knutzen, Chapter 23).

- A fourth instrument is the institution of regionalised benefits. This involves a variation in benefit rates or eligibility criteria vary from one region to another. The idea is not a new one, and as soon as unemployment began to swell in the 1960s certain countries had considered – albeit via a centralised decision-making process – modulating benefits depending on economic conditions in the regions concerned: the worse the situation, the more purchasing power had to be redistributed via unemployment benefits, and *vice versa*. Policies like these ran up against two problems: how, realistically, to ascertain the criteria for such differentiation; and how to avoid windfall effects that would only widen existing inequalities. As a result, the redistribution of purchasing power was left to the State via taxation and government spending, especially insofar as it would have been difficult for insurance-based compensation schemes to have been altered along such lines. Today, it would appear that the objective is somewhat different. Alongside the benefits distributed by employment services are assistance mechanisms put in place by local authorities – mechanisms which complement these benefits or will even replace them over time. It is therefore logical that public employment services team up with local authorities to try to smooth out the various systems and thus to enhance social and economic effectiveness.

An illustration of such shifts is the informational co-operation in Denmark. There, the public employment service is heavily decentralised at the regional level (OECD, 2001a). This decentralisation is accompanied by a high degree of tripartism, since at this same regional level there are Regional Labour Market Councils (RARs) administered by the regional level of the public employment service, bringing together the social partners, the counties and the relevant State administrations. Such decentralisation makes it possible to tailor Danish labour market policy as closely as possible to the constraints and opportunities of each agent. The principle here is to make compatible three objectives that could readily come into conflict: high labour-market flexibility; generous social benefits, thus creating a safety net; and measures to activate the supply of employment to respond as quickly as possible to the demand for work (the "golden triangle" principle) (*idem*).

In the mid-1990s, however, the reform of unemployment benefits led to an increase in the financial difficulties of municipal administrations. When unemployed people exhaust their entitlement to benefits, municipal assistance programmes are in fact the only option open to them. This is why any cuts in benefits increases the financial responsibilities of the communes. Accordingly, the public employment services brought the municipalities into the RARs, as they were preparing to tackle the problem. Moreover, these Regional Councils now manage the unemployment insurance funds. Such a dialogue would have been impossible at the national level, with 275 municipalities; but it was possible at a regional level, with an average of some 20 municipalities having a certain uniformity of resources and expenses. Everyone stands to gain from such a partnership. Municipalities are better able to get their viewpoints across and to formulate a strategy in liaison with the RARs, allowing them more fully to meet the challenge of social protection. The public employment service benefits from the municipalities' sharply focused approach to problems of protection, and in particular from their knowledge of the target groups (see Chapter 3 by Hendeliowitz).

But whatever form it takes, the decentralisation of public employment services alone does not ensure new governance of employment. This entails not only new relationships with local authorities but also, and first and foremost, a new attitude on the part of these public services.

The September 2001 *Joint Statements of the European Public Employment Services* (PES) *on Their Role in the Labour Market* (European Union, 2001b) clearly highlight the type of attitude change that is required. A first statement was in 1998 within the same European framework, situating the role of the PES as essentially one of bringing the unemployed back into the mainstream through a social treatment of their situation. Three years later, however, the public employment services present their role very differently. They find that the coming challenges in the job market will be a chronic shortage of certain skills, the institution of new forms of activity, the effects of population ageing, and so on. From this, they conclude that their action must be based on a forward-looking vision of economic and social development, in respect of which they must highlight both the potentials and the limitations. Their missions as expert authorities consist in ensuring the transparency of the labour market; providing personalised services both to job-seekers and to potential employers; and performing the tasks incumbent upon a State that is governed by social law and ensures equal opportunity for all.

The *Statements* add that this way of working towards economic and social development is meaningful only if it is approached from a regional perspective so as to be both operational and flexible (*idem*); and if it is carried out in agreement with the partners of these territories, so as to be relevant and effective. Such a statement, coming from organisations often criticised for having a rigid and administrative vision of labour markets, shows that their own reform is meaningful only if it begins with a radical change of attitude on their part, in a shift towards effective decentralisation.

Lastly, such decentralisation, which is generally supported by substantial computerisation (as in Belgium), entails the development of territorial engineering capacities. In France, where the public employment service is responsible for preparing action plans, this took the form of an incentive to take stock of local employment situations and an obligation to draw up a departmental employment plan. The result was a major project, starting in many cases with fairly technical discussions about how to identify the skills present or absent in a given territory, and subsequently the possible bases of development of the local environment, entailing the participation of agents outside the PES (European Commission, 2001a).

A new division of powers

The redistribution of powers from central authorities to the various subnational territorial levels (or, more exceptionally, to certain private entities) constitutes the very essence of decentralisation. A number of countries have effectively transferred functions such as adult vocational training, active employment measures, programmes to create new service sector jobs, etc., to the regional or local levels. Spain is a fairly good example, having decentralised to the regional level a set of related powers in the realm of employment (*ibid.*).

Apart from the case of training and certain active policies, however, decentralisation of an entire category of powers is rare. The most frequent case remains the decentralisation of certain functions, with other, related functions continuing to be performed centrally. In the United Kingdom, for example, implementation of welfare-to-work programmes was devolved to local actors, while responsibility for programme regulation and general scheduling remained with the central government. In Australia, active policy measures are implemented by a "Job Network" made up of representatives of the private sector and community services and are supervised by local outposts of the federal Department of Employment and Workplace Relations (DEWR).

In addition, some functions are almost never decentralised, except perhaps only partially and for only certain aspects of implementation. For example, in Belgium, which is one of the countries that has taken decentralisation the farthest, unemployment compensation is still administered solely at the federal level, whereas all other aspects of employment policy are decentralised at the level of the three regions – Brussels, Flanders and the Walloon Region (see Chapter 7 by Vrijens).

So why has the decentralisation of powers not been extended as far as would be logically feasible? Three reasons could be suggested:

- Labour mobility is considered essential if a nation's employment systems are to operate smoothly. But for workers to be mobile, an entire portion of the labour market organisation – information systems, entitlement to benefits, recognition of qualifications, etc. – must be uniform across the territory in question. States are reluctant to decentralise such mechanisms, because to do so would immediately hamper labour mobility and make solutions to certain local crises even more problematic.
- A second reason involves the financing mechanisms for employment and labour policies. In some countries, and especially those in which the social partners play an important role, such policies are financed by contributions and take an insurance approach. This creates entitlements or control options for beneficiaries or their representatives that prevent these resources or mechanisms from being used in any other way. The possibilities for decentralisation are limited despite being in theory suitable for a range of

mechanisms. In Canada, for example, in which five regions enjoy seemingly complete devolution of labour market policy, the federal government continues to bear responsibility for financing active market policies. This is because the funding comes from the federal employment insurance fund, which prompts the government to administer programmes that benefit young people, women and native populations.

- Lastly, an entire category of employment and labour policies is based on equal rights for all. The rights to employment, work and replacement income are devised differently from one country to another. But wherever these rights are widely recognised, the proponents of decentralisation will be suspected of seeking to introduce variations in the effective enjoyment of such rights. The trend towards decentralisation will thus be hindered.

It is therefore not surprising that the devolution of powers has not been as great in the realm of employment as it can be in other areas of public policy. But here too, and in the case of decentralisation of public employment services, devolution is only a tool, and what is most important is the dynamic that it can trigger. Even if these transfers are limited, the key will be to know whether they result in any other changes in behaviour at the decentralised level, and in particular whether they enable labour market agents to achieve synergy, engage in joint stock-taking and lend mutual support.

It would be difficult to make the United States a textbook case in view of the particular nature of US federalism and the magnitude of the American private sector, which should preclude any brash generalisations. But if there is one country in which decentralisation has spawned numerous local partnerships, then clearly it is the United States. Two recent laws have in fact expanded decentralisation in the production of social services, including labour training and development (OECD, 2001a). The 1996 Personal Responsibility and Work Opportunity Reconciliation Act has been conducive to vertical co-operation between the federal, state and local levels for the implementation of labour development programmes (*ibid.*). The Workforce Investment Act of 1998 encouraged state and local governments to manage their services or even to have them managed by private- or third-sector bodies (*ibid.*). Non-profit organisations have been seen to play a significant role in co-ordinating public services. While the first law puts the emphasis on labour development, the second focuses rather on investment in the job search process and training in preparation for employment. But both clearly pursue the same objective: to provide training resources and options closely attuned to local problems. From this standpoint, these laws are in line with a movement that begun more than 30 years ago.

Indeed, the first law on job training, the 1962 Federal Manpower Development Training Act (MDTA), had made job training a federal programme, and one aimed essentially at individuals who were particularly disadvantaged. Since it was administered centrally, it was unable to mobilise a great many NGOs deeply involved in solving such problems, and as a result it left gaps or, conversely, created overlaps. Accordingly, the Comprehensive Employment Training Act (CETA) set up local co-ordination boards and arranged for a redistribution of federal resources. But there was little private sector participation, especially in terms of the supply of training services, which compromised the nature of the vocational training dispensed in standard classes. In 1982, the Job Training Partnership Act (JTPA) tailored job training schemes to the needs of local employers by tapping in as much as possible to their own systems of training.

Both of these recent laws have ripened the decentralisation process by achieving an almost total decentralisation of federal resources and instituting systematic opportunities for partnership at the local level. The effect of this "localisation" has been to create a systematic linkage between training programmes and the obligations undertaken by businesses and workers alike – a linkage that is extremely loose when such situations are approached from a central level. As a rule, the local labour development board (which generally comprises a majority of local members) organises a one-stop shop for access to training programmes, the director of which is recruited after a competitive selection process. These offices perform functions as diverse as preliminary skills assessment, providing information about available services, assistance in applying for unemployment compensation and training programmes, etc. In addition, the local boards sign contracts with various potential service providers (businesses, non-profit organisations, public training agencies, etc.), which exhaustively set forth their functions, obligations and responsibilities. Lastly, the local boards can provide education vouchers which they fund out of their own budgets and provide to persons seeking training (see Chapter 19 by Eberts).

Strengthening co-operation

Today, a fairly different approach to decentralisation is to strengthen co-operation between national and local authorities without necessarily altering the institutional framework. This co-operation may take the form of joint assessment of local needs, but implementation of certain initiatives as well, in which case contractual provisions become essential.

Here, Finland offers an example of the first type of co-operation. Like all other European Union countries, and following the Luxembourg process, Finland prepared a National Action Plan for employment. But in doing so, Finland considered that the plan would hardly be meaningful if it were not underpinned by specific regional approaches, although neither should be an aggregation of the myriad local plans which would not yield the desired effect. It was therefore decided to have three regional centres that formulate a regional action plan for employment, working in tandem with the various ministries. Once the regional plans were completed, the national plan was drawn from them, but above all the public employment service was asked to work towards their implementation. Ireland and Portugal have also taken similar approaches, with regional employment plans forming the basis for the National Action Plan for Employment (European Union, 2001a).

Austria offers another example of decentralisation via a strengthening of partnerships between various territorial levels. In Austria, there has been no transfer of powers from the federal government to other levels, the central government remaining officially in charge of both economic development and the organisation of the labour market. Nevertheless, in 1994, a substantial decentralisation of the public employment service (*Arbeitsmarktservice*, AMS) had been conducted in such a way that AMS agencies at the regional and district level could co-operate effectively with authorities of the *Länder*, who also held certain powers in the realm of economic development. Implementation of two mechanisms called for by the European Union – the National Action Plan for Employment and the Territorial Employment Pacts – enabled the Austrian government to try out a new method of implementing employment policies, based on partnerships at the various levels (*Länder* and districts) between the public employment service and local authorities, and on vertical partnerships between those levels. It is incumbent upon the National Action Plan for Employment to conduct a general analysis of the labour market and to set objectives in close collaboration with the social partners. The regional level, and thus regional partnerships, are responsible for analysing specific aspects of regional labour markets; for co-ordinating PES initiatives concerning the supply of labour with the spontaneous or provoked behaviours of the demand for labour; for creating additional jobs for the unemployed, etc. (Campbell, 2001). The main contribution of these regional partnerships has been to widen the scope of traditional partners in employment policy. While in Austria these have essentially been limited to the social partners, local authorities joined in as well, beginning with those of the *Länder*, along with associations representing target groups such as women and the disabled, NGOs such as Caritas and even unemployed persons' movements. A second positive effect has been to strengthen the capacities of PES agencies (AMS) and local development agencies (OAR) (see Chapter 21 by Förschner).

Co-operation between local agents can also lead to an institutionalisation of decentralised structures at the local level. In Belgium, the Walloon Region has in recent years set up a number of institutions that are instrumental in decentralising employment policies: *Maisons de l'emploi*, local development agencies, skills centres, and so on. In general, the procedure was as follows. First, local people availed themselves of experimental opportunities offered by the central government and in this case financed by the European Social Fund.

Second, the Walloon Region institutionalised these experiments, extended them and turned them into a network of decentralised actions in the field – a network consolidating regional government resources and resources from the PES (FOREM) and local interests, both public and private. Here, the best illustration is probably that of the *Maisons de l'emploi*, which have become cornerstones of the management of jobsearch activities and of the human resource strategies of businesses, and which now have substantial resources to carry out their missions.

In another example from Belgium – a partnership between the three regions (Brussels, Flanders and the Walloon Region) and the federal government – co-operation takes the form of joint projects involving "first job", "social economy", "transition" and "service employment cheque" programmes (European Union, 2001a). Along those same lines, Italy has been setting up job centres based on partnerships between the State and the regions, and one-stop shops for small businesses.

Finally, it should be pointed out that such partnerships usually entail institutionalising co-ordination bodies, or even mediation bodies, which can be created at the initiative of local agents or of the central government. In Belgium's Flemish Region, for example, two types of structures co-exist: district platforms and sub-regional employment committees (OECD, 2001a). The former were created at the initiative of local agents, but economic and social administrations take part in their work as well. But the starting points have shifted considerably. The platforms work very closely with the Ministries, and the sub-regional committees play an essential brokerage role by combining and even consolidating employment mechanisms to assist target groups (see Chapter 7 by Vrijens).

The growing role conferred on the social economy

In a number of countries (Denmark, Ireland, Italy), the emphasis on the social economy and economic solidarity is put forward as a manifestation of the decentralisation of employment policies, for two reasons. Enterprises that are part of the social economy are considered to be major job creators, because they are involved in the development of services and because they treat job creation as an end in itself and not as a means. Such businesses are generally small and highly integrated into the local environment, and as such they reflect a sector with a high degree of decentralisation, both in terms of its structures and its operations.

Some countries have thus considered that through closer association in the implementation of active employment policies, and particularly of programmes that create new services and jobs, they were decentralising a portion of their jobs policy. This is the case with Greece, in which most new job creation, in the area of new personal services in particular, is done via associations, and which has adjusted its mechanisms accordingly (European Union, 2001a). But this line of reasoning needs to be tempered in two respects: barring statistical problems, the number of jobs created is often lower than what is claimed, unless this social economy sector is defined very loosely; and a whole segment of the sector is highly integrated and centralised (see Chapter 24 by Svenningsson).

The evaluation function

Decentralisation creates a new context for labour market agents, who have to deal with new decision-making centres and new procedures, whether these are formalised or not. It is therefore necessary to evaluate the impact of these new institutional adjustments, and this can be done in two ways.

The first way is to test the value added by decentralisation at national level: does it enhance the country's performance in terms of improved rates of participation and employment? This sort of analysis is for the time being not very common because it is very difficult to identify the role of the decentralisation variable amongst the different variables that explain the level of participation and employment rates in a particular economy. It is imperative in this case that the statistical indicators be extended by means of complex econometric adjustments involving instances of multicollinearity and heteroscedasticity, apart from the small number of observations available over time. For the time being, this is more a matter for university research than public policy studies, and very few examples can be found to date.

The second way is to test the way local authorities are using their new competences and how effective they are at achieving their objectives. To some extent, it is a matter of assessing how the new responsibilities are used, and this is all the more important insofar as one of the most commonly advanced arguments for decentralisation is based on tighter control over decision-makers. Furthermore, in many cases local authorities continue to tap into national funding streams, and as a result they are accountable at both the central and local levels. To achieve this, two instruments are necessary: transparency of decision-making – taking us back to the structure of the devolution process mentioned above – and the possibility of evaluating those decisions.

Who should determine evaluation indicators?

While evaluation is already complex at the national level, it is even more so at sub-national level, and for one simple reason: when the effectiveness of the policies they implement is under scrutiny, local authorities (or local employment services) can always contend that such policies only influence the choices of labour market agents, and that the effects of those policies are filtered or even thwarted by economic trends, decisions taken with regard to other localities, or changes in people's behaviour.

Another difficulty is that of setting objectives. If the objectives of employment policies are set at the central level, no one contests the fact that the choices involved are those of the central authority, lest the debate be opened on the nature of the chosen objectives.

Turning to the setting of the objectives of the public employment service, even if decentralised, the problem becomes more complex: in addition to objectives received from the centre and related to the responsibilities of the public service, there is an additional need for indicators related either to conditions specific to the locality in question or to additional policies for that locality.

In respect of actions undertaken by decentralised authorities, a further issue must be considered. Should evaluation indicators be set by those same authorities or by the central level? Here, logic would suggest that decentralised authorities be left to set the evaluation criteria for their own actions, which would allow them to emphasise indicators sensitive to such actions and relatively less influenced by their environment. But in this case, it is to be expected that the chosen indicators will be geared more toward deploying resources than attaining objectives. Conversely, two reasons justify a centralised choice of evaluation mechanisms: the funding of local actions by central resources, which would be conducive to ensuring that those resources are used properly; and the desire to promote labour mobility within as wide an area as possible, which would require that local authorities all share the same objectives, making allowances if necessary for differences stemming from local structural characteristics.

Objectives should therefore be set after joint stock-taking, which is only normal in view of the expected benefits of any process of evaluating government actions: securing quantified information must also be used as an element of collective learning and mediation in the implementation of public policies.

What is the scope of possible indicators?

A first series of indicators are relatively unproblematic to use since they are consistent with the deployment of resources in the field, which falls clearly within the realm of decentralised authorities' unshared responsibilities. These include:

- deadlines for setting up mechanisms in the field;
- deadlines for approving financial assistance;
- coverage rate of target populations by the programmes for their benefit.

A second category of indicators is proving more problematic. These indicators reflect national objectives which must be taken into account irrespective of the territory in question, which makes them partially open to challenge insofar as they involve responsibilities exceeding those of local authorities. These indicators, for example, will cover issues of equal opportunity in the labour market:

- access of target groups to the labour market;
- access of target groups to integration programmes;
- access of target groups to training programmes.

Here, the difficulty will be to formulate an indicator that takes initial conditions into account. For example, the use of an indicator measuring the access of disadvantaged groups to training programmes depends on the density and quality of training programmes in the locality being studied. The quality of such indicators will therefore be inversely proportional to contestability of their basis, which suggests the need for transparency regarding the manner in which they are compiled.

The last category of indicators is even more problematic as it not only implies technical difficulties but also introduces issues surrounding discretionary choice. Beyond objectives set nationally, and which therefore cannot be ignored at the decentralised level, the question arises regarding indicators that a local authority sets for itself. If an authority intends to create new jobs in the realm of services to families or the elderly, it is logical to assume that it would be sufficiently cautious when formulating indicators for those indicators to yield good results, thereby stripping the evaluation function of any relevance. The meaning of these indicators could then be twisted, so that they would become indicators of resources at best. If, for example, an authority introduces as an indicator the number of tourism-related jobs created (Campbell, 2001), knowing that such jobs tend to be temporary and of poor quality, the only thing that the indicator will actually measure is the authority's ability to have put in place the mechanism in question. Once again, this shows the tendency mentioned above for a decentralised authority that controls only some of the outcomes of its actions to prefer indicators of means over indicators of results.

The relevance of governance indicators

Governance indicators are only used moderately. Yet such indicators are to be recommended as they would not give rise to excessive difficulties of interpretation. Since one of the objectives of decentralisation is to take better account of economic and social concerns as they relate to employment, it would logically be possible to assess effectiveness through the closeness of the cooperation found between economic and social agents. But purely formal indicators in terms of meeting places or data-matching are not enough; it is also necessary that such information lead to shared, joint knowledge likely to promote mutual initiatives amongst these agents. More generally, this last condition is, in a sense, the ability of an environment to innovate, which leads back to one of the aims of decentralisation. This consists in finding more innovative solutions to problems than is possible with centralised approaches, for which such innovation is not an easy option. It is also reminiscent of the debates surrounding the constitution of social capital at the local level in response to (un)employment problems (see OECD, 2003).

Among the indicators generally cited at this level are:

- A series of indicators relating to the institution of effective partnerships between all of the agents concerned over a given period (number of agents, number of meetings, volume of resources contributed to set up a network, each agent's effective involvement in the network, etc.).
- A series of indicators relating to the conversion of information into knowledge and capacity for action (the number of documents produced jointly, number of actions undertaken jointly, etc.).

The limited value of benchmarking

Insofar as, in any given country, decentralisation creates numerous systems of labour market governance for each local authority, it would be possible here to envisage an evaluation mechanism based on comparisons between them, *i.e.* benchmarking. Theoretically, this could be done in two ways: by ranking the results of the actions of the various authorities, emphasising the ones that rank highest and lowest; or by determining the upper and lower boundaries of efficiency, to which individual actions and authorities could be assigned.

The exercise would be ambiguous without precautions regarding the construction of the indices. It is difficult to consider that products are comparable, knowing that they can be perceived – and therefore ranked – differently, depending on the time frame of the analysis. Let us consider two authorities wishing to boost the employability of young people via training – one using apprenticeship-based programmes, the other setting up training programmes with a more academic orientation: it is a known fact that in the short term the first authority will enjoy better results than the second, but that after a few years this outcome might be reversed.

An additional difficulty relates to the differences in the initial environment. For example, a territory that is better endowed with the ability to implement policies (*e.g.*, through financial institutions, training facilities, etc.) will have more success with back-to-work initiatives than a territory that is not so endowed with relevant resources and institutions. In this case, benchmarking may in fact explain nothing at all, or – even worse – it may conceal the true factors of effectiveness.

These two difficulties are cumulative. Let us compare the effectiveness of local policies that enlist intermediate associations to promote the gradual return to work of the long-term unemployed. The preferred success criterion would be the rate of re-entry into the competitive labour market after leaving the intermediary labour market (ILM), but the rate would not be the same depending on the length of time, be it six months or a year. The target populations and labour markets within which these organisations operate are not the same. It is therefore necessary to make the criteria more complex in order to take these variations into account, and probably to add additional comparative criteria such as the association's image and how programme participants perceive it. At best, then, this leads to a plurality of criteria, but above all the risk is that they cannot be aggregated simply, thereby precluding true benchmarking and taking us back to the second subset of criteria cited above.

The difficulties and problems of decentralisation

Whatever its ascribed virtues, decentralisation is still more a means than an end in itself. The experiments underway highlight the numerous difficulties that arise from decentralisation, and thus suggest recommendations for improvement. These difficulties are of two types:

- conceptual difficulties, involving the possibility of tackling employment in a local framework;
- other implementation difficulties, involving the possibility of mobilising strategic partnerships within that framework.

Conceptual difficulties

Defining job strategies at the local level means identifying the scope for action in a clear and relevant manner, thus raising a number of problems: Is the territory to which a strategy applies relevant? Is the concept of local employment valid? Do local strategies not entail risks vis-à-vis labour legislation?

The relevant territory

Decentralisation generally results in a shift of powers from one territorial level to other existing levels. But the reasoning behind the decentralisation of actions to promote employment does not necessarily correspond to the territorial criteria underlying a country's administrative organisation. The decision-making environment for employment-related issues may extend far beyond the confines of a city, a county, a province or even a region, and the smaller the territorial focus of decentralisation, the greater this risk will be. There are four ways of addressing this shortcoming.

- The first is to accept that the territories in which partnerships are established through decentralisation will entail several dimensions. Such was the case with Belgium's experiment with sub-regional platforms for employment in the Flanders Region, in which communes could join forces as they saw fit to implement job strategies, and in which a given commune could be part of more than one platform if it felt it belonged to more than one territorial grouping. But by proceeding in this way, the potential gains in effectiveness were negated in terms of accountability, and the option was soon abolished (see Chapter 7 by Vrijens).

- The second method is to approve the setting up of new territorial entities deemed to correspond to genuine local labour markets – markets to which communes or municipalities do not generally adjust. Such was the case with the policies of pays (historic areas) in France, with successive French governments – right- and left-wing alike – encouraging the institution of a new structure that was assumed to correspond to commuting patterns, and that therefore constituted a genuine local job market. But by stopping short of substituting this new echelon for the old ones, and by leaving decentralised powers with the latter, the result was administrative overload. More wisely, it was then decided to encourage communes to join together, allowing them to determine the geographic area within which they agreed to exercise some of their powers jointly (see Chapter 21 by Förschner).

- The third method is to differentiate the decentralisation of employment-related powers. Powers directly related to integration would be left to highly localised territorial levels, while those involving vocational training would be handled by larger territorial entities. Logically, this choice could be explained by economies of scale, but also by the fact that the quality of certain services depends on the level at which they are organised, even if such redistribution may result in a loss of clarity regarding the division of powers. This choice can also be explained by the fact that employment problems do not present the same characteristics, depending on the size of the territory in question. "Neighbourhood jobs" can be administered by relatively circumscribed communal territories, while jobs entailing highly specific skills or related to international specialisation can be analysed and recruited for only in a far wider context, such as that of a region (see Geddes, Chapter 22 and Stewart, Chapter 17).

- The fourth method is to harness contractual arrangements. Since it impossible to define an optimal distribution of powers, local authorities would be encouraged, via appropriate financial measures, to get together and share the exercise of powers in a coherent manner. This is probably a pragmatic policy and an effective way to realistically support the decentralisation of powers in the realm of employment. A good illustration of this is provided by Italy's patti territoriali, which have enabled communes that had previously tended to act separately to co-operate so as to promote employment. This contractual technique can also be used to induce co-operation between entities at different levels, such as regions and cities. Contracts have thus emerged as vehicles of vertical as well as horizontal co-ordination. So why are certain observers reticent about the use of these contracts? Because contracts instituted by the State can have a double bias: the State can postpone the fulfilment of its obligations, citing macroeconomic constraints; and the State can make very steep demands on territorial authorities in exchange for its own commitments, which can strip decentralisation of the desired flexibility (see Chapter 6 by Dau).

The notion of local jobs

This difficulty of having to match areas relevant to employment with areas delineated on the basis of institutional criteria leads to another problem – that of so-called "local" jobs. All too often, moves to decentralise actions to promote employment are justified by the need to pay more attention to local jobs, which national programmes tend to sideline. Arguably, such an attitude is both ambiguous and dangerous.

The notion of local jobs must be used carefully. Only certain jobs have specifically local dimensions, such as those involving neighbourhood services. But rather than local jobs, it would be better here to speak of local employment conditions, insofar as the existence of any given job can be explained both by macroeconomic factors and by factors linked to the immediate environment of the labour supply or demand, and thus by local factors.

The term "local job" can be understood in two different ways. While the second seems relevant, the first would appear far more slanted. When the analysis of decentralisation is based on jobs whose *raisons d'être* are wholly local, strategies are concentrated exclusively on neighbourhood or integration jobs. Moreover, such a slant was uncovered by the assessment of European policies in the Local Action Plans for Employment and Territorial Employment Pacts. It was noted that actions for employment were concentrated solely on neighbourhood jobs, or within the social economy as these promote social inclusion. Local considerations are essentially synonymous with the fight against exclusion – so much so that the new regulations of the European Social Fund virtually equate local development with the fight against exclusion (Article 4, §2 of the Regulation on the ESF). This bias can also be seen through a reading of the National Action Plans for Employment that European Union countries submit to the Commission for review, many of these national plans reducing decentralisation to actions promoting integration and the social economy alone.

But while one of the expected effects of decentralisation is to promote social integration more effectively, decentralisation cannot be reduced to that alone. To do so would be to forget that the purpose of decentralising employment-promotion actions is to enhance the competitiveness of territories by endowing them with sustainable, productive jobs. Introducing a gulf between these two objectives of the decentralisation of employment actions leads to unsustainable development and reduces decentralisation to the management of a segment of society rather a segment of the economy which would depend on the central government alone. An imbalance of this sort was revealed in Belgium, where the bulk of the decentralisation initiatives undertaken by the Walloon Region led to integration actions that were out of phase with long-term economic actions. In that particular case, the problem – symptomatic of weak governance – stemmed from the fact that the decentralised institutions, such as the local development agencies, did not genuinely work in partnership with economic agents (see Chapter 14 by Simonin).

The right to work versus labour law?

According to some observers and managers, the decentralisation of employment initiatives introduces a bias in favour of the right to work to the detriment of labour law. Such decentralisation can in fact entail the creation of "free areas" with terms of employment departing from conventional labour law, a lowering of social contributions, etc., so that job creation causes increasing breaches of labour law and worker protection. In Europe, this issue has taken the form of a debate over "bad jobs" *versus* "good jobs": to boost employment, some countries would not hesitate to accept the creation of "inferior jobs". Ultimately, this could backfire – both against "bad jobs", which in most cases are doomed by technical progress, and against other workers, who must stand up for their rights in an environment in which those rights have increasingly been questioned.

These arguments are far from convincing, especially since the effect of many decentralised actions is to improve equal opportunity for certain particularly disadvantaged social groups or categories of job-seekers. But it would be wrong to underestimate a more debatable aspect arising from the bending of the rules. It would be fairly aberrant if decentralisation, through repeated derogations and suspensions of guarantees, created a sort of social dumping presenting no real benefit for the territories involved.

Obstacles to implementation

Because decentralisation entails the mobilisation of local agents and the creation of synergies from their information and their actions, it must allow for the creation of strategic partnerships for employment.

A first series of difficulties can stem from a poor functioning of the partnerships – and thus from poor governance of employment – to which decentralisation is supposed to contribute. The causes can be manifold: failure to identify – or to represent – the relevant agents, high management costs, a poor information system and the chance that some agents will derive windfall effects at the expense of others, thus inevitably damaging the partnership, etc. (see Chapter 8 by Boni). On a more theoretical level, it is fair to say that partnerships involve principal-agent type relations, each person being both the principal and the agent of the other, which can just as easily result in positive synergies as in negative divisions. Not all these difficulties can be attributed to decentralisation, but the way in which decentralisation is organised can either prevent them or be conducive to them. Examples of this include:

- Decentralisation cannot attain its objectives if there is no synergy between the agents of economic development and agents of integration. But here the greatest risk is that the agents of economic development will be marginalised within decentralised structures, which would lead local partnerships to administer integration functions alone.
- Conversely, if decentralisation does not bring agents such as pro-integration associations, community development organisations, etc. into the discussions on employment, it will leave by the wayside people who might well be able to offer strategic vision in the realms of development and employment.
- With regard to this partnership dimension of decentralisation, a number of recommendations may be made on the basis, in particular, of experience in the United States. This has involved *e.g.* developing mutual accountability, having as the main target people looking for jobs or activities, agreeing on qualitative and quantitative products, having sufficient flexibility on the part of financing bodies – or negotiating it at the outset.

In addition, developing territorial employment pacts is a good way of mobilising and consolidating the right networks of partners for employment. In Austria, for example, the territorial employment pacts initiated by the European Commission have been used as a framework for creating the required partnerships. But it is interesting that this policy has not been confined to hopeful commentaries. Central government has set about mobilising local actors by providing them with certain financial means, creating an independent central agency which can help them to formulate their objectives by setting out its own recommendations in the form of advice instead of rules to be followed, and by allocating them structural funds obtained from the European Union. Amongst all these mechanisms, the creation of the independent agency seems to have played a very major positive role.

A second difficulty can arise *if decentralisation is more cosmetic than strategic.* Decentralisation can in fact result in one of two clearly distinct outcomes. In one case, it sets up a strategic partnership which allows each participant to improve the information available to them, the quality of their decisions and their synergy. In other cases, decentralisation leads an agent to enjoy more information and take the decisions he deems best from his point of view without exerting any positive influence over the decisions of others. Here, decentralisation loses its strategic character and becomes cosmetic at best – and this is precisely what can happen if decentralisation is aimed at the public employment services without prompting those services to work in partnership with other local agents in the employment system (see Chapter 8 by Boni).

The way to prevent such a risk is to guide the decentralisation of objectives, orchestrating synergies between the various agents involved. This is predicated on enhancing the notion of objectives. In addition to employment policy objectives, there should be objectives defining the quality of the desired system of governance: among these, once again, are the linkages between economic and social agents, the capacity to transform information into knowledge for action, and the constitution of genuine social capital for employment.

A third difficulty stems from the lack of flexibility that goes with the implementation of decentralisation – at both national and local levels. The notion of flexibility is in many cases very clearly identified at local level, if only in terms of the globalisation of credits that decentralisation implies. But it is much less well identified at central level, and the new ways in which both local government and administrations work will only produce results if management methods change at central level too. The cases of Denmark and Italy show, in particular, that public finance management has to change in order to gain in flexibility and rapidity. Also, when countries produce guidelines concerning their national objectives (Denmark), here too it is preferable that the objectives be defined in a manner sufficiently flexible for the territorial level to yield added value (see Chapter 14 by Simonin).

A fourth difficulty can stem here from a *poor interface between the vertical networks involved in decentralisation*. All too often, decentralisation is viewed solely through the perspective of horizontal associations of agents in the territory in question. But decentralisation cannot disregard vertical dimensions, even if these are redeployed. States continue to proclaim objectives that they are pledged to maintain regarding labour mobility and equal rights. Moreover, they use their resources to ensure the required equalisation. Regions often proclaim options regarding desired competitiveness in a global economy, and this has repercussions on the training and skills that need to be sought.

Decentralisation can therefore not succeed if a bottom-up approach is substituted blindly for a top-down approach. In a sense, both must now be managed in an intelligent manner. This entails solving problems, many of which can be acute:

- Guaranteeing local authorities genuine decision-making ability through the reality of the powers afforded them, and thus financial resources and flexibility in their use. But the arrangements that have been put in place do not always meet these needs. The decision-making capacities of local authorities are impeded by continued oversight from above, a lack of financial resources and a lack of flexibility in the use of legal and financial resources.

- The potential for State guidance, in particular through the statement of objectives and implementation of financial incentives. But the State's ability to provide guidance is in many cases hampered by the poor quality of information at the local level or its local administrations' own cultures.

Solving the *financial problems* raised by decentralisation constitutes a fifth difficulty, as has already been suggested. If decentralisation does not consolidate public budgets at the local level it deprives local authorities of the necessary financial flexibility and can strip the planned partnerships of their content and their meaning. If decentralisation does not provide a minimum of resources for co-ordination, expertise or even evaluation, it forces agents to spend the bulk of their time looking for financial expedients or trying to shift these expenses on to others.

But an important obstacle comes here from the *financial cost*. Most mechanisms probably consider that any redistribution of powers should be accompanied by a redistribution of the corresponding resources, so that the process can be seen as a zero-sum game. In the realm of administrative organisation, however, there are numerous ratchet effects which in many cases make it impossible to offset increased funding at one level by a corresponding reduction at another level. Moreover, central levels never abandon their responsibilities completely, if only in order to maintain controls or effect the equalisation that they alone can perform. To this must be added the cost of training or investment. Lastly, to institute actions at lower levels may in some cases lead to an abandonment of potential economies of scale. For all these reasons, it would be vain to disregard the cost effect of decentralisation. It could even be considered that decentralisation at constant cost is, for the centre, rather a means of offloading expenses that local authorities will have trouble assuming.

Even so, decentralisation can also be expected to generate scope effects. Thus, all of the services at the local level that deal with integration could benefit from improved synergy between their respective units, and thus from better control over their costs.

It is important, finally, to stress what decentralisation involves in terms of staff training (see Chapter 6 by Dau). This requires both central and local level civil servants to learn a new public management culture. For the former, this means substituting guidance, advice and evaluation responsibilities for the traditional management functions, while for the latter it is a question of moving to a risk-taking culture when previously it had been sufficient to carry out instructions, of adopting objectives-based management instead of being content to oversee processes. The situation in Italy has provided a clear example of the importance of this learning process, without which decentralisation would complicate things rather than improve them.

Conclusion: the three debates involving decentralisation

Decentralisation addresses the desire to bring employment governance more closely in tune with contemporary labour market trends, and to make it more efficient from the standpoint of resource utilisation. To succeed, it must enhance the strategic content, flexibility and accountability of employment policies deployed at the local level. Can it be said today that the decentralisation movements that have featured continuously in employment policies in recent years have in fact succeeded?

Decentralisation is supposed to enhance the strategic dimension of employment policies by incorporating a large number of agents representing diverse dimensions of employment. By doing so, it can lead to joint actions and create synergies in time and space between hitherto unconnected initiatives, thereby improving effectiveness and efficiency.

But it is not always perceived that way in the field, and it may seem like a loss of means, a source of dilution of responsibility or – what is worse – as helping mainly to spur the creation of jobs in ILMs but not of sustainable employment, which does not correspond to the intended strategic goal.

This raises a number of questions: does decentralisation succeed in persuading labour market agents to work with the local authorities? In particular, does it successfully bring economic agents into strategic initiatives? Does it have local information systems capable of yielding relevant assessments?

Decentralisation is supposed to give employment policies the flexibility they lack when they are centralised, by enabling a sharper identification of needs, more relevant responses and participation of target groups in the implementation of initiatives for their benefit.

Here too, the reality has in some instances been different. It often takes a long time to set initiatives in place, and employment policies at the local level focus on the least difficult or least risky actions, and this is reflected in a bias concerning the indicators used, with indicators of means tending to take precedence over indicators of results.

As a result, several questions arise: Is it effective to devolve powers? Can the resources allocated be used flexibly, which might run counter to auditing requirements or requirements for the allocation of public appropriations? Are local authorities prepared to run the risk of flexibility, with all its implications? Do capture effects exist at the local level, on the part of certain employment system agents if not of the target groups?

Decentralisation must be accompanied by a clarification of responsibilities in order to be effective and sustainable. Because new agents and new resources are harnessed, it is essential to clarify responsibilities in order to avoid their shortage of them in the future.

Decentralisation puts the responsibilities of local authorities on centre stage without necessarily doing away with those of the central authorities, and it adds interfaces with numerous decision centres that are controlled by neither group. In such a context, three instruments appear essential if responsibilities are to be clarified:

- clear statement of comprehensible and feasible objectives;
- establishment of a system of indicators regarding these objectives;
- implementation of agreements between the agents destined to become partners in such policies.

Insofar as this implementation is difficult and entails a gradual learning process, pragmatic initiatives, in which contracts can play a role, ought to be adopted. This requires a new culture, on the part of local and central authorities alike – one very different from the traditional cultures of public management: *if decentralisation is to make a difference, local authorities must consider themselves to be civic innovators, and the central authorities support instruments. This is a necessary condition if decentralisation is not to give rise to a new local bureaucracy that the central authorities would content themselves with managing. It is the way to avoid the pitfall facing any decentralisation: innovating without being able to define responsibilities, or conferring new responsibilities which do not contribute to innovation.*

Bibliography

BALLOCH, Susan and TAYLOR, Marilyn (2001), "Conclusion – Can Partnerships Work", in S Balloch and C.U. Ciborra (1996), *Teams, Markets and Systems: Business Innovation and Information Technology*, Cambridge, Cambridge University Press.

BEHRENZ, Lars, DELANDER, Lennart and NIKLASSON, Harald (2001), "Towards Intensified Local Level Co-operation in the Design and Implementation of Labor Market Policies: An Evaluation of some Swedish Experiments and Reforms", in J. de Koning and H. Mosley (eds.), *Labor Market Policy and Unemployment: Impact and Process Evaluations in Selected European Countries*, Aldershot, Edward Elgar, pp. 256-290.

CAMPBELL, Mike (2001), "Partnerships in Austria: Enhancing Regional Co-operation in a Decentralised Policy Framework", in OECD (2001), *Local Partnerships for Better Governance*, Paris.

EUROPEAN UNION (2002a), *Evaluation of the Preparatory Measures for a Local Commitment for Employment – Acting Locally for Employment*, DG Employment.

EUROPEAN UNION (2002b), *Thematic Evaluation of the Territorial Employment Pacts*, DG Employment and ECOTEC.

EUROPEAN UNION (2001a), *Évaluation des Plans Nationaux d'Action pour l'Emploi*, DG Employment.

EUROPEAN UNION (2001b), *Joint Statements of the European Public Employment Services (PES) on Their Role in the Labour Market*, Directorate-General for Employment and Social Affairs, Unit EMP/A.3.

GOODIN, Robert E. (ed.), (1996), *The Theory of Institutional Design*, Cambridge, Cambridge University Press.

GREFFE, Xavier (2002), *Le développement local*, Éditions de l'Aube, Aix.

GREFFE, Xavier (2001), "Devolution of Training: A Necessity for the Knowledge Economy", in OECD (2001), *Devolution and Globalisation: Implications for Local Decision-Makers*, Paris.

GREFFE, Xavier (2000), *Gestion publique*, Éditions Dalloz, Paris.

GREFFE, Xavier (1999), *L'emploi culturel à l'âge du numérique*, Éditions Economica, Paris.

GREFFE, Xavier (1998), *Économie des politiques publiques*, Éditions Dalloz, Paris.

GREFFE, Xavier (1997), *La formation professionnelle des jeunes*, Éditions Economica, Paris.

IGAS (2002), *Politiques sociales de l'état et territoires, Rapport annuel*, La Documentation française, Paris.

KOOIMAN, Jan (1993), "Socio-Political Governance: Introduction", in J. Kooiman (ed.), *Modern Governance: New Government-Society Interactions*, Sage, London.

LE GRAND, Julian and BARTLETT, Will (eds.) (1993), *Quasi-Markets and Social Policy*, Macmillan, Houndsmills.

LIN, Nan (2001), *Social Capital: A Theory of Social Structure and Action*, Cambridge University Press.

MOSLEY, Hugh and SOL, Elsa (2001), "Process Evaluation of Active Labor Market Policies and Implementation Regimes", in J. de Koning and H. Mosley (eds.), *Labor Market Policy and Unemployment: Impact and Process Evaluations in Selected European Countries*, Aldershot, Edward Elgar.

MOSLEY, Hugh, KELLER, Tiziana and SPECKESSER, Stefan (1998), *The Role of the Social Partners in the Design and Implementation of Active Measures*, ILO.16, Geneva.

MOSLEY, Hugh, SCHÜTZ, Holger and BREYER, Nicole (2001), *Management by Objectives in European Public Employment Services*, Discussion Paper FS101-203, Social Science Research Centre (WZB), Berlin.

OECD (2003), *The Non-profit Sector in a Changing Economy*, Paris.

OECD (2001a), *Local Partnerships for Better Governance*, Paris.

OECD (2001b), *The Well-being of Nations: the Role of Human and Social Capital*, Paris.

OECD (2001c), *Devolution and Globalisation: Implications for Local Decision-makers*, Paris.

OECD (1999), *Decentralising Employment Policy, New Trends and Challenges*, Paris.

OECD (1997), *The Public Employment Service: Belgium*, Paris.

OECD (1996a), *The OECD Jobs Strategy: Enhancing the Effectiveness of Active Labour Market Policies*, Paris.

OECD (1996b), *The Public Employment Service: Austria-Germany-Sweden*, Paris.

OECD (1996c), *The Public Employment Service in Denmark, Finland and Italy*, Paris.

OECD (1993), *Partnerships: the Key to Job Creation, Experiences from OECD Countries*, Paris.

OSBORNE, David and GAEBLER, Ted (1992), *Re-inventing Government. How the Entrepreneurial Spirit is Transforming the Public Sector*, Addisson-Wesley, Reeding, Massachusetts.

POLLITT, Christopher and BOUCKAERT, Geert (2000), *Public Management Reform. A Comparative Analysis*, Oxford University Press, Oxford/New York.

SABEL, Charles and O'DONNELL, Rory (2001), "Democratic Experimentalism: What to do about Wicked Problems after Whitehall", in OECD (2001), *Devolution and Globalisation: Implications for Local Decision-makers*, Paris.

SIMONIN, Bernard (1997), "Politiques de l'emploi : évolutions, acteurs et territoires", in J.P. Delevoye (1997), *Cohésion sociale et territoire*, Commissariat Général au Plan, Paris.

SMITH, Steven and LIPSKY, Michael (1993), *Nonprofits for Hire: The Welfare State in the Age of Contracting*, Harvard University Press, Cambridge Mass.

TUROK, Ivan (2002), "Innovation in Local Governance: The Irish Partnership Model", in OECD (2001), *Local Partnerships for Better Governance*, Paris.

ISBN 92-64-10470-4
Managing Decentralisation
A New Role for Labour Market Policy
© OECD 2003

PART I
Chapter 3

Denmark: Anchoring Labour Market Policies in the Regions

by
Jan Hendeliowitz
Head of the Public Employment Service, Storstrøm Region

Unprecedented positive trend in the Danish labour market

Today unemployment in Denmark is at its lowest in the last 25 years. Approximately 5% of the workforce are registered as active jobseekers. In addition, the number of persons working in welfare-to-work schemes and unemployment-related leave-of-absence schemes has shrunk considerably in the past five years and has now reached a historic low.

Compared with other OECD countries, Denmark is one of the countries that have experienced the most marked fall in unemployment in the past ten years. In fact, Denmark has now lower unemployment figures than the United States.

The relatively low unemployment rate should be seen in the light of a high female participation rate. This has resulted in Denmark's activity rate becoming one of the highest in the OECD countries. At the same time, the employment rate, i.e. the number of adults in actual ordinary employment, is also one of the highest. Finally, it should be noted that the youth unemployment rate is one of the lowest in the OECD countries.

In comparison with other OECD countries with similar positive labour market trends, e.g. the Netherlands and the US, Denmark comes out convincingly within several parameters. In spite of a lower registered unemployment rate, the Netherlands have markedly lower activity and employment rates and a higher youth unemployment rate. The US has unemployment and employment rates almost identical to Denmark's. But pay-rate variations have a wider span in the US, where the minimum wage approximates 50% of the actual minimum wage in Denmark, while unemployment insurance and social benefits are far below Danish standards.

The trend in the Danish labour market is therefore close to being exceptionally positive. The fall in unemployment has taken place at a time of high activity and employment rates. Denmark has managed to reduce a very high youth unemployment rate. The gap between male and female unemployment has tapered off, as have the variations in unemployment seen between various skills groups. In addition, regional variations in unemployment are now much lower. Unemployment insurance coverage continues to be high and comprehensive, and the actual minimum wage is one of the highest in the OECD.

Limits to the general economic capacity for growth

This has coincided with the relatively weak increase in money wages in the past 10 years. Falling unemployment seems not to have caused an increase in bottleneck problems or other wage-inflationary, structural problems in the labour market. This development in the labour market should, of course, be evaluated relative to the general trends in the Danish economy.

During the 1990s, Denmark managed to balance income and expenditure in the Danish economy and keep them balanced with a surplus on the balance of payments and the national budget, concurrent with a constant two to 3% annual growth in the gross national product. Both domestic and foreign debts have been considerably reduced to a stable level. The Danish economy has no difficulty in meeting the EMU convergence criteria. Growth and a balanced economy together with a significant reduction in unemployment, increasing employment and moderate wage and price rises distinguish Denmark from the main part of the other OECD economies, seen over the past 10 years.

The general international economic boom has had a considerable impact on the development of the Danish economy. It is nevertheless striking that the upswing in Denmark, which accelerated in 1993-1994, set in earlier than in the other OECD countries and that the downturn in the international economy in autumn 2001 has not yet led to a corresponding recession in Denmark. Unemployment continues to fall, and particularly corporate sales to other countries, which are apparently less sensitive to fluctuating market conditions than previously assumed, continue to enjoy a reasonably positive trend.

The positive trend in the international economy cannot alone explain the favourable trend in Denmark. The political and economical measures taken in Denmark in the past 10 years can be ascribed to important separate causes.

Overall, there has been a national political consensus about the fiscal policy for the past 15 years. Although economic development did not gain momentum until the change of government in 1993, the scope of economic policy had already been outlined. The so-called "potato diet" in 1986, which suddenly curbed domestic consumer spending and increased the public tax yield, had a very positive effect on the balance of payments and the public economy trends. But the "potato diet" also curbed economic growth. When the Social Democratic Nyrup government (SPD) came into power in 1993, unemployment had reached an all-time high. In 1993, the government boosted the economy, primarily by allowing mortgage loans to be re-mortgaged. This measure spurred economic growth.

It is many years since the overall economic policy and its aims were a cause for political conflict in Denmark. The prevailing mood is consensus about ends and means, which has made it possible to take continuous and consistent economic political initiatives with rather positive effects.

A decisive factor for the positive effects of the economic policy has been a properly functioning labour market. In the beginning of the 1990s, economists tended to estimate the "natural" unemployment rate in Denmark to be 7-8%. Any percentage below that figure would lead to rising inflation owing to increasing bottleneck and mismatch problems in the labour market.

The adaptability of the labour force – including the jobless, in particular – was not deemed sufficient to meet the corporate demand for labour if increased demand resulted in an unemployment rate below 7-8%. Limited professional and geographical mobility, skills deficiencies, motivation and incentive problems owing to the generous unemployment insurance system, individual social problems, etc., were stated as the reasons for the high degree of structural unemployment.

It was therefore necessary to supplement the general economic policy with a more targeted labour market policy that could alleviate these structural problems in the labour market and cause a significant reduction in the "natural" unemployment rate.

Reduction in structural unemployment

The labour market reform, which took effect in 1994, had precisely this primary purpose. As described above, Denmark succeeded in reducing unemployment to a rate considerably below what was, in the beginning of the 1990s, considered the level of structural unemployment. Furthermore, the reduction in unemployment disparities according to occupational groups, age and gender and geographical units was also given particular policy attention.

Evaluations show that the labour market reforms policies have been crucial elements of the country's successful economic policy over the past 15 years.

Labour market policies have increased labour force adaptability and readiness for change, reduced the average unemployment period, reduced long-term unemployment and, on the whole, eliminated youth unemployment. This has led to a considerable reduction in structural unemployment and been a decisive factor in the continued economic growth and price stability in Denmark.

In connection with the implementation of the labour market reform, the Danish Ministry of Labour initiated a comprehensive evaluation of its implementation and effects. The final evaluation report – published in 1998 – was a general analysis of the reform's effect on the functioning of the labour market (Danish National Institute of Social Research, 1998). The Danish National Institute of Social Research, which conducted the analysis, concluded that they could not rule out that the reform had had a significant effect on structural unemployment. Since then, the OECD (1997), the Danish Council of Economic Advisers (2000) and the Danish Ministry of Finance (1997) have demonstrated that the reduction in structural unemployment is, to a large degree, ascribable to the Danish active labour market policy.

Overall, there has been a political consensus about the principal lines taken in the Danish labour market policy, a consensus which also goes for the country's overall economic policy framework. The labour market reform was adopted by the Danish Parliament with broad political support and general backing from the social partners. The adjustments and modifications effected since 1994 have also been adopted by the Danish Parliament, by substantial majorities and with general support from the social partners.

Against this background, it is striking how much the political debate and the media have focused on the labour market policy since the implementation of the labour market reform. The labour market reform was essentially the end product of the so-called "Professor Zeuthen Committee". This committee was appointed by the Conservative Schlüter government (CL) in 1991-1992 and included representatives from the social partners, ministerial officials and experts. The committee had completed its work immediately before the change of government (SPD) in 1993, but the succeeding Social Democratic Nyrup government adopted the committee's recommendations in general and implemented the labour market reform in 1994.

Aim and effect

The labour market reform comprised two elements: an administrative reform and a welfare-to-work reform.

The administrative reform entailed that 14 regional labour market councils with representatives from the social partners and the county and municipal authorities became responsible – the Danish public employment service (PES) acting as executive body – for implementing regionally based labour market policy initiatives within the framework of centrally decided overall aims and the economic limits set by the Danish National Labour Market Council and the Danish Minister of Labour.

The welfare-to-work reform meant that the period in which insured jobless people were entitled to support in the form of either unemployment benefits or subsidised jobs and training would now have a fixed duration, so that participation in work-to-welfare schemes no longer reinstated a person in his entitlements to unemployment benefits. The aim included a gradual reduction of the benefit period over a number of years. Concurrently, activities aimed at the jobless were to be more individualised and the concept of an Individual Action Plan was introduced. All jobless people became entitled and obliged to receive an individually agreed action plan, to be drawn up in co-operation with the public employment service and to include the initiatives agreed by the jobless person and the PES in order to restore the jobless person to stable, ordinary employment.

The condition set out in the administrative reform – namely that the labour market policy should now be implemented on the basis of the regional labour market councils' evaluation and prioritisation of each region's specific requirements based on centrally prescribed, region-specific budgets – was seen as an important novelty. It was expected that the reform would bring about high levels of local and regional autonomy and self-management.

The labour market councils came to replace the former regional labour market boards, which had largely been made up of the same group of representatives and had primarily served as advisors to the director of the regional PES regarding his management of the regional employment service.

The welfare-to-work reform also attracted attention. It was very ambitious and made great demands on the PES' administrative capacity, proposing more direct demands on jobseekers to take co-responsibility for their situation, requiring them to obtain ordinary employment in order to retain their entitlement to unemployment benefits.

To the general public, the labour market reform has primarily become synonymous with the labour market policy initiatives taken towards the insured jobless. But the labour market reform also applied to the non-insured jobless, who were, in principle, afforded the same rights and obligations, with the individual action plan as the pivot of initiatives. The same instruments are available for activities aimed at the non-insured, but the provisions of fixed-term benefits and activation periods do not apply to the non-insured.

While the administrative responsibility for implementation of labour market initiatives lies with the labour market councils and the PES, the political and administrative responsibility for the non-insured lies with the municipalities. This means that, in practice, Denmark has a dichotomous labour market system that, in principle, places the general administrative responsibility for the jobless on the authority that finances their subsistence in the form of unemployment benefits (primarily the central government) or social assistance benefits (the municipalities, 50% being reimbursed by central government).

As mentioned, a stocktaking of today's labour market shows a considerable improvement in the unemployment situation, primarily for the insured jobless, whereas non-insured unemployment has not been reduced on the same scale.

It would be a possible conclusion that the relative increase in the group of non-insured jobless people was caused by the introduction of fixed-term benefit periods in the unemployment insurance funds, which could result in a loss of benefit entitlements for many long-term unemployed. There are, however, no indications that many jobless benefit claimants lose their entitlements to unemployment insurance after expiry of a job activation period and are forced to claim social assistance benefits. But tightening the requirements for unemployment insurance from 26 to 52 weeks of ordinary employment – introduced as part of the labour market reform – combined with the fact that "municipal job activation" no longer counts as a qualification for entitlement to unemployment benefits means that this option is not available to a large number of weak jobless recipients of social welfare benefits, who would previously have been eligible for membership of an unemployment insurance fund.

Concurrent with the falling unemployment rate, focus has increasingly been directed towards the measures taken to help the weakest groups on the labour market, who find it particularly difficult to obtain ordinary employment, even in a general situation with high demand for labour.

The concept of the flexible labour market covers an increased effort towards these weak groups whose working capacity is often reduced. For them, the usual rehabilitation measures have been supplemented with special instruments, such as sheltered and flexi-time jobs. One of the main recent developments in Denmark is that, despite increasing employment and falling unemployment, the number of persons of working age with transfer incomes has not been reduced proportionally. This circumstance is often used to argue that real unemployment has not been reduced.

Contrary to most OECD countries, the situation in Denmark is that those excluded from the labour market are increasingly supported by public transfer incomes in the form of disability pensions, rehabilitation benefits, sickness and unemployment benefits, permanent social assistance benefits etc. This is, of course, a societal problem that must be addressed, but it is not a traditional labour market policy issue, since most of these groups do not belong to the actual labour force.

Hence this issue cannot be used to argue that the labour market policy's success story in Denmark is only a qualified truth. If anything, the successful results of the ordinary labour market policy have provided prospects and an economic scope for focusing on the groups reliant on public transfer incomes to help them reintegrate the labour market.

It thus appears that the recent labour market policy emphasis on more active and "dichotomous" criteria has contributed greatly to the extremely favourable development of the labour market in the past decade.

Regionalisation and central co-ordination

Allegedly, the regional focus of labour market policy – including an extended target and management system, in which the central framework and guidelines are defined by the Minister of Labour and the National Labour

Market Council and then, with wide limits, filled in by the regional labour market councils and the PES – has been steadily diluted.

Significant amendments and restrictions in the legislation on jobseekers' rights and obligations have taken place. The entitlement period, during which jobless people receive unemployment or welfare-to-work benefits in step with falling unemployment, now has a fixed duration and has seen a gradual curtailment. There has been a tightening of the rules and guidelines for the timing and scope of job activation. Concurrently, the economic focus on job activation has meant that more fixed and stricter limits have emerged, including the average price per "activated" person. Today, all expenses relating to activation of the insured jobless are financed by the labour market councils through the PES, within a centrally decided framework.

Concurrently, the central authorities' requirements for fixed targets, results and follow-up exercises have become more rigorous. But it would be incorrect to draw the conclusion that the scope of the regional labour market policy has been greatly restricted. Today the Danish labour market policy is regulated by a very finely tuned and balanced interaction between central and regional levels, which seems increasingly convincing, according to the outcomes of the measures taken.

In a state-financed system regulated by the social partners such as the Danish labour market system, it is necessary to balance the many-sided interests and considerations while persisting in the principal aim of the initiatives, *i.e.* to optimise the effect of the labour market policy initiatives taken in the regions, within the targets and economic framework defined by the Danish Parliament and Government at national level.

Today, this is established through a continuous dialogue and interaction between the central level (the Labour Minister, the National Labour Market Authority and the National Labour Market Council) and the regional level (*i.e.* the labour market councils and the PES regions). Central aims, interests and considerations are balanced against regional requirements and targets, whereby the social partners, the central and local authorities become involved in the policy-making and subsequent implementation of policies (Danish National Labour Market Authority, 2002).

The OECD LEED Programme's recent analysis of the role and function of the Danish labour market councils concluded that Denmark had succeeded in establishing a very smooth political institutional framework for regional labour market initiatives (OECD, 2001). This is because its regional labour market councils and their composition and interaction with the central level, work to ensure that the actors on the regional labour market all pull in the same direction. The fact that the regional level forms part of the national framework is considered an advantage in relation to the possibilities of co-ordinating the labour market policy with the general economic policy.

The establishment of a political and economic framework for the labour market policy has in recent years been supplemented with an administrative management system in a performance contract concept that annually establishes the correlation between targets, results, efforts, resource consumption and economic productivity.

This combination of a smooth and coherent political regulatory system and an administrative management system should not be characterised as centralisation in the negative sense of the word. It is a question of continuous professionalisation of the control and management of a very complex institutional framework, where the social partners' interests at central and regional levels are balanced against the government's and the Danish Parliament's overall aims and framework for the labour market policy through governmental administration with central (the Danish National Labour Market Authority) and regional institutions (the PES) to service citizens and businesses at the local level.

Challenges to future labour market policies

The challenges to future labour market policies should be considered in conjunction with the emerging problems on the labour market in the years to come.

The most important problem is the development and composition of the workforce relative to the expected demand for labour. There is a risk that the workforce may shrink in the upcoming decade, if the present retirement pattern and the general activity rate remain unaltered. This is simply the consequence of the demographic composition of the labour force.

We should therefore focus on reducing senior employee retirement from the labour market and ensuring better employment prospects for the groups who have difficulty entering the labour market, *i.e.* primarily immigrants and the most vulnerable jobseekers. This must coincide with the imposition of even more rigorous adaptability requirements on the entire labour force, which exacerbates the underlying tendencies to expel people from the labour market.

The labour market policy should be developed so that tendencies to expulsion are countered by initiatives aimed directly at the employed labour force, *e.g.* by increased workforce training and competency development. These measures should be aimed directly at the situation and needs of the individual regions and industries, since the development in Denmark is becoming increasingly differentiated, both in geographical and in sectoral terms.

The initiatives in adult and continuing vocational education at regional and local levels will be of increasing importance for the adaptability of the labour force. Labour market re-conversion will increasingly be effected by shedding existing jobs and establishing new ones. It is interesting that the number of persons affected by unemployment during one year has not fallen in line with the general reduction in unemployment. Many workers lose their jobs, but find new ones with other companies. The labour market policy can support this adjustment through a greater exposure of job openings on the labour market.

In autumn 2002, the PES launched the "Digital Employment Service", which, via a public job and CV bank on the Internet, will increase all jobseekers' prospects of finding a job and opportunities for employers to advertise their vacancies. The digital employment service, supplemented with various more or less specialised private job portals will, no doubt, become an important instrument in ensuring the necessary strengthening of job turnover on the Danish labour market.

The shrinking labour force trend will, in itself, improve the more or less marginalised groups' prospects on the labour market. The integration of immigrants in the labour market has good prospects of succeeding, but presupposes far more targeted and labour-market-oriented initiatives, to be directed both at the individual situation and competencies of the immigrants and at the employers and Danish employer culture. The same applies to the prospects of the other marginalised groups on the Danish labour market. In this field also, the initiatives taken here must also be directed at both the individual person's situation and at employers.

The crucial question, then, is whether Denmark's labour market policy capacity and systems are geared to meet these challenges.

In terms of administration and organisation, we have a sound basis in the national labour market system under the Ministry of Employment, to which the social partners at both national and regional levels in the National Labour Market Council and the regional labour market councils contribute. The digitalisation of the PES gives the employment service regions better opportunities for handling job turnover on the labour market. The establishment of a more one-pronged labour market system, in which employers and jobseekers are serviced in the same place, will probably render job turnover even more efficient.

The welfare-to-work initiatives aimed at jobless peoples who are unable to obtain ordinary employment directly can, no doubt, become more targeted and efficient. It is necessary to develop even more selective and individual welfare-to-work initiatives and improve the targeting of actual job openings on the labour market. Other actors, *e.g.* private consultancy firms, should also be involved, based on performance-related pay, in order to restore specific target groups to ordinary employment faster and more efficiently.

Although the variations in unemployment have, for most significant factors – regions, unemployment insurance funds, gender and age – narrowed down considerably, it is crucial to maintain the regionally focused and anchored labour market policy, because this is one of the most important causes of the positive effects of active labour market policy.

The regionally focused labour market policy defines the framework and the targets of the labour market initiatives taken by regional and local actors. The frameworks and targets – balanced against national priorities – are established through a dialogue between the social partners and local and regional authorities in the regional labour market councils and are based on common insight and knowledge of the situation and trends on the regional labour market, primarily produced by the PES regions labour market analytical centres.

In Denmark, adjustments have been carried to the targeting system to promote suitability of policies to the local and regional context. The traditional tripartite system has evolved to make room for local and regional authorities in the regional labour market councils, and all take part in a complex negotiation process to reconcile local and national objectives and fix on an agreed basis the annual targets for the ALMPs. The local community at large is consulted on the main local priorities as part of this process.

Without these common aims and frameworks for regional labour market initiatives, it would be very difficult to ensure efficient interaction between the many regional and local actors in the labour market effort. It is therefore a precondition for the continued development of good results on the Danish labour market that the regional labour market policy framework for the initiatives is maintained and developed in step with the involvement of an increasing number of actors through a coherent policy network.

In conclusion, the regionally anchored labour market system still has a great potential for meeting the challenges on the labour market in the years to come.

Bibliography

DANISH COUNCIL OF ECONOMIC ADVISERS (2000), "Dansk Økonomi" (The Danish Economy), Copenhagen.

DANISH MINISTRY OF FINANCE (1997), "Finansredegørelse 1997" (Financial Statement and Budget Report), Copenhagen.

DANISH MINISTRY OF LABOUR (1986), "*Arbejdsmarkedet og arbejdsmarkedspolitikken*" (The Danish Labour Market and Labour Market Policies), Copenhagen.

DANISH NATIONAL INSTITUTE OF SOCIAL RESEARCH (1998), "Arbejdsmarkedsreformen og arbejdsmarkedet. Evaluering af arbejdsmarkedsreformen III" (The Danish Labour Market Reform and Labour Market. An Evaluation of the Third Danish Labour Market Reform), Copenhagen.

OECD (2001), *Local Partnerships for Better Governance*, Paris.

OECD (1997), *OECD Employment Outlook*, Paris.

OFFICIAL SWEDISH REPORTS (1979), "Sysselsättningspolitik för arbete åt alla" (An Employment Policy Aimed at Procuring Jobs for All), Labour Market Department, Stockholm.

ISBN 92-64-10470-4
Managing Decentralisation
A New Role for Labour Market Policy
© OECD 2003

PART I
Chapter 4

The US: Decentralisation from the Bottom Up

by
Robert Straits
Director of the Workforce Development Board,
Kalamazoo and St. Joseph, Michigan

Shifting powers

During the past thirty years the United States has shifted employment and training programme administration from the federal level to the states. The states to varying degrees have further delegated responsibilities to the local level. Previous employment and training legislation reflected the policy position of centralised control at the federal level. By the early 1970s, the political mood changed towards decentralisation because some policy makers believed that local decision-makers could do a better job in selecting service providers and as a result the needs of programme recipients would more adequately be addressed. The degree of the transition in authority was debated. As in the case of most legislation the 1973 policy shift was a political compromise and neither of the major political parties was completely satisfied with the outcome.

After Congress passed the new Employment and Training legislation, and the president signed it, the Department of Labor wrote regulations arguably capturing the intent of congress. Regulations are notorious for being too restrictive according to individual congressional representatives and, at times, are barriers to accomplishing the primary purpose of Congress. It appears to the local observer that the writers of regulations take the most conservative approach, believing it is easier to "loosen" rules that are demonstrated to be inhibiting, than it is to tighten rules once a programme has been implemented. Regulations also provide legislators cover, which generally means they can be purposefully unclear or be written to protect elected officials from being accused of a lack of diligence. However, there has been some fraud and abuse in employment and training programmes, and regulations also offer a guide to help minimise future problems.

A shift away from central control was also a counter measure because to date the "War on Poverty" conducted by the federal government had not accomplished what some believed was intended. There were still unemployed and poor people. Consequently, changes in employment and training measures were important because the old approach was generally considered ineffective (although few legislators could agree on what was meant by effective) and expensive. These "new era" changes were classified as "de-categorisation" and "decentralisation". Thus they reportedly gave state and local governments more discretion in how federally funded employment and training programmes would be operated. The degree to which programmes were intended to be decentralised has been a matter of opinion. From the local perspective there was belief that there was still too much control maintained by the federal Department of Labor, but the evolving decentralisation was a good first step.

Prior to 1973 the federal government determined how employment and training dollars would be allocated from Regional Offices that covered five or more states. The Regional Offices requested proposals from local governments and community-based organisations (CBOs) and according to predetermined weighting of factors, made funding awards. Unfortunately, there were many instances where the factors did not include informed criteria.

Moreover, a problem related to the system that existed was the type of service being provided. Skill training was provided on the basis of recipient interest or the availability of donated equipment and not on the demands of the local market. Participants completing training were not obtaining jobs in the area in which they had been trained. There was a disconnection between what employers were looking for and the type of training being offered.

Decentralisation was accomplished by identifying "prime sponsors" to oversee the programmes at the local level. Prime Sponsors were units of local government that had taxing authority in order to cover any disallowed costs (expenditures not accepted under the regulations). The Prime Sponsor had to have a population of at least 200 000, which was not a concern for larger cities and counties, but smaller counties needed to either join with adjacent jurisdictions or become what was known as the "balance of state".

Where two or more political areas joined together they were required to have inter-local agreements establishing the relationship between the jurisdictions and establishing which unit of local government was ultimately liable for any "disallowed costs". If the political jurisdictions became apart of the "balance of state", the state was responsible for the expenditure of funds and controlled the management of programmes at the local level including the selection of service providers and monitoring for compliance with the regulations. In balance of state areas in particular, many battles were fought over local authority and the selection of service providers. The most challenging were in the rural areas of the states where contiguous political jurisdictions, having a history of competition, were forced together.

From de-categorisation to the one-stop concept

The other pillar of change was de-categorisation. Under the preceding legislation funds were often allocated based on the characteristics of targeted populations. The proliferation of programmes resulted in an overlapping at the local level. Organisations providing similar services were not co-ordinating services, resulting in duplication and other inefficiencies. De-categorisation meant that federal appropriations would not be earmarked for specific programmes. It became the responsibility of the Prime Sponsor and the locally established Advisory Council to determine the needs of the target populations and how they would be addressed. Any race or ethnic group that made up at least 2% of the local population needed to be proportionately reflected in service delivery, but "mainstreaming" was preferred to segregated programmes. This was a significant improvement over past employment and training programmes. A downside was the policy that applicants were required to document that they were "economically disadvantaged" in order to receive services.

The Local Advisory Council was established to provide over sight of local employment and training programmes and serve as a check on local government Prime Sponsors. The intent was to have a cross section of the community sitting on the Advisory Councils, including advocates for targeted groups. Advocates would ensure the needs of individuals with special needs were taken into consideration by the Prime Sponsor when preparing the local Employment and Training plan laying out how the funding would be expended at the local level.

During the 1980s and 1990s, policy changes "tweaked" the fundamental system that was put in place in 1973. The most significant changes were the increased emphasis and role of the private sector. This was to ensure the training provided had relevance to the local labour market and that those who did the hiring had a stake in the development of local employment programmes. Based on the "marketing" of the changes in policy the private sector was led to believe their input would make a substantial difference in programme design and outcomes. Although there have been positive changes, most private sector representatives soon realised the many constraints attached to federal funding and the lack of flexibility actually available. These restrictions have frustrated many volunteers from the private sector and dampened the possibility for financial support it was hoped would fill in funding gaps.

Most recently, federally-funded employment programmes are emphasizing universal access, a "one stop" concept, and a partnership with the private sector. Many employment professionals have expressed concern over the potential loss of any extraordinary effort to assist the "most in need" in a universal access delivery system. Concerns may be heightened because of reductions in the federal financial commitment as individuals with greater needs cannot compete on a level-playing field. Many local advisory boards have instituted local policies that emphasise targeting resources beyond self-help to individuals with significant barriers to employment. It was feared that programmes at the local level driven more by employer interest than jobseeker needs could negatively impact the marginally unemployed; however, economic conditions have proven to have the most significant influence on employment opportunities and employer influence has seldom been an issue.

Unfortunately even in the new legislation the opinions of the central government have been at the expense of local creativity and practicality. The new legislation provides for the co-location of agencies providing similar services. This forced "one stop" design is well intended and from the top down may appear a most efficient use of resources. In reality, clients are not clustered in one geographical area and multiple one stop centres may not be cost effective. A more reasonable approach may have been to encourage electronic co-location or other approaches determined by the local area. This might have been accomplished by defining the desired outcome and not prescribing the method to be used.

Funding constraints

By the twenty-first century, pressures to reduce taxes and to give states more authority shifted greater responsibility for employment and training policy away from the federal government and toward the states. The states feeling budget crunches of their own are now beginning to suggest that the local communities start relying upon the local tax base and private sector to fund programmes important to them. Unfortunately, this change in approach was not strategic but rather reactive. Local employment programmes have not been developed to compete for funding that has been supporting public safety, roads, and public works projects.

Small reductions in federal funding during periods of low unemployment were tolerable, but as unemployment started to drift higher, cries for more assistance have been met with deferral to the state and local policy makers. Complicating matters has been the fact that the federal government remains intent on using dwindling federal contributions to accomplish multiple federal objectives.

There have been many adjustments to employment policy during the past thirty years, but interestingly the balances between federal, state, and local control have evolved slowly. Even now, the shift to state "authority" is not without many strings attached to federal funding. If a state fails to achieve 17 performance standards two years in a row the federal government can withhold funding. And despite evolutionary advances it has been the federal government that funds "silos" by not instituting common reporting requirements, common cost definitions, and clear programme outcome standards.

At the local level, it appears the state is becoming an extension of the federal arm and in some cases it has made programme delivery more complicated because of the addition of state policy, rules and regulations without a corresponding reduction in federal requirements. When the state adds a few state dollars to the pot, the local programmes are faced with the awesome task of attempting to accomplish state objectives in addition to the federal objectives. This is particularly troubling when the state and federal objectives are not compatible.

The evolution of local community involvement in deciding training needs, selecting service providers, and within parameters determining how funds can be expended, has been a process driven by societal attitudes regarding the role of government and our perception of where limited funding should be targeted. Any evidence that the local community can do a better job in addressing the employment and training needs at the local level has been lost in this larger struggle. It is within this context that the three levels of government are wallowing in murky water.

The states are required to submit a state plan to the federal government for funding. The state plan is expected to be a consolidation of local plans that takes into consideration the variances in key indicators such as labour market, educational levels, public assistance rate, and economic growth. The fact that conditions at the local level are extremely fluid can be lost when the plan is viewed as a stable rather than an evolving process. If one or two major employers go through a merger or close their doors, the impact is substantial. The same is true when there is major investment in local development or a local employer dramatically expands. Where such changes are diluted at the state and federal level these local issues are dynamic and consequential.

Funding constrains local development and exploration in a number of ways. There are limitations on the amount of funds that can be expended within a programme, by a cost category, and during the year allocated. Each of these restrictions offers an array of challenges to the local administration of programmes.

The federal government generally approves funding for a specific period of time, usually the budget year, and expects that the funds once allocated will be expended during that period which on the surface may appear to be a reasonable requirement. However, at the local level there are required procurement procedures and the monitoring of programme compliance as well as performance that must be taken into consideration. There is also the up and down of issues such as the fluidity of unemployment and changes in employer needs. It is extremely rare for employers to project out their hiring needs three or four years in advance, but they know their needs today.

For service delivery agencies that are in compliance with rules and regulations and who are performing in accordance with desired outcomes a two-year procurement cycle can become an unnecessary exercise. It becomes an exercise because most of what is sought in the procurement process has to do with ability to manage and comply with federal programmes. This compliance is learned and measured by monitoring. It takes a number of years to develop a service provider into a "qualified" recipient of government funds and unless a community has a number of such entities (most do not) who wish to compete for the local dollars there is little value to keep them on their toes every two or three years.

Technically the federal government monitors the state. The federal monitors often need to visit the local programmes to determine if the state is passing along applicable rules and regulations and the programmes are operating as the federal government intended. The states also send monitors to the local programmes to assess various processes. The states handle their monitoring differently, but most spend two or three annual cycles visiting local programmes and following a guide on systems such as management information systems, fiscal record keeping and reporting, local administrative procedures such as inventories and procurement. It is seldom for either federal or state personnel to provide technical assistance or review quality measures such as staff qualifications and experience.

Perhaps the most unreasonable requirement from the local perspective has been a myriad of unrelated requirements that are imposed on organisations that receive federal funds. It would appear that the federal government is attempting to accomplish considerably more than the specific programme allocation intended. Compliance with the Clean Water Act and Equal Employment Opportunity reporting are just two examples of how legislation is often convoluted to go way beyond, no matter how well intentioned its purpose. Other requirements such as prevailing wage requirements and maintenance of effort are more related to employment and training policy.

Recommendations

The United States' employment and training programmes are becoming more decentralised and adapting to changing needs and desires of society. This devolution is viewed by many as a by-product of political pressures to reduce the role of the federal government rather than an attempt to improve services by improving efficiency, increasing stability, and making employment programmes more meaningful to the recipient. Regardless of whether the reasons for devolution are strategic or political they have been less than advantageous from the local perspective.

More deliberate steps could be taken to build upon the past, including:

Focus on the customer. There is a tendency to be driven by the rules and regulations at the expense of the reasons the programme exists. From the local perspective, the most valuable employment programmes are the ones that meet the needs of the jobseeker and employer. When the customers are satisfied the programme is accomplishing what was intended.

Government programmes will never be as simplistic as the private sector credo of "make a profit", but keeping the focus on the primary goal of satisfying the customer should be the litmus test for all programmes. In recent national surveys the employer customers are mostly not aware of the major employment and training programmes existing in their communities. The job seeker customer is often aware of programmes that are available and when shown respect plus opportunity have given programmes high marks, regardless of who administered them.

Clarify outcomes. Multiple performance standards often work at cross-purposes and make the desired outcomes questionable. For example, wage gains can work against retention rates. If a programme operator wants to demonstrate significant wage gain they recruit individuals who had low pre-programme wages and these recipients are often without a substantial work history and more likely to have low retention rates. Other standards such as "work first" direct programmes towards a one size fits all mode, when the reality is that each recipient is a unique individual and some are better served in skill training before seeking work.

There are a number of essential systems and procedures that compete with the desired outcomes for staff time and priority. Some examples are management information systems, financial record keeping standards, procurement procedures, and organisational certifications. Often these systems and procedures were intended to improve the matching of jobs and people but have taken on a life of their own. Record keeping and reporting need to be simplified and become useful tools for the management of programmes.

Commit for the long term. We know our labour market is fluid and dynamic. It has been under constant change and hopefully will continue to be ever changing. The local area needs to have the resources that will ensure they are evolving with the market and preparing the labour force for the jobs that will be there. Our political leadership needs to recognise labour market programmes are not short term quick fixes, but rather a necessary component of an evolving economy. The same is true for individual training and it cannot be limited by a specific number of months or years. There must be a National commitment to the long term continuous improvement of the labour force. This commitment needs to assure long term funding and provide the technical assistance necessary to prepare the local infrastructure and build the local capacity. This would include the development and maintenance of uniform fiscal and management information systems.

Improve governance. Governance needs to be improved through better communications, co-ordination and participation. Labour policy must eventually be co-ordinated with social and economic policy, but a first step should be to co-ordinate existing labour policies. Policy makers need to know and be communicating with the local programme operators and with each other to enforce consistent understanding and application of policy. Limiting the layers of government and bureaucracy and clarifying roles is critical to improving overall governance. Local government has the most important role of delivering services. Governance needs to be improved through better communications and enhanced co-ordination and collaboration. Each player needs to have ownership of the final outcome.

The central government should provide funding and ensure oversight. The state or regional level may be best suited for the role of a clearinghouse for best practices, providing technical assistance or linking with organisations that can.

Empower. The inability of an employee to perform his or her job is generally attributed to their lack of information, their lack of skills, or their belief that they have no influence over their work. When we identify the barrier as a lack of information we educate the employee. If it is a lack of skills we provide training. And when the employee feels the job is out of his or her control we should be empowering them. In order to obtain optimal performance and build local capacity the same approach is essential. Local elected and appointed officials have a responsibility to ensure the staff is educated, skilled, and empowered. Funding sources have a responsibility to ensure local officials are educated, skilled and empowered.

Be Accountable. There are a number of levels of accountability. The most important level is that of the service provider to those receiving services. We must continuously ask the recipients if we are meeting their needs.

The recipient of the service also has a responsibility to make use of the opportunities they are provided. Showing up to classes, actively participating, following through on job interviews are ways a recipient demonstrates accountability. Employers also need to make a commitment to publicly funded programmes by volunteering expertise on Workforce Boards and hiring the recipients who are products of the system.

In addition to the recipient, the service provider is also accountable to the local authorities for the quality and quantity of service provided and in turn local authorities must be held accountable to funding sources. Funding sources should be held responsible for ensuring technical expertise, information and assisting the local operators with continuous improvement models.

Finally, the ultimate success of employment and training programmes will be measured by responsiveness to local community needs. This will occur within parameters established by the funding source, if programmes have been integrated into the local community and there is meaningful participation of the local community in decision making.

ISBN 92-64-10470-4
Managing Decentralisation
A New Role for Labour Market Policy
© OECD 2003

PART I

Chapter 5

Germany: The Challenge of Taking an Integrated Approach in a Centralised Framework

by
Hartmut Siemon
Director, Employment Agency of Leipzig

I.5. GERMANY: THE CHALLENGE OF TAKING AN INTEGRATED APPROACH IN A CENTRALISED FRAMEWORK

Germany's special conditions with three governmental levels (Federal, States, local, i.e. municipalities) and its tripartite social security institutions are keys to understand labour market policies, their development, their financing and their implementation. Financing of labour market and social security policies comes from various sources (taxes and social security payments) at various governmental levels and from the private sector via social security institutions.

Social security payments (unemployment insurance, pensions and health) from the western part of the country have partly been used to finance expenditures in the East in recent years. Thus the burden of re-unification is to a great deal financed via the social security systems and thus contributes to make labour expensive. On the other hand the flow of money used in the East German States financing the unemployment benefits, active labour market measures and pensions helps boost local and regional consumer demand. Any change in labour market policy (financing, implementation, etc.) has to take into account this East/West difference. Discussions in Germany on the reform of labour market policies are always a discussion about resources flowing from West to East too.

Germany's system of reform resistance is well known and a never ending story for journalism and scientists – see for the example the survey on Germany "An Uncertain Giant" in *The Economist* newspaper (December 2002). Especially in the field of labour market policy, we have a long standing tradition of inflexibility via an (informal) great coalition between the two great left and right parties (CDU and SPD) as well as between the relevant entrepreneurs associations and the trade unions. As *The Economist* says in the above-mentioned overview:

> "Most analysts readily agree on what is wrong with the German economy. First and foremost, the labour market is far too sticky. Second, taxes and social-security contributions are too high and profits too low. Third, and not unconnected, social security payments, pensions and health-care arrangements are too generous. And fourth, there is far too much red tape. Frustrated businessmen often say that in English-speaking countries everything is allowed unless specifically forbidden; in Germany, it is the other way round."

It is important to note that local governments have the smallest budgets of all state levels concerned with labour market policies. Their scope of action depends on:

- their ability to develop and follow an integrated policy approach – needed to combine different (financial) sources with multidimensional effects;
- the realisation of partnership building on the local level between different actors and institutions from the private, the civil and the (different) governmental fields;
- the flexibility of the institutional framework set by state or federal level; and last but not least
- their own innovativeness and their will to take their future in their own hand and to overcome social dependency.

The Hartz Commission and the German experience

Against this background, the Hartz Commission – elaborated by a pool of different civil society actors like representatives from trade unions, entrepreneur organisations, consultants, researchers, municipal and federal governmental level – was one of the few more principal approaches to tackle the German disease on this field.

Two of the planned four Hartz laws have already been implemented, and two will follow later in 2003. They all seek to modify the above-mentioned institutional framework for local actors, including the role of municipalities and of enterprises which delivers services like training courses and other active labour market measures.

From a local point of view, the following three items ("modules") proposed by the Hartz Commission are relevant:

- merging unemployment assistance and social assistance (module 6);
- establishment of job centres (module 1);
- transforming regional employment offices into competence centres for new jobs and employment development (module 11).

Merging unemployment assistance and social assistance

The co-existence of two social benefit systems leads to considerable administrative costs and lack of transparency. Lacking co-ordination and accountability regarding integration efforts may impair the speed of placing people in new jobs. In order to avoid these interfaces in future, every person drawing benefits will be allocated to a single office and receive a single type of payment. In future, there will be three different types of benefits:

- Unemployment Benefit I is the original benefit financed from unemployment insurance contributions. Entitlements will, in principle, correspond to current regulations with regard to the duration of payment and the amount paid. The Federal Employment Service continues to be responsible in this field. The unemployed will be given help and advice in the job centre.
- Unemployment Benefit II is a tax-funded, need-based type of benefit to safeguard the unemployed person's income once unemployment Benefit I is no longer paid or if the qualifying conditions for unemployment Benefit I are not fulfilled. A pre-condition is that this person is capable of working. Those drawing unemployment Benefits II are covered by social insurance. The duration of benefit entitlement is not limited. The responsibility rests with the Federal Employment Service. The job centre will be the office to be contacted in this case.
- The social allowance (paid by the municipalities) will correspond to the current social assistance for those persons who are not able to work. The social welfare offices (on communal level) will continue to be responsible in this area.

Thus the responsibility – at least financially – for unemployment costs would be on the federal level. This change would imply a major overhaul of the German social security system. It will be particularly important to see how the co-operation on local matters between the national agency for employment and the local governmental bodies is implemented and how the integration of other local/regional actors in the processes will be organised.

Establishment of job centres

In the future, job centres will be the local agencies for all services related to the labour market. The employment office will transform its organisational structure into a job centre. The nation-wide introduction of this scheme for main offices as well as local offices will be given top priority.

Besides the original services provided by the Federal Employment Service, the job centre will integrate labour market-related counselling and support services (social welfare office, youth welfare office, housing office, advisory office for drug addicts and people with debts, interface to personnel service agency, etc.). The processes in the job centre are aimed at determining quickly the need for counselling and support services and early implementation of the measures required also via the personnel service agency (PSA). By splitting up the vacancies in accordance with the job family concept, the likelihood of securing a job placement will be improved.

The central organiser will be the clearing office. This office will organise customer control and take over administrative work to relieve the placement officers. More facilities for self-information will be provided for customers in need of information. Persons in need of advice receive tailor-made offers from placement officers. Unemployed persons who may only be placed with great difficulty and who are in need of support will be taken care of by especially trained case managers.

Placement officers will be relieved from administrative and minor work. They will concentrate on making contact with businesses and securing vacancies in the sector they have been assigned to. In addition, they will give advice to job seekers. Their scope of action will be extended through independent action budgets and IT services.

The job centres and the placement workers will develop an adjusted service profile for the companies they have been assigned. They will be in charge of small and medium-sized companies according to sector specific criteria. Major companies will be allocated to specific contact persons. The competence centres will take care of major accounts. Service lines will guarantee that both employers and job seekers can reach the job centre. A "code of good practice" will safeguard the quality of services vis-à-vis both sides of the market.

Thus the general orientation of the activities in the job centres is on two target groups – job seekers and employers.

Transforming regional employment offices into competence centres for new jobs and employment development

To achieve the objective of full employment, labour market, economic and social policy initiatives must be co-ordinated. For this purpose, a new set of instruments will have to be created, which will make a more efficient contribution towards the creation of new jobs and the development of new employment opportunities. The regional employment offices will be converted into competence centres whose tasks in the area of employment policy will be funded by taxes.

In order to link labour market and economic policies, competence centres will not replace local initiatives but rather co-ordinate them across administrative borders offering complementary solutions and resources to federal states, municipalities, companies and chambers of commerce and industry. They will put to use their competence in the area of labour market policy for the following tasks:

They will be the principal contact point for job centres in counselling small and medium-sized companies (employment counselling, support for setting up new plants, growth initiatives and counselling services for start-ups). They will also be liaison offices for state governments, co-ordinate cross-regional training programmes and conduct trend and regional labour market research.

The competence centres will create transparency on the further training market by certifying the institutions of training opportunities and the service these offer. They will determine impending qualification bottlenecks and set up suitable framework programmes. The competence centres will establish their own consultancy areas where the teams will give advice to the job centres as far as the operative implementation of job-creating measures is concerned.

The general orientation on cluster structures will help develop an integrated locally-based strategy of economic development, social inclusion and promotion of integration in employment. It will be of particular importance for the system to be implemented in an innovative and flexible manner, and for a real co-operation between the different state hierarchies, institutions and actors that operate in the economic and social fields to arise.

Leipzig's integrated approach of economic clustering and promoting integration

Most approaches to reform the system of employment promotion do not answer the question of where the unemployed should best be placed? The Leipzig concept of regional development via personnel development aims to combine new ways of promoting both employment and cluster-oriented development of companies. Central to this idea is the concentration on (existing) cluster structures in the region. The Leipzig development strategy states that:

"Leipzig is encountering a remarkable rise in its economic potential with considerable opportunities for future growth. In order to make the best of these opportunities, all partners in the economic process need to work together to ensure that Leipzig can make the best possible use of the anticipated positive development.

The medium and long-term direction of the economic policy of the City of Leipzig requires an universal approach – following the slogan 'Strengthen the strengths'. The goal is to increase the economic power of the city in the medium term. Activities will be focused, amongst others, on growth-intensive clusters, that have partly already developed – or, in the case of the automobile industry, are currently developing. By turning away from the watering-can principle and focussing public means, core growth areas will be further developed and have effects that will reach beyond the limits of the industries concerned (…).

The development goals are tackled (…) through:

- *concentrating on clusters as driving forces of economic growth;*

- *innovation and technology policies to ensure future growth and to strengthen endogenous processes;*
- *attracting investors and improving the quality of the location to extend the supra-regional sector;*
- *supporting regional development through personnel development."*

Due to the decisions by Porsche and BMW to invest in the area and the human resource movements and follow-up investments that followed, the Leipzig region is now facing the challenge of providing future investors and established companies with sufficiently-qualified staff at the right time. The medium-term goal is to prepare the pre-selection processes, usually time-consuming and taking up a lot of resources, according to the qualification profiles provided by the clients in such a way that vacancies can be filled fast. This will allow the new investors to use more resources in their actual field of business.

The benefit for the region is evident: i) increasing movement of people from unemployment or social benefit to jobs in the companies; ii) opportunities for improving the overall employment situation of the region; iii) offsetting the effects of human resources movements; and iv) improved personnel marketing and marketing effects for the region.

In summary, the main instruments of this regional development strategy based upon personnel development are: i) concentration on growth cores within clusters; ii) concentration of regional competencies in competence centres; iii) early involvement of companies and start-ups; iv) provision of adjusted personnel services; v) implementation of appropriate qualifying strategies; vi) arrangement of consistent gateways from profiling to placement; vii) network of competent firms and actors for flexible local/regional personnel management; and viii) service for quick replacement of vacancies.

Implementing the strategy: an example

The goal of local employment and economic development policies has to be the identification, promotion and activation of "cluster-related" qualification and competence potentials. Training and qualification measures co-ordinated with the job centre play a role, as well as targeted training measures for a concrete demand (e.g. recruiting professional staff for BMW, Porsche and other companies). The aim is to define a market-related applicant profile and find targeted jobs for as many people as possible in the primary job market.

The advantage for companies, especially small and medium-sized ones, planning to set up business in Leipzig, is the opportunity for a qualified pre-selection of staff according to the demands of the customer even before the move is made. If necessary, training can be provided through improved co-ordination between the training companies and the customers. Because the applicants will be graded according to the criteria provided by the customer, the necessary level of skills and thus the acceptance of the potential employer is ensured. The selection process needs to fulfil exclusively the quality criteria defined by the labour market.

In 2001, at the initiative of the City of Leipzig after the decision of BMW to invest in a new plant in Leipzig, the PUUL GmbH was set up as a one-stop shop to offer personnel to entrepreneurs and new investors in the region. The rationale was that: i) regional co-ordination and co-operation bring about a combination of different competencies, resources and finances; ii) local and regional actors active in the region help not only to deliver the needed human resources but also to market the region as an innovative one; and iii) use the human resource movement between and to companies to initiate an active approach to promote integration for those previously unemployed and depending on social welfare.

To implement the strategy, a steering committee was set up, which included all relevant local and regional actors such as: chamber of industry and commerce; chamber of handicrafts; regional office of the national unemployment insurance organisation; investors; city administration; federal government; European social fund agency. Working groups have also been set up around specific themes, such as: initial training; vocational qualification; staff profiles; and funding sources.

The juridical form was a private limited company – much more flexible than public normal governmental forms. The main financial sources for the practical work of the PUUL have to be differentiated: i) the start up money for the PUUL and a minimum financing for the on-going structure was delivered by the City of Leipzig; ii) the qualification, profiling and all other services delivered via the PUUL or its networks are either paid by the customers (companies) or – until now mainly – via projects and – as far as they are entitled – via funding of individuals through the unemployment office and the funding of the European social fund.

The regional actors hope to achieve via this co-operation:

- *increasing numbers* of the target group of unemployed people and people on social benefit will find jobs in the primary labour market because of the assessment services (reducing insecurity for companies);
- vacancies can be filled more quickly due to *shorter processing times;*
- the above mentioned target groups receive *improved professional orientation* and will find jobs faster;
- *targeted use of human resources development,* based on diagnosed results rather than on the watering-can principle widely used in training measures, because a detailed individual profile of strength and weaknesses is created for every participant and training resources can be used tailored to the needs;

- the *recruitment process for small and medium-sized companies can receive professional support*, leading to a better quality of staff in the companies while spreading the investment costs over many shoulders;
- the skill-oriented diagnostic process which needs to be developed in the medium term for special target groups (*e.g.* people on social benefit) will lead to higher chances for qualification or finding a job, at the same time reducing fluctuation through wrong choice of staff (for example, avoiding too high or too low challenges, matching job and person-based on skills and interests). The average time people spend in unemployment can be reduced for some people through faster, skill-oriented person-job-matching;
- there is an opportunity to improve the *overall employment situation in the region*, from a socio-political point of view, as well (for example, young unemployed people and those on social benefit schemes, single parents, older unemployed people, re-socialisation cases etc.);
- *improved personnel marketing* in the region and a *marketing effect for the region* (as this currently is a unique project with a highly innovative character), this also improves regional marketing;
- fast counter-action to the movement of human resources in the Leipzig region.

The Leipzig experience shows that it is possible to build efficient partnerships in Germany, provided that there is enough flexibility in using financial resources, in defining the target groups and that it is possible to adjust the state- or federal-funded programmes to the local defined projects and needs. To ensure success, efforts must be devoted to integrate entrepreneurs (including already existing companies, start-ups and new investors) and organisations dealing with social inclusion and promotion of integration in local/regional networks.

ISBN 92-64-10470-4
Managing Decentralisation
A New Role for Labour Market Policy
© OECD 2003

PART I
Chapter 6

Italy: Opening the Circuits

by
Michele Dau
Director-General, National Council for Economy and Labour (CNEL)

Decentralisation of employment policy: the main results

In Italy, the last few years were characterised by an important reform process oriented towards the administrative decentralisation and the modernisation of the public administration and of the labour market. In particular, since the Law No. 196/97 – which has introduced the temporary contracts in Italy's legal system – and after the three Bassanini Laws and the recent Constitutional Reform (Law No. 3/01), the progressive attribution of competences and functions, traditionally centralised to the regions and the local level took place.

This new course occurred in the second part of the 1990s, after a period in which labour and development policies were strongly centralised due to the crisis in public finances and to the commitments set out in the Maastricht Treaty in anticipation of European Monetary Union. In 1993, there was a national social concertation pact among government, trade unions and employers: the objectives were inflation control, incomes policy (wages, taxes, levies, etc.), reform of labour market and reform of national collective bargaining. Besides, in 1995, a reform within the social security system (particularly to the national pension system) was introduced. This was a crucial element to curb the public deficit. The most significant aspects of new framework were: *a)* introduction of a contributions-based system in old-age pension for all workers with a length of service shorter than 22 years; *b)* reduction of contribution-years based pensions; *c)* introduction of supplementary pension insurance.

Decentralisation processes began in 1996 with three major trends: *a)* renewal of the institutional system in labour sector; *b)* reform of the laws and bargaining labour rules; *c)* new territorial actions of employment and growth promotion. In this connection, a very strong decentralisation and liberalisation process towards regions and provinces took place. It also featured a new role for the private sector.

The decentralisation to the regions was completed in 2001 with a reform of the Constitution. In this new framework:

1. The management of Labour market policies is now shared between regional and central authorities, so that the exclusive responsibility of the State no longer prevails.
2. The central State is from now on solely in charge of the following: immigration rules, determination of the essential levels of services related

to civil and social rights for all citizens, determination of rules for different labour contracts, social security (national pension system).

3. The other following policy areas are managed through shared legislation among central State and regions: health and safety in working places; traditional and new professions; supplementary pension insurance.

To implement this reform in 2001-2003 a new government prepared and approved a "white book" on labour market reform and a new action on labour market rules to simplify private job placement services and extend flexible jobs (rules and rights).

Table 6.1. **Distribution of tasks before and after the reform in Italy**

Ministry of Labour	Regions (21)	Provinces (103)	Private sector
a) Before the reform (1996)			
Political guidelines. Planning and co-ordination of labour policies. Government management of employment offices.	School counselling. Professional training.		
b) After the reform (2001)			
General political and administrative guidelines. SIL (Informative Labour System): planning, management and development.	Planning. Co-ordination of actions aimed to labour supply and demand matching.	SPI (local employment services): management, information supply to SIL.	Job placement services.

Source: Author for the OECD.

Which are the most relevant effects of this new situation? Firstly there are some positive aspects: policies and actions closer to local levels are now possible, and more engagements to support disadvantaged people in the labour market. But here also, a very critical aspect of the reform related to SPI (the local employment services). These agencies make use of the same human resources as the old public employment offices, which creates several remarkable training and organisation problems, especially in some southern provinces, where unemployment is higher.

All the reforms of the laws and of bargaining labour rules are to introduce more formal flexibility in the labour market. In 1996 started private temporary – employment agency work, the new forms of co-ordinated continuous collaborators (the so-called "co.co.co.") and more part-time incentives. In 2003, by the Law No. 30, were introduced new profiles, such as project-related contracts, staff leasing, job on call, job sharing and moreover flexible part time rules, simplification of employment office reform (SPI and private job centres), and company branch transfer (outsourcing). The important effects of these new rules are more flexibility and employment, and more jobs in an increasingly dynamic labour market. On the other hand weaker protections and social insurance have arisen.

The third direction of new policies for decentralisation in Italy was a new territorial action of employment and growth promotion. Between 1996 and 2003, economic programmes were negotiated with two specific instruments: the "territorial employment pact" and the "assisted area agreement".

About 230 such local pacts bring together private and public organisations at local level: these comprise labour bargaining to bring about flexibility and lower wages and new investments by private companies and public investment (infrastructures and financial incentives to new companies). About 20 are the agreements launched towards the re-industrialisation of specific areas. These agreements have similar contents, rules and objectives than the pacts.

To summarise the results of this policy, it can be argued that some pacts and agreements worked well, with partnership of private and public actors and organisations, and with more participation and transparency in public policies. On the other hand it is necessary to underline that most pacts and agreements did not work speedily: they produced too much bureaucracy because they were promoted by the local level and later managed by the central State.

Better adaptation of local policies to local conditions and needs

One of the important effects of these reforms is in terms of cultural exchanges. After years of hostile pressure to simply deregulate, the value of positive, sustainable reforms and actions is now appreciated because they lay a solid basis to reach the targets set by the Lisbon and Stockholm European Councils. Significant differences exist between EU member States, and in Italy also between northern and southern regions, in terms of employment, economic growth and participation rates. Decentralisation of employment policy and structural reforms continue to be needed in all members States, because they are necessary to cope with the accelerating economic and social restructuring associated with globalisation, technological process and the development of an inclusive knowledge and information society and economy. The achievement of these goals, will only be possible through creating more and better jobs, investing in human capital, promoting the training policies to raise skill levels and concentrating the efforts above all on the weaker categories.

These are the reasons why, in the last few years, in an attempt to keep in line with the Lisbon strategy, Italy's governments have tried to achieve an improved co-ordination, even at the local level, between structural and economic policies, employment and social policies, given their well-recognised complementary nature. From this point of view, an attempt was made to further the partnership role even for local development purposes, relying on strategies that – through a bottom up process and the convergence of all the institutional, social and private actors towards the definition of a common growth target – proved closer and more in keeping with territorial needs and requirements and, just on this account, more effective in terms of employment growth and improvement of the quality of life.

Participation of civil society and private sector actors in decision making

In recent years, this led to the experimentation of a few concrete initiatives including, in particular, the promotion of the negotiated planning instruments – with special regard to territorial pacts and area contracts – and the development of partnerships for the management of the European structural funds. On the whole, it would seem that the decentralisation of the development policies and the function of the social partners have been considered as highly positive both with reference to the concrete instruments that have already been introduced and viewing them as potentials to be enhanced. In fact, on a number of fronts it is being stressed that, in order to attain the development goals, the utmost relevance should be attached to a reversal of trend in the decision-making process and the contemporaneous involvement of local actors, having a more in-depth knowledge of the different situations and being more likely to meet the different requirements.

What are the limits to flexibility in decentralised frameworks?

In any event, if we are to draw wider lessons from the recent trends towards labour policy decentralisation in Italy, one should not underestimate the need for and, at the same time, the difficulty of co-ordinating the development actions conceived for different areas within the country with the overall national economic policy. In fact, while they may represent examples of excellence, closed systems rarely favour dialogue and exchange.

Hence the need to promote the mobility of entrepreneurs and workers must be borne in mind, with special regard to a few given groups. Likewise, it is crucial to invest in forms of training moving over and above the territorial boundaries. Hence, further efforts should be made in order to achieve a greater dissemination of good practices and an improved exchange of information, while the social partners and other labour market institutions should pay greater attention to employment growth and the construction of employment relationships. This will enable the creation of an open circuit among local realities that, through decentralisation efforts, will succeed in contributing to the implementation of general development and employment policies guaranteeing the smooth operation of enterprises but with a continued effort to promote the interests of the workers.

PART I
Chapter 7

The Flemish Region of Belgium: Moving Decentralisation One Step Further

by

Marion Vrijens
Director, Ministry of Economy and Employment

The policy framework

In order to boost the employment rate, the Flemish authorities strive for an efficient, well-balanced policy mix. The Flemish approach is focused both on labour supply (increasing employability through further training and intensive guidance for jobseekers) and labour market demand (promoting entrepreneurship and job creation, for example). Special consideration is also given to diversity, equal opportunities and the need to modernise the organisation of work. Another key aim is to improve the quality of labour, the key idea of which is not only to create more jobs but also to create *better* jobs. This provides the background for the development initiatives to improve local governance.

Increasing the employment rate

The primary aim of the Flemish employment policy is to increase the number of people in work on the basis of the "active welfare state" principle. The main policy indicator is therefore the employment rate. This represents the share of employed inhabitants in the working-age population (15 to 64-years-old). The aim during the present government's term of office (up to 2004) is to increase the employment rate from 63.3% (in 2001) to 66.5% (in 2004). In the longer term (towards the year 2010), the idea is to achieve an employment rate of 70%. This target figure was set at the March 2000 EU Summit in Lisbon. The Flemish Government and the social partners agreed, in late 2001, to enshrine this target in the so-called "Vilvoorde Pact". As the unemployment rate is fairly low in Flanders (3.7% in 2001 compared with an EU average of 8.3%), this target also calls for incentives to be given to the current non-economically active population (including the 55 to 64-year-old category).

Both *preventive* and *active* measures are being taken in a bid to achieve this aim. The preventive approach involves offering jobseekers intensive guidance and training during the early stages of unemployment so as to prevent a situation of long-term unemployment. The active approach entails providing jobseekers and the economically inactive with incentives and training to look for work rather than passively relying on unemployment benefits.

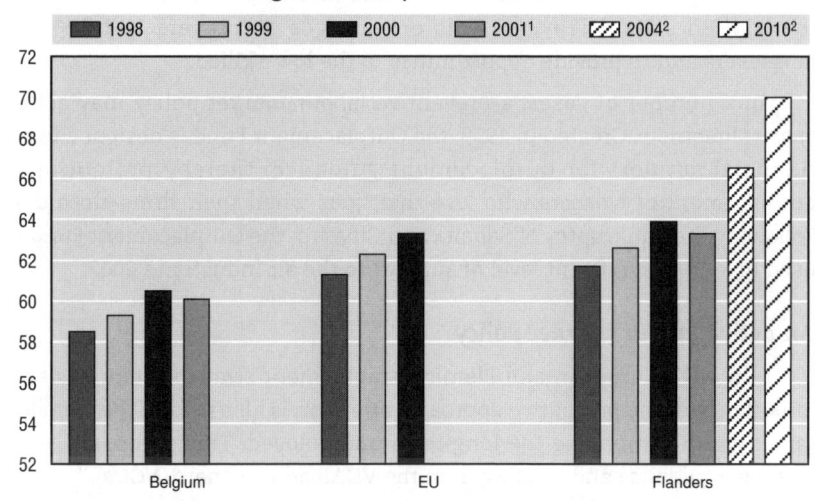

Figure 7.1. **Overall employment rate (as a percentage of the population aged 15 to 64) in Flanders**

1. Temporary estimate on the basis of the first three quarters of 2001 in the NIS survey.
2. The figure for 2010 refers to the target in the Vilvoorde Pact and the EU Summit in Lisbon, the figure for 2004 indicates the Flemish intermediary target.

Source: Eurostat, NIS Labour Force Survey.

A preventive approach to unemployment

Prevention is better than cure: this saying also applies to the labour market. For a few years now, the preventive approach to unemployment has featured as a priority in the European employment strategy (EES). The importance of the preventive approach is also recognised in Flanders. Preventing people out of work from entering long-term unemployment can help deploy human capital as effectively as possible. In Flanders the trajectory approach (or "pathways to integration") is the prime instrument used to implement the preventive approach to unemployment. The Flemish public employment service (VDAB) applies the trajectory approach to offer guidance to jobseekers during an early stage of their unemployment. Services are tailored to jobseekers as much as possible so that the usual division between job-seeking and training is broken down in favour of an integrated system of guidance. The focus is primarily on young and low-skilled jobseekers. The aim of reaching *all* jobseekers at an early stage of unemployment is hampered to some extent by a lack of capacity and resources.

The VDAB lends support to jobseekers in finding work by relying on state-of-the-art ICT applications: jobseekers can register to access the VDAB website and consult the extensive job and training databases. Special terminals are also available in VDAB offices and other locations frequented by jobseekers.

In co-operation with the federal government, financial support is provided to offer guidance and training to young jobseekers. Specific types of vocational training or work experience are used to set them on the right track. Premium systems are also used to provide incentives for the recruitment of low-skilled school-leavers. This encourages employers to hire young jobseekers and to provide opportunities to the low-skilled.

In a number of cases, a preventive labour market policy may actually *prevent* inactivity. Created in 1999, the Outplacement Fund is designed to offer financial support for outplacement guidance, thereby promoting the outplacement of workers who lose their jobs when their firms close down. Following the bankruptcy of Sabena and Citybird, the Outplacement Fund was used to lend a significant level of support to the air industry in 2002.

An active labour market policy

Although European and Flemish employment strategies emphasise the importance of the preventive approach, attention is also paid to the "remedial" target group comprising the long-term unemployed. This group, too, enjoys intensive guidance and training from the VDAB and partners (NGOs).

"*Social workplaces*" have been developed for the most difficult target group. A specific form of employment organisation and tailor-made guidance are used to offer employment to individuals that are only able to work within a sheltered environment.

The *work experience programme* WEP+ offers specific training plus work experience to the unskilled long-term unemployed and those receiving a guaranteed minimum income benefit. The *training business* system allows young companies the opportunity to hire individuals from target groups on special terms. They qualify for a wage subsidy for a four-year period that tapers off on an annual basis (80-60-40-20% of the wage cost). The system of "*insertion interim*" involves employment agencies providing the long-term unemployed and those with a guaranteed minimum income benefit with a temporary two-year employment contract.

The system of "*individual in-company vocational training*" offers jobseekers tailor-made training to prepare them for a job requiring a specific profile. Subsequent to in-company training (one to six months) the employer offers the jobseekers a permanent contract. This way, employment and training for jobseekers is bound up with filling vacancies that are difficult to fill. Hence individual vocational training is a key instrument in matching supply and demand as part of the effort to eliminate labour market bottlenecks.

In a drive to reduce unemployment, policy-makers often used to rely on specific employment programmes for direct job creation purposes. Both in terms of budgets and beneficiaries, such programmes still constitute an important part of Flemish labour market policy. They are primarily aimed at providing employment for the long-term unemployed and low-skilled in non-profit organisations and public services. In the year 2001, some 50 000 (or 1.3% of the economically active population) were still employed under such programmes in Flanders. In order to improve the quality of employment, the Flemish government has sought to convert a large number of these posts into regular jobs, so as to offer better wages and working conditions plus more job security to the employees involved. Between January 2001 and January 2002, roughly 7 700 jobs in the welfare sector were converted into full-time jobs.

Incentives for the labour market participation of older people

The European Commission has placed a lot of emphasis on achieving the "active ageing" goals. During the year 2001 EU Summit in Stockholm, it was agreed that the employment rate among the "elderly" (55 to 64-years-old) should be increased to 50% by the year 2010. Currently, Belgium and Flanders barely reach half that percentage, owing to the long-standing policy of early retirement for employees through systems such as interim pensions, and the historically late appearance of women on the Belgian and Flemish labour markets. Together with the gradual ageing of the population, this has major implications for the functioning of the labour market and the social security system.

Increasing the employment rate among the elderly is a top priority for the Flemish Government. Together with the Flemish social partners, an *action plan* has been devised to promote employment among the elderly. One of the initiatives featured in this action plan involves lending support to specific projects for validating the experience of older jobseekers or facilitating their employability.

Diversity and higher employment rates for target groups

The Flemish Government adopts a diversity policy and the social partners emphasise on proportional labour market participation (employment equity). In the process of increasing the overall employment rate (see above), special consideration is needed for a number of "target groups" whose level of labour market participation is below average. Owing to disadvantages and discrimination, some individuals, such as women, elderly, members of minority groups and the disabled, are often faced with exclusion from the labour market.

In order to promote the labour market participation of men and women, attempts are being made to extend childcare facilities. How serious this issue is being taken is reflected in the fact that Flanders has already achieved the European "benchmark" for 2010: childcare facilities for 33% of children aged under three. Between 2001 and 2004, 2 500 extra childcare places will be created each year. The European benchmark for creating childcare facilities for children aged over three (90% by 2010) has been given institutional expression in Flanders by providing pre-school education starting from the age of 2.5.

Further training

Lifelong learning is one of the top priorities set by the European employment guidelines. The Flemish authorities, too, acknowledge that lifelong learning is a precondition for the effective employability of employees and jobseekers and for horizontal and vertical mobility on the labour market. The Flemish government and social partners have made a commitment to increase the number of people aged between 25 and 64 in continual training from 7.1% in 2001 (EU average 8%) to at least 10% in 2010.

A key lifelong learning policy target involves guaranteeing an *appropriate starting qualification via initial education*. This is of key importance for ensuring a smooth transition from school to the workplace. Consequently, a key aim is to reduce the number of young people leaving secondary school without proper qualifications. Under the heading of the "Vilvoorde Pact", the Flemish government and the social partners are committed to halving the number of early school-leavers by 2010. The Flemish Education and Training Minister has adopted the mid-term target of reducing the number of early school-leavers by 20% by late 2004. Various measures have been adopted with a view to achieving this target.

A *modular system* has been adopted for technical and vocational education dividing the knowledge and skills to be acquired into smaller modules, which are evaluated separately. This ensures that even early school-leavers receive some kind of qualification. As part certificates may represent an important experience of success for young people, the modular system can help prevent students losing interest in school.

The number of unqualified secondary school-leavers may also be reduced by work-and-study schemes. Such initiatives allow students to combine part-time education with in-company training, thus making for a smoother transition from school to workplace.

Education and training requirements are not limited to initial education. Businesses, too, are encouraged to invest in human resources. The Flemish system of *training vouchers* offers companies financial support for the costs (generally 50%) of employees undertaking training courses offered by recognised training providers.

Emphasis on information technology

Launched in 2001, the *"basic IT skills programme"* seeks to improve Flemish jobseekers with basic skills in the realm of computer technology and new communication systems such as cell phones and e-mail. For this project, the VDAB uses a mobile training facility, the so-called "learning mobile". In order to provide incentives for the use of ICT in the working and educational environments, the Flemish authorities support the European Computer

Drivers Licence (ECDL). Jobseekers have an opportunity to receive the ECDL free of charge.

Further efforts and additional funding have helped ensure that the European benchmark of one computer for ever 10 secondary school students in Flanders will be achieved in 2003.

Modernising the organisation of labour

The process of modernising the organisation of labour aims for the best possible balance between flexibility and security. A key Flemish policy initiative in this area is the reform of the system of career break incentives. These Flemish premiums (average € 100 on a monthly basis) top up the payments of the federal career break system (now called "time credit"). The new system shifts the focus to autonomous career management by the employee, with emphasis on lifelong learning and work life balance.

The incentive system is applied on a widespread basis in the Flemish Region. As the number of people taking career breaks rose from 67 600 in 2000 to 79 100 in 2001 (+17%), it is obvious that the temporary (often part time) career break caters for a social need. This group of people taking career breaks represents 2.5% of the Flemish working population.

Promoting entrepreneurship

The Flemish authorities support young companies in various ways and seek to streamline administrative procedures so as to provide more opportunities for the Flemish entrepreneurial spirit.

Young companies can rely on the *Flemish Guarantee Fund* to supply them with risk capital. The "Matrix" network for SMEs was set up in 2001 to encourage *external business advice* and networking between business advisers. Projects have been developed to stimulate the entrepreneurial spirit amongst young people in both secondary and higher education.

The interaction of the Flemish authorities with businesses and citizens takes place via "one-stop-shops". These offices offer assistance in all employment-related matters. The number of different offices is thus limited, but bundles the provision of services and makes them more accessible.

The local and regional dimension of the employment policy

The regional dimension of the labour market is of prime importance for Belgium, in view of the major differences between the regional job markets. In Flanders, a great deal of attention is also paid to sub-regional and local labour market policies, hence the crucial importance of a partnership between the various key players and levels. The Ministry of Employment of the Flemish government developed two important initiatives to come to a decisive decentralisation of some aspects of the employment policy.

Locally, the *local job centres* play a key role. They are designed as one-stop-shops providing citizens and businesses with a whole range of services concerning employment. Moreover, they offer a framework for co-operation between the various key players (VDAB, local authorities, the welfare sector, NGOs). By the end of 2003, 140 job centres will be opened in Flanders: each Flemish municipality (or group of municipalities) is supposed to have its own local job centre by the year 2004.

The *Sub-regional Employment Committees* (in Dutch: STCs) are responsible for co-ordinating labour market and employment policies in the 13 Flemish sub-regions. The STCs offer policy advice and are responsible for facilitating networking activities. Owing to the greater local input in policy-making, their role as a forum is set to be broadened in the future.

The potential of the service economy, the valued-adding economy and socially responsible companies

The employment policy adopted by the Flemish authorities also takes social and environmental considerations into account. These issues are addressed through the concept of a *"value-adding economy"*. The concept allows for a critical assessment of labour market policy in terms of its contribution to the quality of life, social cohesion and ecological balance. In order to support the emergence of such a value-adding economy, a number of specific projects have been initiated.

The *TRIVISI project* seeks to provide incentives for the emergence of *socially responsible companies* in Flanders. Working groups, surveys and conferences provide opportunities to make detailed investigations of themes such as *diversity, learning companies* and *stakeholder management*. The expert knowledge built up by these pioneering groups has been converted into products that can put into practice on the shop floor. In order to enhance the project's impact, the business community is involved in the process whenever possible.

An ambitious *social economy-related* co-operation agreement was sealed between the various Belgian policy-making levels in the year 2000. The aim is to double the number of jobs in the social economy. A social economy consultation platform was created and the "Trividend" fund was devised to supply companies operating in the value-adding economy sector with risk capital.

Relational and care services constitute important factors in the pursuit of a higher quality of life. The Flemish authorities are endeavouring to develop a *local services economy* to cater for the large demand for neighbourhood services. This local services economy is being given concrete expression through the so-called "service vouchers" being promoted in co-operation with the federal government. The local job centres act as hubs in this connection.

A key component of the mould-breaking agreement the Flemish government reached with the social partners in 2000 is the need to create an increasing number of jobs in the social profit sector. The agreement is designed to cater for the requirements of people working in the social profit sector in relation to the pressure of work and the risks of burn-out.

Two cases of decentralisation of labour market policy

This second part will address the issue of whether decentralisation and a decentralised approach represent an added value to reach those objectives in the field of labour market policy.

The importance of a local approach to the employment market and employment in a broader sense of the word is no longer challenged by the Flemish government. However, the way in which this approach can be supported by higher parties requires new amendments. After all, for a too long time the local level has been considered as the level of execution of ideas decided upon centrally, which pay little attention to the existing diversity in the scale, composition or dynamics of the local employment market. Therefore there should be prior discussions about policy measures that have an impact at the local level. Furthermore, these policy measures should be flexible so that there is adequate room for a local interpretation and monitoring. Incentives from the Flemish government should allow links and a balance with the local situation on the labour market. The Flemish government wants to establish a structural repartition of competences. Therefore, an intensive dialogue and exchange of information between the Flemish government, the local and supra-local levels authorities has been set up.

The towns or municipalities themselves can autonomously decide on their role in the employment policy framework. However, concerning the position of local governments, the Flemish authorities have one central task to co-ordinate the local employment policy. This co-ordinating function requires a process of interaction, making cross connections, monitoring social processes in order to monitor the local developments, and achieving an integrated employment policy in the broadest sense of the word. The local co-ordinating role must ensure that the policy measures of different governments achieve the maximum results in different fields at the local level. This exclusive role goes together with the co-ordinating role of the VDAB at the level of the labour market policy. The administration and the VDAB must reinforce each other and must be developed in a complementary way on the Flemish level as well as on the local level. This complementarity must be expressed in the development of the local job centres. In the local governments, particular attention is paid to towns and urban areas. In this respect, Antwerp and Ghent have particular priority as they are areas of special needs.

One Stop Job Shop

From 1999, local job centres have been established. The job centres have two important functions:

- on the one hand, they must provide a universal basic service as a right for all jobseekers, either with or without the monitoring of the route to a job by the VDAB;
- on the other hand, they are responsible for bringing supply and demand together in the new jobs in services, which will be co-ordinated by local authorities.

The work of a job centre is based on one file per user. It streamlines the procedures, the co-ordination between the services and levels of government, and the computerised approach. It must have a clear and open attitude, based on secure rights. This will benefit the service to the user. Jobseekers must be able to go to the job centre for a range of services with a low and broad threshold, ranging from information, registration and re-registration, consulting WIS and KISS for qualified intake, screening and mediation, or for a job in the service sector. The emphasis is made on a rapid, efficient, tailor-made service provided by a consultant and/or online.

An integrated, ready-made approach also requires proximity. Therefore the job centres are established at a municipal or inter-municipal level, and in cities, even at a (clustered) local level. The concept will be the same for every location. The method of operationalisation and the breadth of the provision will depend on the local situation, and on the parties present and activities carried out.

Universal basic services constitute a guaranteed right for all jobseekers. Each jobseeker is guaranteed to get (as well via counsellor, as by self-service as on-line):

- general information;
- registration and self-management of his file;
- automatic matching with job offers;
- orientation test, vocational ability and skills tests;
- WIS (work information system) and KISS (candidates information and selection system);
- mediation or reference to guidance councillors.

The new pillar Service-Economy in the Local Job Shop stands for: *i)* the prevention of dead-end jobs for the unemployed; *ii)* stimulating the emergence of new jobs, *e.g.* neighbourhood services, collective jobs, service-oriented jobs; and iii) bringing demand and offer together in this field.

The Local Job Shop has two directors, one for the organisation of the integrated basic service for job-seekers and the local authority for the organisation of the new economy.

VDAB, as director of the integrated basic service is responsible for: i) the integration of the services of the partners to guarantee an integrated basic service for all job-seekers; ii) stimulating the co-operation between basic service and guidance of job-seekers; iii) taking initiatives to stimulate job-seekers to come to the job centre; and iv) development of new products and services.

The local authority, as director of the new economy jobs, is responsible for: i) stimulating the co-operation between the partners on the co-ordination of the partners in the field of new services; ii) the inventory of the offer of new services; iii) the search for the most appropriate executers for the new services; iv) the development of a vision on local employment policy; and v) the development of new opportunities in the field of new services.

At the Flemish level, the job centre concept is developed on the basis of flexible architectural plans, with including fixed basic aims, a financial organisational frame, a uniform code of behaviour and equal criteria for the guidance-model in view of legal security of the jobseeker. A steering committee, composed of representatives of local authorities, of VDAB, the ministry is represented by a delegate of the minister. It discusses the developing process and the emerging problems. This steering committee has the function of a co-ordination platform between the main directors, VDAB, local authorities and the ministry.

At the *local level*, the local partners have the responsibility for mutual tuning between the services. VDAB and local authority stand for stimulating the establishment of a network. This has to result in the creation of a Forum Local Development. This Forum is chaired by the local authorities and consists of the local authority, VDAB, federal labour market insurance services, social partners and NGOs. Those partners have to develop an agreement and engagements on mutual co-operation, relation between the two functions, and so on.

At the end of 2002 there were already 95 Local Jobs Shops operational. Still another 40 locations should open in the course of this year. In the meantime a decree is being discussed in the Parliament as to give this project a legal foundation. Until now, the process is set up as a *de facto* co-operation.

Some observations

Without any doubt, one can say that this policy leads to more co-operation between different partners at both geographical administrative levels, and that the services come closer to the client. There are also more stimuli for linking the labour market initiatives to related domains (*e.g.* mobility, poverty). Within this concept there is also an important drive to create new jobs (particularly in the field of the social economy).

The local authorities and other local partners experience a lack of policy autonomy in the Local Job Shop, especially concerning the universal basic services. VDAB at the other hand has to make equal job offers to all job-seekers in Flanders. This creates tensions between VDAB and the local actors in the operationalisation of the universal basic service.

Another point of particular interest is the possibility for differentiation between cities and communities. Differentiation in size is experienced as relevant due to the differences concerning the financial capacity and the complexity of tasks and functions between cities and communities.

A specific point relates to the monitoring of the Local Job Shops. Therefore a programme has been developed which is temporarily implemented in a few pilot regions. Monitoring is of crucial importance for the Local Job Shop as well as for the entire programme in view of the implementation of essential adjustments.

Sub-regional socio-economic policy

The *Sub-regional Employment Committees* (STCs) were established in the 1970s as tripartite advisory bodies of the VDAB. They were reformed five years ago. Their role is to undertake a regional analysis of the labour market, identify main problems and priorities and act on these as giving advice to the VDAB and the minister about the policies to implement. The STCs also have a co-ordinating function at sub-regional level and it is anticipated that they will help identify employment actions in the regions they serve. Their tasks are:

- to develop each year a plan for the regional labour market, including an advisory opinion on the regional VDAB plan and an advisory opinion on the implementation of ESF objectives in the region;
- to foster consultation and co-operation between actors in the region (between social partners, between social partners and regional actors);
- to promote and develop innovative actions and initiatives with regard to human resource development for target groups and the social economy.

There are 13 platforms in Flanders. Their composition is tripartite, with representatives of employers, trade unions, Flemish and local government. Also the VDAB and the local "living forces" are represented in the sub-regional employment committees, as well as representatives of education.

The sub-regional committees have a professional supporting structure with a co-ordinator, two-three project co-ordinators, a secretary and an administrative officer. There is also a co-ordination structure at Flemish level. Every two months the chairpersons of the sub-regional employment committees come together with the representatives of the social partners and the representatives of the minister and ministry. This platform organises the top-down and bottom-up flow of information and communication.

After four years, there are already some results to be shown. In the field of diversity and employment equity: there are more than 550 concrete affirmative action plans in companies; in all regions there are platforms established on diversity and employment; there is evidence of innovative projects and networking.

As far as the "value adding-economy" is concerned, there are regional incubation centres established for social economy; in several regions, there are platforms for exchange of experience on social economy and there is regular concertation on issues of competition with the regular economy. Also in the other areas of the Flemish labour market policy, such as the preventive approach, concrete actions have been carried out.

Some observations

Positive aspects of the committees are:
- A forum for dialogue and concertation between various partners in labour market policy (*e.g.* to define priorities).
- The provision in top-down and bottom-up information between policy makers and the partners on the field.
- Networking with other relevant policy areas, such as welfare and education.
- Special attention must be given to:
  - evaluation and monitoring; currently, a monitoring project is being developed;
  - integrating social and economic development: a challenge for the near future;
  - the importance of co-ordination and exchange of experiences.

Some conclusions

Decentralisation adds to effectiveness of labour market policy in Flanders. Decentralisation is an effective method of governance because it:
- optimises communication on employment policy (top-down);
- optimises the catchment of policy signals out of the regions (bottom-up);
- adds to the solution of complex employment problems (innovation and concertation).

But decentralisation asks for accountable partners:
- on regional level with a vision on the region, with professionalism and initiatives and with willingness to ensure transparency;
- on the central level with responsibility for creating favourable policy conditions (i.e. supporting structure) and with a consequent attitude toward input out of the region.

It is important to stress out that many of the dynamics of the regional employment policy depends on trust between the partners. Not only in the region itself but also in the region towards the central partners and in the central level towards the regional partners. But trust is not easy to build; it is something to work on. Therefore, there is a need for an agreed common framework, between the partners in the region and between the regional and central partners with agreed objectives, with monitoring and measurable indicators, and with agreed procedures.

PART I
Chapter 8

Poland: Opportunities, Mistakes and Challenges of Decentralisation

by

Michał Boni
Foundation CASE

Setting up labour market policy

The systemic transformation in Poland begun in 1989, and opened new possibilities to build democracy and a market-based economy. It also revealed problems in the labour market, including unemployment. At the time, forecasts concerning the labour market situation were not precise as both experience and abilities to forecast all the outcomes and side effects of transformation were severely lacking. However, the first rapid wave of unemployment growth (almost three millions of unemployed people at the end of 1993) highlighted the need for many policy initiatives to be adopted.

In the meantime, the legal framework for the design and implementation of labour market policy has been set up. A social system with rules for the definition of unemployment and benefit entitlements, as well as those regarding job search guidance and the like has been established. The responsibilities of the state towards the unemployed have been defined together with the broader economic policy framework to regulate unemployment. It was a continuation of a welfare state model in which it is the state itself, through its central government, is bearing the fundamental responsibility for various social tasks. However this model evolved at a later stage, when shared responsibilities with local governments, and with the social partners, became essential conditions for the delivery of employment policy.

The so-called Labour Fund was created through contributions made by employers and subsidies from the state budget. Its purpose was to finance unemployment subsidies and active labour market policy. Financial assistance from the EU and the World Bank supported the swift establishment of employment services. In contrast to developed western OECD countries, the newly-established PES in Poland had to learn the managerial procedures for assisting the unemployed. The basic framework for modern job brokerage services and guidance were created, as well as labour market intelligence, standards for the delivery of employment services, co-operation with the social partners. Indeed, in the Polish labour market, trade unions, employers and local governments were all new actors. From the very beginning, partner co-operation was significant, and a dialogue within a four-party model became the basis for the activities of employment councils: this was applicable from the level of a region (*poviat*) to the central employment council and advisory committees to the Minister of Labour.

New ideas and the experience gained throughout the 1990s have spurred the implementation of more complex instruments of labour market policy. Local variations were noticed between parts of the country in connection with unequal economic potential, qualifications of the indigenous population, and varying traditions of citizen participation in the public life. Furthermore, specific programmes for preventing unemployment have been designed to address the needs of special risk groups: young people entering the labour market without or with little qualifications, the long-term unemployed, women re-entering the labour market after long spells of inactivity, disabled workers, or workers made redundant as a result of large plant closures in the former state-owned sectors of economic activity (often in so-called "old industries").

The local and regional approach to active labour market policy was a significant achievement of the employment services. Throughout the 1990s, local PES offices were expanding at a rapid rate. Likewise, the Ministry of Labour and Social Policy maintained and extended the functions of this administration supervised by the National Employment Bureau, as a separate central institution shaping general policy rules. Just after one year of being in operation, the employment services were employing some 5 000 staff. In the next years increasing unemployment was matched by the respective growth of PES staffing levels: some 10 000 in 1992, over 13 000 after separating employment services as special administration in 1993 up to almost 20 000 in the years 1997 and 1998 (lowest unemployment rate below 10%). Following the administrative reforms implemented in 1999, staff numbers within the PES began to drop drastically. The administration now employs about 16 000 agents.

During the period of low unemployment and high numbers of PES staff, one agent of the employment services was to take care of about 120 jobseekers. Currently, there is a ratio of one agent for over 200 registered jobseekers. Ironically, the lack of budgetary funds for the PES has resulted in the direct recruitment of PES staff from the ranks of the unemployed as an active labour market policy measure. This is done within the framework set by subsidised employment (public works, interventions). Through this form of recruitment, some 1 200 individuals became members of the PES at the beginning of the 1990s. They were almost 5 000 in 1996 and are currently 3 500 to 4 000.

Early results

A mistake made during the first decade of labour market policy intervention was the excess of passive measures, focusing on securing the income of unemployed people. There was hence no real activation. Furthermore, the process of de-activation was also stimulated, which represented a further mistake. This was done firstly through a lowering of the age for pension eligibility, which weakened the social insurance system. Later, the creation of a system of subsidies and pre-pension benefits aimed towards helping industrial restructuring and maintaining social peace created an enormous burden for the Labour Fund and curtailed its financial ability to shape active labour market policy.

In fact, the mistakes were to some extent unavoidable, as it seemed that the social partners were not only accepting these measures fully, but were also to a certain extent, lobbying for their use on a wide scale.

The government was responsible for labour market policy, and hence for these mistakes. However, new thinking emerged and the necessity for a shared responsibility of the various partners was taken into consideration. The spirit of partnership thus emerged in the context of local labour markets being at stake.

Accessibility of job offices in each *poviat*, numerous job clubs and subsidiaries of job offices set up in *gminas* illustrated the importance of an active labour market policy at the local level. The possibility for complex local-level actions, involving an active participation of the social partners and local authorities had to compensate for the lack of consistent plans and a lack of broader country-wide actions. For many years, there were difficulties in integrating educational and training policies with labour market policy instruments, not to mention the poor linkages with economic development. The major reason behind the failure to link various policy strands was that for many years, the Ministry of Labour was perceived as the sole body responsible for the labour market. Thinking about relations between the fiscal, legal (*e.g.* rules for registering small enterprises) or educational (vocational training not delivering suitable qualifications due to poor technical equipment in the schools) was very limited.

One of the most significant ideas was to create a basis for co-operation of the local governments and employment services in the regions threatened with high unemployment. The key element was the need to support the development of infrastructural investments in these regions – water supply, sewage processing, telephone lines, etc. The pre-condition was a direct input from the *gmina* or a group of *gminas*. Once it was established that the investment was meeting specific criteria, state budgetary reserves could be released and subsidies from the Labour Fund could be paid in parallel to subsidise public works and reintegrate the unemployed in the labour market. During the period 1994-2001, over 2 billion PLN were spent for this at purpose; the contribution from local governments amounted to one and a half billion PLN. *Voivodships* contributed some 100 million PLN; private sector donations totalled some 460 million PLN, and the share of Labour Fund to finance public works was 107 million PLN. This investment allowed for the implementation of 5 350 initiative in almost 500 Polish *gminas* (over 20% of the total number of *gminas*).

A particularly weak element of the local labour market policy implemented by the social partners was the poor consideration given to the needs of local employers in the labour market policy. Perhaps the reason was inadequate organisation of the employers. Similarly, non-public entities and institutions of the labour market did not develop at any significant scale, except establishments for adult training, but even this exception applies mainly to larger agglomerations, while access is still limited in smaller towns. However, their development was not stimulated by either local governments or the public employment service (PES).

To evaluating Polish achievements in the area of labour market policy, one has to take into account the three important stages that characterised it. The first phase, lasting from the beginning of the transformation until the end of 1992, was the time for identifying the problems related to growing unemployment, for building a basis for labour market management and seeking partners for implementing the strategy of unemployment prevention. It was also a time characterised by the supremacy of protective actions (with an excessive use of all kinds of unemployment benefits) over active measures, the importance of which was hard to evaluate.

The second phase (years 1993-1998) was a period of increased care for the development of employment services, for the design of a first set of complex unemployment prevention programmes, for focused labour market management, as well as growing expenditures for active labour market policy. Moreover, the growing educational aspirations among younger generations led policy-makers to move forward the labour market entry of some 600 000 individuals through active labour market policy. This was also a period of rapid economic growth (some 4-5% yearly GDP growth during the period of 4-5 years) achieved due to the economic activity of small and medium enterprises. This in turn resulted in a high absorption of labour and a reduction of unemployment to around 10% (this was the EU average at the time). Moreover, economic restructuring also came to a halt at the time, but was re-initiated in 1998 and has lasted until now. The level of expenditures for active labour market policy was relatively high, from 11% of the total Labour Fund expenditure in 1993 to almost 24% in 1998.

The third period began in 1999 and has lasted until now. It is characterised by lower economic growth with GDP down to 1% in 2001, more people entering the labour market (and therefore higher expenditures from the Labour Fund to help graduates into employment, as indicated above). There was also a drastic decrease of funding from Labour Fund monies allocated to active measures (and therefore a relatively modest use of programmes for professional activation, as shown in Table 8.1), particularly in years 2001 and 2002, a weakness in the growth of small and medium enterprises, a collapse of the employment services due to poor timing and ill-prepared concept for integrated solutions in the area

Table 8.1. **Number of participants and efficiency measure for active labour market programmes, Poland, 1999-2001**

Tasks	Year 1999 Participants	Year 1999 Re-employment rate (%)	Year 2000 Participants	Year 2000 Re-employment rate (%)	Year 2001 Participants	Year 2001 Re-employment rate (%)
Total	**556 500**	**50.2**	**452 072**	**49.8**	**234 759**	**48.6**
Training measures	146 037	50.6	108 711	49.1	51 176	44.5
Intervention works	174 669	65.1	132 930	66.4	64 846	67.8
Public works	77 881	13.2	56 328	14.2	32 874	13.3
Social insurance refund	2 400	–	1 384	77.8	1 086	89.4
Graduate refunds	68 271	73.3	53 974	71.7	26 362	73.5
Graduate internships	64 697	39.5	72 862	36.3	45 867	35.2
"Socially beneficial" jobs	1 046	19.4	931	26.2	632	44.6
Special programmes	9 880	25.2	11 593	60.2	4 972	62.4
Total loans	11 598	–	7 338	–	3 737	–
For the unemployed	9 055		5 507		2 955	
For employees	2 543		1 831		782	
Other tasks	–	–	6 021	43.3	3 207	30.5

Source: Polish Ministry of Economy, Labour and Social Policy.

of decentralisation of the labour market policy. However, new promising labour market programmes such as the EU Sectoral Operating Programme – Human Resources Development, to be financed by the European Social Fund in the period 2004-2006 should benefit Poland following its entry into the European Union.

It should be stressed that despite high economic and employment growth, and despite multiple actions undertaken by the PES, labour market policies did not manage to achieve two goals. The first one is the goal of complexity coming from mutual relations between the spheres of education, social support and economic stimulation, which should be flexible in terms of realising clients' needs, and responding to local needs. The second aspect relates to the efficiency achieved through the synergies of various initiatives such as those undertaken by local governments, employment services, committed employers, trade union members. These should eventually allow employment promotion rather than protection to come to the fore.

Raising governance issues

Next to the constitutional debate, a debate started in 1996 regarding the appropriate governance model. Questions were raised concerning the tasks and responsibilities between public authorities of different levels and characters, and the move towards decentralisation. There were specific concerns about the possible effects of decentralising labour market management. The framework for the reforms that was discussed revolved around the need to create strong regions, new *voivodships* down from 49 to about 8 to 12. Eventually, the final number agreed was 16. Another matter for discussion was the creation of a second level of local government – the *poviat* – equipped with all functions necessary for development-oriented social processes aimed at the realisation of educational, health, employment, cultural, security and justice (courts of law) needs.

Proponents of a decentralisation of active labour market policy stressed that local measures would facilitate the participation of local community actors in policy design and delivery and that a climate of social trust would be fostered as a result and help build social relations. What was sought was an integration of the actions of local businesses, educational and training establishments, job centres and local social policy players. Consolidation of the actions was to increase their efficiency. It also seemed that this policy stance would encourage some financial engineering, *i.e.* a combination of local government funding, fund coming from the private sector, mutual funds active in the areas of local economic development as well as public monies through the Labour Fund in particular. A pre-condition for the success of such a local labour market management model was mutual trust among partners, maturity of the local authorities and transparency of local finance visible through an autonomy in creation of own funds by the latter. The decision to limit income redistribution via the state budget was to be compensated with a guarantee for mechanisms to mitigate the threat of financial disparities between localities.

During the debate held between 1996 and 1998 (the ruling coalition changed after the 1997 parliamentary elections) criticisms were expressed, less against decentralisation, than against the PES. It was argued that this institution was in danger of becoming subordinate to local and regional governments and would hence lose their autonomy.

The National Labour Office, the Ministry of Labour and Social Policy as well as numerous labour market experts held that within the new policy framework, government remained the key actor and that it would prevent the system from reacting swiftly and flexibly to sudden changes in the labour market. It was assumed that the lack of a decision and approval by the Ministry of Finance would limit the opportunities for strengthening the *poviats' own funds*. Therefore these would be turned into clients of the central state budget, and of the Labour Fund in particular. In such case, the Fund would be planned and allocated by the government using a suitable algorithm; constraints would limit the possibilities of creating reserves for unplanned situations and realisation of important projects, not planned before). It was also feared that distributed supervision over labour offices would not help standardisation of actions procedures and methods used, and would also negatively affect the quality and number of staff of the employment services. Realisation of nationwide programmes would therefore involve a lack of control and positive stimulation.

In turn, earlier experience of co-operation with local governments has shown that these are not ready to understand all aspects of local labour markets and labour market policy design. Their tendency for making excessive a use of public works, an instrument which from the second half of the 1990s proved rather inefficient, was limiting understanding and acceptance for actions like training-for-work or expanding the network of adult education.

In many cases, there was also concern over the fact that the conditions for obtaining additional finance from the Labour Fund would essentially be based on high levels of unemployment in a given *poviat*. Hence, assuming limited budgets available to the *poviats*, these could to some extent be tempted to maintain high levels of unemployment. The only way to limit moral hazard amongst some 360 entities would be to create a subordination to the regional *voivodship*-level authorities. However, this proposal was rejected during the debate on decentralisation. The winning model was the one that strengthened the *poviats* by granting them decision-making powers – without consideration of the necessary financial support towards the implementation and consistency of individual policies, for example executed at *voivodships* and central level.

Negative opinions were not taken into consideration during the political debate that took place within government and in parliament. The discussion was even more difficult when the voices for a cautious approach towards decentralisation of employment services were viewed as standing against the development of democratic principles. In such an atmosphere no one was really listening to any warnings concerning the effects of the implemented changes, which was undermining support for their application at that particular time.

The circumstances were as follows: decreasing pace of the rate of economic growth, a high demographic tide entering the labour market, a lack of possibility to absorb new labour, especially in an inflexible market, unclear results of the implemented educational reforms, hardly oriented at supporting adult education, and problems in the realm of public finance. Together with the sharp increase of subsidies and pre-pension benefits (de-activating tools) expenditures – almost 700 million in 1998, 1.15 billion in 1999, 2.2 billion in 2000, over 3.3 billion in 2001 and planned 5 billion in 2003 – these problems led to reduced expenditures for active forms of labour market policy. The dipersion of the PES activities at the time, the lack of co-ordinated supervision, either from the level of *voivodship* or the country – additionally weakened the efficiency of labour market management and made integration of the policies that would have improved the situation impossible.

Hence, a decentralised labour market management, through a reform introduced in the above context, did not bring the expected results.

The lack of finance to introduce the many necessary functions at the time when the Labour Fund entered a crisis, *i.e.* in 2000 and 2001 (with funds for active forms over two times lower than in 1998) destroyed the trust between the social partners, local businesses, public agencies, and the local employment services. The level of participation amongst the partners decreased, instead of increasing as hoped. As the result, it was not possible to find mechanisms for building local coalitions and priorities for local labour markets, adjusted to the situation and needs of the local communities. Additionally, staff turnover in the employment services increased radically as many specialised agents left. Many new, untrained staff joined the PES at a time of a partial collapse of the organisation's HRM practices within the organisation).

The result of the reforms was a weakening of the institutional and merit position of the PES at *voivodship* level. At that particular territorial level, the PES is not allowed to supervise the self-governing, the *poviat*-based PES. This is because constitutional rules do not allow for any supremacy of self-governing structures of one level over another.

Visible structural inefficiency of the public employment services becomes problematic not just in relation to high unemployment but also due to the necessary – in the perspective of Polish accession to the European Union – readiness of the Polish labour market institutions to absorb financing from the European Social Fund in the years 2004-2006. Indeed, this will be necessary with the view to implementing the tasks of the Sectoral Operating Programme – Human Resources Development (some 1.2 billion euro).

Challenges for the future

In this connection, what challenges should be faced and what actions should be taken in the immediate future?

One crucial issue concerns the final architecture for the PES, which implies a necessary clarification of the roles and scope of activities, autonomy and supervision of the offices at the level of the *poviat*, as well as the strengthening of the position enjoyed by the offices at the *voivodship*. It is a prerequisite for embedding their activities within a regional development policy framework. It would then enable the creation a main axis for labour market policy, that is the promotion of employment with the use of regional economic potential and resources or support by European Union structural funds in order to reduce the inequality between the Polish regions. It seems important that the bill for the social treatment of employment (planned by the government for 2004) allows for a better integration of policy preventing social exclusion with labour market policy (jobs as a means out of poverty – even if subsidised to some moment). This might be achieved on the level of *poviat* by creating Social Integration Centres, but also combining efforts of social welfare and labour market policy.

What is needed is a redefinition of the role of local government and scope of its responsibilities for some elements of labour market policy. Better consciousness of the local governments (missing so far) concerning the "soft" factors of labour market management, such as the improvement of employability (1st pillar of the EU employment strategy), support for the development and quality of school and adult education, support for professional career development through increased importance of labour market information and job guidance, including the accessibility of such services to their potential clients, are all factors that might lead to increased effectiveness of labour market policy.

It also seems important to stimulate financially and legally the development of agencies other than the PES. Whether in the area of non-governmental organisations or in business, these could complete the services not only to unemployed job seekers but to the workforce as a whole. Moreover, access to public finance (*e.g.* bidding for contracts from local governments or employment services affiliated to the *poviats*) could lead to increased efficiency, not to mention integration within the local community.

In order for the local government to participate in shaping and implementing local labour market policy in the area of workforce development, it is necessary that financing and revenue-raising tools be clearly defined. Similarly, if the *voivodship* level of government is to play any significant role in regional economic and social development policies, its financial and income generation rules must be fully transparent.

There is no doubt that rules regarding the social dialogue should be renewed, so that local and regional co-operation of different partners (not only the ones represented by traditional model: trade unions, employers' organisations and public authorities) is not only of a purely cosmetic function. An impulse might be the introduction of pre-defined tasks, for example co-operation of local and regional employers with employment services and educational institutions towards the establishment of the qualifications and professional skills of graduates expected by employers.

A significant impulse for stimulating social co-operation would consist of resorting to the rules of citizen dialogue, *i.e.* integrating reflecting in the numerous institutions of citizenship-based society in the institutional architecture of active labour market policy.

Finally, the key for the success of the labour market management reforms involving is its implementation in an environment that understands and promotes the decentralisation philosophy. Therefore, necessity is another key concept for the future governance of labour market policy, next to the issue of responsibility, not only for labour market and social policy but also balanced growth. Economic efficiency is a result of the transparency of rules for financing defined goals and building a climate of social trust. This in turn helps negotiations with trade unions concerning the pact for development and makes labour market laws more flexible. Hence, a feeling of local or regional community of interests is created as the social partners realise that a decentralised public policy does not undermine their position.

This chapter has shown that there is still much more to be done in Poland until the decentralisation process brings real effects and until capital (in its narrow, economic sense) can be added to social capital to truly support the development of human capital.

PART II

Reconciling Flexibility and Accountability

> One of the most difficult challenges faced by decentralised frameworks is in guaranteeing public accountability. Decentralisation implies a sharing of responsibility for decision-making among a number of actors, and to agree on an accountability framework politically acceptable to the various government levels involved is rarely an easy task. Yet there are ways to reconcile accountability and administrative flexibility.

ISBN 92-64-10470-4
Managing Decentralisation
A New Role for Labour Market Policy
© OECD 2003

PART II

Chapter 9

Flexibility and Accountability in Labour Market Policy: A Synthesis

by

Hugh Mosley
Social Science Research Centre Berlin (WZB)

This chapter presents a framework for examining the relationship between flexibility and accountability in labour market policy. The first section discusses the concepts of flexibility and accountability. The second section examines accountability mechanisms and problems in managerial decentralisation within the public employment service. The third section addresses these issues in the context of political decentralisation and multi-level governance. The fourth section discusses flexibility based on privatisation through contracting out. The fifth section presents some conclusions.[1] A central thesis is that different types of governance structures in labour market policy have their own distinctive accountability frameworks with characteristic accountability standards, mechanisms and processes.

Accountability and flexibility

Accountability

In its most general sense accountability can be defined as "being accountable; liability to give account of, and answer for, discharge of duties or conduct; responsibility" (Oxford English Dictionary). This definition suggests several basic elements of accountability about which we should inquire in a concrete organisational setting: who is responsible to whom for what, whereby the latter refers not only to the task to be performed but also in particular to the applicable accountability standards. A variety of different types of accountability standards are discussed in the literature on public administration (*e.g.* legal, political, bureaucratic, fiscal, professional, results, process accountability, etc.). As is evident from this definition, accountability is a relationship between two or more actors, for example, government agency and ministry, local office and regional headquarters, provider and purchaser, employee and supervisor, and it is as a rule an asymmetrical relationship.

Accountability standards

Four basic types of accountability standards can be identified, that have varying weights in different types of public administration regimes and accountability frameworks (Wirth, 1991; OECD, 1999a):

- *Legal accountability.* Public agencies are expected to act on the basis of the rule of law and in conformity with applicable regulations. The values at stake do not solely refer to a uniform and equal treatment but also to democratic legitimacy. More decentralised and flexible forms of governance in labour market policy, which blur the traditional public-private distinction, may come into conflict with the norms of legal accountability, especially in countries with strong traditions of administrative and social law.[2]

- *Fiscal accountability.* A second accountability criterion is correctness and economy in the use of public monies. Public bureaucracies are expected to minimise costs and account for expenditure in terms of legislative mandates. The finance ministry or budget and accounting office in each country is the guardian of this traditional accountability standard, which like legal accountability, may act as a restraint on or come into conflict with more flexible forms of governance and other accountability criteria.

- *Performance accountability.* Here the primary criterion is output-oriented effectiveness and efficiency: whether declared goals have been achieved and whether the results justify the resources committed. In modern organisations, this standard is central to external (political) accountability and to the internal accountability of operative units to higher organisational levels.

- *Public accountability.* Democratic public administration requires not only political accountability to elected government officials but also responsiveness to the needs and preferences of citizens as consumers (*e.g.* the Citizens Charter in the UK) and to other stakeholders (*e.g.* employers, trade unions, clients).[3]

Accountability frameworks

Different types of governance structures in labour market policy have their own distinctive accountability frameworks with characteristic accountability standards, mechanisms and processes. In more traditional systems of public administration, the accountability framework emphasises legal and fiscal accountability and the separation of administration and politics, whereas flexible systems give greater emphasis to decentralisation, managerial discretion, performance measures, quality standards and consumerism in accountability frameworks. Our primary focus in this chapter paper is on accountability in the latter sense of performance and public accountability.[4]

Accountability frameworks establish accountability relationships by assigning responsibility for tasks to someone (person or organisation) and giving another an interest and supervisory role in overseeing the discharge of this responsibility (Davies, 2001). Within an organisation such as the public employment service (PES) there is an internal chain of accountability relationships between organisational levels. For example, the local PES office (director) is accountable to a regional office, which in term must answer to the national office. Depending on its own governance structures, the national PES is typically held externally accountable to the ministerial (political) level on the basis of a national framework plan or agreement.[5] Area-based networks and partnerships, whose constituent organisations are typically accountable to different government departments, levels of government, and non-governmental organisations, are a special case because their activities are subject to multiple accountability chains with overlapping and possibly inconsistent accountability frameworks (OECD, 2001; see also OECD, 1999a).

Conflicts and tradeoffs in accountability standards

Accountability standards may conflict.[6] For example, a strict interpretation of legal and fiscal accountability may be an obstacle to increased discretion of managers at the operative level to promote improved performance. In this case, however, the conflict is not between flexibility and accountability but between two different accountability standards. Thus accountability to demands of an agency's clientele for improved services may conflict with ministerial pressure for cost reductions even at the expense of service quality. Participation of employers' organisations, trade unions and other non-governmental organisations in governance may be inimical to managerial efficiency, if there is a lack of agreement on goals, or if these organisations are themselves also providers of the services about which they have to decide. Moreover, organisational units such as a local PES office may experience accountability conflicts between, for example, their responsiveness to local communities (*e.g.* in a local partnership) and the goals and requirements for which they are accountable to their own organisation.

Finally, it should be noted that accountability frameworks impose substantial costs for keeping and auditing financial and administrative records, programme monitoring and evaluation and contract management on organisations. These costs have to be reasonable in terms of the total cost of the activity being audited. We rightly complain of excessive "red tape" when accountability standards are unreasonable (*e.g.* requiring competitive bidding for the purchase of a relatively inexpensive equipment, documentation and approval of reimbursements for small items, inflated evaluation requirements for relatively small programmes). In this case, overzealous accountability standards are inconsistent with efficiency goals. This is a problem in multi-level governance and partnerships, in which different government departments and levels of government as well as diverse private organisations are involved. Not only do the participating organisations have their own relatively inflexible accounting and record keeping systems, but also especially smaller organisations may be heavily burdened or deterred from participation due to inflexible accountability requirements.

The Polish Agency for Enterprise Development (PARP), which is charged with implementing pre-accession EU structural funding in Poland, has adopted a flexible approach to accountability that is instructive in this respect.

PARP faces the task of central management of contracts that vary greatly in size and in the type of organisations involved (public, private, non-profit). Small and medium sized contracts with non-governmental organisations are subjected to less stringent accountability standards for reasons of efficiency and to foster innovation (see Chapter 15 by Gęsicka).

Flexibility trends in governance

In the past two decades traditional hierarchical forms of public employment service organisation are being challenged by innovative "new public management" strategies borrowed from the private sector: decentralisation, management by objectives, contracting out, competition even within government, customer orientation, etc. Instead of being monopolistic public administrations with sole responsibility for "administering" labour market policies, they are expected to co-operate with other private, public, and non-profit organisations involved in the same tasks. There is a new emphasis on the role of co-operative networks in policy implementation among private as well as public sector actions and on linking labour market policy with social policies and local economic development (*e.g.* "workforce investment boards", territorial employment pacts, local partnerships, "alliance for work" and so forth). These trends toward flexibility in governance raise special accountability problems and offer alternative accountability frameworks at odds with that in traditional hierarchical and rule-oriented public administration (see Mosley and Sol, 2001).

We can identify three major trends toward flexibility in labour market policy governance that give rise to distinctive accountability frameworks and problems:

- managerial decentralisation;
- political decentralisation;
- privatisation.

There has been in particular a strong trend toward decentralisation of labour market policy in the last two decades. By decentralisation we mean the extent to which responsibility for labour market policy is delegated to the regional and local level. Decentralisation entails increased regional and local control over programme design features, targeting and policy mix. It is frequently argued that decentralisation will enhance the adaptation of labour market policy to local needs and enhance co-ordination with regional and local labour markets, social and economic development policies. Another major influence has been the public service reform movement and "new public management" ideas, which advocate greater flexibility for the regional and local or public employment services in the context of a shift toward management by objectives.

At the risk of oversimplification, we can distinguish two major types of decentralisation in labour market policy in OECD countries: managerial and political decentralisation.[7] The former represents a form of intra-organisational flexibility, in which managers in regional and local offices receive greater operative flexibility in implementing national policy objectives (e.g. in France, the United Kingdom or in most Scandinavian countries). Political decentralisation, or devolution, entails not merely managerial discretion but a more far-reaching delegation of responsibility for labour market policy from the national to the sub-national (regional, provincial or state) levels of government, especially in federal systems (e.g. Canada, the United States, Spain). In both types of decentralisation there is an increasingly strong reliance on inter-organisational networks or partnerships at the regional or local level, which co-ordinate the actions of diverse public and private sector actors involved in labour market policy, especially social and local economic development policies (see OECD, 2001).

Privatisation through contracting out is a third major form of flexibility in implementation. Public employment services have traditionally contracted out service provision, for example, for labour market training to external providers. What is new in most recent developments (e.g. in Australia and the Netherlands) is the establishment of networks of purchaser/provider relationships in which responsibility for re-integration services is largely contracted out to external providers. The local public agency responsible for intake services for the unemployed plays only a subordinate role in the contract-based network managed by the labour ministry or labour market authority.

In the following sections we discuss accountability frameworks and problems in organisations with decentralised managerial structures; in partnerships in the context of political decentralisation and multi-level governance; and privatisation through contracting out.

Managerial decentralisation

The MBO model

Decentralisation, contracting and other market mechanisms in public administration reflect in particular the influence of "new public management" (NPM). "New public management" aims to replace "administrative culture" with a "management culture" (Richards, 1994) using a quasi-contractual paradigm adapted from the private sector (Osborne and Gaebler, 1992). Management by objectives (MBO), or management by results, is the common denominator of diverse administrative reforms that aim at enhancing the efficiency and effectiveness of labour market policy through managerial decentralisation.

The basic elements of the management by objectives model can be summarised as follows:[8]

- *Goal definition and performance indicators.* The first step in the management cycle is the establishment of clear goals, operational objectives (targets) and the development of corresponding performance indicators capable of measuring the extent to which these targets have been achieved.
- *Delegation.* Delegation of objectives and resources, in manageable units, to staff at subordinate levels of the organisation.
- *Flexibility.* There is a low density of generally binding rules and procedures. Managers and operating units at regional and local levels are free to allocate resources flexibly between budget items, to vary their policy mix, and even programme design features (*e.g.* eligibility requirements, implementation structures).
- *Monitoring of performance against targets.* Management by objectives requires sophisticated management information systems that regularly measure the progress of indicators toward agreed targets. Moreover, "real-time" monitoring enables managers to intervene immediately in case of under-performance (*i.e.* stronger deviations from the "target track").
- *Performance assessment.* A final performance review at the end of a management cycle is another important ideal-typical component of MBO. At this stage the performance of the operating units is assessed by the next supervisory level. In contrast to traditional bureaucratic administration, the emphasis is on outputs or outcomes against targets rather than on controlling inputs and adherence to detailed regulations.
- *New policy cycle.* On the basis of the performance assessment policy goals, operational targets and performance indicators are redefined or adjusted for the next policy cycle.

In the field of labour market policy, Sweden and Norway have the longest experience with MBO systems in Europe, which were first introduced in the mid-1980s (Niklasson and Tomsmark, 1997). Use of management by objectives in some form is now widespread in EU public employment service organisations. This is a consequence, in the first instance, of the dissemination of performance management in the public sector in the 1980s and 1990s. The spread of management by objective has also been promoted by European Employment Strategy, which since 1998 requires member states to submit annual "national action plans" that document and measure progress toward achievement of the EU's employment policy guidelines. Ten of the eighteen EU PES organisations surveyed were found to use management by objectives: Austria, Denmark, the Flanders regional PES (VDAB) in Belgium, France, Germany, Great Britain, Finland, the Netherlands, Norway, and Sweden (Mosley *et al.*, 2001).[9] Recent PES reforms in Switzerland have introduced strong elements of performance management system. Outside of Europe, this approach to public sector management appears to be strongest in the US, Canada, Australia and New Zealand.

It should be noted that the implications of management by objectives for decentralisation are ambiguous. It does not represent an abandonment of central control of the organisation but rather a refinement. Operating units are typically given a great deal more discretion in the use of funds and personnel and in the mix and management of programmes than in more traditional administrative structures but are expected to achieve centrally set targets or goals in terms of which their performance is assessed. In practice one can observe two clearly different models of PES performance management: the more centralised and hierarchical agency model (*e.g.* France, Great Britain) and the more decentralised self-administration model (*e.g.* Austria, Germany). The agency model entails a strong separation between policy and implementation, a national level "agency" agreement, top-down allocation of targets to the regions, centralised controlling etc. In the self-administration model the PES agency itself enjoys greater policy autonomy *vis-à-vis* the ministerial level, target setting incorporates stronger elements of dialogue, some targets are autonomously set at the regional level, and quantitative targets are only one element in a more consultative style of performance assessment.

In France, the implementation of employment policies remains relatively centralised even after the introduction of management by objectives and some developments in the direction of decentralisation. Thus Simonin (Chapter 14 in this volume) prefers to describe the process as one of "deconcentration" rather than "decentralisation". In particular the placement agency (ANPE) exhibits a top-down management style, although the impact of decentralisation has been greater in other components of the PES. Noteworthy in the French case is that the elements of local flexibility in MBO have only been partially implemented: local actors can choose from a toolbox of relatively rigidly defined national programmes but they are not free to adapt them to local needs or invent new programmes. Moreover, their freedom to allocate expenditure among different types of programmes is limited (see Chapter 14).

MBO and accountability

As is evident from the above discussion, MBO is not only an alternative management strategy but also an alternative accountability framework. In contrast to the emphasis in traditional public sector governance on legal and fiscal accountability, it places more emphasis on performance and public accountability. The central internal accountability mechanism is the contract or "quasi-contract". An external contract or agreement with the responsible ministry specifies the organisational goals and targets to be achieved within a given time period and (in some cases) the resources available. For example, in Great Britain the Employment Service (renamed Jobcentre Plus since mid-2002) concludes an annual Agency Performance Agreement with its department setting forth the targets to be achieved in the current fiscal year and the indicators used to assess performance.

This national agreement becomes the basis for a series of internal agreements between the agency and each of its regional offices and between the regional offices and the district offices for the achievement of specified targets in the delivery of government programmes. Progress toward agreed targets is monitored by the management information system on a weekly or monthly basis. The comparison of tracked results with targets is the basis for performance assessment in the internal accountability relationships between different levels of the organisation and between the agency and its ministry. Management by objectives has emphasised not only political accountability for the achievement of specified goals but also accountability to the users of public services. Thus the Employment Service places on strong emphasis on quality targets for customer service to jobseekers and employers (*e.g.* short waiting times for appointments or accessibility by telephone); service quality is systematically checked by anonymous "mystery shoppers" in local job centres (Mosley *et al.*, 2001).

Such intra- and inter-agency agreements are called "quasi-contracts" because they are seldom legally enforceable; the parties to the agreement (here different levels of the same agency) are in most cases not legal persons. They serve merely to co-ordinate activities and provide an accountability framework that assigns responsibility, reporting requirements, and accountability standards in terms of which compliance is to be assessed (Davies, 2001). From a legal point of view, these agreements are sometimes regarded as being merely symbolic: "In effect, the contractual relationship is simply a hierarchical management relationship with a greater degree of formality about the aims to be pursued" (*idem*). However, when rooted in the culture of organisations and backed by implicit or explicit sanctions for managers and other personnel (bonuses, promotions, distinctions), they can be real and effective instruments of governance. Sanctions, which are usually weak, are in any case less important than the motivation of staff and their identification with the organisation and its goals (Mosley *et al.*, 2001).

Accountability problems and good practice in MBO[10]

The successful functioning of accountability in MBO-type performance management in labour market policy has a number of characteristic prerequisites and pitfalls:

1. The commitment of PES top management and government is important for MBO success. In most cases, the introduction of MBO in the PES was part of a broader commitment at the governmental level to modernisation of the public sector. Without strong leadership support MBO becomes largely inefficient because it is not taken seriously within the organisation.

2. There are frequently failures or disruptions in MBO that are attributable to the political level of government. For instance, there are many examples of government failure to agree some or all of the annual targets in a timely manner. Moreover, because labour market policy is so politically sensitive, *ad hoc* interventions during the course of the annual performance agreement sometimes disrupt PES operations (occasioned, for example, by a new minister, a change of governments, or an election year initiative). For example, the key political importance of the unemployment issues has made the French government reluctant to relinquish control of labour market policy and to resist greater regional flexibility in the use of resources (see Chapter 14 by Simonin). These shortcomings in the practice of MBO are coped with pragmatically by experienced PES organisations; nevertheless they may at some point undermine its credibility and effectiveness.

3. The appropriate time frame is another critical design feature of MBO. A combination of multi-year and annual planning in which annual operational objectives are agreed on the basis of medium-term goals is the most practicable solution for reconciling the need for strategic planning with short-term flexibility.

4. Design features of goals, operational objectives and performance indicators are critical for the smooth functioning of MBO-type PES management systems. PES organisations with MBO-type systems use a moderate number of operational objectives and targets (typically 8-10), which is consistent with the theoretical model of MBO in the literature. But one of the main practical problems of MBO implementation in PES organisations proved to be the development of good performance indicators. In addition to shortcomings in data availability, many countries reported problems finding easy-to-measure and understandable performance indicators for organisational objectives. For example, in France data is readily available only on whether clients are still but not on whether they have entered employment (see Chapter 14 by Simonin).

5. The existence of a strong central controlling unit within the PES organisation is an important condition for the success of MBO. Without reliable data that are collected in "real time", performance cannot be monitored and management intervention comes too late.

6. Another key concern is the "right" level of quantitative target levels. The general consensus is that targets should be "stretching", *i.e.* challenging, but still realistic. In countries with more hierarchical management styles, national targets are allocated to the regional level in a top-down fashion based on some combination of formulae and bargaining. In other PES management systems with a more decentralised style, regional and local offices play a much stronger role in the setting of target levels.

7. Agency problems, especially moral hazard, are endemic to the performance management approach with its strong emphasis on quasi-contracts and achieving quantitative performance targets. Evidence from case studies suggests that there is a strong incentive for "street level" programme managers to produce the "numbers" that are "needed". In many countries administrative data on job placements through the public employment service are not reliable, which in recent years has led to major scandals in Great Britain, Norway and Germany. Regular validation of vulnerable key indicators in the management information system (*e.g.* placements) as well as staff acceptance of the performance management targets are the best remedies against such opportunistic behaviour.

8. The strong management focus of MBO and the concomitant concentration of responsibility for policy at the ministerial level may be at the expense of the participation and influence of other stakeholders (*e.g.* the social partners, clients, providers), and of inter-organisational partnerships.

9. MBO entails costs as well as benefits, including the establishment of new types of organisational structures. In the first place, it requires a major investment of time and organisational resources in an adequate management information and controlling system, although the technical standards of modern information technology facilitate the collection and processing of data, implying lower costs and less red tape than would have been the case in the past. Output- and outcome-oriented performance controlling services, should not, however, only be regarded as an accountability cost: they promote efficiency and effectiveness by improving the quality of information available to decision-makers.

10. The relationship between classical management by objectives and quality management deserves special attention. Above all, the emphasis on quality management is an important response to the perceived shortcoming in the original quantitative emphasis in MBO systems (*e.g.* in Norway), and hence a useful complement to management by objectives.

Political decentralisation: partnerships and accountability

The OECD has highlighted the importance of local networks or partnerships in the implementation of labour market policy in a number of major conferences and publications (OECD 1999, 2001; Giguère, 2003). The US (see Dorrer, Chapter 12 and Eberts, Chapter 19) and Canada (see Rymes, Chapter 11) with their strong federal systems and Spain (Ruiz, Chapter 10) with its far-reaching devolution of responsibility to the autonomous regions exemplify in particular the problems of accountability in a partnership approach to multi-level governance. Since most readers will be familiar with the partnership literature (OECD, 2001), this section focuses on: *i)* institutional complexity in the public sector, to which this groundswell of local partnerships is a response; and ii) the special accountability problems that arise in the case of partnerships as an instrument of policy implementation.

Institutional complexity and partnerships

Institutional complexity in the public sector frequently results in a mismatch between the competence of agencies and jurisdictions and the problem to be addressed. First, responsibility for labour market policy is itself frequently fragmented with different institutional actors responsible for major functions in the re-integration of the unemployed: job placement, training and other active measures, administration of unemployment benefits. In eight OECD countries (Belgium, Denmark, Finland, Ireland, the Netherlands, Portugal, Sweden, Switzerland) job brokerage and responsibility for active programmes are concentrated within the PES and benefit administration is the responsibility of separate agencies. In other countries such as France and the US, responsibility for placement services and active measures are assigned to two or more separate institutions. Moreover, there is frequently an even more complicated division of labour in federal systems with devolution of substantial responsibilities to provincial or state governments (*e.g.* Canada and the US). Actor constellations in labour market policy have recently become even more complex due to the increasing role of local authorities in welfare to work programmes for the clientele of social assistance recipients and efforts to form new linkages between labour market and local economic development strategies. Finally, there has been a growing recognition that there is a territorial dimension to unemployment that requires involvement of a broad spectrum of public and private local actors.

National responses to these structural problems of policy implementation have varied. What is required is an effective co-ordination between the different government and private actors involved in a policy domain. Network-based, co-operative approaches should not, however, be regarded as an end in themselves but are a more or less appropriate response to co-ordination problems in a given national institutional setting. Moreover, such co-operative forms are only one option. Another would be institutional reform that reallocates responsibility and resources between different agencies or levels of government in order to achieve a better fit between government and the problems addressed. For example, responsibility for labour market policies and related issues might be concentrated in one agency or level of government. Thus in Great Britain the new Jobcentre Plus network now puts responsibility for welfare to work programmes for social assistance recipients and all labour market policies for other unemployed people in a single agency. Promotion of co-operation between organisations at the local level is another, more flexible approach. Such partnerships have a number of distinct advantages for policy-makers: 1) they are relatively easy to implement in comparison with cumbersome institutional reform (and easier to alter or end); 2) they entail very low costs – usually only start-up and co-ordination costs,[11] whereas the potential gain from better co-ordination of labour market policy appears to be relatively large; 3) they are in form extremely flexible and thus highly adaptable to local conditions; 4) they include private as well as public sector actors, promising synergetic effects and may engender a long-term gain in "social capital".

The Austrian territorial employment pacts (TEPs) illustrate these points (Huber, 2002; Campbell, 2001). The TEP-model is extremely varied and thus hard to define: It may exist at the provincial or at the local level, be primarily concerned with policy co-ordination or with policy implementation, be concerned with any type of institutional problem or policy area, and may include any type of actor. In most cases, the TEPs are based on agreements between the PES and the provincial authorities and are concerned with co-ordination of labour market policy with other policies within the framework of the Austrian National Action Plan. The Austrian scheme offers a relatively small staff subsidy to stimulate the development of TEPs at the regional and local levels. This relatively small subsidy appears to have leveraged disproportionately large amount of co-operative activity at the regional and local levels. The Austrian TEPS are not organisations in a formal sense (their own staff and budget is relatively small) but primarily inter-organisational networks.[12] The two levels of the Austrian model, the provincial and local levels, appear to have somewhat different functions with the former being concerned more with policy co-ordination, especially between the AMS and regional governments, and the latter more focused on policy implementation. The "hidden agenda" in Austria appears to be to improve the co-ordination of labour market policy with regional and local economic development, functions that in Austria are largely the responsibility of different institutions (the AMS and regional and local authorities).

Although there are strong cultural and institutional similarities between Germany and Austria (strong national PES organisations, a federal system in which provincial (*Land*) governments are primarily responsible economic development, a strong tradition of social partnership etc.) the actual focus of the activities of TEPs has been quite different in Germany. In Austria, the TEP model focuses above all on co-ordination between the PES and provincial governments, whereas in Germany TEPs have been primarily a variety of local employment initiative (Gerlach and Ziegler, 2000). The regional-level policy co-ordination function of the Austrian model is of little relevance to Germany because this is already carried out in other informal and formal ways, especially the "Alliances for Jobs" (see Neumann, 2000) and other corporatist bodies at the regional level (*e.g.* the role of the social partners and regional and local governments in the PES governing bodies). There is, moreover, an abundance of other (unsubsidised) local employment initiatives in Germany, especially at the municipal level.

Accountability in multi-level governance

Partnerships and other inter-organisational networks are, in this perspective, intermediary institutions in labour market policy at the regional or local level. In most cases they were established in response to national or EU programmes that address co-ordination problems in national policy frameworks and seek to foster area-based coalitions of public and private actors to address local employment, social and economic development issues. This embeddedness in their national policy framework is constitutive for their accountability and accountability problems.

The basic accountability problem of area-based networks or partnerships has been identified by the OECD literature. The partnerships themselves are in an organisational sense relatively weak. They have influence and an impact largely through the actions of their members. The constituent members are, however, not as a rule accountable to the partnership or its board in a hierarchical sense, or as purchaser and provider. The constituent members are typically government agencies, which are accountable to different government departments and levels of government and non-governmental organisations. Their activities in the partnership are subject to multiple accountability chains: each partner is accountable to its own governing body or agency; to the partnership; and to its local public (OECD, 1999a, 2001).

These accountability chains are not of equal status for the organisations involved. For government agencies at all levels of government, the accountability framework and accountability chain imposed upon them by their own governing body clearly has priority and constrains their participation in and commitments to the partnership. This is even more strongly the case insofar as the MBO management style imposes binding (regionalised) performance targets on local operating units. This means, for example, that we would only expect a local PES office to participate in an area based network or partnership to the extent that there are net benefits. For public sector entities the criteria in terms of which their interests are defined are complex and derived to a large extent from the institutional framework in which they operate (*e.g.* formal or informal performance indicators), which also imposes important constraints on their behaviour (laws, regulations, financial and personnel resources etc.).[13]

If the accountability ties of the constituent members are asymmetrical, as this analysis suggests, participating organisations are in the first instance ultimately responsible to the accountability chains and standards of their own separate organisations. Their commitment to the partnership will have a lower priority, depending on the degree of flexibility in setting local targets and designing local programmes that they have and the compatibility of partnership goals with those of their own organisation. For example, in the US, each of the programmes co-ordinated by the Workforce Investment Boards and delivered in "one-stop shops" has its own separate funding source at the state or federal level and its own "accountability stream" with separate reporting requirements and rigidities in developing local programme packages (OECD, 2001). Sometimes there are clear conflicts in organisational goals. Thus in eastern Germany, the PES subsidies the outward mobility of unemployed skilled workers as a response to severe labour market imbalances; this strategy is heavily criticised by state and local governments as inimical to regional economic development. On the other hand "double counting" from joint projects with local partners aids the PES in achieving its own operational targets: local German PES offices count ALMP programme entrants and report placement rates as their own, even when there is a significant share of co-financing of their activities by state governments and local authorities.

One solution might be better high-level co-ordination of national policy frameworks (Giguère, 2003). This is, however, difficult to realise because the inconsistencies between government agencies and levels of government reflect not only the co-ordination problems of large organisations with a complex division of labour but also different policy perspectives and institutional interests. Nevertheless, in specific areas in which government seeks to promote partnership at the regional or local level – as noted above most major partnerships are government sponsored – programme design must give careful consideration to the institutional incentives (and disincentives) for co-operation. For example, in Germany in the late 1990s, the PES endorsed in principal improved co-operation between local authorities responsible for social assistance and its local offices in providing services to this target group, but co-operation remained purely voluntary. The PES did not introduce performance standards that encouraged placement of social assistance recipients or even monitor their participation in PES programmes. In fact, budget cuts led the PES to further restrict eligibility for its programmes in a way that reduced the number of social assistance recipients and undermined existing patterns of co-operation in some PES (Mosley and Schütz, 2001). This was not an information problem but a problem of political will. After a scandal over falsified placement statistics, a reform commission recommended a mandatory one-stop-shop for all unemployed people. In this case, voluntary co-operation failed and is to be replaced by a merger of the separate organisations.

The partnerships themselves are in some sense in an accountability dilemma. They themselves are subject to complex accountability demands, although their constituent organisations may, for the reasons discussed above, have only a conditional commitment to the partnership. The complexity of accountability for the Irish partnerships illustrates this point:

> *Accountability is a complex matter for the partnerships. They are effectively accountable to different interests and in different ways: to their funders through their detailed monitoring and financial reporting procedures; to local residents and local*

groups through community representatives on the board and community forums; to other social partners and state agencies through their board representatives; and to many other individuals and organisations actively involved in particular projects through their working groups and organisational committees (Turok, 2001).

At least four different types of accountability relationships are documented here: *i)* the government agency that sponsors and funds the partnership and imposes its own accountability requirements; *ii)* the constituent partners represented on partnerships board; *iii)* the local public; *iv)* providers and other participants in the partnership's programmes.

The existing literature has identified a number of weaknesses in the governance of partnerships that may undermine accountability, for example, unclear or inconsistent goals, blurred distribution of responsibility among partners, poor monitoring, failure to separate strategic planning and participation as a provider, and evaluation criteria that emphasise policy results instead of their contribution to governance (OECD, 2001; Giguère, 2003). These are of course critical views that might be applicable to performance assessment in any context. Moreover, these problems are not surprising given the heterogeneity of the partnerships, their organisational weakness, and the subordination of their members to other accountability frameworks.

The territorial employment pacts, and most other partnerships, were established under national or EU programmes and are accountable, in the first instance, to these agencies. The partnerships themselves are, in this respect, "policy-takers". Whether these shortcomings of the partnerships in a given case represent accountability failure depends on the accountability framework and standards imposed by programme design and legislation on which the partnership is based.

There are also examples of good practice in institutional design in this respect. For example, in Austria the responsible ministry issues "guidelines" for TEPs that establish criteria for the goals and strategy, and organisation of the co-operation as well as quality standards for its work programme. The relatively small number of TEP contracts in Austria makes it possible to flexibly manage TEP contract on an individual basis.

The Italian territorial pacts are required to meet very stringent requirements with regard to the tasks and responsibilities of each partner and the terms and conditions of the partnership agreement. Every application needs to contain:

- all the activities to be carried out, with their time-schedule and methodologies;
- the institutions responsible for the attainment of every project;
- the specific commitment of each partner;

- the financial means required for the different types of activities, the sources of funding, legislation applicable and the available risk capital;
- the agencies in charge of monitoring and evaluating results, as well as their methods (Melo, 2001).

The same is true for the US Workforce Investment Board (WIB), which formalises the relationship with its service providers in a memorandum of understanding that establishes an agreement "concerning the agreed-upon roles and responsibilities of the subcontractor (...) to ensure the effective and efficient delivery of workforce services to prevent duplication, and to co-ordinate resources in the local workforce development area" (Eberts and Erikcek, 2001).

Programme accountability standards may be more or less adhered to in practice. The adequacy of programme standards in partnership design is a central evaluation issue in assessing partnership programmes. Nevertheless, the accountability standards applied to partnerships and other co-operative implementation structures should be appropriate and reasonable. As noted above, accountability has costs as well as benefits. This means, for example, that the stringent MBO-standards of performance accountability used in national PES organisations described above are unrealistic for partnerships, given the heterogeneity of their membership, their limited organisational resources and their members' priority commitment to the accountability frameworks of their own parent organisations.

The accountability framework of the Workforce Investment Act in the US can be regarded as an attempt to adapt performance management to the special tasks and problems of multi-level governance. It establishes a common performance accountability framework for programmes implemented by state, and local governments and private sector partners. There is a small set of "core" performance indicators for different target groups, with state and local governments free to include additional indicators beyond these minimum requirements. Importantly, the core indicators (*e.g.* entering employment; retention after six months; earnings) are largely gathered at low cost from unemployment insurance wage records. Formal performance agreements with the states establish performance targets and provide in principal for sanctions. In this complex and decentralised system there have been formidable problems both in developing comprehensive data and information systems and in reconciling differences in the definition of core indicators (*e.g.* job placement). The accountability framework is also a major concern in current debates in the US over reform of the Workforce Investment Act. State and local officials frequently criticise federal regulations and accountability requirements for limiting flexibility and impeding adaptation of programmes to local needs (see Eberts, Chapter 19, and Dorrer, Chapter 12).

Accountability problems in multi-level governance in Canada are aggravated by the pattern of asymmetrical devolution through labour market development agreements: whereas some provinces have assumed full responsibility for active programmes within the funding and client eligibility guidelines of the national government ("full transfer"); in others the provinces are involved only in planning, while actual delivery is the responsibility of the federal government ("co-management"). Finally, no agreement has been concluded with Ontario and active programmes continue to be delivered as in the past by the federal government. A national accountability framework (targets, performance measurement, reporting requirements etc.) for this complex administrative structure is incorporated in the labour market development agreements concluded with the provinces. As in other federal systems, there are problems with the integrity and comparability of performance data exchanged across multiple governmental levels (see Chapter 11 by Rymes).

Since 1994 Spain has devolved responsibility for labour market policy to the regional "autonomous communities". In the area of labour market policy these are now responsible for the management of active policies and placement services, although the regulation and allocation of funds for these policies is controlled by the national labour market authority (INEM). Unemployment benefits are a national responsibility. The regional authorities are also responsible for local economic development. As in other decentralised political systems, the difficulties of establishing a common information system and data exchange for the multi-level governance system has given rise to accountability problems. In the course of decentralisation, some regions opted for their own information systems with different data bases and software. In fact, what began as a computer project (SISPE) ended as a broader management reform project. In the process of agreeing common definitions of a number of basic concepts (claims, job offers, duration of unemployment, job matching etc.) administrative practices as well as information systems had to be adapted to ensure compatibility (see Chapter 10 by Ruiz).

Privatisation though contracting out

Privatisation through contracting out is perhaps the most widespread form of privatisation in labour market policy. It aims at achieving heightened efficiency and flexibility by outsourcing employment services to external providers. New public management strongly advocates contracting out in the public sector on the assumption that the market sector is more efficient that the public sector. The issue here is not whether the public sector should assume responsibility for providing a service but whether it should be provided by its own employees "in-house" or by external providers. Long practiced in many countries in the area of training and job creations programmes, this approach is now being increasingly used in placement services, which in most countries is one of the few labour market services still provided "in-house". In a few countries, governments now contract out provision of comprehensive "re-integration services" for some target groups to external providers (*e.g.* Australia, the Netherlands).

In the Netherlands, the new Centres for Work and Income (CWI), into which the residual functions of the old PES offices were merged, provide only basic labour market services. The CWI is a one-stop shop, responsible for both benefits and basic services for both social assistance and unemployment benefit recipients. "Basic services" are: collection of information to determine benefit eligibility, assessment or profiling into streams based on proximity to the labour market, referral of clients requiring intensive services to the appropriate benefit agency. For ready-to-work jobseekers (Stream 1), placement services and labour market information system are provided by the CWI. Responsibility for other clients (Streams 2-4) requiring more intensive re-integration services is contracted out to external providers. The purchasers in the Dutch system are not the local CWI agencies but the benefit agencies, *i.e.* the municipalities, which are responsible for social assistance beneficiaries (and for clients ineligible for benefits), and the UWV, the agency responsible for unemployment and disability benefits. The Dutch government allocates funds to both to purchase re-integration services for their respective clienteles in a competitive tendering process. In 2002, a total of 162 re-integration companies participated in the tendering process for UWV contracts and contracts were awarded to 41 companies; the 10 largest companies have a market share of ca. 80%. The service contracts are structured by a combination of target groups, region and, in many cases, by sector.[14] Since clients have a choice of re-integration companies, the contracts do not guarantee a fixed number of clients. The tendering process of the 537 municipalities is highly fragmented in comparison with that of the insurance carrier (UWV) (see Chapter 13 by Sol).[15]

Accountability and contracting out

The accountability framework in a privatised system based on contracting out is relatively truncated in comparison with that in more hierarchal systems based on managerial or political decentralisation. The primary focus is on the provider and the primary instrument is the set of performance standards and reporting requirements specified in the contract itself, for example, in the Netherlands the number of clients from a specific target group receiving services, drop-out and placement rates, average costs etc. The accountability framework for assessing the overall performance of the market system for employment services is in comparison relatively underdeveloped. There are clear MBO-type performance criteria and annual targets for the CWI, the public component of the Dutch system, but not for employment service provision as a whole. In the Dutch case, this neglect is due in part to the fragmentation of the system (multiple purchasers), but it is a reflection of the general assumption that market processes per se yield efficient results. Flexibility through contracting out raises a number of characteristic accountability issues. Typical performance accountability issues relate in particular to market failure and transaction costs in the tendering process and to principal-agent problems in service contracts.

The tendering process for re-integration contracts entails in essence a national planning process for active policies for the coming period in the cumbersome form of a large batch of invitations to tender. It places tremendous demands on the purchasers for information about labour market developments and the needs of jobseekers, which may be unrealistic. In the Netherlands, for example, the UWV, the unemployment and disability insurance carrier, is regarded by many as being a bureaucratic organisation without sufficient knowledge of the labour market to carry out this task properly (Struyven and Steurs, 2002). Contracting out systems in which government is the single or dominant purchaser should meet performance accountability standards comparable to those applicable in public provision.

Contracting out may be subject to market failure on the supply side if competition in the provision of integration services markets is limited or non-existent. Thus the fact that the 10 largest companies in the Netherlands have an 80% market share suggests that this may be the case even in a very densely populated country with a well-developed transportation infrastructure. This is particularly likely in smaller towns and rural areas, or for specialised labour market services. In Australia, the labour ministry itself is the provider of last resort, if no suitable private contractor is available. Careful monitoring of the tendering process in detailed markets segments for re-integration services is necessary for early detection of such problems.

As the Dutch case illustrates, competitive tendering of re-integration services can entail very large transaction costs. In the selection and award phases of the 2002 tendering process, 162 companies submitted over 5 000 tenders, amounting to more than 450 000 pages of text. High transaction costs are greatly augmented by the practice of an annual contracting cycle and considerable turnover in the Dutch model (three years in Australia) (see Chapter 13 by Sol).

Market competition in service provision undoubtedly leads to efficiency gains but mistakes in the calibration of the system may also produce adverse effects. The Dutch framework contracts entail considerable commercial risk for providers because they do not guarantee a specific number of clients. Moreover, both the Australian and the Dutch models use a variety of performance contracting in which service providers are paid in part based on outcomes, i.e. placements. This subjects them to an unpredictable commercial risk from unforeseen labour market developments that may adversely affect placement rates. Finally, short-term contracts may not be the appropriate model for provision of high quality services. Quality firms in the business sector maintain long-term and co-operative relationships with key suppliers that correspond more to the model of relational than spot contracting. Re-integration services require specialised skills and social networks that are developed over time and not easily replaceable.

Adverse selection or "creaming" is a typical abuse found in contract provision of services, especially results-based contracting. Providers select among eligible persons those who due to personal characteristics (qualifications, attitude, etc.) can be prepared in the shortest possible time for achieving programme goals. Positive results are maximised by recruiting insofar as possible the most promising within the contractual target groups and avoiding poor risks. The Dutch contracting procedure now seeks to constrain this effect, for example, by defining target groups more narrowly, by increasing the proportion fixed payments for hard to place target groups, and by limiting the number of clients not processed (see Chapter 13 by Sol).

In terms of performance accountability, the Dutch model emphasises heavily the tendering process but does not appear to incorporate any systematic evaluation or benchmarking of providers performance in awarding contracts. In this respect too, the Australian model with its "star system" of regression-based, nationwide benchmarking of the providers of integration services is an interesting contrast.

Contracting out may also pose a dilemma for political accountability: ministers and government can contract for the delivery of services to external providers but they remain ultimately politically responsible for the outcomes, even though they have in practice much less control over and possibilities for intervening in the actions of an independent contractor than they would have over subordinates in a government agency. Public accountability in the sense of the rights of clients may also be adversely affected since only the purchaser of the services, i.e. the government agency, has a legal claim to services of a specified quality under the contract. Thus important legal rights under administrative law (e.g. Ombudsman or procedural rights) may not be applicable to contract providers. Alternatives such as contractual grievance procedures need to be specified. Moreover, the non-governmental status of contractors means that their operations cannot be subjected to the same degree of scrutiny by parliament or by public auditors, as is the case for governmental agencies (Mulgan, 1997).

Conclusions

Four basic types of accountability standards can be identified, that have varying weights in different types of public administration regimes and accountability frameworks: i) legal accountability; ii) fiscal accountability; iii) performance accountability; iv) public accountability. Our primary focus in this paper is on accountability in the sense of performance and public accountability.

A central thesis is that different types of governance structures in labour market policy have their own distinctive accountability frameworks with characteristic accountability standards, mechanisms and processes and that accountability problems (and solutions) are specific to these organisational settings. We can identify three major trends toward flexibility in labour market policy governance that give rise to distinctive accountability frameworks and problems:

- managerial decentralisation;
- political decentralisation;
- privatisation through contracting out.

There has been a strong trend toward decentralisation in the last two decades. Two major types can be distinguished: managerial and political decentralisation. The former represents a form of intra-organisational flexibility, whereas political decentralisation, or devolution, entails not merely managerial discretion but a more far-reaching delegation of responsibility for labour market policy from the national to the sub-national levels. Management by objectives is the common denominator of diverse administrative reforms that aim at enhancing the efficiency and effectiveness of labour market policy through managerial decentralisation. Most OECD countries use some variant of this approach in their public employment services. The implications of management by objectives for decentralisation are ambiguous: it does not represent an abandonment of central control of the organisation but rather a refinement.

MBO is not only an alternative management strategy but also an alternative accountability framework. In contrast to the emphasis in traditional public sector governance on legal and fiscal accountability it places more emphasis on performance and public accountability. The central internal accountability mechanism is a national performance agreement that is the basis for a series of internal agreements between the agency and each of its regional offices and between the regional offices and the district offices for the achievement of specified targets in the delivery of government programmes.

The successful functioning of accountability in MBO-type performance management has a number of prerequisites and pitfalls. For example, it requires a limited set of clear and consistent goals and operational targets; a strong central controlling unit that provides reliable data collected in "real time". Accountability frameworks also have their characteristic problems. Agency problems, especially moral hazard, are endemic to the performance management approach with its strong emphasis on quasi-contracts and achieving quantitative performance targets.

Partnerships and other inter-organisational networks are intermediary institutions in labour market policy at the regional or local level, especially in multi-level governance systems. They address co-ordination problems in national policy frameworks and foster area-based coalitions of public and private actors to address local employment, social and economic development issues. The basic accountability dilemma of partnerships is that the constituent members are typically government agencies or non-governmental organisations that are subject to multiple accountability chains. Participating organisations are in the first instance accountable to their own organisations. The partnerships themselves are in an accountability dilemma: they themselves are subject to complex accountability demands from their members, from the agency that has sponsored and funded them, and from the public, although their constituent organisations may only have a conditional commitment to the partnership.

The territorial employment pacts, and most other partnerships, were established under national or EU programmes and are accountable, in the first instance, to these agencies. The partnerships themselves are, in this respect, "policy-takers". The adequacy of programme standards in partnership design is a central evaluation issue in assessing partnership programmes. The accountability standards applied to partnerships and other co-operative implementation structures should be appropriate and reasonable. This means, for example, that the stringent standards of performance accountability (MBO) used in national PES organisations are unrealistic for partnerships, given the heterogeneity of their membership, their limited organisational resources and the primary commitment of their members to the accountability frameworks of their own parent organisations.

Privatisation through contracting out is a third major form of flexibility in implementation. Public employment services have traditionally contracted out service provision. What is new in most recent developments (*e.g.* in Australia and the Netherlands) is the establishment of networks of purchaser/ provider relationships in which responsibility for re-integration services is largely contracted out to external providers. In such delivery systems an accountability framework is imposed on providers through specifications in the contract itself, whereas the accountability framework for assessing overall performance of the delivery system is relatively underdeveloped. Typical performance accountability issues relate in particular to market failure and transaction costs in the tendering process and to principal-agent problems in contract performance, for example, "creaming".

Notes

1. The author would like to thank Holger Schütz at the WZB for helpful comments on an earlier version of this paper.
2. See Pollitt and Bouckaert (2000) on the special importance of juridical accountability in the continental Rechtstaat tradition.
3. See Mosley et al. (1998) for an examination of tripartism in the governance of public employment services.
4. Requirements of fiscal and legal accountability remain of course important but take on in part new functions. For example, traditional financial and compliance auditing are replaced by performance accounting, in which expenditures are related to outputs ("value for money"). Moreover, the substitution of flexible budgets for input-oriented, line-item budgets greatly simplifies financial auditing. See Pollitt and Bouckaert (2000).
5. On the distinction between external and internal accountability, see Davies (2001).
6. See Pollitt and Bouckaert (2000) for a general discussion of "trade-offs, balances, limits, dilemmas and paradoxes" in public administration reform.
7. Pollitt and Bouckaert (2000) coin this distinction in the course of their more general discussion of decentralisation in public administration.
8. Like other elements of NPM, has been implemented in different ways and with different degrees of stringency, this "ideal type" is adapted from Richard's (1994) account of the UK experience.
9. This classification is based on two core criteria: 1) *ex ante* setting of goals, operational objectives and quantitative performance targets; 2) measuring and reporting the actual level of performance of operating units against these objectives. Four other PES organisations, Spain, Portugal, Ireland and the Walloon regional PES (FOREM) in Belgium, have adopted elements of MBO, however use of *ex ante* quantitative targets is selective or there is no clear evidence that they actually play a central role in steering and controlling the performance of PES operating units.
10. See Mosley, Schütz and Breyer (2001) for a more detailed discussion of these issues.
11. The OECD has estimated annual operating costs to vary between € 88 000 and € 185 000 per year (OECD, 2001).
12. The OECD estimates the annual average operating costs for the Austrian TEPs to be only about € 165 000 (OECD, 2001).
13. While national targets in MBO may condition their co-operation, increased flexibility in programme design and mix should make it easier for them to co-operate with other actors. See Behrends et al. (2001).
14. In 2002 there were 22 target groups (plus several sub-categories) 60 sectors and 6 regions that formed the basis for contract batches (Struyven and Steurs, 2002).
15. The Australian privatisation model is different in some important respects: it has a simpler structure because there is only one purchaser, the Labour Ministry, in the simpler Australian system. In effect, the Dutch system regards social assistance beneficiaries and unemployment and disability benefit beneficiaries as two separate markets. Moreover, in Australia the guarantee of a minimum number of clients in contracts with providers precludes allowing clients to freely choose between competing providers, even where more than one provider is available.

Bibliography

BEHRENZ, Lars, DELANDER, Lennart and NIKLASSON, Harald (2001), "Towards Intensified Local Level Co-operation in the Design and Implementation of Labour Market Policies: an evaluation of some Swedish experiments and reforms", in J. de KONING and MOSLEY, H. (eds.), *Labor Market Policy and Unemployment: Impact and Process Evaluations in Selected European Countries*, Edward Elgar, Aldershot.

CAMPBELL, Mike (2001), "Partnerships in Austria: Enhancing Regional Co-operation in a Decentralised Policy Framework", in OECD (2001), *Local Partnerships for Better Governance*, Paris.

DAVIES, Anne (2001), *Accountability. A Public Law Analysis of Government by Contract*, Oxford University Press, New York.

EBERTS, R. and ERIKCEK, G. (2001), "The Role of Partnerships in Economic Development and Labour Markets in the United States", in OECD (2001), *Local Partnerships for Better Governance*, Paris.

GERLACH, Frank and ZIEGLER, Astrid (2000), "Territoriale Beshäftigungspakte in Deutschland – neue Wege der Beschäftigungsförderung", *WSI-Mitteilungen 7/2000*.

GIGUERE, Sylvain (2003), "Local Partnerships in the OECD: A Tool to Improve Local Governance", *Acting Together at Local Level: More and Better Jobs, Better Governance*, proceedings of the European Forum on Local Development and Employment, Rhodes, Greece, 16-17 May 2003, European Commission/Employment Observatory Research-Informatics.

HUBER, Peter (2002), "Evaluating Territorial Employment Pacts in Austria", paper presented at the OECD Conference on "Evaluating Local Economic and Employment Development", 17-18 November, Vienna.

MELO, Alberto (2001), "A New Approach to Economic Development in Sicily: Planning in Partnership", in OECD (2001), *Local Partnerships for Better Governance*, Paris.

MOSLEY, Hugh and SCHÜTZ, Holger (2001), "The Implementation of Active Policies in the German Regions: Decentralisation and Co-operation", in J. de Koning and MOSLEY, Hugh (eds.), *Labor Market Policy and Unemployment: Impact and Process Evaluations in Selected European Countries*, Edward Elgar, Aldershot.

MOSLEY, Hugh and SOL, Elsa (2001), "Process Evaluation of Active Labor Market Policies and Implementation Regimes", in J. de Koning and H. Mosley (eds.), *Labor Market Policy and Unemployment: Impact and Process Evaluations in Selected European Countries*, Edward Elgar, Aldershot.

MOSLEY, Hugh, KELLER, Tiziana and SPECKESSER, Stephan (1998), *The Role of the Social Partners in the Design and Implementation of Active Measures*, ILO, Geneva.

MOSLEY, Hugh, SCHÜTZ, Holger and BREYER, Nicole (2001), *Management by Objectives in European Public Employment Services*, Discussion Paper FSI01-203, Social Science Research Centre (WZB), Berlin.

MULGAN, Richard (1997), "Contracting Out and Accountability", *Australian Journal of Public Administration*, No. 56, pp. 106-116.

NASCHOLD, Frieder and BOGUMIL, Jörg (1998), "Modernisierung des Staates. New Public Management und Verwaltungsreform", in U. von Aleman, R. Czada and G. Simonis (eds.), *Grundwissen Politik*, Band 22, Leske and Budrich, Opladen.

NEUMANN, Godehard (2000), "Bundnisse für Arbeit in Deutschland-Ein Überblick", *WSI Mitteilungen 7*.

NIKLASSON, Harald and TOMSMARK, Lars (1997), "Zielsteuerung der Arbeitsmarktpolitik in Finland, Norwegen und Schweden", in C. Riegler and F. Naschold (eds.), *Reformen des öffentlichen Sektors in Skandinavien*, Nomos Verlagsgesellschaft, Baden-Baden.

OECD (2001), *Local Partnerships for Better Governance*, Paris.

OECD (1999), *Decentralising Employment Policy. New Trends and Challenges*, Paris.

OECD (1999a), "Managing Accountability in Intergovernmental Partnerships", Paris.

OSBORNE, David and GAEBLER, Ted (1992), *Re-inventing Government. How the Entrepreneurial Spirit is Transforming the Public Sector*, Addisson-Wesley, Reeding, Massachusetts.

POLLITT, Christopher and BOUCKAERT, Geert (2000), *Public Management Reform. A Comparative Analysis*, Oxford University Press, Oxford/New York.

RICHARDS, Sue (1994), "Devolving Public Management, Centralizing Public Policy", *Oxford Review of Economic Policy*, Vol. 10(3).

SCHMID, Günther, SCHÖMANN, Klaus and SCHÜTZ, Holger (1997), *Evaluierung der Arbeitsmarktpolitik. Ein analytischer Bezugsrahmen am Beispiel des Arbeitsmarktpolitischen Rahmenprogramms in Berlin*, Social Science Centre Berlin (WZB), Discussion Paper No. FSI 97-204, Berlin.

STRUYVEN, Ludo and STEURS, Geerts (2002), "The Competitive Market for Employment Services in the Netherlands", OECD Working Paper, OECD, Paris.

TUROK, Ivan (2002), "Innovation in Local Governance: the Irish Partnership Model", in OECD (2001), *Local Partnerships for Better Governance*, Paris.

WIRTH, Wolfang (1991), "Co-ordination of Administrative Controls: Institutional Challenges for Operational Tasks", in F.X. Kaufmann (ed.), *The Public Sector – Challenge for Co-ordination and Learning*, De Gruyter, Berlin/New York.

ISBN 92-64-10470-4
Managing Decentralisation
A New Role for Labour Market Policy
© OECD 2003

PART II
Chapter 10

Spain: Modernisation through Regionalisation

by
Dolores Ruiz
National Institute for Employment (INEM)

The Spanish labour market

Figures on employment in the past few years have improved the outlook on the Spanish labour market. The current situation is that there are 16.4 million employed persons, 3.4 more jobs than six years ago. In 2002, the unemployment rate declined by over eight percentage points. Employment increased by a further 256 000, half the total in the European Union. Furthermore, 78% of new employees are women. These are signs that reforms in the last five years are paying off. However, there are still fundamental problems in the Spanish labour market so that employment issues continue to receive special policy attention.

The principal features of the Spanish labour market can be summarised as follows:

- high rate of temporary jobs (one third of the active Spanish population);
- low rate of activity, compared with European Union countries, and low rate of employment (the employment rate is still only 58%, due to a low female employment rate of 43.2%);
- large difference between figures for employment and unemployment, by sex, by regions and by age;
- high job turnover, which has repercussions for job security and in worker training and qualifications;
- low rate of part-time workers, which at 8% is much lower than the European Union where part-time work generally been on the increase over the past few years. This is especially concentrated among female workers;
- the unemployment rate is still high at 11.5%.

In general, despite the fact that figures on employment have improved, largely thanks to the economic boom the Spanish economy has enjoyed, the high number of unemployed workers, as well as the low employment rate, is of major concern, a concern that is shared by European institutions.

The institutional instruments in employment policy

By law, employment policies are under the government's responsibility (LBE L51/80) and the National Institute for Employment (INEM) endorsed the responsibility for the management of employment policy. Currently, a draft bill for a new Employment Law is being considered, which this chapter will refer to later.

The INEM is an autonomous agency attached to the Ministry of Labour and Social Affairs. It was created by Royal Decree Law 36/78 of 16 November 1978. Its structure and functions are laid down in RD 1458/86.

The INEM is structured and organised into:

- central services, constituted by governing bodies (General Council and Executive Committee, where the administration and social agents are represented, and the Directorate General) and by the basic central structure;
- territorial services, constituted by managing bodies (provincial directorates of the INEM), territorial management bodies (600 employment offices, as well as professional training centres and sections and departments of the provincial directorates) and institutional participation bodies (INEM executive committees of the provinces).

The functions carried out by the INEM can be grouped into the following broad areas:

1. intervention in the job market, handling placement services and adjusting employment supply to demand;
2. promoting employment, adopting programmes and measures to enable incorporation into the job market of those seeking work;
3. vocational training;
4. management and monitoring of unemployment benefits.

Active labour market policy includes all actions that seek to help, facilitate and promote the integration of jobseekers who are willing and able to work into the labour market, and to help them stay there. Therefore, actions taken by the INEM itself or in co-operation with other institutes can be considered active policies, except handling unemployment benefits, which is clearly a passive policy as its goal is to try to offset the needs of those who have lost a previous job. In addition to INEM, within the framework established by the national administration, the autonomous communities and local authorities implement active policies related to employment and training.

It is important to highlight two important events in the regulatory framework that led to a reconsideration of the public employment service in the mid-1990s:

1. the abolition of the placement monopoly of INEM in job matching between workers and enterprises (Act by Royal Decree 18/93, implemented by Law 10/94) with the authorisation of private placement agencies (RD LG 1/95, RD 735/95) and temporary employment agencies (Law 14/94; RD 4/95);
2. co-operation of the territorial administration in the management of the employment and training policies.

With regard to this latter point, it is important to note that in Spain, the state and autonomous regions are assigned responsibilities for applying employment policies by the constitutional judicial framework and by the distribution of constitutional competencies between the three levels of the civil service: national, regional and local authorities. Basic labour legislation and the general planning of the economic activity is the exclusive responsibility of the state; specifically, the regulation of the conditions of the labour market in dialogue with the social partners, the social protection system, active employment policies, within the framework of the European Employment Strategy (EEE). The regional governments apply the basic labour legislation and also have the responsibility for the promotion of the economic development in their territory. They seek to develop their own policies using their own resources and manage the resources that have been transferred by the national authorities, adapting them to their local needs. The Spanish Constitution allows the regions to develop their own job-promotion programmes. Each autonomous region develops specific actions adapted to its territorial area and financed from its own budget.

How Spain is tackling the regionalisation of the public employment services

The development of the Spanish constitutional pattern, based on the transfer of competencies to the regional authorities, began in 1984. It is foreseeable that in the current year, this process will be completed, and the new system of the public employment service (PES) implemented.

The objectives sought with the regionalisation of the PES are:
- bring the public employment services closer to the public;
- offer better services to citizens;
- integrate all active policies and bring together all the actors who participate in the labour market.

The background for the regionalisation are the following. The Spanish Constitution dates back to the year 1978. Prior to this, Spain was a country that was totally centralised in its planning and administration. Active policies and brokerage services were exclusively carried out by the INEM. However, in 1978, 17 regional Autonomous Communities were established in Spain. The Constitution establishes a very well defined framework of powers, distinguishing between those belonging to the State and those belonging to the Autonomous Communities. By virtue of this distribution of powers, the State in entrusted with the legal regulation of all the labour and employment issues and the legal regulation and the management of social security, while the autonomous communities are entrusted with the management of employment policies.

A few years ago, the INEM began the devolution of active policies to the Autonomous Communities: first, the management of vocational training (an essential element of active policies) and from the year 1996 the remainder of active employment policies, when the Autonomous Communities began to set up their own PES. These integrate all the devolved measures within their own policy framework carried out by virtue of their autonomous status, in such a manner that the maximum result is obtained from all the resources available. Currently, professional training is directly administered by 16 of the 17 Autonomous Communities.

The devolution of responsibility for employment services has presented a number of challenges such as: *i)* achieving a uniform basic employment policy throughout the country; *ii)* maintaining a labour market, that allows for geographic mobility outside the regions; *iii)* sustaining and reinforcing collaboration with the unemployment benefits system which remains the responsibility of a different administration (INEM); *iv)* diffusing current information throughout the country.

The distribution of powers between the State and the Autonomous Communities is currently as follows. The state responsibilites, through the INEM, include:

- the management of unemployment benefits;
- the regulation of passive and active policies. This is the principal mechanism for attempting to obtain a common basic policy throughout the whole labour market;
- the budgeting of funds for financing active policies;
- the control of the operative programmes of active policies financed by the INEM, even when they are executed by the Autonomous Communities. Both the budgeting of funds as well as the control of the operative programmes are useful instruments for guaranteeing a certain uniformity in the managerial systems;
- international relations in the field of active policies and employment in general;
- the maintenance of a State database of all jobseekers, job offers and employment contracts within the whole Spanish territory. This is an instrument that is necessary for maintaining a labour market with brokerage that allows for geographic mobility across regions;
- the administration of the subsidies given for hiring workers, in the form of a reduction of the social security taxes;
- the elaboration, in co-operation with the Autonomous Communities, of guidelines for the National Action Plans (NAPs) for Employment (especially those that have a preventive approach and activation);

- the follow-up by the NAP of these guidelines;
- the co-ordination of active policies.

The responsibilities of the Autonomous Communities are the following:

- the management of active policies and brokerage services: the matching process;
- the administration of all employment subsidies;
- design and execution of their own policies, in accordance with the powers established in their Statutes of Autonomy. Each Autonomous Community regulates and finances them independently, and does not have to be accountable to the State. However, they are under the obligation to provide enough information for inclusion in the NAP;
- participation in establishing the criteria used for the distribution of funds for active policies among all the territories;
- Organisation of their public employment services in an efficient manner. The State guarantees their autonomy in this field.

The process of devolution has been governed by a series of basic principles to which the newly established regional public employment services must adhere:

- a free public employment service;
- equal opportunity for all citizens when accessing employment, without detriment to the existence of positive discrimination authorised by the law (*e.g.* rules for the employment of disabled people or disadvantaged groups);
- free movement of workers throughout the Spanish territory;
- geographic mobility for employment purposes to all those that wish to move to another territory;
- unity of the labour market, without detriment to the diversity of the territories;
- participation of the social interlocutors in the PES.

Each of the Autonomous Communities can choose the organisational form they wish to adopt for the PES, as long as they the principles cited above are applied.

Devolution of responsibility to the regions was accomplished according to a number of procedures to ensure compliance with these principles and the efficient management of the public employment services:

1. The transfer of powers is carried out by means of a Royal Decree enacted by the government, which provides the Autonomous Communities with all the resources that were hitherto used by the INEM. There is a transfer of personnel and material resources. Subsequently, the Autonomous Communities can use more resources, but at their own expense.

2. The network of employment offices is transferred, although personnel from the State Administration remain at these offices administering unemployment benefits so that citizens will not have to go to two different offices or two different counters as a result of the transfer process: one to request unemployment benefits and the other to search for work. This serves to promote the co-ordination of active and passive policies.

3. Collaboration agreements are been signed with the administration of the Autonomous Communities to guarantee certain actions, including the submission of statistical information necessary for maintaining the national database. This also helps guarantee the unity of the labour market, free movement, as well as equality in accessing employment and geographic mobility. Initially, the funds necessary for financing the active policies regulated by the State but carried out by the Autonomous Communities were not transferred (i.e. funds to finance training, subsidised employment, etc.). These funds continue to form a part of the annual budget of the INEM, in such a way that each year, the Spanish Parliament approves the amounts allocated to these policies. Once the total amount is approved, the territorial distribution is carried out according to objective criteria that must be agreed between the central administration (INEM) and the Autonomous Communities, gathered at the Sectoral Conference described below. Naturally, on many occasions the interests of the Autonomous Communities do not coincide. They may even be opposing, but an agreement must be achieved; if not, there is no allocation of funds. Over the years, a series of criteria have been established, somewhat different for the different policies items, which are repeated each year. Once each region receives their share of the funds, they have a certain margin of flexibility for shifting funds, but this is limited: for example, they cannot reallocate funds earmarked for job creation in favour of disabled jobseekers towards general retraining measures. At the end of the period, each Autonomous Community must prove that the funds have been spent on what they were destined for – within their margins of flexibility – and in accord with the applicable state regulations.

4. The decentralised Spanish state has equipped itself with an important political instrument which controls key aspects of the public employment service: the Sectoral Conference. It is made up of the Minister for Labour, who chairs it, to whom the INEM reports on, and the Labour Secretaries (the same level as the Minister in the respective Autonomous Communities), who are responsible for the regional PES organisations. Among its powers are the approval of the criteria for the allocation of the funds between the territories so as to finance their active policies; the approval each year of the NAP, or planning the design of certain activities. For example, in 1999 it ordered the General Directors for Employment, who supervise the PES, to

set up four working groups the results of which would form the framework of the necessary reform of the PES. These working groups studied the following issues:

- co-ordination between active and passive policies;
- computer compatibility and common information system for the PES;
- centres for professional training with national competences;
- elaboration of the NAP.

The results of their work, together with the Agreement signed in 1998 with the social partners on the reform of the PES, have been main instruments for shaping the future of the PES that is now being undertaken.

Management reform: an example

Of all the working groups mentioned above, it may be worth focusing on the second: computer compatibility and common information systems for all the PES. In accordance with the conclusions of this group, the SISPE (Information System of the Public Employment Services, or *Sistema de Información de los Servicios Públicos de Empleo*) project was initiated in July 1999.

The SISPE project began as a computer project and it eventually became a project for the reform of the management of employment policies and a common placement service throughout the country. It is led by a steering committee in which all the Autonomous Communities, chaired by the INEM, and different working groups for the management of active policies and the computer systems participate.

It may appear as surprising that what was initially a computer project turnedi out into a management reform project. When the active policies were devolved and the regional PES organisations were established, the INEM provided the Autonomous Communities with all the computer infrastructure and the infrastructure for the management of brokerage and employment. However, some Autonomous Communities opted for their own information systems, with different database managers and different applications. This gave rise to different systems, some compatible and others not.

It was necessary to seek a common tool so that all PES staff and relevant actors could speak the same language. When work began, policymakers soon realised that the issues had more substance than thet had initially anticipated. For example, there are certain issues regarding the administration of job offers and jobseekers, that are not regulated by law but only in management manuals. This is not a problem in practice if there were only one PES organisation, but it is a problem when there a numerous regional offices with sometimes conficting interpretations.

Basic issues such as what is understood by a jobseeker and how the time spent unemployed is calculated had, in many cases, different interpretations (something which each country applies in a different manner, and this is why sometimes the NAP prevention indicators give results that are very difficult to compare between different countries); other issues included, for example, how job offers are administered, how brokerage services are provided or, if they cannot be filled within one region, how they are communicated to other regional offices. This led to the conclusion that it was necessary to reach an agreement in the conceptual definition of all these cases: claims, offers, matching process, career guidance, etc. It took one year's work to define conceptually all the processes that affect the brokerage services, because all the aspects of this process have been agreed and accorded between all the administrations of the Autonomous Communities and the State (INEM). As a result, certain aspects of the PES administration and some of the computer applications had to be modified.

An agreement was reached to define the common information throughout the country so as to guarantee the free movement of workers, geographic mobility and equal opportunities. The agreement sets out what is needed in real time and batch processes: regular reports and the information required for the control of the employment plan or for the justification that the INEM must annually give to the ESF, or collaboration with partners of the PES.

Next to the definition of these issues, the connectivity tools were clarified; the communication networks are already available and verification tests are being carried out between the State database and the databases of some Autonomous Communities.

SISPE became a model for institutional collaboration in the eyes of both the State as well as the Autonomous Communities. There are even sectors, for example, in the field of health service, that are requesting a project of this type. This is an added value, not trivial, in view of the tension that exists between the central and regional governments in decentralised States.

Reforming the PES further

In summary, the regionalisation of the PES and the successful response to the challenges posed by the regionalisation process is based on certain basic principles:

1. The State uniformly legislates within all the Autonomous Communities on active and passive policies financed with State funds.
2. The funds that finance the active policies belong to the State and are not transferred at the source. They are allocated in accordance with the criteria that have been jointly agreed.

3. The Autonomous Communities must give account to the State of how they have used the Funds. Those not used are returned.
4. The State controls the common information databases of job offers, jobseekers, placements, completed with all the information provided by the Autonomous Communities.
5. Co-ordination and co-operation mechanisms have been established between the State administration and the Autonomous Communities (Sectoral Conference, SISPE Project).
6. Integrated services are guaranteed for all citizens, due to the coexistence in the all offices of mechanisms for the administration of both unemployment benefits as well as active policies.

The Spanish case is perhaps a clear example of how reality anticipates legal regulation. Thus, the totality of the regionalisation process of the PES has been developed without new legislation. The Spanish Law on Employment dates back to the year 1980, and did not contemplate the new regionalised reality, the membership of Spain in the European Union, nor the co-financing of active policies by the European social funds, nor the European Employment Strategy (EES). It actually consolidated the INEM, the PES that acted as a monopoly.

A new legal regulation that takes these developments into consideration is necessary; this should take advantage of and exploit the experience of nearly ten years of collaboration with the Autonomous Communities in the administration of employment policies. It should also integrate in a coherent manner all the parties involved in job-matching, like placement agencies, that must always act under the umbrella, the directives and the criteria set by the PES.

For this reason, the government, on 25 May 2003, approved the Draft Bill of the Law on Employment, which is being widely discussed between the Autonomous Communities and the State. The bill incorporates all the principles that have been mentioned in this report and the wealth of co-operation obtained in this time with the Autonomous Communities. It recognises that employment policy is a combination of decisions adopted by the State and the Autonomous Communities, which have as their aim the attainment of full employment. It consolidates, amongst the general objectives, the preventive approach against unemployment, in accordance with the European Employment Strategy, and it seeks to maintain the unity of the labour market, guaranteeing at the same time the free movement of workers. It draws on the Sectoral Conference as the central instrument for the co-ordination of employment policies: it must annually elaborate the work plan for the PES, which establishes the specific objectives of the action to be taken, and evaluate the results obtained. It confirms the necessary local dimension of employment policies, in accord with the European directives, invoking the need for the local entities to promote the participation of all the social and economic partners, integrating their action in a co-ordinated manner, in line with that set forth in the communications issued by the Commission.

The Law lays down the folowing principles for the organisation and operation of the PES:

- co-ordination and close collaboration between all the regional units of the PES;
- participation of all the social partners;
- integration, compatibility and co-ordination of the information systems;
- existence of a sole site on a telematic network that lists all the employment and training opportunities, complying in this manner with the conclusions of Barcelona relative to this issue and the recent resolution by the Council regarding mobility and qualifications;
- collaboration with other entities that may facilitate the re-integration into the labour market of people in difficulty;
- permanent improvement of the PES so as to adapt to the needs of the market by taking advantage of the new technologies, with sufficient human and material resources that allow for specialised and personalised attention to employers and jobseekers.

The Law defines the principles applicable to brokerage. And, likewise, the necessary co-ordination of active and passive policies, advocating stimulating action in the fight against unemployment, or what is the same, that the PES must provide, together with an income, training or other active policies for the smooth and rapid reintegration of the unemployed into the labour market.

ISBN 92-64-10470-4
Managing Decentralisation
A New Role for Labour Market Policy
© OECD 2003

PART II

Chapter 11

Canada: Partnerships across Levels

by

Don Rymes
Head of the Alberta, North-West Territories and Nunavut Region,
Human Resource Development Canada

Since the mid-1990s, Canada has made long strides in establishing and strengthening collaborative partnerships in support of programme management and delivery. While this experience has been successful, along with this progress came certain challenges around the need to balance programme flexibility and innovation in governance on one hand, and accountability requirements on the other. This paper highlights three examples to demonstrate Canada's success in implementing decentralisation initiatives. The main focus is the transfer of responsibility for the design and delivery of active labour market programmes from the federal government to the provinces and territories, and aboriginal organisations. The government of Canada's recently extended Supporting Communities Partnership Initiative to respond to homelessness is also highlighted as an example of the federal government's work towards the development of collaborative partnerships with local governments and community-based groups. Finally, Annex A provides an overview of accountability and evaluation systems under the Labour Market Development Agreements, and briefly outlines some preliminary evaluation findings.

The labour market and the institutional context

While most of Canada's 31.4 million people are concentrated in relatively few urban centres in the south, a significant number live and work in small communities and remote areas, including those in the north. In response to local conditions and the natural environment, strongly differentiated labour markets have arisen across the nation.

Canada is a culturally diverse nation with a constitution that explicitly recognises its linguistic duality and multicultural character. While most Canadians use English, there are over 6.7 million Francophones, 81% of whom reside in the province of Quebec. People with Chinese, Italian, German and Punjabi roots are the next largest groups in Canada.

In the early 1990s, Canada experienced higher unemployment rates, reaching 12% in 1992. In recent years, the unemployment rate has declined. In December 2002, the national unemployment rate was 7.5% and regional rates ranged from 5.1% in Alberta, 7.0% in Ontario, to 18.5% in Newfoundland and Labrador. The rate for youth is typically about twice that for adults 25 and over, while Aboriginal Canadians generally face considerably higher rates of unemployment. Thus the economic and labour market context for employment services in Canada varies a great deal geographically, from one group to another and over time.

Despite the current global economic downturn, Canada's economy will continue to enjoy strong growth in the years ahead. But its workforce will grow at a much slower rate than in the past, and future labour supply will be inadequate to meet the demands of the economy. Canada is already facing structural skills shortages in a range of occupations, such as nursing, engineering and management. Shortages are also occurring in many skilled trades, including plumbing and construction. Immigration currently accounts for more than 70% of net growth in the Canadian labour force. Over the next decades, immigration will play an even greater role; by the year 2011, it is expected that immigration will account for all net labour force and population growth.

A number of factors are contributing to this situation. The Canadian population is ageing overall, and population growth rates will continue to be low. The next cohort of youth workers will be smaller than in the past. Too many Canadians are currently outside the workforce: there is a sharp divide in labour force participation rates for low-skilled and high-skilled Canadians (56% vs. 79%).

In 2002, the government launched its Innovation Strategy with the release of two companion documents: *Achieving Excellence: Investing in People, Knowledge and Opportunity* and *Knowledge Matters: Skills and Learning for Canadians*. *Achieving Excellence* presents and searches for ways to build a stronger, more competitive economy. In *Knowledge Matters*, the government outlines a national skills and learning framework that seeks to address current and future labour market challenges, namely around demographic pressures and the demand for a highly skilled workforce. The government has made a strong commitment to work in partnership with other key labour market players including provinces and territories, in order to meet these goals.

Under Canada's constitution, governmental powers and responsibilities are divided between the federal government and the ten provinces (and three northern territories). Federal powers relate primarily to economic and financial policy, international affairs, defence, immigration, criminal law, etc., while provincial powers relate primarily to education, health, social assistance, and municipal institutions. Notwithstanding this constitutional division of responsibilities, there are various national regimes, such as public health and pensions, that have long involved both orders of government working together. Furthermore, the federal government makes significant financial transfers to the provinces for health, social assistance and post-secondary education programmes.

Training and active labour market policy have historically been treated as a joint federal-provincial responsibility. Income support for unemployed individuals has been provided by the federal government from contributions made by employers and workers to the national Employment Insurance fund. Active labour market programmes have also been provided by the federal government from this fund, as well as from general tax revenues. Provincial governments, on the other hand, have provided income support – social assistance – for those not eligible for Employment Insurance. The provinces have also provided active labour market measures for their clients, although until the 1980s such measures were not very extensive.

Both orders of government have offered special employment and training-related services to particular groups, notably recent immigrants, women, youth, people with disabilities, ethnic minorities, older workers, and Aboriginal Canadians. The national employment service in Canada has long provided services through federal and provincial (and often municipal) governments working together. In addition to local government offices, aboriginal organisations, contract agencies including government-funded technical colleges and schools, private vocational institutes, non-profit community groups, labour groups, employers and other organisations have all played essential roles in the provision of employment-related services.

Through the National Homelessness Initiative, the government of Canada has partnered with communities and other levels of government to help remove barriers to the participation and inclusion of homeless people, to help them move out of the cycle of homelessness and prevent those at risk from falling into homelessness.

Case study 1: the Labour Market Development Agreements

Employment Insurance Reform

During the mid-1990s, the federal government embarked upon a fundamental reform of its income support and labour market policies. At the core of the labour market reforms was the introduction of a new Employment Insurance (EI) Act, which also provided the authority to enter into federal-provincial/territorial Labour Market Development Agreements (LMDAs), and represented a whole new phase in the provision of active labour market programmes and services. The new EI programme, and the active labour market programmes associated with it, were contained in this legislation and were adopted in 1996. The modifications related to active measures had five major objectives:

- To broaden the range of clients eligible for active programmes to include those who have had an EI claim within the past three years or for parental or maternity benefits, within the past five years.
- To increase expenditures for active labour market programmes by re-investing some of the savings on income support payments into these active programmes.

- To ensure that active measures generate "economic returns" by aiding clients to become employed as quickly as possible. In this regard, the new legislation underscored that the success of interventions is to be determined by two, inter-related, measures: i) the number of EI clients participating in active labour market programmes successfully re-employed; and ii) the savings to the Employment Insurance account. This represented the first time that an accountability-for-results framework for active measures was enshrined in legislation.
- To ensure that programme decisions be made at the local level. The legislation also stated that active labour market programmes should be established in co-operation and partnership with the provinces, employers, community-based and other interested organisations.
- To increase the flexibility of programme interventions and ensure they are responsive to labour market conditions.

Federal withdrawal

In late 1995, the Prime Minister committed the federal government to withdraw from labour market training for EI clients. This commitment prompted federal-provincial discussions leading to a proposal by the federal government in May 1996 to transfer responsibility for the design and delivery of active measures for EI clients to interested provinces. Interested provinces could deliver active programmes to EI clients and receive federal funding (approximately C$ 1.5 billion in total for 1996), as well as acquire federal staff and resources in order to screen clients and provide employment counselling and placement services.

The proposal for provinces to enter into negotiations for Labour Market Development Agreements, and the agreements that were subsequently signed, required that the active labour market programmes delivered by provinces be similar to those specified in the federal legislation. The federal government also reserved the right to decide funding levels and client eligibility.

The federal government retained sole responsibility for managing the EI fund and delivering income benefits. Furthermore, the federal government also retained three components of labour market policy:

- *National labour market information exchange.* This enables it to maintain and improve the national system of labour market information and labour market exchange to, among other objectives, support the inter-provincial mobility of labour.
- *Pan-Canadian activities to be funded from the EI fund.* These activities total about C$ 250 million annually and are undertaken in response to special labour market problems or situations that affect either Canada as a whole or a significant area of the country.

- *Active labour market measures for non-employment insurance clients with special needs.* These would include youth, people with disabilities, Aboriginal Canadians, older workers, and recent immigrants.

Full-transfer and co-management models

Not all provinces were interested in assuming responsibility for designing and delivering active labour market programmes. Consequently, two quite distinct types of agreements emerged: full-transfer and co-management. No agreement has been concluded with the Province of Ontario, and Human Resources Development Canada continues to deliver active labour market programmes and services in that province.

The full-transfer model involves provinces and territories assuming responsibility for active labour market programmes within the federal funding and client eligibility constraints. Typically, but not exclusively, this type of agreement has been reached with the larger provinces or those that had more experience in designing and managing active labour market programmes. Full-transfer arrangements are currently in effect in five provinces and two territories, comprising about 43.5% of Canada's population.

Under the co-management model, the provinces play a significant role in planning of active labour market measures, but the responsibility for actual delivery of programmes is left to the federal government. The joint management model is currently in operation in four provinces and one territory, representing approximately 18.6% of Canada's population.

The emergence of distinct full-transfer and co-management models means that the delivery of the national employment service and labour market programmes in Canada is not uniform and a high of degree of "asymmetry" has emerged across jurisdictions.

Federal requirements

Although the agreements gave provinces wide latitude with regard to the programmes they might design with federal funds, the federal proposal required provinces to meet seven policy objectives set out in its 1996 legislative reform of the Employment Insurance programme. These objectives require that active measures must:

- be results based;
- incorporate an evaluation of outcomes;
- promote co-operation and partnership with labour market partners;
- involve local-decision making;
- eliminate unnecessary overlap and duplication;

- encourage individuals to take personal responsibility for finding employment; and,
- ensure service to the public in either official language, where there is significant demand.

Given these federal objectives, the agreements negotiated contain mechanisms to ensure that the objectives are met, regardless of whether an agreement is full-transfer or co-management. All agreements contain annual numerical targets for clients served and savings generated to the EI account. These targets ensure that provincial active programmes are results-based in that they reduce the dependency of individuals on government assistance. Each agreement also includes an accountability framework. Annex A provides an overview of the performance measurement strategy, including the LMDA accountability framework.

Case study 2: Aboriginal Human Resources Development Strategy

Aboriginal Canadians

Aboriginal people represent a significant and growing segment of the population in Canada. About 1.3 million people of aboriginal ancestry – more than 4% of the population – live in Canada. In addition to diversity of languages and dialects, the Aboriginal population is diverse in terms of ancestry, history and culture. Traditionally, Aboriginal people have depended on nature for survival and continue to have a very special relation with it. Aboriginal peoples live in urban centres, rural communities and remote locations. This group accounts for a large proportion of the population in the northern and western regions of the nation.

The aboriginal population is significantly younger than the Canadian population: 65% of this population is younger than 29 years of age, as a result, the number of aboriginal entrants into the labour market is growing rapidly. Aboriginal peoples are generally under-represented in the labour force, among the 25-44 years old, unemployment rates are three to five times the national average.

Aboriginal people face multiple barriers to successful labour market integration. Over 55% have not completed high school, and many lack adequate foundation skills such as literacy and mathematics. In addition, many aboriginal people live in remote locations, where there are limited job opportunities and possibilities for career development. In the workplace, problems may arise from lack of understanding of cultural differences.

Aboriginal Human Resources Development Agreements

The Aboriginal Human Resources Development Strategy (AHRDS) was launched in April 1999 in the context of Gathering Strength – Canada's Aboriginal Action Plan, announced in January 1998. The five-year, C$ 1.6 billion strategy, is part of the government's commitment to improve Aboriginal people's access to jobs and address a broad range of human development needs in Aboriginal communities. The Strategy contributes to increasing aboriginal people's self-sufficiency by transferring more control over the design and delivery of employment-related programmes and services to aboriginal organisations. The Strategy's initiatives are designed with the goal of reaching all eligible clients which includes all status and non-status First Nations people, the Inuit and Métis communities residing off and on reserves.

The specific objective of the Aboriginal Human Resources Development is to support Aboriginal organisations to develop and implement labour market, youth and child care programmes that are designed to address the local and regional needs of Aboriginal people. The programming:

- assists aboriginal individuals to prepare for, obtain and maintain employment;
- assists aboriginal youth (individuals normally from 15 to 30 years of age) in preparing for, obtaining and maintaining employment and in making a successful transition into the labour market, thereby resulting in increased employment; and
- increases the supply of quality child care services in First Nations and Inuit communities, thereby raising the availability of distinct and diverse services in these communities to a level comparable to that of the general population.

This programme expands the employment opportunities of aboriginal people across Canada while accommodating the uniqueness of aboriginal groups in various communities. To meet this needed flexibility, the aboriginal organisations are given the authority to make decisions that will meet the needs of their communities while being accountable for clear performance results. The Strategy's specific initiatives work towards the enhancement of: capacity building, good public administration, and a results-based accountability system. This Strategy, also contributes to the long-term goal of increasing aboriginal self-sufficiency, by enabling aboriginal people to build stronger communities and find long-term employment.

The AHRDS was designed in partnership with aboriginal leaders and organisations, five of which signed accords with the government. These Accords establish the framework for community level agreements with aboriginal organisations across the country, to ensure access to aboriginal-delivered human resource programmes and services for aboriginal people regardless of status or residence. To date, 79 Aboriginal Human Resources Development Agreements (AHRDAs) have been concluded with aboriginal organisations.

Each AHRDA outlines general and regional specific terms and conditions through which an aboriginal community can access federal funding to design and deliver employment solutions that are best suited to local needs. AHRDAs require that each community account for the results of its programme spending. The AHRDAs integrate all aboriginal programming into one initiative, including labour market and youth programmes, schemes targeted at aboriginal people living in urban areas as well as measures for people with disabilities and childcare needs. They are flexible to ensure that aboriginal organisations have the authority to make decisions that will meet the needs of their communities.

Another component of the AHRDS is the Aboriginal Human Resources Development Council, launched in January 1998, to enable aboriginal organisations to build a broad network with leaders of the federal and provincial government and the private sector. The prime objective of the Council is to encourage private-sector investment in aboriginal human resources development. Private and public sector leaders, labour, academia (both aboriginal and non-aboriginal) address Aboriginal human resources issues at the national level. The Council mandate, scope and activities are driven by Council membership. Initiatives include human resource planning, networking, joint opportunities and employment.

Labour market programming historically did not have an aboriginal-specific component. Aboriginal communities were not involved in programme design, but remained part of a target group. Funding was demand driven and there was no long-term commitment. Between the 1980's and 1999, when AHRDS was introduced, a number of initiatives were implemented to increase aboriginal communities and organisations' participation in the design and development of labour market programming.

In transferring funding and responsibility for skills development, employment initiatives, and income support programmes to aboriginal communities, the federal government recognises that aboriginal people best understand their own needs and are best able to design and implement effective labour market programmes and services. While under the AHRDS, aboriginal organisations integrate social and economic programmes to the local level, a number of federal government departments and agencies continue to co-ordinate programme and policy efforts at the national level.

Case study 3: National Homelessness Initiative

Homelessness in Canada

Canada is known around the world for its high standard of living, yet homelessness is an urgent problem in far too many of our communities. In 1999, the rise in homelessness was deemed a crisis in Canada with homeless people facing a multitude of barriers to participation and inclusion in society. This rise in homelessness stood in stark contrast to Canada's reputation as a caring society.

Today's evidence suggests that homelessness continues to grow in Canada's major urban centres and increasing numbers of Canadians are at risk of homelessness. Evidence suggests two reasons: homeless individuals and families face barriers (*e.g.* federal/provincial/territorial cutbacks and weakening social security system) to get out of homelessness and more people are falling into homelessness due, in large part, to increased housing costs and poverty rates, growing economic disparity, and reductions in assistance benefits.

Supporting Communities Partnership Initiative

In 1999, the government made a commitment to improve the quality of life for all Canadians and launched the three-year, C$ 753 million, National Homelessness Initiative (NHI) to address a growing social problem in Canada's urban centres. The 2003 federal budget announced an extension of the NHI for an additional three years and $ 405 million to build on the progress to date, broaden partnerships, and invest in transitional and supportive services and facilities to help homeless people become more self-sufficient. The NHI's core objective is to help communities develop a comprehensive "continuum of supports", ranging from immediate shelter to services vital to independent living, that address the multifaceted and diverse needs of homeless people and those at risk of homelessness.

Fundamental to the NHI's objectives and design is the importance of partnerships across and between all orders of government, as well as among community and not-for-profit and private sector interests. The causes, symptoms, and outcomes of homelessness are multifaceted, and interventions are required from a broad range of partners with resources and expertise in fields ranging from health to justice. A community-based approach facilitates the development of collaborative efforts, which aim at both helping homeless people while supporting communities' efforts to achieve this goal. This approach underpins the NHI principle that reducing homelessness is a shared responsibility.

A community-based approach was adopted for several reasons. No single actor – whether government, voluntary or private – could effectively address homelessness. With well-developed programmes and activities already in place in several cities, communities were recognised as the best "location" for different stakeholders to join forces, build partnerships, attract investments, and ensure co-ordination of efforts among service providers. Moreover, as the nature of homelessness varied widely, not only between regions or provinces, but among communities themselves, a flexible approach was needed. Across Canada, local solutions reflecting local realities and needs would form the basis of an appropriate and effective national response.

The Supporting Communities Partnership Initiative (SCPI) was designed as the NHI's centrepiece to support local, integrated community-based action in communities with a demonstrated homelessness problem. Eighty per cent of SCPI funds are targeted to the 10 major cities most affected by homelessness. Additional funds are allocated to communities to develop a Community Plan that identifies current community resources and gaps in service, and establishes priorities for helping the homeless in their community.

The five long-term objectives of SCPI, are as follows:

1. to reduce significantly the number of individuals requiring emergency shelters, transition and supportive housing. For example, sufficient health services, low cost housing, discharge planning, early intervention and prevention initiatives;
2. to ensure that no individuals are involuntarily on the streets by providing sufficient shelters and adequate support systems;
3. to improve the social, health and economic well-being of people who are homeless;
4. to help individuals move from homelessness to self-sufficiency; and,
5. to help communities strengthen their capacity to address the needs of their homeless population.

Under the SCPI programme design, communities are expected to generate 50% of the funding from sources other than federal programmes. The SCPI will match a community's contribution to a maximum of the total national allocation available to that community. The community contribution may include funding from other partners, such as, provincial and municipal governments, private sector donations, charitable donations and in-kind services.

Municipal involvement has been pivotal to the success of the SCPI. Evaluation findings indicate that the SCPI has led to more municipal participation in homelessness issues, which, in some instances, has resulted in additional resources to local service providers for specific projects. In 12 cities, the municipality has become the community entity taking on the planning, decision-making and administrative responsibilities for the delivery of the SCPI. In most, if not all, SCPI-designated communities and municipal governments are closely involved in the planning, development, and implementation of homelessness activities.

The SCPI is a unique delivery model and a demonstrated success of an integrated policy approach to human investment. Evaluation findings indicate that the SCPI presents "a new face of the federal government" that is "being embraced enthusiastically" by communities. These findings also strongly support the effectiveness of the SCPI's community-based model and its flexibility to address a wide variety of circumstances and needs. This underscores the applicability of the SCPI as a potential model for the government to address other social and economic issues.

Community organisations, provinces/territories, municipalities, and experts have indicated that the SCPI, together with Youth funding and Urban Aboriginal Housing (UAS) funding, has enabled communities to effectively address emergency needs, and improve conditions for homeless people. These tools have enabled communities to mobilise local assets and partnerships into concerted strategies reflecting community realities and needs.

The United Nations has praised Canada for its efforts to address homelessness. The SCPI was nominated as a Best Practice in the UN-Habitat 2002 International Awards. The Awards recognise initiatives that have made outstanding contributions to improving the quality of life in cities and communities around the world.

Balancing programme flexibility and accountability requirements

The NHI represents a unique model for the government of Canada and a considerably different approach from the work traditionally carried out by Human Resources Development Canada's (HRDC) regional offices. It is a government initiative that involves a new community-based approach, multiple partnerships, and a new approach in working with provincial/territorial governments and communities.

In facilitating community action and ownership in response to the problem of homelessness, communities "own" their plans and projects while the Federal Co-ordinator on Homelessness (Minister) and the federal government are recognised as playing a leadership role. This poses a unique set of challenges for the delivery of the NHI. As such, considerable investment is required to ensure an appropriate balance between controls and flexibility.

The federal government is further challenged to address capacity issues at both community and at the federal service delivery network level. The need for compliance and stringent federal accountability requirements was recognised as a significant risk to the government's ability to work with community partners who may have limited capacity and is contradictory to the SCPI's flexible approach.

In response to this risk, a strategic decision was taken to manage administrative requirements more effectively in order to ensure the most innovative and effective responses to homelessness. A SCPI "light" agreement helped to reduce the administrative burden for low risk proposals less than $ 25 000 (this represents 129 SCPI projects to date, 17% of the total projects) and has allowed the government to partner with organisations that might not have had the necessary capacity to administer the projects under the SCPI requirements.

ANNEX

Performance Measurement under the Labour Market Development Agreements

The overall objective of active labour market programmes established under the Employment Insurance (EI) Act, is to help maintain a sustainable employment insurance system and a national employment service. The Employment Benefits are established to help insured participants obtain employment while a national employment service is maintained to assist workers in their search for suitable employment and help employers find suitable workers. The reduction of dependency by individuals on employment insurance in the short and long term is considered a key factor in the measurement of the effectiveness of the these active labour market programmes. The EI Act stresses the importance of focusing on results in order to ensure active measures are implemented effectively.

The performance measurement strategy under the Labour Market Development Agreements (LMDAs) enable managers to track progress, measure outcomes, support subsequent evaluation work, and, to enhance programme effectiveness, identify best management and administrative practices. The performance management strategy is comprised of the following key components:

1. Accountability Framework: the EI Part II Activities Accountability Framework developed in the context of the LMDA negotiations primarily focuses attention on three short-term indicators: clients employed, unpaid EI benefits (resulting from EI claimants returning to work earlier than expected), and the number of active EI claimants served. This framework applies to employment programmes provided at the local, regional and national levels by Human Resources Development Canada (HRDC) and by provinces and territories.

2. Evaluation of LMDAs: Part II of the EI Act requires that active labour market programmes be established and implemented within a framework for evaluating their success in assisting persons to obtain and maintain

employment. The legislation stipulates that the federal government work in concert with the provinces and territories in establishing this framework. To these ends, specific clauses in each of the LMDAs contain provisions for the development of an evaluation framework to guide ongoing monitoring and assessment.
3. All transfer LMDAs contain provisions which require provinces and territories to submit audited financial statements on an annual basis. These statements, certified by the provincial or territorial auditor general, outline costs for active labour market programmes and associated administrative costs.

Formative evaluations

Formative evaluations, undertaken during or shortly after the first year of implementation of each agreement, were designed to supply information on changes to the design and delivery structure necessary for achievement of the stated objectives. Of the thirteen formative evaluations scheduled to take place, twelve are completed. The main findings are highlights below:

Harmonisation of programmes and services. Most jurisdictions reported that, in general, there is still room to improve the co-ordination of programmes. The consensus was that programmes were mostly complementary, with no apparent overlap as the programmes targeted either different clients or the same clients at different stages in the process of returning to work.

Local flexibility. Most jurisdictions report that active labour market programmes are sufficiently flexible to be adapted to local needs. In most jurisdictions these programmes are viewed as broad in scope and flexible in interpretation, thereby allowing decisions to be tailored to the circumstances of the community.

Co-operation and partnerships. Despite some inevitable adjustments in work processes, LMDAs have contributed to growing partnerships between and within governments. This has demanded a large investment of time and energy from all involved.

Access to programmes and services. Individuals knowledgeable on the delivery of the programmes and focus group data suggest that active labour market programmes have been highly relevant to the needs of the EI client group, and that the majority of active EI claimants are being reached. Evaluations indicate that access is more difficult in rural or remote communities where distance and market size pose a challenge to service delivery. Evaluation results also suggested that, because the EI Act specifically defines the client group to be served, many individuals who might benefit from an intervention are not eligible.

Client satisfaction with programmes and services. Most clients report a high level of satisfaction with the quality of service associated with programmes and services. Over three-quarters of participants rated service as good or excellent, while only 1 in 10 expressed dissatisfaction.

Impact on individuals. Most formative evaluations measure incremental impact. In general, self-employment assistance and targeted wage subsidies had a positive incremental impact on both employment and earnings. Training shows positive significant impacts on earnings in a few jurisdictions. In the short term, reliance on income support appeared not to have been significantly reduced through participation in these programmes, except for self-employment assistance participants who have reduced their reliance on EI. More definitive results will be available from the summative evaluations.

Impact on communities/employer. Evaluation findings suggest that active labour market programmes have been perceived favourably and that community groups have been pleased with the LMDAs' emphasis on community capacity building and helping people get back to work. Evaluations suggest that programmes may have already had some impact on local employment.

Monitoring and accountability. Information exchange is an area requiring further work. Data integrity and data capture systems continue to present a challenge given the complexities and incompatibilities when exchanging data between provinces/territories and HRDC. In general, day-to-day reporting of management information was problematic (*e.g.* producing client and intervention activity reports). HRDC and provinces/territories are working together to manage and resolve these issues.

Summative evaluations

Summative evaluations, scheduled for the third year of the implementation of each LMDA, or shortly thereafter, are designed to measure cost-effectiveness and the longer-term impact of active labour market programmes in assisting individuals to prepare for and maintain employment. Beyond this period, LMDAs require that evaluations be conducted on a three to five year cycle.

Eight summative evaluations have already commenced and are now at various stages of completion. It is expected that the remaining five will be launched in 2003. Summative evaluation findings are usually available about one year following the initiation of the evaluation process. The key objective of these evaluations is to answer the questions: have active labour market programmes produced impacts on individuals, employers and communities?

To ensure that these evaluations adhere to the highest quality standards, an Expert Panel was assembled, bringing in the best minds in the field, to provide clear direction on a state-of-the-art methodology. The panel's mandate was to review the proposed summative techniques and processes and provide clear direction on developing and applying a state of the art methodology. The panel members met with evaluators and programme officials, including regional managers, to brainstorm the summative evaluation methodology. The panel submitted a final report in September 2001. This report was shared with evaluation staff from federal, provincial and territorial governments and was a topic of discussion at an international conference held in Ottawa, Canada, in November 2001.

Under the LMDAs, provincial/territorial governments each establish a joint Management Committee with the federal government to oversee the effective administration and implementation of the agreement. The Management Committee is responsible for the completion of all evaluations of the active labour market programmes and approval of evaluation reports. The responsibility for undertaking evaluations is delegated to a Joint Evaluation Committee, consisting of officials from both orders of government.

Each Joint Evaluation Committee supports and oversees the evaluation activities of the active labour market programmes under the LMDA. This Committee fosters a partnership approach to evaluation between the federal and the provincial governments. Moreover, the committee provides technical expertise in all aspects of evaluation including the approval of detailed reports on methodology, protocols, survey instruments, timelines and budgets, updates, briefs, summaries, revisions of draft findings and evaluation reports.

Common indicators

Summative evaluations are expected to provide results on a set of indicators common across all regions. These are outlined in one to 11 below. In addition to these, summative evaluations provide the flexibility for provinces and territories to develop and measure additional indicators which may be relevant to each region's respective economic or labour market conditions:

1. *Employability and integration.* The objectives of active labour market programmes are to assist eligible clients to find and keep employment. A broad measure includes anyone working in the post-programme period. A breakdown between full-time and part-time as well as proportion of weeks worked in the post-programme period provides an indication of the extent of employment. The duration of employment spells provides a measure of sustainability of employment. The most comprehensive measure of labour market integration is the total annual hours worked in the post-programme period.

2. *Self-reliance/independence from government support.* An objective of the active labour market programmes is to reduce dependence on government transfer payments. Independence can be measured in terms of total and average amounts of EI and Social Assistance (SA) received and the number of weeks where EI and SA was received in the post-programme period. The total proportion of income accounted for by EI and SA provides another broad measure of dependence.

3. *Economic well-being.* Economic well-being is largely determined by the amount of money earned from employment. Individuals may be working longer hours and have more sustainable employment, but this may not translate into positive impacts on their economic well-being. Change in employment earnings would allow an indication of potential impacts through comparison with non-participants. Since family structure has such a significant relationship with economic well-being, both individual and family earnings/income should be examined.

4. *Quality of life.* Publicly funded training and other active labour market programmes are designed to prepare individuals to find and maintain work, and lower dependence on government transfer payments. There is also interest in realising full social externalities from these programmes, a measure of social well-being that includes substantial economic effects as well as some aspect of quality of life. Two themes – satisfaction and motivation – have been identified to measure aspects of quality of life.

5. *Investment in human capital (skills and literacy).* Education is an important variable in determining success in the labour market. Education levels of participants can be compared to that of the total labour force/total unemployed. This will show whether clients have a relative advantage or disadvantage in the labour market to find and keep employment. Education can be used as a proxy for literacy and is a key factor in determining earnings impacts for clients. Occupational coding of employment both pre- and post-programme will provide an indication of improved skills or improved opportunity for clients to maximise their employment contribution.

6. *Employment equity/employment barriers.* An important question is the extent to which active labour market programmes are assisting clients who are less job-ready and to what extent the interventions are effective. Analysis of employment equity groups, older/younger workers and those facing barriers will provide indications of this. Distribution of client groups compared to the total labour force/total unemployed would indicate the accessibility of programmes and services to these different groups.

7. *Labour market adjustment.* To what extent can active labour market programmes be seen as a significant lever on the supply side of labour

markets? To what extent are these programmes assisting the adjustment process of the supply side by addressing issues such as: displaced workers; skills shortages (by training in demand occupations); and labour mobility.

8. *Community impacts.* This relates to how active labour market programmes assist communities: through job creation in the communities; helping economic and social infrastructure; and improving partnership and collaboration among various stakeholders in the communities.

9. *EI Savings.* To the extent that investment in active labour market programmes increases employability and earnings for participants, there will be a reduced demand for EI. The longer-term incremental impact will be measured using the individual client usage of EI in the post-programme period.

10. *Cost-effectiveness.* The initial step in cost-effectiveness analysis is to document the programme impacts. How participants' earnings, employability and reliance on government transfers were affected are some of the impacts measured. The second step is to determine the costs associated with the programme delivery, and to compare them with the impacts achieved.

11. *Follow-up to formative evaluations/emerging issues.* One important objective of the formative evaluations was to assist programme managers and field personnel to fine-tune programme design and delivery. The formative evaluations have identified areas of concern and improvement. The summative evaluations will study whether these, or other emerging issues, have been addressed since the completion of the formative evaluations.

ISBN 92-64-10470-4
Managing Decentralisation
A New Role for Labour Market Policy
© OECD 2003

PART II

Chapter 12

The US: Managing Different Levels of Accountability

by

John Dorrer
National Center on Education and Economy

For over 30 years, workforce development programmes in the United States have been steadily decentralised. The Comprehensive Employment and Training Act of 1972, the Job Training Partnership Act of 1983 and the Workforce Investment Act (WIA) of 1998 successively assigned powerful roles and responsibilities to state and local governments and encouraged strategic planning to solve local labour market problems.

The aims of decentralisation are to fit better programme designs and services delivery to the demands of local labour markets and needs of client groups. Decentralisation has also encouraged local partnerships encompassing transportation, childcare, housing and other social services. By integrating community-based and diverse governmental resources, states and local areas have been able to address broader employability and social development aims in the context of workforce development programmes. Recently, some states and local areas have sought to align better economic and workforce development resources to support sectoral and cluster-based job creation and growth strategies.

Decentralisation creates formidable political, managerial and technical challenges in practice. Roles and responsibilities assigned among the levels of government and the other stakeholders of the workforce development system are rarely without conflict. State and local administrators have welcomed federal resources but have seen federal regulations as intrusive and the demands of federal oversight bodies as burdensome. State and local officials have routinely argued that federal programme regulations including accountability measures limit flexibility and impede adaptation of programmes to local circumstances including the integration of employment and workforce development programmes funded from multiple sources. Those at the federal level have argued with equal enthusiasm that federal investments demand high standards for accountability. They attribute the lack of innovation at the state and local level to a failure to maximise the innovation potential embedded in most federally funded workforce development initiatives. Federal officials are quick to point to examples of high performing, innovative programmes and service strategies resulting from significant risk taking and creativity displayed by state and local organisations.

The Workforce Investment Act expires in September 2003 and is up for reauthorisation. Federal, state and local government officials along with numerous other stakeholders are once again engaged in intense debate about reforming the workforce development system. The five-year operational experience and performance record of 50 states and over 600 local workforce boards under the policy and regulatory framework of WIA provides a track record to inform policy and system change. In a statement before the US House of Representatives, Emily Stover De Rocco, Assistant Secretary of Labor identified WIA as a "ground-breaking piece of legislation that has sparked dramatic improvements in the delivery of employment and training services nationwide". She went on and proclaimed:

> *"Now our challenge is to build on these reforms in order to make the Act even more effective and responsive to the needs of local labour markets and to strengthen the innovations that many states and local communities have developed to serve business and individuals with workforce needs."*

The challenges of balancing flexibility and accountability will, no doubt, remain central in the debates over the next few months. Major reform proposals call for further deregulation, devolution of authority to states and modifications to the performance accountability system. While states and local areas have made use of more flexible programme designs and service integration strategies, performance accountability systems have remained more rigid and continue to focus on individual programmes. Reauthorisation of the Workforce Investment Act presents an opportunity to align better policy goals, programme co-ordination and service integration objectives with the performance accountability system.

While previous legislative battles have centred on balancing roles and responsibilities among federal, state and local levels, the reforms of WIA seem to be more focused on strengthening the roles of states at the expense of local control. Economic, political and institutional forces will continue to assert powerful influences on the reform process and the final shape of these reforms is not yet known.

Key innovations advanced by WIA

The period from 1992 to 1998 was marked by an extensive review and analysis of workforce development strategies and programmes culminating in the passage of the Workforce Investment Act of 1998. A rapidly growing economy with tight labour markets and skill shortages helped to focus serious attention on reforming the US. workforce development system. One of the underlying thrusts for reform was to bring about greater coherence and alignment among a patchwork of over 150 separate federal employment and workforce development initiatives. There was widespread perception that workforce programmes were duplicative with overlapping responsibilities and inefficiency. Furthermore, the fragmented nature of the systems discouraged access by job seekers and employers. Reforming and aligning this unwieldy system would proof to be more difficult meeting with politically and institutional resistance from some reluctant partners.

WIA reaffirmed the respective roles of the federal, state and local governments in planning and implementing workforce development programmes. The basic system of workforce regions at the sub-state level was maintained. WIA provided for cities with a population of 500 000 or more with automatic designation as a service area while sub-state regions of 200 000 population were designated provisionally. It also preserved the role of business leadership for local workforce boards and extended it to state boards in hopes of achieving more responsiveness and greater accountability on the demand side of the labour market.

WIA also brought forth a longer-term strategic orientation to planning and accountability. The quest for programmatic coherence, streamlined service systems and vastly improved customer services across the spectrum of employment and workforce development programmes demanded new visions and bold approaches. WIA introduced a participatory planning process calling upon states and local communities to craft a more comprehensive, integrated approach for organising and delivering employment and workforce development services. States were required to develop a five-year strategic plan. States could also choose to develop a "unified" plan encompassing 13 different federal employment, education and training programmes under a common planning and accountability framework. While some states made attempts to create unified plans, most did not because of the considerable complexity involved in bridging regulatory and policy differences of separate programmes.

The planning process was also envisioned as a way to achieve more effective collaboration and partnership-building between the state and local levels. The local elected officials and the local workforce boards, working with the business community, service providers and community-based organisation leaders, were expected to shape the vision and customise the system to better respond to specific local labour market needs. The planning process led by the governor and state board in collaboration with local elected officials and local boards sought to secure the partners' endorsement of the vision, along with performance goals and the critical strategies needed to attain them. The plan was expected to provide a roadmap with quantifiable milestones. This five-year strategic plan was intended as a management tool that all stakeholders could use to guide the evolution of the workforce investment system and to assess progress toward the agreed upon goals. As economic conditions changed requiring revisions in planning assumptions and strategies, plan modifications were encouraged to ensure that these plans remained relevant in guiding the evolving workforce development system.

WIA also called for bold systems changes and innovation in service delivery. A network of one-stop career centres was to be established to integrate services of multiple partners and funding streams and to improve access and efficiency for both job seekers and employers. One-stop career centres included the public employment service along with job training, adult education and vocational rehabilitation service providers as mandatory partners. States and local areas had considerable flexibility in expanding the one-stop partners and adapting the delivery system to fit local needs.

One-stop career centres were envisioned as high quality, accessible service environments offering information, guidance and resources for a spectrum of job seekers including dislocated workers, low wage and disadvantaged workers as well as employed workers seeking to upgrade their employment situation. Services would be provided based on needs beginning with low intensity information and job placement assistance and leading to the issuance of individual training accounts for those unable to find employment because of a lack of skills. An important accountability innovation introduced by WIA required education and training providers who wanted to qualify to receive training funds to provide outcomes data so that consumers could compare the efficacy of training programmes.

Partnership development and service integration in one-stop centres was given considerable emphasis. Guidance from the federal level for administrative, management and performance accountability systems development, including more specific directions for financing the one-stop operating costs, remained ambiguous however and caused considerable hesitation and delay in implementing one-stop career centres.

The performance accountability framework

The general public, legislative bodies and the executive branch demand accountability for public investments. WIA makes a bold accountability declaration in the Statement of Purpose of the Act.

> "The Act provides for activities that increase the employment retention and earnings of participants; and increase the occupational skill attainment by participants and as a result improve the quality of the workforce, reduce welfare dependency and enhance the productivity and competitiveness of the Nation."

One of the key challenges to the successful implementation of WIA was the design and development of a performance accountability system to assess the effectiveness of state and local programmes. Federal, state, and local officials along with non-governmental groups, including community-based organisations, labour unions and business groups had considerable involvement in the design of the system and in reaching final agreement on performance measures. Inclusion was seen as a means to create widespread acceptance and "ownership" of the system.

Separate performance indicators were identified for youth and adults based upon recognition that distinct programme investment strategies and outcomes would apply to each group. Core indicators of performance focused on outcomes were adopted and new customer satisfaction indicators were included in the new system.

The core indicators of performance for adults consisted of:

- entry into unsubsidised employment;
- retention in unsubsidised employment six months after entry into employment;
- earnings received in unsubsidised employment six months after entry into employment;
- attainment of a recognised credential relating to achievement of educational skills and occupational skills.

Core indicators of performance for youth (aged 14 to 18) consisted of:

- attainment of basic skills, work readiness or occupational skills;
- attainment of secondary diploma or equivalent;
- placement and retention in post-secondary education, advanced training, military service, employment of apprenticeship.

Reliance on unemployment insurance wages records ensured that employment and earnings data would be consistently collected in a more efficient manner. Levels of customer satisfaction would be measured through surveys conducted upon completing participation in workforce investment activities. By gathering feedback from job seekers served by the one-stop centre and the employers who hired them, planners expected that such input would be central to forging a continuous improvement culture making services more responsive for the two primary actors in the labour market.

Policymakers clearly understood that if flexibility in programme design is to benefit the state and local level, more flexibility would be needed in specifying the accountability system. WIA encourages states and local areas to specify additional performance indicators reflecting innovative or distinctive services delivery approaches and partnerships. Levels for core and customer service performance measures including any additional measures proposed by states was to be expressed in "objective, quantifiable and measurable form" as presented in a formal multi-year plan. Furthermore, such measures needed to show continuous improvement over an initial three-year period.

Before the plans of individual states were approved at the federal level, a negotiation process between federal and state officials was called for. The process was to yield a formal performance agreement. Key factors and conditions driving the negotiations process and influencing the final agreement included:

1. promoting the achievement of high levels of customer satisfactions with services provided by the workforce development system;
2. comparing performance levels with other states, including taking into account economic conditions, needs of populations served and types of service strategies adopted;
3. evidencing of continuous improvement in performance measures.

Agreements reached could be renegotiated as a result of changes in significant factors, including economic and labour market conditions or needs of populations seeking services.

The planning process provided for incentives and rewards based upon negotiated performance standards. Meeting and exceeding standards resulted in states receiving incentive payments. If states failed to meet negotiated performance levels, sanctions would be applied. Prior to sanctions however, the first line of response from the federal level called for the provision of technical assistance and the preparation of a formal performance improvement plan. If a state failed to meet its negotiated performance targets for two years in a row, the Secretary of Labor could reduce by up to 5% the amount of the grant that would be payable to the state by the federal government. Funding withheld under these circumstances would be re-invested for technical assistance and additional performance improvement planning.

If performance failure occurred at the local level, the states assumed the responsibility for technical assistance and performance improvement planning. If the performance failure persisted in the second year, the governor could make revisions to local area workforce plans, choose to restructure the local workforce board and eliminate local partners from the one-stop career centres deemed responsible for poor performance.

In building the performance accountability system under WIA, there was also a more intense pressure on the federal government to take an active role in accountability systems development. Not only would federal officials sit in judgement of state efforts, they would be asked to share more responsibility for getting results. In 1993, the Government Performance and Results Act (GPRA) was enacted. This important federal legislation shifted the focus of government decision-making and accountability. Advocates sought for government agencies to move "away from a preoccupation with the activities that are undertaken – such as grants dispensed or inspections made – to a focus on the results of those activities, such as real gains in employability, safety, responsiveness, or programme quality". Under the Act, agencies are required to develop multi-year strategic plans, annual performance plans, and annual performance reports.

Under GPRA, annual performance plans are intended to inform the Congress and the public of:

1. annual performance goals for agencies' major programmes and activities;
2. measures that will be used to gauge performance;
3. strategies and resources required to achieve the performance goals;
4. procedures that will be used to verify and validate performance information.

These annual plans are to provide a direct linkage between an agency's longer-term goals and mission and day-to-day activities.

Annual performance reports are required to report on the degree to which performance goals were met. The issuance of the agencies' performance reports provide the opportunity to assess federal agencies' actual performance for the prior fiscal year and to consider what steps are needed to improve performance and reduce costs in the future.

Leadership and participation of the business sector in planning workforce development programmes represent another important dimension of accountability. Both the Job Training Partnership Act (1983) and the Workforce Investment Act (1998) provided strong business leadership to ensure oversight of workforce development programmes. There were high expectations that workforce development investments would become more responsive to labour market and employer needs as business leaders at the state and local levels framed strategies and assessed performance of workforce development initiatives. Business participation in governance and oversight of the workforce development system has been uneven and problematic according to some business advocacy organisations.

During the mid-to-late 1980s, the growing quality and customer service movement embraced by business and industry impacted upon public service systems, including employment and workforce development programmes. For the first time, accountability focused on the "customer" satisfaction and system responsiveness to meeting customer needs. Surveys and measurement systems were adopted on a widespread basis to provide quantifiable feedback on how well services responded to customer expectations and measured up against quality standards.

Performance accountability challenges: data systems and technology

An effective performance accountability system requires development and maintenance of complex database systems and sophisticated information technology infrastructure. Reliable and retrievable data that accurately reflects service inputs and the outcomes from the workforce investment system is the foundation an accountability system.

One of the major challenges for the decentralised, multi-partner workforce development system has been to design, implement and maintain data and reporting system in a cost-effective manner. As mandated and voluntary partnerships for services delivery have evolved under a decentralised system, the challenges of aligning and integrating information and data system have become formidable. Some states, such as Texas, Pennsylvania and Florida, have made major investments in building comprehensive information systems that serve the needs of multiple partners and service providers and thus permit comprehensive tracking of participants and management of multiple programmes within one management information system.

For most states and local areas, the development and implementation of comprehensive management information systems including multiple partners remains a formidable and expensive undertaking. Too often, the federal funding sources of local partners define basic outcomes, such as what constitutes a job placement with variable definition. There is a significant variance in policies related to confidentiality and data sharing among partners. Finally, the design, development and maintenance of comprehensive management information systems add considerable expense severely taxing smaller states and local areas with limited resources.

WIA requires each state to prepare an annual progress report detailing progress on core and customer satisfaction performance measures for the state overall as well as individual local workforce areas. States are also expected report on evaluation activities and progress with any additional indicators included in the plan. Along with reporting on the progress of core and customer satisfaction, states are required to report detailed information, including:

- number of participants who have completed training;
- entry in to unsubsidised employment related to training;
- wage at entry into unsubsidised employment, including wage replacement for dislocated workers;
- cost of workforce investment activities;
- retention and earnings received in unsubsidised employment 12 months after entry;
- core and Customer Satisfaction Performance for public assistance recipients, out-of-school youth, veterans, displaced homemakers, older workers and individuals with disabilities.

Reports showing individual state performance are published annually and used by funding sources, including the legislative branch, to judge the efficacy of workforce investments. State-by-state comparisons of performance are used in developing performance improvement strategies. Many states and local workforce boards have developed performance accountability systems and evaluation strategies that exceed the minimum requirements set for under WIA. Organisations such as the Workforce Excellence Network have been established by states and local areas to "promote, establish, implement, and utilise methods for continuously improving the workforce investment system".

WIA reform proposals: responding to some of the early lessons

The Workforce Investment Act has been in place for five years. As part of its reauthorisation, significant reforms are expected to be implemented. Fifty states and over 650 local workforce boards have a demonstrated track record in highly variable economic, labour market, institutional and political circumstances. The US economy has moved from high growth and tight labour markets to a prolonged downturn with rising unemployment. Along with the return of federal deficits, state and local governments are facing extraordinary budget challenges as revenues are not keeping up with expenditures. These conditions will certainly influence WIA reforms particularly as they impact the flexibility in resource utilisation.

A number of substantive proposals for improving the flexibility and accountability of the system are being advanced. Business, labour and community groups have all taken an active part in pushing for reforms to make WIA more responsive to the needs of their constituencies. While the final shape of reforms and outcomes are not yet certain, major efforts of key Congressional committees and proposals from the executive branch have identified bold changes centred on flexibility and accountability. A full vote by the US House of Representatives and separate action of the US Senate are still pending before final approval of these reforms.

Among the key reform proposals that have been advanced are:

Further consolidation of funding streams. Primary funding streams authorised under the Workforce Investment Act include funds for adults, youth and dislocated workers. A separate source of funding supports the public employment service. Effectively and efficiently integrating these funding streams to align resources and programme services has proven to be problematic leading to duplication and inefficiency. To give states and local areas greater flexibility, combining these funding streams into a single grant is proposed.

Along with streamlined programme administration, combining funds would result in states and local areas shifting resources more easily as needs and economic conditions change. While such flexibility for allocating resources may be welcomed by state and local government officials, advocates for disadvantaged populations and dislocated workers fear that their constituencies may lose priority standing and fail to get their fair share of workforce development resources absent targeting provisions.

Expanded waiver authority/block grant authority. To encourage greater flexibility and reduce impediments to programme and service integration at the state and local level, the Workforce Investment Act permits waivers to regulatory provisions. Over 30 states have made use of waivers in better adapting WIA to state and local circumstances. Proposals have been put forward to further ease statutory restrictions and encourage states to make more use of waiver provisions. Among the Administration's reform proposals is a provision that would allow governors to apply for block grant authority. Under a block grant authority, governors would have complete discretion on how to administer specific programmes funded under WIA. Key areas where governors would be able to exercise discretion are in sub-state funding and governance structures shifting considerable authority from the local to the state level. Such authority would remain in force as long as negotiated performance measures are met. Failure to meet such performance levels would result in sanctions and loss of authority.

While expanded waiver provisions and block grant authority would maximise flexibility at the state level and help to overcome constraints to service integration, local officials are concerned that such broad authority resting at the state level would shift resources over time. Shifting resources from the local to the state level would undermine the ability to address workforce development problems and opportunities including the integration of job creation and workforce development investments.

Technical improvements to the performance accountability system. States and local areas have expressed continued frustration with the performance accountability system under WIA. Separate measures for youth, adults and dislocated workers were perceived as excessive and burdensome. Proposals call for adoption of eight indicators that are now being developed by the mandated federal partners as part of a common measures initiative for employment and job training programmes. For adult programmes, these new indicators are job entry, retention in employment, earnings increase and efficiency. For youth programmes, proposed indicators are placement in employment, education or military, attainment of degree or certificate by participants, literacy and numeracy gains, and efficiency. Also, as a part of the common measures initiative, there are further efforts to develop common definitions. Currently definitions of key terms and measures such as "entered employment" are defined differently by one-stop career centre partners as well as other federally funded service systems that collaborate with one-stop centres.

Common performance measures and definitions will help to improve service integration and more efficient operations. Some states and local areas are distrustful however and would like to have a more active role in specifying the new performance indicators and definitions. State and local areas are particularly concerned about the introduction of a new efficiency measure (cost per programme participant). There is fear that such measures would encourage high volume-low cost services over more intensive training and human capital investments.

The new common performance measures proposal would also eliminate customer satisfaction indicators (employers and job seekers). At time when there should be more intensive focus on meeting customer needs and providing high quality services, the elimination of these measures would undermine long-term investments and strategies to give more voice to the customers of public services.

National performance goals. Previously, negotiations between states and the federal government to arrive at performance targets for WIA were judged to be too rigid. A new proposal calls for the establishment of long-term national performance goals. National targets would be established to form the basis for state-level negotiations. This approach would call for state negotiated levels averaging the established national targets. In addition to creating a more challenging negotiating framework, reforms are proposed so that the negotiation process would more rigorously take in to account local labour market conditions and the characteristics of individuals served, including factoring in the rates of job creation or loss.

State and local areas want to be reassured that the adoption of national performance goals will not undermine state and local flexibility. Some state and local advocates are proposing the use of national regression models that would more thoroughly account for participant demographics and local economic conditions in order to avoid creating disincentives for working with hard-to-serve populations.

Conclusion

Efforts to decentralise and decatagorise workforce development initiatives have yielded considerable flexibility and opportunities for innovation. As result, states and local areas have made significant progress in programme coordination and service integration. More comprehensive, high performing systems should lead to better access for more workers and employers. Furthermore by aligning resources and service, those with the largest employability and skill deficits should reap the greatest benefit. The Workforce Investment Act has served as an important catalyst and an organising framework for the development and implementation of more ambitious labour market and human capital development strategies. Formidable challenges remain however and more reaching reforms are needed.

As the workforce development system evolves and adjusts to new economic and demographic realities, the 30-year collaboration between federal, state and local levels must continue to effectively harmonise strategies, resources and systems. Taxpayers have a right to expect a full accounting of the investments made on their behalf. Performance accountability systems must determine if we are using our scarce resources wisely and inform us how we could do it better. As decentralisation and de-categorisation provide us with greater flexibility, accountability systems must also reflect the more complex nature of interventions and investments associated with integrating services and resources. Performance accountability is especially important at the state and local level where providers have a more intimate accountability as their work is most visible to consumers. In re-authorising the Workforce Investment Act, policy-makers must ensure that its visionary ambitions are supported by a performance accountability strategy and system that befit the endeavour.

Bibliography

MALONEY, Christopher (2003), "State Touts Success, Points to Weakness in OMB Plan", *Employment and Training Reporter*, Vol. 34, No. 28, March 24.

NATIONAL CENTER ON EDUCATION AND THE ECONOMY (2003), Draft Position Paper for Local Workforce Organisations on Reauthorisation of the Workforce Investment Act., Washington DC, March 2003.

STOVER DE ROCCO, Emily (Assistant Secretary of Labor) (2003), *Testimony before the Committee on Education and the Workforce*, Subcommittee on 21st Century Competitiveness, US House of Representatives, March 11.

US DEPARTMENT OF LABOR, EMPLOYMENT AND TRAINING ADMINISTRATION (1998), "Overview of the Workforce Investment Act of 1998".

ISBN 92-64-10470-4
Managing Decentralisation
A New Role for Labour Market Policy
© OECD 2003

PART II
Chapter 13

The Netherlands: Tackling the Trade-off between Efficiency and Accountability

by
Elsa Sol
University of Amsterdam

Market flexibility, competition and deregulation are the new buzzwords behind the recent attempts to instil change in the field of labour market re-integration policy.[1] Many European countries have been experimenting with market forces in this field of policy, with the purpose of reducing government bureaucracy, improving the operation of the labour market and achieving improved harmonisation with labour demand. In the Netherlands, the private re-integration market has been in effect since 1 January 2002. As of that date, the public employment service (PES) was profoundly reshaped

The introduction of the market for re-integration service provision has not been particularly smooth. The full establishment of a competitive market for the delivery of public services was preceded by successive stages of privatisation of public re-integration activities, over a period of approximately ten years. After a period of several decades, during which the PES was wholly under ministerial control, the government decided to hive off the PES. In the early 1990s, the PES became an independent administrative body. Control of the body was transferred to a tripartite board, made up of representatives of the government and of employer and employee organisations. The government monopoly on labour exchange was lifted, so that from then on, private recruitment agencies and re-integration companies were allowed to operate alongside the public re-integration service. Dissatisfaction with the results of this phase led the government to take back control of employment policy – now combined with social security policy – at the end of the 1990s, and to fully liberalise the re-integration branch. The section of the PES which offered re-integration services was privatised.

The changeover to an open market has been subject to criticism, however. Despite the reduced responsibility of the government in the delivery of services, the public still holds the government accountable for the results. The primacy of politics is currently at the heart of the labour market policy debates. New rules are coming into effect which, analogous to the concept of corporate governance, are being termed "government governance". Transparency and accountability are the new key words in this respect. By providing improved accountability, the government hopes to regain the legitimacy of its actions with the public.

Government governance, while initially an abstract concept for an integrated approach, is also an operational concept that is having an effect at various levels. Attention is being paid to regional and local government as well as central government. Job seekers who are very distant from the labour market, in particular, are often forced to rely on the local level for a successful re-integration. At the local level, the situation is currently being managed by municipalities, which are acting as principals of private re-integration companies. These municipalities are being held accountable for achieving a satisfactory re-integration.

Public accountability is coming up against limits, however. A great deal of tension is arising from the conflict between, on the one hand, the demand for accountability and, on the other, the problems faced by the government in collecting sufficient information in the private re-integration market to enable it to comply with its obligation of accountability. To a certain extent, these tensions can be reduced by involving the clients more closely in the policy feedback loop. The purpose of this chapter is to examine the tension between flexibility and accountability.

The next section will explore the various steps taken towards privatisation in the Netherlands, which eventually led to the public re-integration task becoming fully liberalised. The following section will examine the process of "marketisation" and the tense relationship arising from the attempt to reinstate the primacy of the political arena. It will describe the shifting demands on contracting between principals and re-integration companies. The final section will suggest several options for reducing the tension between public accountability and market flexibility.

The transition from hierarchy to market

In order to reduce dissatisfaction regarding the realisation of public employment services and to regain the declining legitimacy for the functioning of public organisations, the Dutch government implemented reforms intended to enable the "marketisation" of the employment services. In these new forms of public organisation, a "quasi market" takes the place of traditional forms of co-ordination. Contracting out and principal-agent separation were employed to create and enhance competition. The transition from hierarchy to market took place in three steps.

The first step: decoupling policy and implementation

The job centres were traditionally in the public sector, within an institution which was separate from the social security structure. Under government control, however, the PES proved unsuccessful in practice in the areas of efficiency, customer-friendliness and innovation in service provision. Employers, in particular, complained about the lack of, and poor quality of, service provision by the job centres, and the government saw a growing number of job seekers, who, despite a large budget, were receiving unsatisfactory service from the PES.

When it became apparent that internal re-organisations had not solved the problem, the decision was taken to implement a more radical solution in the form of privatisation, "tripartisation", decentralisation and removal of the public monopoly. In 1991, the job centres were hived off from direct government control. With the establishment of a tripartite PES board of management for the independent administrative body, the government tried to meet the demands of the social partners, in order to increase the basis of support for the policy. The idea behind this change was that the PES government department would start using public funds more efficiently as soon as it was cut loose, following the example of the business community. The business experience of the employer organisations and trade unions in the board of management could be of great use in the management of the job centres. Furthermore, decoupling policy and implementation fits in with the ideological trend of reducing the size of the top-down civil service: by separating the policy-making civil servants from the job service providers, the number of state civil servants was reduced by several thousand. The results of the tripartite PES were poor. One of the structural mistakes of the Manpower Services Act of 1990 which caused problems for the tripartite PES was the lack of proper accountability for the regional organisation units in the decentralised organisational structure. Moreover, supervision of expenditure was inadequate. The lack of supervision of expenditure on job creation schemes from the European social fund (ESF) was notorious. When the PES was evaluated in 1995 regarding the characteristics of effectiveness and efficiency of the service provision, the results turned out to be paradoxical: an increase in the mediation and training results, but at a considerably higher cost, and disappointing results for hard-to-place job seekers. The evaluation report was highly critical, and thwarted the further expansion of the tripartite organisation. The government then withdrew from the tripartite board of management.

During this period, the government had little control over the actions of the PES. There was little motivation to improve the range of re-integration tools available, although experiments were being carried out with new re-integration techniques (such as work experience). The lack of competition for the job centres also meant that there was no incentive to be cost-efficient or to invest in new products. Employment services were assessed by the government purely quantitatively on the number of people who found work with the help of the job centres, on the basis of targets set for itself by the tripartite board of management. Apart from those for the weakest groups, the quantitative targets were all met. Typical for this period was the fact that the PES board relied on its own organisation for the realisation of the tripartite policy. The PES controlled the methods of re-integration, and even owned the job centres and training institutes in which these methods were implemented. This meant that there was no level playing field with other – private – re-integration service providers.

The second step: purchaser-provider split

The second step in the introduction of market forces followed in the mid-1990s. Demand and supply were separated by creating purchasing relationships between the public principal and the contractor (internal marketisation). This step came as a response to the disappointing evaluation of the PES, but primarily as a corollary of changes in the implementation of the social security system, under which greater attention was being paid to re-integration. The new regulations ensured formalisation of the principal-contractor relationship between the ministry and the PES and for embedding in the funding structure. From 1996 on, the PES received a basic contribution for the basic service provision. For the rest of its services, the PES received a performance-related budget. In preparation for the subsequent marketisation, the municipalities – as the bodies implementing the National Assistance Act and the Employee Insurance Implementing Body (and its precursors), as the parties responsible for the re-integration of job seekers and occupationally disabled – were deemed to be the purchasers. They were obliged to source 80% of their re-integration services from the PES (so-called "truck system").

Insufficient preparation was given to the implementation of building-in market-like elements. Accountability towards the principals, in particular, turned out to be a bottleneck in practice. The staff of the public job centres in the regions were not used to being accountable for their actions. There was a lack of clarity regarding how accountability should be evidenced to the principals. Moreover, different principals requested a different form of accountability. The necessary accountability information was unavailable, inaccessible to others or only partially reliable. There was a high level of independence among the staff on the shop floor, and a great deal of information was locked away inside people's heads. Bottlenecks included the uneven progress of organisational changes and changes in the information provision, due to the turnaround in the way in which accountability had to be rendered after the introduction of purchasing relationships. PES was working with an outdated system which could not be linked up. There was no clear picture of how many people actually found employment through the efforts of the PES' resources.

At the end of the 1990s, several private re-integration companies became active in the market, and started offering services to public agents. The market was a quasi-market, with a limited number of powerful clients on the demand side and for the time being, a limited level of competition resulting from restrictions on entering the market.

There was criticism from private intermediaries of the privileged position of PES and there were increasing demands for a market for re-integration services without entry restrictions, in which public and private intermediaries could compete with one another on a level-playing field. Social security implementing bodies made limited use, in 1997 and 1998, of the option to purchase private re-integration services; they were only allowed to spend 20% of their budgets freely. As of 2000, the obligation on purchasers to purchase re-integration services from PES was lifted. This resulted in a painful loss of market share for the PES.

The third step: privatisation

The next step in the privatisation process followed in 2002. Under the Work and Income Implementation Structure (SUWI) legislation, the government ordered that re-integration services be moved fully into the private sector. This decision was part of a political exchange on the implementation of the social security system. As a public provider, the PES was split into various parts and then wound up. The re-integration section of PES was hived off to become an independent government company, known as Kliq. A number of basic responsibilities, such as intake and placement services, remained in public hands and were bundled together in the Centres for Work and Income (CWI), which took over these tasks from the former PES.

The private re-integration market was a fact. Customers on the demand side of the re-integration market were the municipalities, employee insurance bodies, employers and, on occasion, private individuals. Private re-integration agencies acted as the providers on the supply side. The municipalities and the body arranging the benefit payments to job seekers and occupationally disabled persons (UWV) were now required to purchase services for their clients in the market, using tendering procedures. More recently, employers themselves have also started acting as principals. They have been given greater responsibility for the re-integration of their employees who have become occupationally disabled. Since 2002, legislation has been in effect which has also made employers responsible for the re-integration of their own employees with a different employer (known as second-track re-integration).[2] New legislation has also introduced financial incentives for municipalities in respect of the demand for re-integration services. The UWV has not (yet) started working with financial incentives.

The winding up of the PES also resulted in the formal end of management by the employer and employee organisations. Several factors explain the end of the tripartisation. The decision making process amongst the partners was slack at the national level, there were no clear central goals and tripartite PES lacked an incentive structure.[3] Since 2002 – as was the case up to 1990 – the state has had sole responsibility for governance, now not simply of the PES but also of the social security structure.

The market. What now?

The privatisation operations of the PES were an expression of a more general trend towards privatisation which has been prevalent during the past several decades. Apart from cost-cutting considerations, a new vision of governance in the public sector also played a role. The public sectors are influenced by an international trend towards reforms captured by the terms "managerialism" or "new public management". The reforms have had a number of components, including management by objectives, corporatisation and privatisation, competitive tendering and outsourcing, separation of purchasers and providers, and greater client and customer focus. These reforms are intended to apply private sector management principles to the public sector on the grounds that the public sector is inefficient and ineffective in comparison with the private sector. Key concepts in this approach include decentralisation, flexibilisation, efficiency and contracting out.[4]

This privatisation development – which together with privatisations in other fields of government has resulted in hundreds of quangos (according to Audit Office estimates, 3 200 in the Netherlands in 2002) – has not been without its critics. The intended gains in efficiency and effectiveness, resulting from independent government departments using public funds more efficiently and effectively, were accompanied by a loss of responsibility across large swathes of central government.

One of the first influential criticisms of the functioning of the independent administrative bodies (i.e. quangos) was contained in a report from the Audit Office in the mid-1990s (National Audit Office, 1994). The main point of contention concerned the number of quangos, which it was argued, was growing uncontrollably. It was also pointed out that there was a limited amount of information available for the purpose of accountability. In more than 30% of cases, it was not indicated clearly for the bodies which objectives they were supposed to meet, and furthermore the Audit Office noted that the objectives for the other 68% were "formulated in insufficiently concrete terms". It is notable that the Audit Office report contains little or nothing regarding the efficiency or effectiveness of the functioning of the quangos or regarding policy implementation by these organisations. The criticism was limited to the question of the extent to which a number of administrative-organisational conditions had been met, which would enable the bodies to operate effectively and efficiently (Leeuw, 1997).

As a response to this criticism, the cabinet called for a re-instatement of the primacy of the political arena. This call led to reforms of the government machinery. Whereas until quite recently, government authorities focused on policy-making and, where necessary, managing crises and incidents, in recent years, attention had noticeably shifted to improving governance in an increasingly wider context.[5] In addition to processes aimed at controlling operations, policy-making processes are also important in this respect. Transparency of these processes, which may extend over an entire policy chain (from policy-making to the ultimate implementation of policy), was becoming increasingly essential. And while building in financial incentives for the implementing departments was a key aspect in the financial reforms – which focused on a "new public management" and primarily the principal-agent model – the key focus of governance is the ability to implement ministerial accountability (for policy, operations and finances). The key word in this operation is accountability. This relied heavily on the concept of corporate governance. In the Netherlands, attention to corporate governance focused primarily on increasing the transparency of the policy implemented and accountability of the corporate executives towards the stakeholders. The involvement of stakeholders was to be increased by removing obstacles, such as protective constructions, and by improving accountability. Transparency was to be increased by including not only information on the corporate results, but also regarding the manner in which these results are achieved. With this corporate governance model as a guideline, the search started for a public variant. This variant, identified as "government governance",[6] is defined as safeguarding the interrelationship between management, control and supervision by government organisations and by organisations set up by government authorities, aimed at achieving policy objectives efficiently and effectively, as well as communicating openly thereon and providing an account thereof for the benefit of the stakeholders.

Central government is concerned with policy objectives set by parliament. The minister is responsible and also accountable for achieving these objectives. The essence of a sound governance, from the perspective of the ministerial responsibility, is that there are enough safeguards enabling the minister to bear ministerial responsibility. A sound public governance requires public accountability in respect of management as well as control and supervision. These four elements are collectively referred to as government governance. And it is specifically the connection of these four elements which is supposed to prevent lop-sided growth taking place, so that the emphasis switches to legitimacy, for example. As there are various processes – such as benefits payment, employment mediation, training and education, and often linked to a variety of institutions – playing a role in achieving the objectives, re-integration in the labour market requires good governance, with a harmonisation between the various processes which results in an efficient and effective re-integration.

Seen in this light, privatisation means that clear agreements are needed regarding the chain of accountability, particularly regarding the division of authority and responsibility, and the information flows needed. After all, if the accountability is not properly arranged, either because it is not sufficiently clear who is responsible for what, or because the information flows are insufficient, the ministerial accountability – and thereby the primacy of government – is at risk. The Audit Office indicated that arrangements had not been made in a satisfactory manner with many of the independent administrative bodies. The independent administrative bodies implement public tasks, and the Lower House of Parliament must therefore be able to hold the minister accountable for these. To this end, the organisation must be governed and controlled, and accountability must be rendered for these activities to the interested parties, in many cases through a supervisory body set up on behalf of the interested parties. The government's grip on the internal governance system increased.

However, there have been some losses in accountability from the reforms (Mulgan and Uhr, 2000). Most notable have been various restrictions in the scope of ministerial intervention and therefore accountability. As a result of the reforms, and in the light of new public management the reformers have been highly critical of what is seen as the "interference" or "intervention" of politicians in matters which are better left to the operation of competitive markets or delegated to managers unconcerned with political popularity. In the interest of economic efficiency, the right of ministers to intervene has been curtailed. To the extent that services such as the private re-integration companies have their own responsibilities, and are not subject to political direction, they are not accountable to citizens via the political process. This applies equally to less far-reaching privatisations. Purchaser/provider splits and contracting out have sought to impose an institutional divide between ministers and service deliverers, bridging the gap with formal, contractual agreements in place of an unlimited right of intervention (Mulgan, 1997). This accountability deficit has not stopped the government from trying to get a grip on the re-integration companies, if not directly then by tightening up the contracts. The limited accountability is expressed clearly in the developments affecting contractual principles.

Tendering and contracting in practice

Two studies have been published into the most recent tendering procedure and the way it was implemented.[7] The studies show that earlier criticism on the first round of tendering for 2001 had definitely been acted on in the tendering process for 2002. Three mechanisms had been built in to protect the client's interests and prevent creaming. The first of these is a greater differentiation by target group. A second mechanism is built into the system of payment, the statutory obligation to hold the companies accountable for their results has been translated into "no cure, less pay", varying by target group. The more difficult the target group, the greater the percentage of the fixed payment and the higher the bonus on placement. For the more easy-to-place target groups – for example job seekers needing training of less than three months – the system chosen was one of no cure, no pay. A third mechanism against creaming is the requirement in the tender document that the percentage of clients not processed must be very small; this is known as the dropout rate. The companies must then assist a certain proportion of the accepted clients back to work (placement rate). As a result of this and other modifications, the tender document became a very large (127 pages) volume, without it actually having removed all the risks of less-objective evaluation of tenders and quotations. One concomitant disadvantage was that, with the detailing and expansion of the tender document, a new obstacle had been created for new and smaller providers.

Research was also carried out into the progress of private tendering itself. This consists of two phases, the selection phase and the awarding phase. The selection phase is intended to exclude unreliable and poor-quality companies from submitting offers. In 2002, a total of 162 re-integration companies took part in the selection phase, which together submitted 3 491 tenders. These companies submitted a total of more than 270 000 pages of text! In practice, the selection of most economical provider was almost never made on substantive grounds (experience and professionalism of staff), but much more on the grounds of the bureaucratic skills of the re-integration companies. It was therefore still unclear as to whether the most economical providers went through to the awarding phase. During the awarding phase, 83 of the remaining companies submitted a total of 2 272 bids. These contained another 175 000 pages of text, and again resulted in a major administrative burden. The awarding criteria were the price, dropout rate, placement rate, throughput time, target-group and regional specificity of the bid.[8] The tendering was not on persons/participants but on "trajectories". A trajectory includes the following services: intake, interview and drafting of re-integration plan, diagnostic stage, reinforcing availability for work, placement, placement support and follow-up. Analysis of the awarding revealed that the soft criteria (target-group and regional specificity) were difficult to interpret. The attempts to offer smaller or more regionally operating companies more opportunities than in the previous round turned out to be unsuccessful. There were no indications in this second round that preferred suppliers had been given preference. Questions could also be raised concerning the limitation of creaming, in view of the fact that companies with high dropout rates were also awarded orders. Eventually, the purchaser entered into a contract with 41 companies. The 41 companies received contracts for a total of 60 489 trajectories. The distribution of trajectories among the re-integration companies showed a major shift when compared to the previous year. The ten companies with the largest number of trajectories had a market share of almost 80%, while in the previous round this had been 85%. The total number of trajectories was distributed more evenly in 2002, among more companies than was the case in 2001. The number of companies increased from 33 to 41, including 18 newcomers.

Finally, an analysis was made of the content of the contracts entered into. It was revealed that the average agreed dropout rate was 7%, and the average agreed placement rate was 57%. Combining both these percentages showed that, of the 45 787 trajectories which the UWV purchased as a minimum, at least 24 368 must result in a placement. These two percentages also varied greatly. This also applies to the prices and throughput times agreed in the contracts. These results indicate that the market is not yet stable. Freedom of choice has increased for the client, because UWV contracted several companies for each participant.

On the basis of the research, the UWV has announced new modifications for tendering in 2003. In order to reduce the administrative burden for both the UWV and the re-integration companies, it has been decided to switch to a public procedure, in other words without prior selection. In addition, the regional criterion, which produced little effect, has been withdrawn for the 2003 tendering procedure, and the number of target groups has been reduced. The emphasis in the 2003 tendering procedure has been placed heavily on placement. This means that re-integration companies will be assessed on their results, i.e. placement. The starting point is full results-oriented funding. A no cure, less pay funding system will only apply to the more vulnerable target groups (target groups who require more intensive services). The ratio is that 40% of the orders will be contracted out on a no cure, less pay basis (and therefore 60% on the basis of no cure, no pay), whereas under the 2004 tendering procedure, this will be increased to 70%. There will also be a number of tendering procedures per year. The first contracts will be entered into as of 1 July 2003.

In this way, attempts are being made in the Netherlands to tackle the problem of creaming and insufficient competition amongst re-integration companies by tightening up the criteria in the tendering procedure. Risks will always remain, however, because discretionary space is needed in order to be able to serve clients. This space could be abused, resulting in less attention for the protection of client rights. In the next few years, clarity must be achieved on how to deal with this problem. A great deal depends on the manner in which the UWV fleshes out the framework contracts[9] at the client level, and what the re-integration company and the client then do with this. In practice, there are signs that the public principals and the re-integration companies are putting the blame for creaming on one another. The UWV is being accused of not selecting clients properly in terms of re-integration prospects, as a result of which the re-integration companies are being left with too many difficult cases and are unable to meet their contract targets. Client organisations have already indicated that the UWV/municipalities as principals should be focusing more attention on the supply and supervision of clients.

The conclusion must be that contracts for public services increasingly provide rights for ministerial intervention or for scrutiny by review agencies.

The attempts to gain a greater hold on the re-integration companies – and contract formation with them – have also followed on from the fact that the public continues to hold the government accountable for (alleged) abuses, regardless of whether the ministers have a direct institutional responsibility or not. The public are not prepared to accept a devolution of accountability for administrative reasons away from ministers to other agencies public or private contractors. This applies to every level of government. National assistance clients can apply to the municipalities in the event of (alleged) abuses. The municipalities therefore then complain that the central government has given them the responsibilities but not the resources for realising local governance, and they also complain that central government also continues to interfere greatly with the implementation.

The inherent uncertainty of the incomplete (in terms of information) contracts results in continued risks. Contracting out inevitably involves some reduction in accountability through the removal of direct departmental and ministerial control over the day-to-day actions of contractors and their staff. Indeed, the removal of such control is essential to the rationale for contracting out because the main increases in efficiency come from the greater freedom allowed to contracting providers. Contracting out involves a trade-off between political accountability and efficiency (Mulgan, 1997).

Conclusions

Public accountability requires a stronger grasp on the entire policy chain. With this objective in mind, the government has tightened up the requirements, to such an extent that some people are already referring to an accountability bureaucracy. At the same time, this same government has set in motion a process to privatise government departments for the sake of flexibility, efficiency and effectiveness, and to limit itself to its core tasks. In its need for accountability, the government – central and local – is coming up against the limits of its information options. Mulgan and Uhr (2000) refers to an accountability gap, in other words a gap between the information requirements of demanders and suppliers of accountability. The government only has a limited grasp on the private market parties, even if they are performing a public task.

Public accountability can manifest itself in more ways than simply as ministerial accountability, however. Another form of public accountability is where the public is the account-demander. This bottom-up accountability requires the participation of the public. This role of the public is in line with the shift in responsibility to lower levels which has been taking place in the past decades. This is expressed not only in the increased responsibilities given to the municipalities for the re-integration of their job seekers, which has turned them into the biggest principal in the Dutch re-integration market, but also in the increased responsibility of employers and employees for re-integration ("Gatekeeper Improvement Act", 1 April 2002; "Carrying your Own Risk for Sickness Act", 1 March 2003). This role takes shape especially at the local level, where different processes converge. In addition to marketisation, which restructures responsibilities to enhance flexibility and accountability, successful re-integration requires co-operation between actors involved in the re-integration chain. Co-operation directed towards the creation of trust and support between the actors involved is an alternative to juridification. In the consensus-oriented Dutch society, co-operation is fostered, for example, by the SUWI-act of 2002. It offers the municipalities the opportunity to create regional platforms: "municipalities promote by co-operation with other municipalities in the regional labour market the creation of regional platforms in which they consult periodically on matters of work and income other actors active in the labour market" (Article 23 SUWI-act). The role of the (bigger) municipalities as an initiator and director of this consultation process is consistent with their wish to see their increasing responsibilities in the policy domain of re-integration translated into more power. These regional platforms offer the opportunity to give immediate substance to public accountability. The consultative structures can – once trust has been formed – develop into a partnership in which joint responsibility for the improvement of the re-integration process is at the forefront. In order to achieve this type of local governance, lessons from the past must be drawn, especially from the failure of the tripartite co-operation in the beginning of the nineties. The main lessons are that clear goals must be formulated, that supervision and management must be shared between relevant bodies, and that a clear division of responsibilities must be created in which the actors involved are called to be accountable – also financially – in the case of non compliance. Unlike in business, where the market can enforce compliance of a code that is agreed on, this is not possible in the case of public organisation in the form of a quasi market.

Notes

1. Due to the fact that labour market policy in the Netherlands is currently effectively limited to re-integration policy, only the latter term will be used in the rest of this paper. In the Netherlands re-integration covers a wide range of activities like job brokerage; activation, motivation, and orientation; training; social activation and guidance; medical guidance and assistance; co-ordination.
2. Gatekeeper Improvement Act.
3. This had, in effect, already been the case since the mid-1990s. For an in depth analysis, see Sol (2000, 2003).

4. Contracting out typically implies provision by private sector contractors. However, it may also include in-house provision by public service departments or other public agencies where the right to provide is won through competitive tendering and is governed by contract. Here the term is used for provision by *private* sector contractors.

5. In the Netherlands, compliance with relevant laws and regulations and financial management were the first areas which witnessed this shift of attention. In recent years, this approach has extended from proper and compliant financial management to a control process in which efficiency and effectiveness of government policy and day-to-day operations also play a key role.

6. This term was first introduced in Ministry of Finance (1996), a study report, and published in Ministry of Finance (2000). See also *www.minfin.nl*

7. One study used questionnaires and interviews, and focused on the opinions of the benefit providers and re-integration companies, the other involved statistical analyses of the tenders, awarding and all contracts entered into. See IWI (2003) and TNO Arbeid (2002).

8. In the case of regional specificity, the re-integration company had to indicate what knowledge the provider has of the regional labour market, and what access it has to the market.

9. The term framework in framework contracts refers to the fact that companies cannot rely on a guaranteed flow of candidates. The reason for this is that clients are offered a choice of re-integration companies, which makes it impossible to determine the exact number of clients.

Bibliography

CONSIDINE, Mark (2000), "Governing Diversity: prospects for putting the public back into public service", in D. Glover and G. Patmore (eds.), *For the People. Reclaiming our government*, Pluto Press, Melbourne.

IWI (2003), *De praktijk van het aanbesteden. Een onderzoek naar de uitvoering van de aanbestedingsprocedure reïntegratiecontracten 2002 van UWV* (Tendering Practice. A study into the implementation of the tendering procedure for re-integration contracts for UWV in 2002), IWI, Zoetermeer.

LEEUW, F.L. (1997), "Doorlichting zelfstandige bestuursorganen en beleidsdoelmatigheid" (Study of independent administrative bodies and policy effectiveness), in *Bestuurskunde*, jrg 6.

MINISTRY OF FINANCE (2000), "Government Governance; Corporate Governance in the Public Sector, Why and How?", Government Audit Policy Directorate, Ministry of Finance (*www.minfin.nl*), The Hague.

MINISTRY OF FINANCE (1996), "Government Governance; on the management – control – supervision – accountability cycle", by the Government Audit Policy Directorate, 27 September (*www.minfin.nl*).

MULGAN, Richard (1997), "Accountability and Contracting-out", *Australian Journal of Public Administration*, Vol. 56(4), pp. 106-117.

MULGAN, Richard and UHR, John (2000), "Accountability and Governance", in Glyn Davis, Michael Keading, John Wanna and Patrick Weller (eds.), Discussion Paper No. 71, Series "Governance in Australia".

NATIONAL AUDITING OFFICE (1994), "Autonomous Administrative Authorities and Ministerial Responsibility", Report of the Court of Audit, Part 3.

SOL, Elsa (2003), "Crisis in de Arbeidsvoorziening. Een dubbel probleem" (Crisis in the public employment service. A double problem), in *Bestuurskunde*, jrg 12, No. 2.

SOL, Elsa (2000), *Arbeidsvoorzieningsbeleid in Nederland. De rol van de overheid en de sociale partners*. (Labour market policy in the Netherlands. The role of the government and of the social partners), Sdu, The Hague.

TNO Arbeid (2002), *Evaluatie aanbestedingsprocedure 2002* (Evaluation of 2002 Tendering Procedure), TNO Arbeid, Hoofddorp.

ISBN 92-64-10470-4
Managing Decentralisation
A New Role for Labour Market Policy
© OECD 2003

PART II
Chapter 14

France: Providing Greater Flexibility at Local Level

by
Bernard Simonin
Commissariat général au Plan

A rigid, hierarchical model progressively made more flexible and decentralised

In France, active labour market policy is still very largely the responsibility of central government, in contrast to other social policies, which have now been decentralised. Although the social partners have been responsible for unemployment benefits[1] for over forty years and have used the funds that they manage to finance activation programmes, these have long played only a limited role in comparison with the considerable monies spent by central government on employment-related measures. However, these activation programmes have recently taken on greater importance with the unemployment compensation reform of July 2001 and the creation of the back-to-work assistance plan (*Plan d'aide au retour à l'emploi*, PARE). The future decentralisation legislation that should soon be adopted in order to launch a major new phase in the transfer of responsibilities from the central government to the territorial authorities (the regions, *départements* and communes) should not alter the current balance in this field, as the central government will continue to have general responsibility for employment policy in order to ensure social cohesion.

The central government's main institutional instruments in the field of employment policy were established in the 1960s, even before the advent of mass employment, with the creation of public bodies placed under the supervision of the Ministry of Employment and Solidarity: the National Employment Agency (*Agence nationale pour l'emploi*, ANPE) and the Association for Adult Vocational Training (*Association pour la formation professionnelle des adultes*, AFPA). In the 1980s, the public employment service (PES or *Service public de l'emploi*, SPE) was added to these. The PES is not a separate agency, but is responsible for organising co-operation at the national, regional and departmental levels between the three institutions that work together to implement employment policy, *i.e.* the central and deconcentrated offices of the Employment Ministry, the ANPE and the AFPA.[2]

The operating methods of the employment services have long been characterised by a rigid hierarchical organisation that has left little room for initiatives by the staff of regional and local offices and has not been conducive to developing partnerships with other institutions. In many cases, the primary focus has been on meeting the targets for existing measures set by the central government that have been allocated on the basis of simple criteria for each region in order to contain the level of unemployment. The main task of regional and local offices has been to publicise these measures and ensure that they are used in compliance with the legislation.

From a comparison with the four accountability standards suggested by Mosley (Chapter 9 in this volume), one can thus conclude that a traditional mode of governance strongly marked by the legal accountability still dominated in France ten years ago.

However, like all other French administrations, the PES has had to adjust to the transformation of the models of reference for public action that has been reaffirmed by successive governments as part of the policy for "modernising government". The concept of what constitutes effective government action has gradually shifted from the traditional hierarchical organisation to a managerial approach based on the delegation of power, promotion of initiatives, organisational flexibility and co-operation with outside actors; these means of introducing flexibility must be supported by monitoring and evaluation tools that make it possible to measure results regularly and, if necessary, rapidly modify the programmes offered.

This trend became more widespread in the 1990s as the effectiveness of the main employment policy measures was called into question (by parliamentary reports, evaluation procedures and the work of experts), not only in terms of their impact on the sustainable creation of new jobs, but also their ability to promote the employment of those considered as priority categories (recipients of basic income support, long-term unemployed, unskilled young people, etc.). It was recognised that the central government alone could not define all aspects of the organisational principles that would ensure that the many different employment policy instruments were used coherently and were adapted to users' needs (Simonin, 1997).

Consequently, an effort was made to define improved systems that would derive their effectiveness from the appropriate coupling of traditional employment policy measures with a broad range of individualised services both for job-seekers and companies. The growing use of the concept of the "integration process" ("*parcours d'insertion*") to facilitate the return to work of those with difficulties in the labour market is a good example of this trend, since the PES endeavours to organise, over a given period, a succession of diversified initiatives that are both job-related (training programmes, temporary subsidised employment, job-search assistance, etc.) and more socially oriented, adapted to individual needs.

Uncertainty in the 1990s about which model to adopt

The promotion of this new model has gone hand in hand with a recognition of the benefits of local and regional employment initiatives as the

LEED Programme has underlined for quite many years (see for example, OECD, 1998). These benefits include the adaptability to the diversity of labour markets, the proximity to local actors, the ability to promote initiative and innovation and to mobilise a broad network of actors more easily. However, the relationship between the PES and the other actors at the territorial level awaits further analysis. Similarly, there is still uncertainty about what the internal organisation of the PES should be, both as regards relations between its component bodies (ANPE, AFPA, deconcentrated offices) and relations between the central administration and the various territorial levels.

If we analyse the new employment programmes launched in the 1990s, we can observe that the programme priorities have involved either improving the internal functioning of the PES or better regulating co-operation with the other local employment policy actors. Both approaches call into question the previous hierarchical model. However, the first tends to promote a management model within the SPE, broadly based on the development of management by objectives,[3] as the means of enabling deconcentrated central government offices to translate the government's priorities into formalised local strategies and to assume responsibility for co-ordinating the initiatives of all actors. The second approach is implicitly based on another model – that of "the central government as promoter and partner" (Donzelot and Estèbe, 1994) – in which the central government actively seeks to promote a greater sharing of responsibilities between local actors and views the quality of the co-operation between them as the key to effective government. These two models are not incompatible but, as demonstrated by Mosley, their simultaneous application can generate tensions as indeed happened in France.

We may wonder why the first of these approaches did not prevail immediately, since the central government does not share its legal powers in the field of employment, in contrast to the practice in many countries. There are several factors that can explain why it proved difficult for central government to affirm its comprehensive responsibility for all employment policy programmes and consequently its dominant role in defining local strategies and in co-ordinating the various actors:

- The first factor is directly linked to what has just been said regarding the emergence of a new model for government action. The wish to provide users with diversified services to make this action more effective has obliged the Employment Ministry to work with other institutions, for some of these services were outside the scope of its specific responsibilities and involved other central government agencies and especially the territorial authorities. For example, since the initial decentralisation legislation was adopted at the beginning of the 1980s, the regions (26 regions in France) have had important responsibilities in the fields of economic development assistance and continuing vocational training, and these responsibilities were further increased in 1993. The *départements* (approximately one hundred in France) have numerous responsibilities in the social policy field. In particular, they must finance the programmes aimed at ensuring the social and vocational integration of recipients of the social minimum income (*revenu minimum d'insertion*, RMI), the main allowance provided to the poor, who are often unemployed. The communes (some 36 000 in France, of all sizes) have fewer direct responsibilities in employment-related fields but, given the needs of their unemployed residents and of companies wishing to move into their areas and develop activities there, many communes have come to play an active role. Consequently, it has proved impossible to clarify the respective responsibilities of each level of government using the concept of "separate sets of responsibilities" that had been adopted during the initial phases of decentralisation and which was supposed to make it possible to establish a clear separation between the fields of employment, training, social action and local development.

- The role of the territorial authorities was all the more important because the central government, in order to develop its programmes and multiply the temporary jobs that it subsidises in the non-market sector (several hundred thousand jobs each year), strongly encouraged them to recruit the unemployed for these types of jobs and to finance jointly the many associations that wished to create such jobs.

- As it was generally accepted that the policy decentralisation process, undertaken late in France, was far from complete, many elected officials in territorial authorities thought that it was legitimate to take the initiative of launching programmes in the employment field. This was not formally part of their responsibilities, but they anticipated that they might be given such responsibilities in the future. EU policy, through the European Social Fund in particular, also contributed to encouraging initiatives by territorial authorities in the field of employment and vocational integration.

- Since the 1980s, the many networks of associations providing assistance for the economic and social integration of the poor and unemployed as well as support for the creation of small enterprises have developed many new forms of employment initiatives. They have sought to promote approaches that they considered to be more effective than the standardised programmes of the PES. Some of these initiatives have progressively been recognised by the central government and have become key components of its national employment policy. These associations, which continue to receive financial assistance from central government for implementing such programmes, wished to be recognised as having joint responsibility for running them and for defining policies for their future development, and they have sought to establish equal partnership relations with the central government rather than acting merely as its "subcontractors".

However, it should be pointed out that there was little participation by the social partners in local and regional employment initiatives throughout this period, although their active involvement seemed essential to ensure the programmes' effectiveness. These actors, and especially employers' organisations, often become actively involved in economic development programmes within their area, which naturally have an effect on employment, but they are far less active in vocational integration programmes for the unemployed, which are the core activity of the PES. A number of reports by experts have clearly shown how difficult it is to promote social dialogue on these issues at the regional and even more so at the local level (Casella and Freyssinet, 2000). Often, employers' and especially trade union associations do not have the human resources to participate actively in partnerships at these levels and to create or promote these types of programmes.

In addition, the rapid development of a model of management by objectives within the PES aimed at reconciling flexibility of action for deconcentrated offices with better accountability to Parliament and citizens regarding the effectiveness and efficiency of public policies was hampered by the central government's uncertainty during this period about the degree of freedom that it should grant these deconcentrated offices. At least two reasons can be given to explain this uncertainty:

- In the light of the key political importance of the issue of unemployment in France and the persistent difficulty of reaching full employment, governments have continually sought to keep direct control over the functioning of the main employment policy programmes. This enables them to act rapidly to contain the level of unemployment in the event of an economic downturn. The national evaluations that have been made over the past twenty years have shown that certain types of measures (such as subsidised jobs in the non-market sector) have a more direct and immediate impact on the level of unemployment than other measures that may have more favourable macroeconomic and microeconomic effects in the medium term. This is a powerful factor for maintaining the previous hierarchical model, as is shown by the fact that PES staff are required to comply with a regulatory framework that is often very precisely defined at the national level for all employment policy measures to enable the government to anticipate effectively their impact on the level of unemployment short-term.

- Control of the administrative and financial management of employment policy has often been considered to be insufficient in the past, resulting in budget overruns, transfers of appropriations from one programme to another that had not been planned when the annual finance act was voted by Parliament, etc. This led to considerable distrust, in particular by the Finance Ministry, of any organisational change that would give greater flexibility in managing resources unless it was accompanied by a guarantee of improved management control.

Consequently, until the mid-1990s, the decentralisation process was real, but limited. It was also uneven across the three institutions of the PES, as it was more rapid and far-reaching in the National Employment Agency than in the offices of the Employment Ministry.

This lack of clarity regarding the methods and scope of the decentralisation that the central government was seeking to promote led to very different situations in the various territorial units. In those areas where there were longstanding, high-quality relations between actors, and traditions of operating in networks, local actors were in some cases able to take full advantage of the freedom that they had been given to innovate and organise forms of co-operation that were considered to be effective by all partners. However, the overall results observed at the time in relation to the local implementation of employment policy were more mixed: tensions between institutions regarding the legitimacy of their respective initiatives; overlapping of the services provided; the fact that central government staff sometimes felt that they had been deprived of their prerogatives by local bodies (*Travail et Emploi*, 2000), and more frequently that local actors felt that the central government's talk of partnerships was not being translated into concrete action. For example, a recent report by members of Parliament to the Prime Minister (Robin-Rodrigo and Bourguignon, 1999), while emphasising the progress made in recent years, concluded as follows: "Central government departments, despite the recent reforms aimed at enabling them to facilitate the local implementation of their programmes, still remain very marked by the habit of mass management of national measures. This reflex continues to make them ill-adapted to provide access to the existing range of diversified instruments at the proper time, with a real concern for ensuring that they meet the needs of residents (…). Consequently, we can conclude that there continues to be major institutional difficulties in replacing the approach of administrative interpretation of objectives defined at the national level with a culture of contractual negotiation with local actors".

A clarification of approach in 1998: strengthening the accountability

The clarification of the model that the government wished to adopt dates from 1998. The approach chosen was to reaffirm strongly the prime responsibility of the central government and its departments in the field of public employment initiatives, the existence of national priority objectives and the need for an improved decentralisation of management.

This clarification has led to the following key developments:
- A broader adoption of management by objectives for programmes for the unemployed. This had already been done by the ANPE, but has been extended to the PES as a whole, including central government departments.

- New possibilities given to deconcentrated public offices to make quantitative trade-offs between the main measures aimed at facilitating the employment of priority groups (subsidised jobs in companies, subsidised jobs in the non-market sector, training programmes) to adapt them better to local labour markets and users' needs.
- A clarification and formalisation of the relationships between the various territorial levels for public policy intervention and a definition of the progression of the various stages in the implementation of this new approach. Every year the PES must:
  - ❖ prepare a local diagnostic report[4] on the area's needs and opportunities and the results of previous initiatives;
  - ❖ define at the departmental level the best way of achieving the national objectives in the light of the results of the local diagnostic reports; translate priorities into operational objectives and plan initiatives;
  - ❖ manage at the regional level the system of physical and financial monitoring of the implementation of programmes and the effects of measures on the basis of a series of indicators, and send information regularly to the central administration;
  - ❖ make useful readjustments in mid-year on the basis of the results obtained and labour market trends.
- A significant reinforcement of the procedures used for the management, monitoring, evaluation and statistical observation of the situation of local labour markets and the local use of employment measures.
- A far more precise definition of the respective responsibilities of the various local actors and the possible methods of co-operation between them. This clearly specifies the dominant role of the PES in negotiating with the central government regarding the results to be achieved, the preparation of local diagnostic reports, the definition of priorities and the guidance of job-seekers towards back-to-work assistance programmes. There is also a clearer definition of the possible forms of co-operation between the PES and other local actors; the forms of institutional and financial partnerships; and the conditions in which the PES can allow parts of programmes for which it is responsible to be implemented by other operators (local authorities, other public bodies, associations and firms).

A limited number of strategic objectives well adapted to policy priorities

A discussion of the concrete operating procedures of this overall system goes beyond the remit of this chapter. However, I would like to point out the fundamental change in the PES' approach introduced by the extension of management by objectives to all its component services. Each year, the Employment Ministry sends a circular in November of year n – 1 to all of its services explaining and justifying the government's priorities for year n. These priorities are then translated into a limited number of strategic objectives, and the resources available for achieving these objectives are defined. For example, there are six strategic objectives for 2003.[5]

- to reduce the number of job-seekers who have been unemployed for over two years;
- to raise the number of job-seekers who return to employment before they have been unemployed for one year;
- to reduce the proportion of women among the long-term unemployed;
- to increase employment among recipients of the social minimum income (RMI);
- to reduce the number of young people who are unemployed;
- to fill more of the job vacancies notified by firms in sectors experiencing recruitment difficulties.

These strategic objectives are not defined through negotiation with deconcentrated offices or other institutions, but by the Minister. Some objectives have been set since 1998, while others have emerged more recently, in particular due to the influence of the policies of the European Commission (prevention of long-term unemployment, equal opportunities). The results to be achieved at the national level are also set by the Minister. On the basis of a forecasting model of likely unemployment trends during the year n, if the PES does not change its past policies, a calculation is made for each strategic objective of the positive variances to be achieved in relation to these trends (indicators). These variances represent the expected impact of employment policy initiatives for year n. Their level also takes into account forecasts of economic growth, and if these are favourable, the variances with respect to the previous trend can be high, for the PES will be considered to have significant scope for action, and conversely.

An initial breakdown by region of the results to be obtained is indicated in the same circular. It takes into account both the cyclical trends of regional unemployment, calculated using the same model as at national level, and the region's position with respect to the objective set. For example, a region in which the rate of those unemployed for more than two years has been particularly high will have a larger variance to achieve in relation to the cyclical trends that have been calculated. The regional PES then have two months to analyse these proposals internally and with their partners, and either to accept them or to draft a reasoned note presenting counter proposals. In the latter case, there are discussions between the central administration and the regional PES and a decision is taken bearing in mind that the overall regional objectives must not differ significantly from the national objective set previously. Regional PES can also add their own regional strategic objectives to national ones.[6] The AFPA and the ANPE must also define operational objectives specifying the priority means of action for attaining the strategic objectives.[7]

Once these objectives have been set, the PES can, on the basis of the local diagnostic reports prepared concurrently, define its territorial action strategy and its concrete forms of intervention and co-operation with other local actors.

This deconcentrated (rather than decentralised) organisation of government action in the field of employment can in principle be considered an effective way of reconciling flexibility with the need for accountability. There are a limited number of clearly defined annual national strategic objectives that are discussed with the deconcentrated PES in order to determine how they can be translated into regional objectives; thanks to the diagnostic reports on the needs and economic and social resources of each territorial unit, it is possible to prepare local action plans for attaining these objectives; and the improvement of management procedures and statistical systems, the affirmation of the key role of the central government and the clarification of the legal aspects of co-operation with the other local actors should make it possible to define clearly each actor's responsibilities and assess the results obtained by each one.

It should also be pointed out that, since 1998, when this management system was introduced, the strategic objectives defined each year have usually been largely attained. This was admittedly facilitated by the favourable economic conditions that prevailed until 2001. However, we succeeded, for example, in lowering sharply the number of job-seekers unemployed for over two years, despite the fact that many experts, referring to the poor results obtained in the past, even during periods of growth, had predicted a continuing high level of long-term unemployment.

Nevertheless, the elements available for analysing the functioning of this system show the current limits of its operational flexibility and its ability to ensure accountability as to the results achieved. Furthermore, if this system is compared with countries that have adopted policy decentralisation, one can also question its capacity to involve other actors (territorial authorities, social partners and civil society) in a system that remains dominated by central government departments.

The limits of flexibility

In addition to the fact that strategic objectives are defined from the top down and are a considerable constraint for territorial initiatives, at least three factors significantly limit the scope for action of local actors:

- *The national regulations applying to each category of employment policy initiatives remain relatively rigid.* They generally define specifically the legal framework for the initiative, the target groups that qualify, the average duration of these initiatives, the amount of financial incentives paid to employers to encourage them to hire (for subsidised jobs) and the average amount of funding provided to operators who carry out other aspects of initiatives (training programmes, advice to companies, various types of assistance to the unemployed to facilitate their job search). To use a metaphor, the flexibility consists of the fact that local actors can choose from a toolbox containing many carefully calibrated tools those that seem to suit the local situation best, but they cannot create new tools or slightly change a specific tool in order to adapt it to their needs.

- *The possibilities of making quantitative trade-offs between existing instruments are far from covering all initiatives.* In 2001, of the € 11.5 billion spent on active employment policy (*cf.* Annex 1), the expenditure for measures for which quantitative local trade-offs could be made was € 3.4 billion, or 30%. In particular, financial resources cannot be transferred between initiatives promoting the employment of priority categories (integration policy) and initiatives supporting the creation of new jobs and activities (local development policy). Even for initiatives that only concern priority categories, certain transfers are impossible, such as those involving the resources available respectively to the ANPE, the AFPA and the deconcentrated offices of the Employment Ministry.

- Lastly, with the creation of the PARE by the UNEDIC, the ANPE, which implements the initiatives financed under this programme, has been required to meet new operational objectives, which are often ambitious. Although these are consistent with the strategic objectives presented earlier, the fact remains that the ANPE's means of action seem to be less flexible than was previously the case.

How to interpret these choices?

The choice to give preference in this new setting to accountability rather than administrative flexibility seems to be at the same time political and technical.

It is political to the extent that government reaffirms in this way that unemployment and its impact on social cohesion require a national answer which should adapt to the changes of the economic situation while respecting the primary objective of containing unemployment growth in the context of economic slowdown.

Such a counter-cyclic policy implies frequent changes in the choice of employment policy instruments (measures targeted on young people or the long-term unemployed, focused on the non-commercial sector or the commercial sector, etc.) and in the financial resources allocated to implement them. It also imposes certain limits to the flexibility of the regional and local services if the objective is to ensure that the impulses of the central level are rapidly spread to all other levels.

It was considered that these advantages would prevail over the shortcoming of such a "top down" approach, even if it was clearly understood that the latter would harm a good co-ordination of other local actors: difficulties for the agents of the PES to specify, beyond the short term, the amount of resources available for local programmes; other actors may feel that they are not being heard by national (or regional) decision makers.

This is also a technical choice as it derives from an understanding that the flexibility, necessary for a good adaptation of the government's response to local needs, can only be achieved if from the beginning the internal organisation of the PES allows to evaluate the results of public initiatives in terms of fiscal accountability and other standards of accountability and performance evaluation. However, a significant improvement of internal systems of management control, follow-up and evaluation would be needed in order to progress in this way.

Accountability is still insufficient

Since 1998, there has unquestionably been an improvement in management practices and statistical systems, a certain clarification of responsibilities within the PES and *vis-à-vis* other institutions and an improvement of the legal instruments that define the forms of co-operation between the central government and other actors. Nevertheless, there is also room for further progress in a number of fields. In addition to the improvements that can still be made in management practices, it seems necessary to solve several types of problems that continue to affect the quality of accountability. These are as follows:

- *Performance indicators that only show imperfectly whether the strategic objectives are being attained.* This problem stems mainly from poor knowledge of the employment status of job-seekers when they are no longer registered with the ANPE. The indicators for strategic objectives presented earlier are based on data from the administrative files of the ANPE, the only source that makes it possible to survey the trends and composition of unemployment in France in real time and at all territorial levels. However, the data contained in these files are not always sufficient to determine people's employment status (IGAS, 2000). For example, the fact that job-seekers registered for over two years disappear from the ANPE files does not necessarily mean that they have found a job or that they have ended a long period of unemployment (the first strategic objective). They may have been temporarily removed from the lists because they failed to prove that they were actively looking for employment; quite often, they will register again after a short time but their file no longer shows the real length of their unemployment. Conversely, job-seekers may be counted as long-term unemployed even though they have been working almost continuously; this is the case of persons who are registered with the ANPE but who do not work more than a specific number of hours per month. This being the case, there is always some doubt about the real meaning of the favourable (or unfavourable) results derived from the indicators used.

- *A persistent difficulty in distinguishing between effects due to the economic situation and those due to public employment policies.* In France, we still do not have a satisfactory model that makes it possible to distinguish, even very broadly, between these two types of effects. This is an important issue at the moment, for the social partners would like to be able to assess the impact that the implementation of the PARE is having on preventing long-term unemployment. However, the creation of the PARE coincided with a sharp economic downturn, which led to a certain slowdown of gross flows out of unemployment and a questioning of the effectiveness of the PARE. But what would have happened if growth had continued?

- *Independently of this difficulty, there are insufficient human resources to analyse all of the numerous statistical data that are nevertheless available at the local level.* The government statistical services have provided back-up for the deconcentration process by developing many possibilities for local use of the data available in the management files of employment programmes and in regular statistical surveys on employment trends. A systematic comparison of all these data would provide much, albeit incomplete, useful information on the results obtained. However, this kind of analysis is necessarily time-consuming and relatively complex given the large number of programmes under way. In recent years, there has been a major effort of analysis at the national level to evaluate the net impact of the most important employment-related measures. However, in a more deconcentrated system of organisation, in which the success of government action is based on the effective interaction of many types of existing instruments, we still find it difficult to answer the questions raised by a deconcentrated management by objectives, such as why has the number of women registered with the ANPE for over a year fallen far more quickly than the number of men?

- *The poorly integrated information systems of the central government and the territorial authorities.* As we have seen, the territorial authorities contribute to employment through the training programmes, economic development assistance and aid for the employment of people with difficulties that they finance. When these activities are jointly financed with the central government, there is a more or less shared information system, but when, as is often the case, they are part of a separate programme of the territorial authorities, information general circulates very poorly, making it impossible to have a comprehensive overview of government programmes, even though they have the same or very similar strategic objectives. For example, the strategic objective set by the central government for 2003 of reducing youth unemployment significantly will depend partly on the services provided by the PES, but it will also be highly dependant on the continuing training and the employment assistance programmes provided by regions.[8]

The dominant role of the central government and the creation of partnerships

As we have seen, the fact that the central government has the sole official responsibility for employment policy has not prevented its potential partners from becoming involved in this field, since the strategic objectives are broadly shared by French society, even though there may be differences in the ways that the various actors pursue these common objectives. For example, the central government, through its employment policy, and the regions, through their vocational training policy, both pursue the objective of improving the vocational integration of young people. However, for the central government, success in meeting this general objective is measured by the employment rate, irrespective of the kind of job found, while regions tend more readily take into account new diplomas earned and the level of the job found and the type of qualifications that it entails. Similarly, the central government and the *départements* both promote the vocational integration of the poorest of the unemployed, but the central government's main criterion for success is finding a job, while for departments it is coming off the register of the minimum social income (RMI). Naturally, these criteria are linked, but they are not exactly the same. This brings the issue of "accountability chains" raised by Mosley, where each partner must give account to his own hierarchy in accordance with accountability standards which may differ from one institution to another.

Beyond these minor differences, the main obstacle that prevents the territorial authorities from becoming active partners of the central government is the fact that they consider that the government does not let them participate sufficiently in the decisions that it makes, even though, because of the similarity of their respective responsibilities, these decisions often have a direct impact on the financing and content of the territorial authorities' own programmes. Some territorial PES have realised this and have opened up their meetings to the representatives of regions and *départements*. However, the most striking example of inadequate consultation was the launch by the central government in the late 1990s of two very large youth employment programmes that involved a large number of training initiatives. The regions were not really involved in these decisions, but the central government later turned to them and asked them to finance these initiatives. Given the interest of these programmes, some regions agreed to do so, but others did not or only provided marginal support.

The relations between the central government and networks of specialised associations in employment assistance programmes for priority categories have been based on different principles. Most associations are highly dependent on public funding to conduct their programmes, and as a result they have no choice but to adopt the operating standards defined by the government. Although the objective of the 1998 Act to combat exclusion was to increase significantly the number of employment assistance schemes run by associations, some associations felt that the new rules imposed by the central government restricted their freedom of action and that their initiatives were being "instrumentalised". This may explain why the Act did not produce the results anticipated. Furthermore, government employment programmes have never really succeeded in linking up with the initiatives of local resident groups, despite many attempts to do so over the past twenty years in connection with urban policies. This situation has not changed markedly in the recent period.

Lastly, as we have already said, territorial co-operation with the social partners has been hindered by their organisational structure, which has until now been focused on the national level.

Two key reforms for the future: the new phase of decentralisation and a new financial constitution

The new phase of decentralisation that will be launched in 2003 will not call into question the central government's responsibility in the field of employment, but it should make it possible to provide better solutions to some of the difficulties mentioned above. The analytical work already done[9] on the need to clarify the responsibilities of the different actors in the many programmes in which several fields intersect (employment and vocational training, employment and social integration) shows that it will not be possible, and certainly not desirable, to move away from partnerships towards a strict allocation of fields of action to each type of actor. On the contrary, the favoured policy is to move away from the approach of shared responsibility, given the confusion that it introduces as to the rights and obligations of each party. This would be replaced by the concept of a steering role for central government, affirming its legitimacy to promote and organise a concerted strategy and co-ordinate its implementation. This approach would necessarily be combined with the principle of contractualisation between the different partners and thus of mutual solidarity.

Another effect of this new phase of decentralisation might be to require the central government to consult with territorial authorities when it creates a new programme. Finally, this phase is leading the social partners currently to envisage significantly restructuring their internal organisation and operational practices in order to give much greater importance to the local and regional dimension.

The organic law on public finance of 1 August 2001 has introduced an equally fundamental reform that will apply to all of central government in 2006. This new financial constitution "provides for three major innovations: it reforms the framework of public management by making it results-oriented, it ensures the transparency of budgetary information and it promotes strategic choices in the field of public finances. New responsibilities are given to ministerial managers, together with a new freedom to ensure that budgets are result-oriented".[10] This general extension of management by objectives throughout the central government does indeed reconcile flexible management and accountability.

The objective is to organise all of the Employment Ministry's initiatives into programmes and sub-programmes for which precise objectives and corresponding resources will be defined, which will be translated into a series of indicators of performance, activities, resources and contexts. Each programme will be a "responsibility centre" (employment policy might be divided into four or five programmes) in which flexible management will be greatly increased since it will be possible to make transfers between all sub-programmes within a programme and redistribute resources between expenditures for operations, intervention and capital investment and, to a certain extent, staff. The clearer objectives and the very fully defined system of indicators should in turn enable Parliament to have a much fuller overview of the contents and outcomes of the programmes when making its decisions.

However, many points remain to be clarified, in particular regarding the respective roles of central and deconcentrated offices and the effects of the reform on the organisation of territorial policies. The Employment Ministry is already experimenting with implementation in two regions. Nevertheless, we may wonder, as IGAS[11] has, about the consequences of this reorganisation of the central government on partnerships within territories: "this new organic law on public finance (…) is based on a highly vertical approach to identifying responsibilities and evaluating public policies. In this regard, how it will interact with the more horizontal approach of territories raises a major question for our institutions (…)".

Notes

1. They exercise this responsibility by managing the national unemployment insurance fund, the UNEDIC (*Union nationale pour l'emploi dans l'industrie et le commerce*).

2. The different roles that they play can be described schematically as follows:
The deconcentrated offices of the Ministry, in particular at the regional level, play a strategic role of defining and promoting regional and local employment initiatives (within the boundaries defined by the central government). They also ensure monitoring and represent the central government in many meetings. They manage and implement certain employment policy measures (at the level of the *département*).
The ANPE is responsible for information, advice, job-search and placement on the labour market. It provides job-seekers with guidance regarding employment policy programmes, manages individual services to facilitate their access to employment and certain incentive measures aimed at encouraging firms to hire those in categories given priority under employment policy.
The AFPA provides job-seekers with training leading to diplomas, assists them in preparing training projects and certifies their job skills.
The annex presents a breakdown of the employment budget by the major categories of programmes funded by the central government.

3. The development of this model in the ANPE is described in Chapter 9 by Mosley.

4. These diagnostic reports concern the 365 "operational action zones of the SPE" (*Inspection générale des affaires sociales*, 2002). Each area covers an average of 70 000 economically active persons, including 8 000 job-seekers, with major differences between rural areas (less populated) and highly urbanised areas.

5. Circular of 22 November 2002 by the *Délégation générale à l'emploi et à la formation professionnelle* (DGEFP) to regional and departmental public employment services and to the Directors-General of the ANPE and AFPA.

6. The approach is still, on the whole, top-down (definition of national objectives apportioned between regions). However, elements aimed at giving greater weight to the regional level have been introduced as this procedure has been developed.

7. The report by Mosley, Schütz and Breyer (2000) gives a precise description of the objectives for 1999 and 2000. The creation of the PARE in 2001 has resulted in changes. Operational objectives have become more numerous and, in my view, impose greater constraints on staff in organising their activities.

8. The annual report of the Inspectorate-General for Social Affairs (*Inspection générale des affaires sociales*, IGAS) for 2002, entitled "The Social Policies of the Central Government and the Territorial Authorities" ("*Politiques sociales de l'État et des territoires*") published in *La Documentation Française*, provides many additional elements of assessment beyond the necessarily very summarised presentation given here.

9. A working group composed of representatives of regions, social partners and the central government drafted a document entitled "*Quelle décentralisation de la formation professionnelle pour demain ?*" ("What kind of decentralisation of vocational training for tomorrow?"), which addresses co-ordination of vocational training with employment policy (working document of the *Comité de co-ordination des programmes régionaux de formation professionnelle et d'apprentissage*, December 2002.

10. Statement of the Minister for the Budget to the press (4 December 2002).

11. Annual report mentioned above.

ANNEX

The Main Components of Employment Policy

Major categories of programmes	Programmes	Expenditure (millions of euros)
Measures for priority categories (long-term unemployed, recipients of basic income support, etc.)	Subsidised jobs in the non-market sector	1 938
	Subsidised jobs in the market sector	1 011
	Training programmes	432
	Aid for programmes run by associations	95
	Programmes for disabled workers	892
Central government participation in training programmes for other categories	Training of young people (apprenticeships, etc.)	2 005
	Payment of trainees, other programmes	618
Support for creating or maintaining jobs in companies	Various programmes	900
Support for the creation of sustainable jobs for young people in the non-market sector	Programme "Youth employment and services to job seekers"	1 998
The specific means of action on the ANPE	Internal operations and services to job seekers	1 080
The specific means of action of the AFPA	Internal operations, training programmes, guidance	748

Source: The draft Bill on public finances for 2003. Active employment expenditure managed directly by the central government has not been included, nor have the expenditures of the UNEDIC in implementing the PARE nor the expenditures of territorial authorities participating in employment policy.

Bibliography

CASELLA, Philippe and FREYSSINET, Jacques(2000), "Les acteurs économiques et sociaux face aux nouvelles responsabilités des régions en matière de formation professionnelle", *Évaluation des politiques régionales de formation professionnelle 1997-1999*, Vol. 1, La Documentation française, Paris.

DONZELOT, Jacques and ESTÈBE, Philippe (1994), *L'État animateur, essai sur la politique de la ville*, Editions Esprit, Paris.

IGAS (2002), *Politiques sociales de l'État et territoires*, Annual Report, La Documentation Française, Paris.

IGAS (2000), *Les acteurs de la politique de l'emploi face au chômage*, 1999 Annual Report, La Documentation française, Paris.

MOSLEY, Hugh, SCHÜTZ, Hosler, and BREYER, Nicole (2000), *Management by Objectives in European Public Employment Services*, Discussion Paper FSI01-203, WZB, Berlin.

OCDE (1998), *Local Management for More Effective Employment Policies*, Paris.

ROBIN-RODRIGO, Chantal and BOURGUIGNON, Pierre (1999), *Le territoire de la cité au service de l'emploi*, Report to the Prime Minister, La Documentation française, Paris.

SIMONIN, Bernard (1997), "Politique de l'emploi : évolutions, acteurs et territoires", in J.P. Delevoye (ed.), *Cohésion sociale et territoires*, Commissariat général du Plan, la Documentation française, Paris.

TRAVAIL ET EMPLOI (2000), *Dossier "Acteurs locaux de l'emploi"*, No. 81, La Documentation française, Paris.

ISBN 92-64-10470-4
Managing Decentralisation
A New Role for Labour Market Policy
© OECD 2003

PART II
Chapter 15

Poland: A New Accountability Framework for Human Resources Development Programmes

by

Grażyna Gęsicka
Vice-President, Polish Agency for Enterprise Development

The public accountability for implementing state policy requires the best possible efficient use of available human and organisational resources, as well as financial assets. Efficiency requires flexible approaches, yet the latter is frequently at odds with such requirements as strict observance of legal provisions, application of precisely specified proceedings at each and every level of the process, record keeping that makes it possible to control every action performed within the scope of programme implementation. This chapter shows that the choice of the approach to implementation of a programme, and therefore the decision regarding the applied controlling tools may, from the very beginning, determine the trade-off between accountability and flexibility involved in the implementation of public tasks. The paper describes the example of human resources programmes implemented by the Polish Agency for Enterprise Development (PARP) and its flexible approach to accountability requirements.

The Polish Agency for Enterprise Development

The Polish Agency for Enterprise Development (PARP) is a government agency established in 2001. The goals of the agency include its participation in implementing programmes focused on developing the economy, and in particular the programmes pertaining to support of: *i)* small and medium-sized enterprises development; *ii)* export; *iii)* regional development; *iv)* application of new techniques and technologies; and *v)* job creation to reduce unemployment, and human resources development.

These goals are implemented through *inter alia: i)* provision of specialised and advisory services for entrepreneurs, central and local government administration units; *ii)* provision of grants and loans for entrepreneurs and for business support institutions; *iii)* helping entrepreneurs access to knowledge, training, and economic information; *iv)* analysing the economic situation and dissemination of the analyses results; and *v)* organising information and promotional events.

Being a government agency, PARP focuses on implementing government programmes in compliance with the outlines and expectations of the government administration. From this perspective, PARP is rather an element of the centralised administrative system. However, the programmes for which the agency is responsible cannot be successfully implemented in a top-down, centralistic manner. PARP does not have an extensive structure having a character of a "special" administration with regional and local offices employing an army of bureaucrats and professionals implementing government programmes. Such a (hypothetical) structure would probably give the government the feeling that it has full control over the process of programmes implementation. Yet, on the other hand, such a structure would entail a great deal of red tape and would prove to be inefficient.

As a matter of fact, PARP being a government agency operates in the environment of hundreds of co-operating institutions and organisations on the contractual (agreement) basis. PARP co-operates with regional and local authorities on the *poviat* and *gmina* levels, with NGOs, with commercial institutions selling their services in an open market. In setting forth the rules for implementation of the programmes entrusted to PARP and in determining their procedures, the agency takes into account both accountability and flexibility. The programmes must be implemented in tandem with all the applicable principles of accountability and fairness with respect to spending and settlement of the use of public funds. At the same time the programmes must reflect the needs of their beneficiaries, who must approve and accept them. Therefore, they must show flexibility in defining the detailed goals and in implementation, facilitating adaptation to the local needs and conditions. Each time, both of these principles must be observed. Failing to observe the first one may trigger accusation for violating the principles of using the public finances. Failing to observe the other one may result in low uptake of the programme by the beneficiaries, who may not be interested in participation.

Implementing European structural funds programmes

The system of implementing the structural funds in Poland assumes the foreground role of the government as the organ responsible for programming, management and financial settlements. Thus, the system is not a decentralised one, where the responsibilities are delegated for instance to *voivodships* (regions). However, the partner role of the regional self-governments of *voivodships*, organisations representing social partners from the business community and NGOs is quite significant in this system.

PARP implements Poland's pre-accession programmes. After the country's accession to the EU, the agency will participate in the implementation of three sectoral operational programmes: Economic Competitiveness, Human Resources Development (HRD), and the Integrated Operational Programme for Regional Development. As part of HRD, PARP will be in charge of:

- supporting managerial staff and personnel of existing enterprises;
- strengthening the co-operation between the academic and business communities;
- promoting new forms of work organisation;
- promoting entrepreneurship.

These tasks will be translated into projects accessible to a wide audience, as illustrated in Table 15.1 below.

Table 15.1. **Implementation of the Human Resource Development Operational Programme in Poland: projects and beneficiaries**

Types of projects	Beneficiaries
• Training related to enterprise operations	• Entrepreneurs, employers, employees
• Post-graduate studies for employees and scientists	• Organisations of employers and employees
• Professional internships in enterprises	• Entrepreneurship support centres
• Internships in R&D institutions	• Persons willing to start-up their business activity
• Subsidised employment in enterprises and in R&D institutions	
• Research and analyses of new forms of work organisation	
• Subsidising of projects related to new forms of work organisation	
• Grants for implementing entrepreneurship supporting projects	
• Advisory and information services for start-ups	

Source: Author for the OECD.

PARP now faces the task of preparing guidelines and procedures to carry out the above-mentioned projects. We will be guided by the following principles:

- the procedures should be as simple as possible, not costly and not too time consuming for both applicants and the implementing agency;
- potential beneficiaries must be familiar with the implementing procedures, which to large extent will be based on the existing legal regulations and on the templates applied so far.

Goals pursued by PARP as part of the implementation process include highest possible efficiency. The efficiency, understood as the best use of the public resources available for achieving the assumed goals, is closely connected with ensuring parallel and scrupulous observance of the principles of accountability and flexibility.

Accountability

While developing rules and procedures related to the implementation of projects and programmes, PARP must take into account its responsibility for the policy goals pursued by the policy and for efficient administration of the public money allocated for implementation of these programmes. With respect to this last issue, the accountability level of the programme should be adequate in terms of its financial volume, in order to facilitate the taxpayers (both Polish and those of the EU) to maintain control over the expenditures

and provide them with information regarding the purposes of these expenditures. Thus, the accountability means:
1. Achieving the goals pursued by the programmes, in terms of quantitative and qualitative impacts.
2. Administrative correctness:
   - observance of law and formal procedures in the process of programmes and projects implementation;
   - professionalism of the implementing entities (personnel, equipment, *e.g.* computer equipment, experience, easy communication with the principal actors of the process, etc.) to ensure efficient and timely tasks implementation;
   - maintaining control over each phase of the process of project/programme implementation;
   - maintaining unbiased criteria for allocating the entrusted funds due to application of relevant formal procedures.
3. Financial accountability:
   - ensuring reasonable, optimal (possibly low, taking into account the complexity of the assumed tasks) costs of the programme administration;
   - ensuring co-financing (matching funds).
4. Accountability towards citizens – taxpayers:
   - consultations with social and economic partners during the phase of programming and implementing the projects, within the scope determined by law and by the decisions of the government agency delegating implementation of the programme;
   - information and promotion of the available services offer;
   - clear, simple and public procedures;
   - information on progress of the implementation and outcomes of the programmes.

Flexibility

Implementing the rules outlined earlier could easily lead to significant formalisation of the projects implementation. The factors of administrative and bureaucratic correctness could take over the programme goals. Therefore, while developing the projects implementation rules it is necessary to strive to make these rules facilitate:
1. Adjusting the projects and tools to the actual needs of individuals and local communities:
   - reaching various groups of final beneficiaries offering them participation in the programmes;

- adjusting the programme tools to the individual needs of the final beneficiaries;
- real time reacting for changing situation, instead of reacting within the timeframes determined in the programme timetable.

2. Co-ordination of actions to promote employment and social policies in local communities:
   - ensuring partnership in programming and projects implementation.

3. Getting the local communities involved in problem-solving since this is not solely an issue for central government:
   - ensuring that the local communities have the feeling of active participation in the projects implementation (among other things, this ensures better supervision over the projects implementation).

4. Innovative approaches with respect to the tools and methods.

Characteristics of the implementing tools in accordance with the criteria of accountability and flexibility

The methods used by PARP to implement the human resources development projects within the framework of the pre-accession programmes include: i) large service contracts implemented by commercial consortia; ii) large contracts of public institutions; iii) small and medium-sized contracts public institutions; and iv) small and medium-sized contracts of NGOs. Each of these instruments offers more or less scope for accountability and flexibility, as shown by Table 15.2.

Accountability

Large service contracts implemented by commercial consortia, as well as all contracts executed by public institutions (labour offices, lifelong learning centres, universities and research institutes) can be expected to fulfil accountability obligations to a high degree. Because these institutions are included in the implementation of the government's policies, they can react efficiently to the goals set by these programmes. Being subject to the administrative rigour, knowing the laws and being in the habit of acting in strict compliance with the legal provisions, they have no problems with observing principles of administrative correctness. Moreover, the public institutions are familiar with the principles of financial accountability and they do observe them. Public institutions are not expected to have any significant problems with respect to co-funding of the projects. The matching funds, once included in the budgets of these institutions, are, as a rule, available in due time and in the required amounts. Furthermore public institutions are usually accustomed to performing their duties towards the citizens-taxpayers: application of public consultation

Table 15.2. **Scope for accountability and flexibility per instrument of programme implementation, Poland**

Type of project	Accountability				Flexibility			
	a) Goals achievement	b) Administrative correctness	c) Financial responsibility	d) Fairness towards taxpayers	a) Adjustment to the needs	b) Co-ordination within the local community	c) Local community commitment	d) Innovativeness
1. Large service contracts implemented by commercial consortia	High	High	High	High	Depends on the quality of the consortium	Low	Low	Low
2. Large contracts of public institutions	High	High	High	High	Depends on the quality of institutions and political culture level of the region	Low	Low	Low
3. Small and medium sized contracts of public institutions	High	High	High	High	High	High	High	Low
4. Small and medium-sized contracts of NGOs	Products of local interest	Low	Low	Depends on the institutions	High	High	High	High

Source: Author for the OECD.

procedures (in most cases within the scope determined by the respective legal provisions), making information concerning the procedures publicly available (to a smaller extent) concerning the outcomes of the implemented programmes. For some other reasons – and in the first place due to high level of professionalism – the units implementing large service contracts (in most cases consortia) demonstrate all these traits.

Projects implemented on the basis of agreements with non-government organisations as well as small contracts with contractors from the commercial sector meet the requirement of accountability only to a lesser degree. Regarding implementation of the policy goals, this issue is usually dominated by direct goals of non-government organisations and by the market-oriented approach of commercial firms. From these contractors we can expect a high degree of administrative professionalism or financial accountability, in particular with respect to efficiency in generating the co-funding for projects. Compared to public institutions, NGOs and small commercial service providers are less inclined to carry out their accountability obligations pertaining to the towards the citizens and taxpayers: application of public consultations procedures, providing making information concerning the procedures and outcomes of the implemented programmes publicly available.

Flexibility

Regarding flexibility, there is no doubt that the size of the projects or contracts does not enhance it. Large contracts in the area of human resources, executed by both public institutions and commercial business entities (consortia) are characterised by low level of co-ordination with other public policy actions addressed to local communities, limited willingness to seek the involvement of local communities in solving their problems using the resources made available through the project, and thus they do not make the local communities feel committed. They also demonstrate a low level of innovation with respect to the tools and methods of acting. In this type of projects, adjustment to the local needs and to the needs of specific groups of beneficiaries depends to a large extent on skills, knowledge and approaches applied by the implementing consortia, as well as, in case of public institutions, on the political culture of the region. Focus on implementing the public goals rather than on bureaucratic fulfilment of the statutory provisions, knowledge of the situation (needs) and the ability to make use of the statistical data, analyses and expertise in the ongoing work, habit of public debate over social problems and public consultations with social and economic partners are the factors supporting adjustment of the projects carried on by the public institutions to the actual needs. The level of accomplishment of these aspects in Poland is varied locally and regionally, and there are differences even among public institutions.

Low flexibility includes also small and medium-sized projects carried out by commercial contractors. Their market-oriented approach means that they are hardly interested in co-ordinating their actions with other projects pertaining to local or regional social policies, and they are hardly interested in seeking involvement of local communities in solving their problems using the resources made available through the project, and usually they do not demonstrate innovative approaches. At the same time, this market-oriented approach makes the contractors deeply interested in adjusting their offer to the needs – this helps them to perform the task more efficiently and get paid for it.

Small and medium-sized projects, both, those carried out by public institutions and those executed by NGOs, demonstrate the highest degree of flexibility. The size of the project alone enables placing it in the environment that is well known to the contractor. No special studies are necessary or expertise to learn what are the needs of *poviat*, *gmina* or specific community (*e.g.* academic, business start-ups, etc.). Within such relatively small communities, it is also easier to establish contacts with potential institutional partners (local authorities, organisations associating entrepreneurs, schools), which may provide advisory or financial support, execute part of the project, provide assistance with project promotion, etc. It is easier to inform the interested parties about the offer that the project includes.

Despite the high flexibility indicator there is an important difference between these two groups of providers. Public institutions demonstrate a low level of innovativeness, while in NGOs this level is very high.

Conclusions and future perspectives

Under Polish current conditions, small and medium-sized contracts for project implementation concluded with public institutions (Labour Offices, schools, lifelong learning centres, scientific institutes) and with NGOs seem to be the most appropriate way to implement the tasks in the area of social policy and employment co-funded by the ESF. Projects of this kind ensure efficient implementation combined with the highest level of application of the principles of public accountability and flexible adjustment to the needs of the final beneficiaries. It is likely that most of the projects for which PARP will be responsible will be implemented this way.

However, this will not be the sole instrument. Each of the implementation methods mentioned in this chapter has its strengths. Large service contracts with commercial entities (consortia) are particularly useful in case of contracts in which certain procedural standards are imposed. In most cases, such contracts pertain to the technical assistance for specific types of beneficiaries. They also prove useful in situations in which high qualification and highly specialised knowledge not commonly available in all social groups and local communities are indispensable, for example, assisting in opening a business by innovative start-ups. Large projects with public institutions are justified if there is a need to closely co-ordinate specific tasks with the regional strategies and programmes. Small and medium-sized projects for commercial institutions are appropriate for projects in areas where the market for contractors providing commercial services is already developed and professional service providers offering better quality than public institutions has been established, for example, some types of training courses and employment agencies.

While developing rules and procedures for programme implementation, PARP includes requirements that increase accountability of the contractors: it sets forth the goals, determines requirements concerning the professional standards and experience of the implementing team, sets forth the principles for reporting, accountancy, information, promotion, etc. It is a much more difficult task to build into these procedures the requirements regarding flexibility during project implementation: contractor contact with the local community, winning the local community acceptance, suggesting other approaches to implemented tasks. There is no doubt that this aspect of PARP activities should be strengthened.

Broader promotion of new pilot actions initiated by local communities, NGOs and other public partners is necessary. An "incubator" of new non-standard projects would be needed. This aspect of PARP activities is not sufficiently covered. Also, it seems that the programmes of the Polish government put less emphasis on the promotion of local initiatives in comparison with the early nineties. It may be that at the time of the creation of new *poviats*, the belief in natural development of those initiatives weakened the will to support them from the very "top". However, this support from the "top" is actually inevitable. The structures of the local government administration (*gminas*, *poviats*) are a necessary but not a sufficient condition for the development of local initiatives. There is a need for favourable political climate for this type of initiative, conscious support for building new local institutions and programmes, assistance in establishing and maintaining them, conceptual efforts and operational support for the existing structures. It seems that the National Development Plan and its operational programmes put too little stress on supporting the development of local and "intermediary" structures. It was assumed that the supply of resources for the programmes would naturally generate contractors, *e.g.* NGOs and commercial firms, and that it would provide an impulse for public institutions to undertake additional actions to implement them. Yet, this may prove to be delusive.

Further decentralisation of the system for implementing structural funds programming, which in the first instance consists in delegating the responsibility for the programming and implementation to the regional self-governments, is necessary. Decentralisation would contribute to increased efficiency of the programmes and better addressing the actual needs. The role of PARP in a more decentralised system would be limited to the following tasks:

- carrying out programmes in the area of systems development, that is development of standards and supporting the network of institutions implementing the projects;
- carrying out national range programmes, which if transferred to the regional or local level would be performed in less efficient manner;
- implementing and promoting pilot solutions;
- monitoring and evaluation of the projects and programmes, development of recommendations and suggestions for the government regarding legal and institutional changes, financing and purposes of the programming;
- information and promotion with respect to programmes, procedures, best practices, maintaining databases and rendering accessible to the public.

In order to make decentralisation possible without harming efficiency and effective management of public money, appropriate preparation of public institutions, commercial firms and NGOs is necessary. For this purpose, training courses for the personnel of future public and non-government contractors are planned along with actions developing and implementing services provision standards for the employment and other social policy programmes, developing procedures and an effective information exchange system.

PART III

New Forms of Governance in Practice

> *Economic development problems and social exclusion concerns have a clear dimension at local level, yet responsibility for labour market policy is often devolved to the regions. Therefore, decentralisation per se does not guarantee better policy co-ordination, and partner relationships between labour market authorities and local actors involved in economic and social development are required to complete the process successfully and improve local governance. Building effective partnerships is a difficult task, however, and new forms of governance are being experimented with to avoid some of the problems met with local partnerships.*

ISBN 92-64-10470-4
Managing Decentralisation
A New Role for Labour Market Policy
© OECD 2003

PART III

Chapter 16

Local Partnerships: Different Histories, Common Challenges – A Synthesis

by

Mark Considine
University of Melbourne

The process of reform in OECD countries has now produced a remarkable range of models, plans and trajectories involving partnerships at the local level (Balloch and Taylor, 2001; McCarthy, 1998; Considine, 2001). At the forefront of these developments is the emergence of new decentralised networks that seek to improve both economic development and social inclusion (see Chapter 18 by Prats-Monné, and Chapter 17 by Stewart). In a number of these cases there is strong evidence suggesting that improvements in job creating, better labour market flexibility and enhanced training opportunities can be incorporated into local development plans (see O'Callaghan, Chapter 20, Eberts, Chapter 19 and Popov, Chapter 25). It is also true, at least in some leading countries, that "the case has yet to be won for partnership as a legitimate means of delivering high quality public services" (Commission on Public Private Partnerships, 2001).

OECD research from the early 1990s has been focused upon the desirability of bringing social partners together to address problems of unemployment (OECD, 1993; see also Chapter 18 by Prats-Monné). These pioneering initiatives were responsible for showing how easily programmes and initiatives can fail if different public and private interests do not achieve sustained forms of co-operation. As a result we are now seeing a new emphasis being placed upon ways to make such projects more *resilient* in the face of changing environmental circumstances, more *durable* across different local iterations, and more able to achieve results that are *sustainable* beyond the first generations of heavily subsidised projects (see Chapter 26 by Cullen). In other words the new frontier is less to do with the desirability of such initiatives than with ways to enhance the local *institutions* used to develop and support them.

In the academic literature on local governance a strong emphasis has recently been given to cities, districts and regions that have developed a "software" of trust, reciprocation and know-how trading among both economic and civic agents (Putnam, 1993; Considine and Lewis, 2003; see also Chapter 17 by Stewart). This literature is interested in the way "social capital" contributes to economic development and how such social capital itself is defined by local actors as a valued asset made up from "networks together with shared norms, values and understandings that facilitate co-operation within or among groups" (OECD, 2001a). Unfortunately this research has also pointed towards conservative conclusions, including the idea that these local systems tend to be path-dependent, or in other words, set on a path by their history and unable to be easily modified. For example, this criticism has been made by some reviewers of Putnam's celebrated study of Italian regions (Feigenbaum, 1995).

But a less determinist view of networks of local actors is one that views them as a structural property that can be altered by deliberate policy and improved governance. If we agree that this form of "organisational asset" is actually a collective good that is made up of a specific type of relationship between individuals and organisations, we can see that the research literature actually has quite a lot to say about how this network can be activated. For example the work of Flap (1991) shows that key social resources include the number or persons (or groups) in one's social network who are prepared or obliged to help one when called upon to do so. Once viewed as an actionable variable (rather than as an historical constraint) this form of reciprocation can presumably be encouraged by supporting the values of co-operation (a cultural strategy) and by enhancing the incentives to invest in reciprocal activity (an economic strategy).

Of course we should also acknowledge that the network research literature, along with the partnerships discourse that has been informed by it, has some serious conceptual problems yet to be resolved. We have already touched upon the greatest of these, the problem of path-dependence. The other one that needs to be kept in mind when devising and assessing actual projects is the problem of network closure. What makes a group strong in social capital terms may be the same thing that makes it exclusive and restrictive. Density of ties between a group of firms and government agencies may well enhance the prospect of economic development, but is can also be a means by which outsiders are kept from participating, some classes of insiders are restricted to limited roles and information flows are confined to one or two well-worn pathways.

We do not need to spend too much time on this theoretical level before we see that the exciting new horizons of "social capital", "partnerships" and "social network" research in fact contains an important conundrum, a conundrum that speaks directly to the challenge we face in developing strategies at the local level. On one side of the conundrum is the observation that networks need significant *internal coherence* and high levels of internal connectivity in order to develop the organisational assets which individuals and groups require for economic development and projects of social inclusion. On the other side of the conundrum is the equally compelling observation that it is probably the quality and effectiveness of links and ties from the local network *outwards to other networks* or domains which ultimately determines how well the network functions in creating innovations, learning from innovations pioneered elsewhere, and gaining access to other critical resources not available locally. As Lin (2001) observes, "To argue that closure or density is a requirement for social capital is to deny the significance of bridges, structural holes, or weaker ties".

Where these questions inform our understanding of the new partnerships movement is precisely at the point where these new developments begin to ask questions about the ingredients of their own success. We may summarise these questions in the manner of the OECD study (2001b) by asking how the partnerships structure themselves to manage local coherence among actors (horizontal governance) and also engage successfully with other key actors at the national level (vertical governance).

The partnership movement

The partnership movement is yet to be identified in a clear and consistent manner across all jurisdictions (Cullen, Chapter 26 and Stewart, Chapter 17). It may be that this will never happen and that instead we will see a series of partnership modes evolve in different countries – perhaps following the already evident welfare state traditions (Esping-Andersen, 1990). Certainly there is some indication that types of partnering reflect different histories of corporatism, social democracy and liberalism. Nevertheless we can certainly say that some broader common aspirations are emerging in these local experiments.

Without exaggerating their virtues, the best of these examples seem to have done the two of the things most commentators agree are necessary – to have generated improvements in levels of local economic development, and to have encouraged the emergence of new forms of governance among public and private actors in order to help support this development. In many of the cases there is also evidence that those involved are attempting to "de-functionalise" local governance systems by building bridges between different programmes and spheres of interest, and by seeking to attack deep systemic problems by using a multi-dimensional approach to such things as health, education and joblessness (Balloch and Taylor, 2001). Obviously there are echoes of previous community development movements in these new experiments. But perhaps because the neo-liberal reforms of the 1980s and 1990s have challenged almost every part of the contemporary political systems in the OECD to rethink the boundary between state and market, the new partnerships are more ambitious and contain much more attention to questions of governance and institutional design than did the earlier models of community development and local economic development. Nor are they as shy as their predecessors in embracing the needs of local entrepreneurs. This important symbiosis between neo-liberal strategies and partnership initiatives is at least as important as the obvious conflicts between the two conceptions of public/private relations. Certainly they both express a common interest in a new model of social action involving the stimulation of individual and collective "enterprising states" (Considine, 2001).

The first evaluations of these projects provide evidence that this process of bridging functional domains and building alliances among state, civil and private actors is a complex process. Much good work has been done to raise awareness and to establish a basic understanding of key concepts and methodologies. "There is evidence of a sophisticated level of understanding of the concept and general appreciation of the practical value of partnership" (OECD, 2001b). The next stage of evolution is to consider how the different *strategies, institutions* and *instruments* of partnership offer alternative possibilities.

What we notice about these different programmes is that they contain a number of common design elements, but rarely are all the elements found in any one example. In other words there are important "family resemblances" but we do not yet have a clear picture of the underlying genetic code or codes. What we do know is that the resemblances involve the following five elements:

- the use of partnerships to link governments and social actors;
- the focus of such partnerships on area-based initiatives;
- a willingness to decentralise public services;
- a desire to enhance local economic competitiveness;
- a desire to foster social inclusion.

The purpose of this chapter is to reflect upon some of the experiences to date of these important reforms and to suggest how they may offer opportunities for better governance in the future. This is primarily an institutional design puzzle (Goodin, 1996) in which we can regard these new arrangements and commitments as a dual structure. On one hand they provide important and distinctive *action channels* through which local and central actors are able to produce important breakthroughs. On the other hand they are themselves a form of closure or sets of *boundaries* against alternative or unwelcome developments. In considering both action channels and constraints we have some choices to make about the kinds of *capacities* we want these systems to develop over time. In the UK case (see Chapter 17 by Stewart) this is evident in the type of leadership that the partnership models develop. In Norway (see Chapter 23 by Knutzen), the choice is much more to do with the ability of county councils to make good use of new budget powers, while in the Swedish example (Chapter 24 by Svenningsson) the new forms of partnering must negotiate a powerful tradition of national policy direction which is only slowly loosening its grip on local structures. In other words, in considering the prospects for partnership we seek to include some consideration of local institutional history and interactive effects of current institutional arrangements, such as the impact of national targets, budget systems and traditions of social partner involvement in national policy making.

The diversity of the partnerships currently being explored is itself a challenge. It is difficult to generalise about such a diffuse set of experiences. Both the UK (Chapter 17 by Stewart) and Ireland (Chapter 20 by O'Callaghan) provide a diversity range of intersecting and overlapping partnership arrangements at local and regional levels. As we know, Ireland is a much discussed example of this pattern of economic and social development. Here we find the central government using local partnerships to help devise re-insertion initiatives for unemployed people. Using a national Framework Agreement, each disadvantaged area forms its own working group made up of community groups, employers and other civic groups (OECD, 2001b). In the first stage of development these initiatives were run on an experimental basis and received little attention from the public employment service (FÁS). Co-operation between the community-based networks and the PES was allowed to evolve at the local level, with policy makers encouraging FÁS staff to work on secondment to the community initiatives. While this trajectory may have insulated the FÁS from the need to make more radical changes to its own organisation, the approach has certainly had the advantage of promoting significant empowerment of community networks, a condition which might well have been jeopardised by forcing a top-down model of bureaucratic reform upon local initiatives. However the local partnerships now have an "anomalous administrative status as quasi-public bodies" and one important new challenge they face is to improve and clarify their "linkages with existing local government structures" (Chapter 20 by O'Callaghan).

In another highly innovative approach, the Italian government has since 1996 been promoting its *programmazione negoziata*, or negotiated plans as a method for fostering development in vulnerable regions such as southern Italy. Melo (OECD, 2001b) points out that two elements create the framework of this approach. The first is use of "territorial pacts" for development in which area-based committees form together to receive national and European funds for development. A second strand includes two special laws, one designed to foster local businesses to modernise or restructure, the other to promote youth entrepreneurship.

In the case of the territorial pacts, the intention has been to encourage the formation of local consortia of businesses, municipal planners, banks and employer organisations to create an integrated development plan. Such plans are typically focused on tourism, local industry, services or agribusiness. Of special interest in the Italian case is the intelligent use of banks as "honest brokers" in the process of assessing projects and recommending funding. As the OECD review (OECD, 2001b) has pointed out, the Italian model has answered a number of important questions in regard to the transparency and fairness of the funding of local partnerships. It has not gone as far as some other examples in supporting the on-going structure of the partnership by creating a sustainable means for meeting costs. Closer alignment of economic goals with the need to address issues of social inclusion is also a challenge in this case.

This relationship between economic and social objectives causes strain in many partnerships and should be regarded as one of the most important "creative tensions" in the partnership movement as a whole. In the Italian cases, the emphasis is most firmly on the importance of economic outcomes, including the creation of new jobs in disadvantaged areas. What can social projects contribute to this outcome under the short term contracts that underpin partnership funding? Those with sympathy for the social agenda but compelled to meet strict output targets for sustainable jobs tend to take the view of one of the administrators interviewed in Sicily (Considine, 2003) – "The thing we find with social projects is that they only grow while it rains" – or in other words, they jobs only last while there is public funding. The challenge is obviously to get a better fit between social projects and programmes that link "civic entrepreneurs" to existing services being run by local and regional governments.

A similar point is made in regard to the Austrian territorial pacts (see Chapter 21 by Förschner). Here we find one of the best examples of capacity building by central government. But there remains "relatively weak co-operation with economic departments and entrepreneurs". The importance of finding a strong link back to the national economic planning departments is critical here. In many countries the social ministries are a "poor relation" in the overall structure of the national government and are confined to dealing with the "effects" of the economy, not its restructuring or strengthening. Undoubtedly one of the key tasks of the local governance structure of the partnerships is to prove the case for local development to these powerful economic departments. The Austrian path offers one of the most optimistic possibilities for achieving this because it includes a central Co-ordination Unit with a responsibility for know-how transfer.

These examples show us that in building partnerships a lot depends upon where you begin. If the starting point is community organisations, NGOs and civic engagement, it may take some time for state agencies, and particularly economic ministries to become integrated. If, on the other hand, the starting point is local industry and employer organisations, it may take time to find a means to include social questions such as training, social services etc.

This suggests that the process of developing partnerships needs to have its own internal strategy of deliberate strengthening through a model of the "learning system" or "expert system" development. It is difficult to generalise across all cases in suggesting how such a reflexive approach might work. However there is much to be learned from identifying the key elements in the models already discussed and using this as a means to draw some conclusions about the "revisability" (Goodin, 1996) of these new institutions – that is, their capacity to change in the face of new needs and demands.

- If the traditional "line accountability" of bureaucracies to legislatures no longer captures the public roles of private actors, where do these new roles fit within the constitutional architecture?
- Do the new partnership agreements or contracts include robust new forms of accountability?
- If "civil society actors" are to be regarded as part of an enlarged democratic sector, what obligations will they assume in relation to non-member citizens?
- Where the main instruments of formal steering and accountability are such things as contracts and performance measures, is there adequate attention paid to creating or preserving cultural capital such as trust, commitment, long term planning, etc.?

At the core of these recent changes we find a strong interest in having private agents become directly involved in the delivery of public services. While this is a general trend in most countries it has a number of quite different manifestations including: i) privatisation involving the removal of a service from the public sphere; ii) contracting-out in which the service remains public but is delivered by private contract; and iii) partnership in which public and private actors share responsibility for the creation of public goods. In each of these cases the turn away from traditional bureaucracy is supported by economic theories of organisation which draw on Agency Theory and Transaction Cost Analysis in order to qualify the advantages of different forms of service provision and different levels of risk (Williamson, 1975; Moe, 1984).

The partnership model and current practice

The architecture of local partnerships and new forms of local governance is complex and subject to rapid change (see Chapter 19 by Eberts and Chapter 22 by Geddes).

Yet when considered from the vantage point of institutional design there are a number of common challenges to do with mandates, accountability, performance measurement, allocation of funds and decision rules. Rather than discuss partnerships as a general concept it therefore makes sense to disentangle these different problems and reflect upon the way these are being addressed in each case.

Table 16.1. **Partnership governance**

Instruments	Issues
Mandates	• Goals must be clear • Timelines must be specified • Contributions need to be explicit • Lead agency must have sufficient authority
Budgets	• Clear published criteria needed for gaining national funding • Allocation system needs to be transparent • Funding should be independently supervised • Adequate funding horizons needed • Incentives needed to allow partnerships to accumulate efficiency savings
Partnership agreements	• Goals and outcomes defined • Partner contributions defined • Horizontal and vertical accountability defined • Decision rules established • Obligations to local and national communities defined.
Project selection	• Avoid duplicating market mechanisms • Emphasise creation of spillovers • Economic viability and political support should be assessed separately.
Performance management	• Goals linked to outcome measures • Partnership indicators aligned with key performance indicators of key public agencies • Indicators included for new development and innovation • Start-up indicators focus on desired inputs • Evolution of start-up indicators toward outcomes indicators linked to incentives
Human capital	• Audit of current brokerage skills needed • Partnerships with training agencies able to improve core competencies needed • Training support needed for board members, NGO representatives, etc. • Evaluation of staff secondments and other recruitment strategies needed

Source: Author for the OECD.

Mandates

In order to achieve sustained local improvement through an integrated approach, local or regional partnerships need to be based upon a clear mandate, preferably expressed in a company charter or trust deed. Clarity of mandate and clarity regarding the authority of the partnership organisation is essential to sustainability. Weak mandates create weak authority structures (OECD, 2001b). In the case of the Danish partnerships the mandate was clear and this helped governmental actors and others to contribute effectively (*idem*). In contrast, the lack of a clear mandate was seen as a problem for the Irish partnerships (*idem*). Without a clear mandate there is a likelihood that there will be conflicts with other government priorities and with other national targets. Such conflicts can never be avoided altogether, but the likelihood that they will lead to blockage and demotivation of the partnership process is highest where the mandate is loose and non-binding.

The elements of the mandate that are most important are those concerning the way governmental agencies will co-operate. The ideal mandate is one in which a lead agency (such as Treasury) has responsibility for bringing all other departments and municipal organisations together under an act of parliament which empowers the consortium to carry our defined tasks. A paradox of the whole movement towards localism and decentralisation is that it requires a powerful patron at the central government level, otherwise the mandate is too diffuse to support long-term actions.

A second question to be addressed in the mandate is whether or not the partnership is actually going to deliver services, or merely acts as a planning organ for existing services. There are some problems with those partnerships which do not evolve past the planning and co-ordinating stage. Although one could imagine a scenario in which one begins with the planning function or with consultation, and then later moves to actual service delivery, the risks involved in being defined only as a "talk-shop" are high. It therefore seems that the best partnerships are likely to be ones in which actual services are included as a core element of the formal mandate. These may be services to ordinary citizens, or services to members of the consortium. The more tangible the service the stronger the mandate is likely to be.

However this need to produce tangible results is not without risks. The OECD study of partnerships (2001b) shows that in several cases the service delivery activity of partnerships may be viewed by the public service as a competitor and as a result these existing public services may resist co-operation or find co-operation difficult. If this results in the creation of duplicated networks there will obviously be serious cost problems. A second challenge for partnership involved in service delivery is that they may not be as competent as existing agencies, may not have the length of experience and skills, and may not be as well staffed as existing public services. It is therefore important to view the involvement of partnerships in service delivery as part of the overall fabric of existing services. In an ideal mandate, the partnership would have clear authority to bring local actors together, foster pathways among existing services and negotiate new services where those are needed.

Budgets

The most important steering device in partnership development is the budget. In practice the budget is a number of different instruments such as bids, approval processes, audits, incentives and rules of allocation. The starting point in most partnerships is some process by which the resources of different actors are focused upon a common set of objectives. While the partnership itself may not be the budget holder, its role in helping co-ordinate resource allocations and bring improved effectiveness to the budget commitments of others is crucial.

The budget question has two dimensions. First, and most importantly, local partnerships need to have influence on the development funds from national and European agencies and the methods for targeting these funds need to be transparent, performance-based and enduring. There are some jurisdictional issues to be navigated here as European agencies are obliged to respect national political imperatives. Nor is it clear that local partnerships have any right to expect a hearing from Brussels if their own national governments adopt either a contrary or blocking position. The new experience of "target-based tripartite contracts and agreements" between the Commission, a member state and a local partnership provide the first strong indicator that this gap might now be addressed (see Chapter 18 by Prats-Monné).

Transparency involves the establishment of clear criteria and the use of an honest system of allocation among contending partnership consortia. The Italians have had success with using banks in this process and the Australians have used law firms to supervise major allocations in the employment services field. In both examples the presence of an impartial broker has helped rescue the budget process from disrepute.

The third aspect of the budget process that is important is the setting of a reasonable time period for the development of partnerships. Unless national and European governments commit to long term funding there is little hope that major private interests will devote resources to new initiatives. The temptation for government is to make time horizons short so that problems can be detected, or so that a greater variety of projects can be tried. But the case evidence suggests that only where time periods of five years or more are anticipated will key actors make commitments. Of course this does not mean that funding is guaranteed at a fixed rate, but merely that partnerships can expect to be able to make submissions for support in the reasonable expectation that funding will continue.

The fourth aspect of the budget process that needs explicit institutional development is the process for allowing partnerships to accumulate their own local resources. It is essential for the durability of partnerships that they achieve some level of financial independence, at least to the extent necessary to employ staff and maintain information gathering activities (see Chapter 25 by Popov). The experience in the case studies suggests that most partnerships remain dependent upon central governments for their survival. Rules are needed for permitting a percentage of funds managed to be reserved for overheads. Such rules need to include provision for an equitable distribution of accumulated funds in the event the partnership is dissolved. Where the majority of such funds originate from government it is important to provide guarantees that any accumulated funds will only be dispersed to public agencies and will not be diverted to individuals. The Austrian case is important in this regard and may provide a useful experience for others seeking a more secure basis for the funding of local capacity (see Chapter 21 by Förschner). There is also much to be learned from the Russian example where local partners take responsibility for funding the core costs of the partnership (Chapter 25 by Popov).

One of the reasons for using the partnership approach to co-ordinate service delivery is that through co-operation, various agencies can deliver services in a more effective manner. This has the potential to save money if clients no longer need to be treated by many different agencies in separate places. Where is this saved resource to be accumulated? In order to ensure that partnerships benefit from the efficiencies they help create, it is desirable for these results to be made transparent. In more formal partnerships involving joint production of services (such as "one-stop shops" or networked services) the "co-operation dividends" created by these forms of co-operation need to be distributed fairly among contributors at both the central and local levels. While it is not necessary for all partnerships to become large budget holders or to accumulate large funds in their own right, the real costs of co-operation should be factored into these budgets. Some evidence exists in the case study literature to indicate that partnerships lack the secure funding base needed to maintain themselves and their core staff on a fully professional basis. As partnering matures as a form of governance we should expect a stronger, results-based link to be forged between partnerships and the various fund-holders (firms, public services etc) who benefit from their efforts.

Partnership agreements

In each of the countries surveyed the partnerships have come into being by a different means. A mixture of "bottom-up" and "top-down" methods is evident and we should expect that to be the case in the future (see Chapter 17 by Stewart and Chapter 24 by Svenningsson). However, one of the side effects of this diversity of initiatives is that it is often less than clear who the partners really are or what their responsibilities might be. Some interests are invited by government to become involved and stay only while government provides incentives. In other cases these private interests are consulted at arms length from the actual partnership and are more like consumers of the partnership service. In other cases the partnership seeks to express a separate governance tradition to the one based on the central state's role. This is part of the story in the US example (see Chapter 19 by Eberts) where "since colonial times, there has been a lingering suspicion of the power of the national government" and so local services seek to express a different, localised, form of democracy. In many of these cases it is not yet clear what the status of being a partner means in terms of legal responsibility, contributions of funds, obligations to adopt policies, and rights to vote on key decisions. What is healthy is that many established partnerships have this question on their agenda and have not stopped asking how the partners fit as "stakeholders", "consumers", "equals" or "owners".

As with other aspects of the local development process we should not aspire to any kind of uniformity but instead seek to improve the strength of alternative models and encourage them to learn from one another. But for sake of clarity, let us suppose that there are two general types of partnering models – let us call one the "corporate partnership" and the other the "consultative partnership". In each case a different kind of agreement should be struck between contributors. In the first type we should expect a defined programme of action controlled by the partners themselves, largely funded by them and controlled by them. In the second type the partners act as a forum for influencing other actors such as the Treasury or the EU fund holders. In both these examples there is a need for partners to be explicit about the level of accountability they will adopt, and then to devise decision rules that are appropriate to that level. As the partnership movement takes shape it would also be desirable to develop and publish model rules and examples of good agreements.

Project selection

The core of all partnerships is the selection of a set of projects that will create prosperity and enhance inclusiveness. In many cases, these projects will involve government support for new infrastructure developments. In other cases, the projects will involve public support for the renewal of private industries through provision of new technology, subsidised plant and equipment or training. And in some other cases, the projects will bring public and private agencies together in a new organisational form to co-produce a service such as aged care facilities or training for young entrepreneurs.

In developing the governance arrangements for such projects a number of important considerations must be included in deliberations. First and foremost the partnership must be clear about the "value adding" that is to take place. It makes little sense and may be self-defeating for support to be given to projects that would have been developed anyway by the existing firms. If the economic viability of the project is so clear and strong that conventional methods could be used to fund it, there is little value in devoting scarce partnership resources to it. While it is tempting for partnerships to select such projects for inclusion in their list because success will be assured and political support easy to achieve, the overall effect upon the local economy will not necessarily be significant in the long term. The exception to this is that in their early stages the partnerships often need to secure a strong reputation among firms, including those with a solid economic base. Helping healthy firms to grow is not a bad method of creating a strong reputation. However the strategy obviously needs to mature from this level towards helping marginal companies to improve and from a focus on single enterprises to a focus on sectors, districts and networks.

The evaluation of projects should therefore include a mechanism for including other lending and project management agencies, or for projects organised for already strong businesses to be supported on a reciprocal or cost-recovery basis. Mentoring, know-how trading and shared use of technology between established and emerging firms in a district are some examples of how partnerships could use such an approach without fear of duplicating existing private capital markets or distorting the normal risk-return payoff for investors. A second consideration in the selection of projects is the creation of spillovers. The concept of spill-over is used to define the part of an economic benefit that does not flow back to the entrepreneur (Stiglitz and Wallsten, 2000). So, for example, if a local firm creates a successful tourist resort there is a good chance that the reputation of the area as a tourist destination will be enhanced. The resort's publicity and marketing will return profits to the firm but also create spillovers for others in the region. Partnerships are an important institutional device for supporting the entrepreneur who is in a position to generate spillovers and one might even argue that the partnership should consider its core purpose to be the identification and enhancement of spillovers, especially where they spill towards disadvantaged groups. Project assessment and evaluation should therefore explicitly target such spillovers. This would also assist partnerships to evaluate their impact in a manner more conducive to the assessment of strategic effects and not just project-level outcomes (Chapter 17 by Stewart).

Performance management

Performance-based management involves the planning, review and improvement of partnership activities using agreed data on both the external conditions and programme effects or impacts. Many of the current examples in the literature indicate problems with the use of performance management techniques. There appear to be two parts to this problem. In some cases the problem is one of rigidity resulting from the fact that public agencies that are part of a partnership structure find themselves unable to adapt their existing performance management system to accommodate new ideas and challenges arising from their partnership work. For example, in Finland, "stringent management by results has made it difficult for the PES to adapt services in the directions favoured by partnerships" (OECD, 2001b). A second problem is the fact that partnerships often have objectives which are difficult to quantify in the one to three year time horizons required in many public service key result areas (KRAs), programme targets and key performance indicators (KPIs). Geddes (Chapter 22 in this book) also points out that in the case of local area partnerships in the UK there is genuine differences of opinion about whether or not conventional performance measures should be used to judge there horizontal structures.

And of course, as with many public services, the work of the partnerships is often concerned with producing effects that are inherently difficult to evaluate. This is a notoriously difficult aspect of the governance process because many variables may influence key indicators such as the rate of unemployment or the level of investment in a locality. Nevertheless, local indicators are an essential element of responsible budgeting and over time can only serve to strengthen the partnership process.

In order to avoid role confusion it is desirable that the indicators of success for local partnerships be aligned with the internal performance indicators of the public bureaucracies involved in the partnership. Ideally this should be part of the process for negotiating the mandate of the partnership. That way it is possible for both to share responsibility for success and avoid blaming others for failure.

Since partnerships are usually concerned with producing effects in a defined territory over a medium term time period, the performance management system for the partnership itself needs to include a mix of input measures and outcome measures. Without short term input measures such as "number of community consultations", "number of project proposals reviewed" there will be a risk that partnerships run off track for long periods before anyone is in a position to take remedial action. But unless there are clear outcome measures built into the budget process, such as increases in local employment and successful inclusion of disadvantaged groups into the local economy, the ultimate effectiveness of partnerships will be difficult to demonstrate to the satisfaction of stakeholders.

It will also be obvious that exact performance measurement will be difficult when comparing the contributions of different members of the partnership. If several public agencies are involved it may be necessary for central agencies such as Treasury to pool the evaluation of this aspect of the work of these agencies. In other words, the government will need to separate this function from the rest of the work of these agencies and give it a set of its own indicators somewhat in the manner of a programme budget. Since there may be a tendency for agencies to try to shift blame for poor performance (or to monopolise credit for good outcomes) there is also a benefit in such partnerships having a chief sponsor or lead agency to exercise responsibility (and have accountability) for making sure that all the agencies make useful contributions.

To avoid excessive competition over results it is also important that KPIs include measures of good governance within partnerships. These measures could for example include feedback on how well partners shared data, learned to navigate one another's IT and planning systems, used meetings to resolve problems and be accountable for decisions, and created improved outcomes for one another at the local level. These kinds of evaluations are identified in the case overview (OECD, 2001b) where a useful distinction is made between the usual forms of programme evaluation and the more sophisticated extra measures needed to comprehend and value the governance aspects of partnerships.

The final important point to note about this aspect of partnerships is that care must be taken to avoid developing a set of indicators that only measures currently accepted issues to the exclusion of all new priorities. While a core of medium term measures of such things as employment levels is obviously mandatory, to avoid the scenario in which partnerships loose their vitality and become only the representation of "last year's priorities", some indicators measuring innovation and new initiatives are essential. This is an essential step towards the development of a "culture of accountability", rather than merely a form of instrumental accountability (Considine, 2002).

Human capital

As well as a different kind of institutional structure, partnerships involve a new form of human agency. Existing skills in project management and negotiation are available to those who work in large organisations. In some of these settings there are forms of relationship management or brokerage which resemble the skills needed in partnerships. However the differences are also great. The skills required to navigate around the different divisions of a large bank in order to help a customer get the best service are quite different to those needed to assist a small firm to navigate among training agencies, public bureaucracies and municipal agencies in order to get a new project approved.

Because the new partnerships involve multi-agency relationships and multi-level approvals, the skills needed to create and sustain partnerships are complex and demanding. Although the rhetoric of the partnership model suggests that contributing agencies are committed to the partnership ethos, in practice many partnerships "suffer from bureaucratic and funding straightjackets which seem to prevent suitable and sensitive partnerships and 'joined-up' solutions" (Coles, 2000). What this means in practice is that success depends upon their being a cadre of professionals able to navigate around obstacles and gain clearances from those in authority in several different organisations.

The broker's skill base is a unique mix of public policy knowledge, awareness of industry constraints and goals, and capacities to communicate effectively and patiently with the local community. In the Irish case there is evidence that secondments from the bureaucracy to the community sector is one valuable strategy for building this skill base. In New Zealand, the employment service has had some success in recruiting people into the administrative rank from older age groups where more diverse life experiences in fields such as teaching, policing, running a small business prove to be a strong base from which to develop the needed negotiating skills to work well with employers and jobseekers.

What the case literature shows us is that unless a concerted effort is made to train and support this new class of partnership brokers, it will soon prove impossible for more complex partnerships to find the necessary executive staff to maintain their operations. It would be useful for one of the key agencies in this field to sponsor a skills audit and a review of training opportunities. Professionals who already have experience in case management, relationship management, project management and other related fields need to be targeted by government and given incentives to undertake training in partnership brokering. It would also be useful for key agencies to promote internships and staff secondments so that skills and "know-how trading" can occur across jurisdictions. The Irish case provides some interesting examples of this kind of intermediation among partnerships to improve advocacy and influence on policy, and to raise standards of partnering (see Chapter 20 by O'Callaghan and Chapter 26 by Cullen).

Conclusions

Partnerships require forms of local governance that are able to satisfy both vertical and horizontal demands. This is difficult to do and we should expect a good deal of negotiation to take place, and perhaps a degree of healthy conflict. We should not expect partnerships to conform to the usual design features of bureaucracy, in either its public or private form. The governance systems that evolve from this movement should be expected to be hybrid in nature. That is to say, they will need some of the characteristics of a traditional corporate structure (chain of command, specialisation, results oriented, management-centred) and some of the characteristics of a community organisation (value-based, inclusive, self-managing). To satisfy the accountability needs of a democratic institution, the partnership structure should include a clear mandate and an agreed budget process, both of which need to be transparent and revisable in the light of experience and according to agreed principles.

Partnerships receiving central funding must expect to have to negotiate their mandate and budget in an open and ethical manner. But to avoid the situation in which partnerships become nothing more than the instrument of central government, there needs to be power vested in the local consortia to help define objectives, express local values and identify valued local priorities. It cannot be assumed that any group of civic associations has all the answers to such questions and like the municipalities these agencies should test their vision of future development against public opinion by conducting open planning sessions, citizen juries and other methods for gaining public input into decisions. A hallmark of a good local partnership would therefore be the quality of the participation and engagement it can generate among the citizenry. Closely related to this is the maturing of relations with local government, a challenge for many partnerships.

The most important practical achievement of partnerships is recognisable in the services they produce. This can be at either of two levels. First, many partnerships seek to co-produce services for ordinary clients such as job seekers and local firms. Second, partnerships produce services for the agencies involved in more direct functions – such as state agencies.

Many of the best examples in the research literature involve partnerships brokering new activities or projects where industry and government have co-operated in building-up local businesses. Often these initiatives have involved creating jobs for previously excluded groups such as unemployed people, refugees or women returning to work. Individual projects are an attractive starting point for most partnerships because they are tangible and easily defined. The more challenging partnership work however, is in the field of on-going services linking public and private providers. Creating new partnerships to deliver or to help co-ordinate multi-dimensional services for the aged, for local businesses, for environmental improvement will all need new skills and more sophisticated forms of institution building.

In the services field there are large untapped opportunities for agencies to get together and develop concerted programmes and joint processes for treating common problems. To avoid the situation where such partnerships become "re-bureaucratised" there needs to be careful attention given to mandate and budget issues, and the training of partnership brokers must become a high priority.

It should not be assumed that the partnership is best suited to deliver all these new services themselves. Often the best contribution they can make is to become a vehicle for existing agencies to co-operate better without the need of a new organisational structure at the local level. It is difficult to make a single generalisation about the alternatives of co-ordination of existing services *versus* creating a new service system around the partnership. Some of the risks of the latter course have been identified above. Much depends upon judgments concerning the state of development of existing services and the capacity of partnerships to win support from them. Certainly there should be a reluctance to create more and more services alongside all the existing systems without a plan to eventually broker a more integrated approach. And whatever the starting point, the strength of the partnership movement remains its capacity to convince local and national actors to develop new governance arrangements that create and capture the benefits of co-operation.

Bibliography

BALLOCH, Susan and TAYLOR, Marylin (2001), "Can Partnership Work?", in Balloch and Taylor (eds.), *Partnership Working: Policy and Practice*, The Policy Press, Bristol.

BARNEY, Jay B. and OUCHI, William G. (eds.) (1986), *Organisational Economics*, Jossey-Bass, San Francisco.

BECK, Ulrich (1992), *Risk Society: Towards a New Modernity*, Trans. Mark Ritter, Sage, London.

BOSTON, Jonathan, MARTIN, John, PALLOT, Tune and WALSH, Pat (eds.) (1991), *Reshaping the State: New Zealand's Bureaucratic Revolution*, Oxford University Press, Auckland.

CHRISTIANSEN, Peter Munk (1998), "A Prescription Rejected: Market Solutions to Problems of Public Sector Governance", *Governance*, Vol. 11, No. 3, July.

CIBORRA, Claudio U. (1996), *Teams, Markets and Systems: Business Innovation and Information Technology*, Cambridge University Press, Cambridge.

COLES, Bob (2000), *Joined-up Research, Policy and Practice: a new agenda for change?*, Youth Work Press, Leicester.

COMMISSION ON PUBLIC PRIVATE PARTNERSHIPS (2001), *Final Report – Building Better Partnerships*, Institute for Public Policy Research, London.

CONSIDINE, Mark (2002), "The End of the Line? Accountable Governance in the Age of Networks, Partnerships and Joined-Up Services", *Governance*, Vol. 15, No. 1, January, pp. 21-40.

CONSIDINE, Mark (2001), *Enterprising States: The Public Management of Welfare to Work*, Cambridge University Press, Cambridge.

CONSIDINE, Mark and LEWIS, Jenny M. (2003), "Bureaucracy, Network, or Enterprise? Comparing Models of Governance in Australia, Britain, the Netherlands and New Zealand", *Public Administration Review*, Vol. 63(2), pp. 131-140.

CONSIDINE, Mark and LEWIS, Jenny M. (1999), "Governance at Ground Level: The Frontline Bureaucrat in the Age of Markets and Networks", *Public Administration Review*, Vol. 59(6), pp. 467-480.

ESPING-ANDERSEN, Gosta (1990), The Three Worlds of Welfare Capitalism, Polity, Cambridge.

FEIGENBAUM, Harvey (1995), "Review of Making Democracy Work: Civic Traditions in Modern Italy", *Governance*, Vol. 8, No. 3, July, pp. 436-437.

FLAP, Henk (1991), "Social Capital in the Reproduction of Inequality", *Comparative Sociology of the Family, Health and Education*, Vol. 20, pp. 6179-6202.

GARDNER, M.R. and ASHBY, W.R. (1970), "Connectance of Large Dynamic (Cybernetic) Systems: Critical values for Stability", *Nature*, Vol. 228, 5273.

GOODIN, Robert E. (ed.) (1996), *The Theory of Institutional Design*, Cambridge University Press, Cambridge.

KOOIMAN, Jan (1993), "Socio-Political Governance: Introduction", in J. Kooiman (ed.), *Modern Governance: New Government-Society Interactions*, Sage, London.

KRASNER, Stephen D. (1983), "Structural Causes and Regime Consequences: regimes as intervening variables", in S.D. Krasner (ed.), *International Regimes*, Ithaca, Cornell University Press.

LE GRAND, Julian and BARTLETT, Will (eds.) (1993), *Quasi-Markets and Social Policy*, Macmillan, Houndsmills.

LIN, Nan (2001), *Social Capital: A theory of social structure and action*, Cambridge University Press, Cambridge.

MCCARTHY, Dennis (1998), "The Genesis and Evolution of the Irish state's Commitment to Social Partnership at the Local Level", in P. Kirby and D. Jacobsen (eds.), *In the Shadow of the Tiger: New Approaches to Combating Social Exclusion*, DCU Press, Dublin.

MOE, Terry (1984), "The New Economics of Organisation", *American Journal of Political Science*, Vol. 28, pp. 739-777.

OECD (2001a), *The Well-being of Nations: the Role of Human and Social Capital*, Paris.

OECD (2001b), *Local Partnerships for Better Governance*, Paris.

OECD (1993), *Partnerships: the Key to Job Creation, Experiences from OECD Countries*, Paris.

ORMSBY, Maurice J. (1998), "The Provider/Purchaser Split: A Report from New Zealand", *Governance*, Vol. 11, No. 3, July.

SMITH, Steven Rathgeb and LIPSKY, Michael (1993), *Non profits for Hire: The Welfare State in the Age of Contracting*, Harvard University Press, Cambridge, Mass.

STEIN, Robert M. (1990), "The Budgetary Effects of Municipal Service Contracting: A Principal-Agent Explanation", *American Journal Of Political Science*, Vol. 34, pp. 471-502.

STIGLITZ, Joseph E. and WALLSTEN, Scott J. (2000), "Public-Private technology Partnerships: Promises and Pitfalls", in P. Vaillancourt Rosenau (ed.), *Public-Private Policy Partnerships*, The MIT Press, Cambridge Mass, pp. 37-58.

VISSER, Jelle and HEMERIJCK, Anton (1997), "A Dutch Miracle" *Job Growth, Welfare Reform and Corporatism in the Netherlands*, University of Amsterdam Press.

WALSH, Kieron (1995), *Public Services and Market Mechanisms. Competition, Contracting and the New Public Management*, Macmillan, Houndsmills.

WETTENHALL, Roger (1997), "Public Administration and Public Management: The Need for Top-Quality Public Service", in M. Considine and M. Painter (eds.), *Managerialism: The Great Debate*, Melbourne University Press, Melbourne.

WILLIAMSON, Oliver E. (1975), *Markets and Hierarchies: Analysis and Antitrust Implications*, Free Press, New York.

ISBN 92-64-10470-4
Managing Decentralisation
A New Role for Labour Market Policy
© OECD 2003

PART III
Chapter 17

Tackling the Challenge of Policy Integration

by
Murray Stewart
University of the West of England

From government to governance

The failings of government

"Governance" is different from government, which is commonly used to refer to the activities of the formal bodies through which society is governed – typically central and local government. The emergence of "governance" reflects the fact that traditional forms of government have weakened under the influence of diverse pressures, the capacity of state governments to plan, fund and manage social, economic and environmental change has diminished, and that the role and function of local government to plan locally and deliver locals services has been eroded.

In many countries there now exists a multiplicity of government and non-government agencies accountable to different government departments for different targets, each with different professional cultures and theoretical frameworks, with different systems of accountability, different financial regimes and all with considerable operational autonomy. It is difficult to overstate the organisational complexity that results, since while there are not only a large number of important organisational actors involved in the policy process, there are also different combinations of these actors involved in the delivery process at regional, local and neighbourhood levels, giving rise to problems of both vertical and horizontal integration. The existence of this disjointed government can be understood in the light of three strands of research – the literature of central-local state relations, the literature of implementation, and the literature of organisational (and inter-organisational) political sociology.

Much of the literature on central-local relations in the last twenty years has focused on the centralisation of state functions and on the dilution of local autonomy and democracy in the face of the quangos of the 1980s and the "new public management" of the 1990s. This literature has emphasised the extent to which the capacity of local governments has been weakened by the loss of statutory powers and duties and by a reduction in financial autonomy. The shift of functions to a range of non-local governmental bodies altered the local balance of power in terms of implementation, and this was matched by an increasing role for the centre in terms of planning and control. A related, although in some ways contradictory, theme has been that of the hollowing out of the nation state. Faced (in the European Union) with the growing influence of Brussels, the shift to agencies of much central government executive activity, and the decentralising tendencies evidenced by a re-emergent regionalism, central government is increasingly focussing on "core executive" functions. As the centre loses its functions, if not its budgetary control, so it becomes more reliant on other organisations for implementation (agencies, local authorities, partnerships, etc.). So while the institutions of local governance have lost their autonomy, central government has lost some direct control. The field has become more unmanageable and less susceptible to consistent management from either centre or periphery. In this changed environment of central/local relations, the traditional mechanisms of control and compliance model do not work. In post-communist Eastern Europe the shift from centralised structures to a more open democratic regional/local system poses similar issues (Reid, 2002).

At the same time, new models of implementation are emerging, and there is greater diversity of delivery systems relying on a mix of market, hierarchy and network. The hierarchical administrative modes associated with a central and local state bureaucracy have been challenged (although not replaced) by reliance on a market mode of governance. This embodied a shift to competitive bidding combined with contractualisation, contract compliance, and increased market regulation. The later new local governance purports to rely on networks, social capital, trust and partnership to draw together the variety of actors. Implementation, however, is not simply a matter of control of agencies with greater or lesser autonomy. There is a large literature which argues that the "implementation gap" emerges for a host of reasons. The top-down flow from policy is often imperfect, including poor communication, inadequate resource allocation, and poor policy specification. The implementation gap may also occur, however, because there is a separate implementation culture which derives from the bottom-up. This is a function of the inevitable freedom of action and scope for discretion which lies with those who implement and who are beyond the reach of the centre. Thus implementation structures, street level bureaucracy, and the discretion open to front line staff, may all distort policy intention.

A literature of organisational sociology emphasises power in organisations and looks to structure rather than agency as the determinant of organisational behaviour and hence successful implementation. Organisations are endowed with the power of their key interests (professional, political, administrative, occasionally users) and the delivery of policy is a function of the power struggles which flow through the "circuits of power". Within complex, multi-organisational delivery systems, government policy is not the sole driver of change, and the behaviour and actions of regulators, monitors, civil servants and others in private and not for profit sectors directly impact on the policy implementation system.

In summary, local governance confronts a realignment of state role and function, the dismantling of long-standing institutions, moves towards a new economy of welfare, an increased vulnerability to global competition and increased visibility of some of the more problematic issues of contemporary urban life. In terms of urban administrative processes there has also been the co-existence of, but tension between, hierarchy, market and network as the ideologies and practices of national governments shift in terms of the most appropriate and effective methods of allocating and managing resources.

The search for co-ordination

The historic failures of government inevitably pose questions about the effectiveness of the cultural, organisational, and administrative mechanisms which are in place to bring about the necessary new capacity building for integrated local governance. The "new governance" literature emphasises the importance of collaboration and co-ordination as the means of building a local institutional capacity to counter the challenges outlined above. Countering the tendencies to fragmentation and disconnectedness requires shifts both in the vertical relationships between centre, region, locality and neighbourhood, and in the horizontal linkages between organisations at different levels of the governance system. For some, this involves advocacy of "whole system" approaches (Wilkinson and Appelbee, 1999; Pratt et al., 1999; Six et al., 1999). These approaches are useful in offering an alternative way to understand and plan intervention within a complex set of interactions. They are based on the premise that complex systems need to be understood in terms of the interactions between parts of the system and its environment. These interactions involve feedback loops, whereby elements in the systems feed influence and information to each other over time. Outcomes are the result of the interaction of a large number of organisations and agents each of which is attempting to respond to a changing environment, by adapting behaviour and by shaping the environment itself. The system is "open" in the sense that there is constant interaction between each organisation or agent and all the other agencies that make up the environment they find themselves in.

Whole systems models are useful in recognising the interdependence of parts of the system of governance, but are less helpful in deciding precisely where to intervene. Systems models are inherently liable to failure as disequilibrium sets in. Holism is desirable in principle, difficult to achieve in practice. In effect, as argued above, all systems have particular drivers which maintain the system in motion and mediate the relationship between the parts and the whole. One of these drivers is the stance taken by central government towards system management, compliance, control and co-ordination. Equilibrium is achieved, or at least sought, through the imposition by government of a dominant administrative perspective which imposes itself on the institutions, norms and practices of governance and establishes common the roles and rules which must be applied to interagency working. Historically hierarchy dominated; then markets. Currently the dominant perspective is that of networks and partnership, the view that the meeting together of stakeholders with differing contributions to make to the solution of the "wicked" problems (Rittel and Webber, 1993) is the way forward. A second driver stems from the fact that the central state cannot address adequately the complexity of these wicked issues. Moves towards a more decentralised system therefore become appropriate – perhaps imperative – for the planning and implementation of programmes. In many countries these two drivers – networked, partnership governance on the one hand, decentralisation on the other – have coincided in the emergence of area-based initiatives, designed to address at the sub-national and often sub-regional level the failures of traditional government.

Area-based initiatives

There is now wide experience of ABIs (area-based initiatives) (Parkinson, 1998; DTLR, 2002). Although the form and function of such initiatives varies widely the broadening experience points to five main functional directions – stimulation of economy and employment, renewal of the physical environment, enhancement of social conditions and social relations, political engagement, and delivery of public services. Whilst it is increasingly acknowledged that a holistic integration is appropriate one or more of these functional directions can often be seen as the leading edge of area-based activity.

Economy and employment

The disadvantage experienced in particular areas can be attributed to lack of work, which in turn leads to lack of earned income and reliance on an inadequate social wage. Whether induced by the disappearance of traditional jobs (coal, steel, and manufacturing) or by the perceived inadequacies of labour supply (educational shortcomings, lack of skills, lack of work experience), economically driven initiatives have in general sought to improve the quality of labour supply and to ease access to the labour market. Demand for labour is less susceptible to policy intervention but area-based initiatives have tried to create more local jobs – historically by attracting investment into or close to disadvantaged areas or by stimulating the creation and growth of small business. Stimulation of the social economy, of community business, and of small business support address this latter issue, the creation of wider opportunities in larger firms the former. A range of labour supply mechanisms – education, work experience, mentoring, job shops, intermediate labour markets, targeted recruitment, and initiatives which attempt to "bridge the gap" or create "pathways to work" attempt to identify the most vulnerable in the labour market. In the UK, historically the Task Forces of the late 1980s and the New Deal for Unemployed of the late 1990s involved initiatives of this kind, whilst currently the New Start initiatives and Employment Zones fulfil the same function.

The physical environment

If the improvement of labour supply represents the favoured approach to economy and employment, then renewal of the physical stock has come close behind, and indeed the bulk of the criticism of past area-based initiatives has been that they have concentrated too much on physical improvements rather than on economic and social improvement. Thus the clearance of derelict land, the improvement of infrastructure and transport access, renewal of obsolescent housing, provision of advance factories or small industrial units has characterised many initiatives and indeed transformed the appearance – though less so the function – of many areas. An architectural/physical determinism has dominated many of the British area based initiatives from the post-war New Towns to the Urban Development Corporations of the 1980s. Many of the housing initiatives – Housing Action Areas, Estate Action, Renewal Areas – were characterised by heavy expenditure on the external residential fabric of areas at the expense of other functions.

Social conditions and social relations

The function of supporting enhanced social interaction and community organisation is rooted in the assumption that there is a decline in the quality of social relations which has brought about the reversal of the fortunes of some neighbourhoods. It is argued that the rebuilding of social capital based on trust and mutual interdependence can achieve neighbourhood turnaround if only the traditional habits of neighbouring and caring could be recreated. There is extensive new evidence about the nature of local social networks from the Joseph Rowntree Foundation research on neighbourhood images (Silburn et al., 1999; Cattell and Evans, 1999; Andersen et al., 1999; Wood and Vamplew, 1999), on the strengths of and pressures on family life – the Bristol-based study by Gill, Tanner and Bland (2000) for example – and on the nature of social cohesion in disadvantaged neighbourhoods (Forrest and Kearns, 1999; Page, 2000).

Much of the evidence focuses on the role of children as a pivotal element with networks mobilising around issues of childcare and schooling. Women play a crucial role. It is important, however, to remember some of the negative aspects of neighbourhood life – relations of trust and dependence built around drugs, crime, abuse and the function of illicit and often illegal power structures in maintaining oppressive systems of social relations (Hoggett, 1997).

Theoretically, this echoes the strong ties/weak ties debate (Granovetter, 1973) and invites discussion of the nature of social capital in building relationships within communities and between communities and the formal organisations of state and society (Woolcock, 1998; Taylor, 2000). In practice we see a huge range of area-based community capacity building initiatives involving community centres, organisational skills development, leadership support designed to invest in social capital and create a new social solidarity.

Political engagement

Political engagement rests on the assumption that the area/neighbourhood is disenfranchised and disconnected from the mechanisms which normally fulfil rights and offer equality in access to goods and services. A lack of information, the absence of aid and advice services in deprived neighbourhoods, the vulnerability of excluded communities in the face of bureaucratic administrative systems combine to deprive some communities of "voice" with the political system offering little redress and the choice of "exit" seldom open to the most disadvantaged groups. This interpretation of disadvantage challenges the processes of traditional representative democracy and argues that local elected councils and councillors have failed the disadvantaged neighbourhood. Initiatives which seek to respond to this challenge should enhance representative processes. In England this means the modernisation of local government (DETR, 2000a) through a range of measures which aim at ensuring political responsiveness, revitalising electoral procedures, providing mechanisms for scrutiny, and enhancing leadership.

The failure of public service delivery in disadvantaged neighbourhoods represents one of the major challenges to public policy. While failure is not confined to the public sector (financial services, retailing, leisure are equally absent), it is the shortcomings in housing management, health, education, environmental management – street cleaning, rubbish collection for example – that are pronounced. In different countries local municipalities are addressing these issue at neighbourhood level already – decentralisation schemes, neighbourhood offices, one stop shops, realigned front line working, for example. There are further proposals to extend this public service improvement programme into disadvantaged areas – neighbourhood management pilots are in progress in order to make services more responsive to local needs, more user-focused, more immediate in delivery.

The form in which initiatives appear, however, is also influenced both by the external environment of national government and regional agencies as well as by the by the micro-politics local inter-organisational working. Central government determines the way in which many initiatives must be implemented and denies local flexibility in implementation. The consequences are that the structures, processes, activities and outcomes are heavily centrally determined and the possibilities of locally sensitive solutions are reduced. Thus area-based initiatives become much more the manifestation of central policies in areas than a reflection of local community based solutions. The specificity of the area becomes diluted, place becomes a less important variable in initiative design, and initiatives become homogenised as programme guidelines determine the form in which initiatives will emerge.

Nevertheless the pursuit of local discretion and autonomy remains an espoused goal in many countries, even if central prescription can determine the shape of local arrangements and in particular establish the rules under which ABIs operate. Certainly in the UK and with increasing frequency elsewhere, partnerships are the required form, with local partnerships engaging local stakeholders in an attempt to develop collaborative, co-ordinated and integrated working.

Partnerships

Understanding partnerships

Over recent years there have been numerous studies looking at area-based partnership working (OECD, 2001; Parkinson, 1998; Geddes, 1998), at community-based partnerships (Skelcher and Lowndes, 1998; Purdue et al., 2000), and at collaboration (Huxham, 1996; Sullivan, 2002; Kantor, 1994). The early work of Macintosh (1993) remains helpful. She distinguished between transformation (working in partnership to convince the other partner(s) of your own values and objectives), synergy (working to produce added value beyond what would have been achieved separately) and budget enlargement (achieved when partnerships generate extra resources).

The impact of partnership working is a function of a number of features of joint working, and it is possible to categorise partnerships along a number of descriptive variables such as membership, status, structures, leadership, agendas, and organisational cultures. "Participatory" groups (Joldersma, 1997), and heterogeneous participatory groups in particular, are more likely to be open, thus increasing the scope for diversity and for generating wider understanding, but reducing the likelihood of agreement about aims and objectives. Such broad based groups have been termed "facilitating partnerships" (Stewart, 1998), so called because their primary role involves negotiation of contentious or politically sensitive issues and facilitation among partners with differing perspectives. Debate may arise either in relation to the ends to be achieved or the means to attain them. They tend to have wide-ranging objectives which are difficult to measure because they encompass macro-level goals or because the programme of specific objectives remains unclear and is subject to ongoing negotiation. They deal with long-standing issues of concern and attempt to address deeply rooted problems. A number of powerful stakeholding partners may be involved and sensitivities relating to the balance of power must be carefully addressed and respected.

"Facilitating" partnerships contrast with "co-ordinating" partnerships which relate primarily to the oversight, in both strategic and practical terms, of initiatives to which a wide range of organisations have committed themselves. Activities are either hived off to task-based bodies or are delegated to departments or sections within one or more of the partner authorities. Such partnerships deal with less politically sensitive and controversial issues and partners generally agree quickly on a broad agenda for the partnership. The lead is often taken by a dominant partner but the balance of power within the partnership is not especially delicate.

Finally there are "implementing" partnerships. They are specific in focus and time-limited in nature. They are responsible for the implementation of pre-agreed projects which are neither contentious nor highly politically sensitive. Project delivery is acknowledged as mutually advantageous to the key partners and the means by which it is to be effected is fairly clear. A key function of the partnership is to secure funding and resources for the projects and to manage the implementation process. Success is clearly defined and easily measured. These partnerships are concerned with pragmatic solutions and specified outputs and partner relations are neither problematic nor highly prioritised on the agenda.

Whilst many people would agree with the simple typology offered of three models of partnership, there is much less agreement about which partnerships fall into which type. Thus some participants in a particular partnership would perceive the structure as being primarily a facilitating one whilst other members of the same partnership would view it as an implementing partnership. This creates ambiguity in discourse within the group and places a premium on creating better understanding of the assumptions and starting points of different members of the participatory group.

Starting points are crucial. Few partnerships start from scratch. They build instead on past relationships and these foundations matter. In any locality – region, city, town or neighbourhood – there is a very particular past, and a unique geography. Every successful local intervention has to be based within the context of unique local circumstances. Research on area-based initiatives argues that there are five important dynamics that affect successful collaboration (DTLR, 2002):

- where the *political geography is clear*, boundaries are long established and at least some common boundaries exist between partner areas of responsibility it is easier to create the basis for collaboration at a strategic level;
- it is easier to build collaboration where there is a sense of shared *identity* and common interest;

- while new initiatives assume a blank canvass, in reality each area is already marked over and over by the *history* of previous initiatives;
- the problems facing local agencies have changed over *time*, and their capacity to deal with them has changed;
- *personalities* are crucial and collaborative working depends on the role of individuals.

Key elements in partnership working

Membership

Membership is crucial to partnerships and success is often a function of which stakeholders participate. Partnerships can be distinguished by whether their membership is open or closed, and also by whether their members are chosen, appointed, selected, elected or invited. The membership of ABI partnerships may be more or less closed according to the national and regional guidance. In addition, procedures may at least tire the smaller initiatives many of whose active members ail come from local voluntary or community organisations, or at most kill off risk as initiative fatigue sets in. The experience of community leaders in area based regeneration (Purdue *et al.*, 2000) is a salutary lesson to those who see community oriented area-based initiatives as the source for a new participative democracy (see above). The evidence from a wide range of studies (Hastings, 1996; Skelcher *et al.*, 1996) is that community interests can become marginalised and that power shifts slowly if at all. Procedures of project appraisal, monitoring, and implementation delay progress and disempower communities with the consequence that community leaders opt out and/or that professionals step in. There is also only modest evidence that local people benefit from the creation of these opportunities to shape their areas. In initiatives which are even more strongly dominated by central government priorities (*e.g.* in schools) the role of local interests such as parents is weaker than central influences such as performance targets.

Leadership

Collaborative and partnership working might appear to diminish the importance of leadership (because partnership may involve the suppression of strong leadership in the interests of consensus building). In practice leadership is as necessary in collaborative ventures as in single organisational developments. In relation to regeneration partnerships a threefold categorisation of leadership can be identified (Hambleton *et al.*, 2001).

- *Designed and focused* leadership provides a clear vision of future direction, a firm manifesto, and a dedicated budget. The leader is high profile, imposes influence and leverage on others, relies on a dedicated staff, offers patronage to supporters, holds office by virtue of personal election/appointment, derives authority from position, and is directly accountable to a constituency of followers. In mayoral models, this leadership is personal and individualised, although it is possible to also envisage designed and focused leadership by a small group.

- *Implied and fragmented* leadership provides a consensual (and often confused) view of direction, operates on an implicit rather than explicit forward plan and puts together packages of resources through joint funding arrangements. Leadership is virtually invisible, depends on a team of secondees/temporary staff, has delegated and often shifting membership, derives authority from collective sanction, and is less transparently accountable.
- *Emergent and formative* leadership relies on implementation to shape policy, reflects pragmatism in developing future direction, uses *ad hoc* resources to make progress, emphasises learning as the basis for further action, derives authority from getting things done, is accountable for what is done not what is said (Huxham and Vanger, 2000).

The conclusions to be drawn from practice is that designed and focused leadership (the mayoral model) can offer a more autonomous leadership dependent on style and representational legitimacy. The fragmented, multi-organisational model, which implies a collaborative approach to leadership, may offer a weak leadership which is subservient to external policy influence and dominated by bureaucratic arrangements. The concept of formative leadership confirms this view of the fragility of partnership structures and processes to procure desired ends.

Nevertheless even those in ostensibly powerful leadership positions (those designed into focused leadership roles) find themselves only partially able to control events, and are susceptible to other influences in the formative stage. Because partnerships are collaborative, directed in practice largely to building consensus, strong leadership can be perceived to be inimical to joint working. In such cases, "strong" leaders are suspected to be taking over. Thus leaders can carry apparently contradictory roles, on the one hand generating collaboration, inclusiveness and consensus, while on the other hand exercising pragmatic but powerful manipulation of diverse interests. There can, however, be a retreat from leadership with those in potentially influential or powerful positions choosing not to exercise their power. The consequence can be a leadership vacuum and slippage into a position where there is effectively no leadership driving forward either strategy or action. This is implicit rather than explicit, fragmented rather than integrative, and such leadership problems can lead to chaos and confusion in inter-organisational relations. The systems of joint working may then break down.

Transaction costs and social capital

Common to all approaches to collaborative working, co-ordination and partnerships are transaction costs. All modes of governance involve transaction costs. Under market rules there are the costs of negotiation and exchange; in hierarchies there are the costs of establishing rules and of ensuring compliance. In network modes of governance (typified by partnerships) the costs are of time expended in meeting, communicating, and sharing. The burden of transaction costs under any mode of governance can be lightened if the parties know, like and trust each other. Granovetter (1985) argues that economic and administrative actions are embedded in social relations. Social norms substitute for the rules which hierarchy demands, the contracts which markets demand, and the interaction which networks demand, and produce a context within which compliance occurs without high transaction costs

Central to the operation of systems of governance, therefore, are issues of trust (Kramer and Tyler, 1996; Hardy *et al.*, 1998). Indeed trust is the key concept raised in all discussions about the attributes of a good partnership. It is less clear, however, whether trust is a necessary input to partnership or is an output from it. That is, can trust be assumed or does it have to be built, earned, won, or given. There are different definitions of trust. For some (Hardy *et al.*, 1988) trust is a proxy for predictability. The greater the degree of trust the more likely is it that actions will be predictable. In this sense, trust underpins economic transactions, endorses the principal/agent relationship and reduces the need for binding legal and costly contracts. For others trust needs to be both formed and fulfilled to generate bilateral trust. Trust can both be rooted in expectations (that something predictable will occur) and in experience (that something has occurred). Granovetter (*op. cit.*) reinforces this view in commenting that trust does not arise "when the transactors are previously unacquainted, where they are unlikely to transact again, and where information about the activities of either is unlikely to reach others with whom they might transact". Trust is therefore generated by both experience and reputation. Trust also lies at the heart of two other features of partnership working: risk and power. In situations where no one partner has the will, resources, or capacity to carry through some task on his or her own, then trust in others minimises risk-taking, since the possibilities of failure or resource wastage are spread. Trust ensures that risks are genuinely shared as opposed to being off-loaded in the case of failure. Furthermore trust reduces the risks of partisan interest group activity, partner disempowerment, or leadership domination.

Power

Leadership and trust lead to considerations of power. Power is a central – if often unacknowledged – feature of partnership working. Partners bring different degrees of power to partnerships – skills, expertise, local knowledge, human resources, but above all money. Those with resources carry most power and the evidence is that the big battalions prove to be the big players. Conversely, those whom many contemporary community or neighbourhood partnerships intend to benefit, have less power and once more there is much evidence of the marginalisation of community sector interests in partnership working (Hastings, 1996; Hastings *et al.*, 1996; Skelcher *et al.*, 1996; Hoggett, 1997; Purdue *et al.*, 2000; Taylor, 2000).

Power may also be exercised in the conduct of partnership business, including the location of meetings, agenda setting, chairing, dress, and norms of behaviour. Once more, the evidence is of the marginalisation of some interests with minority ethnic participants and women often being relegated in importance simply by the operation of a system within which traditional, white, male habits are the norm. Thinking about power also leads to questions as to whether the arrangements for partnership reflect the emergence of a "regime". A wide US based regime literature has now crossed the Atlantic and is increasingly, if hesitantly, being applied to European politics (Stoker and Mossberger, 1994; Lauria, 1997; Di Gaetano, 1999). Regime theory originally argued that private sector interests, in conjunction with public authorities, created some form of growth coalition which pushed forward the interests of the development sector. It is clear that in the UK situation, growth, or at least economic development and regeneration, has proved a major driver of the partnership movement over the last decade, but there is also evidence that there are significant variations in the form and behaviour of the UK coalitions, not least in the extent of their local autonomy and their ability to act independently of a centralised state.

Stakeholder commitment to partnership working

Much management literature points to the pressures militating against partnership philosophy. Provan and Millward (2001) emphasise that individual public service organisations – of which employment agencies are but one – may be involved with network governance, but have specific stakeholder constituencies which "tend to evaluate, reward or punish individual agencies regardless of the network's role in enhancing or limiting client outcomes". There are political and organisational limits to the "extent to which community and network level decisions can be made at the expense of network participants".

A different way of expressing this is in terms of "isomorphism" (Lawton et al., 2000) – the ways in which, and extent to which, organisations are structured by their external environment, incorporating into their behaviour elements which are legitimated externally to the organisation itself. The evidence is that the environment is dominated by those who are perceived to be the key stakeholders to an organisation's planning and delivery processes. These may include resource providers, user groups, fund holders and the external agencies which set accountability or performance standards (e.g. the Audit Commission).

Given that the current climate of performance assessment presents a significant external environment for public bodies it is perhaps unsurprising that public bodies present an ambivalent approach to partnership working. There is widespread agreement that the new public management poses a threat to joint working as accountabilities, regulation, inspection and performance management demand focused and targeted behaviour from a range of public bodies. The literature about public management and managers both demands recognition of the nature of NPM and suggests that it militates against networking and partnership. Considine (2002), in assessing accountability (cross-nationally and in relation to the pubic employment service) argues that "we must expect accountability to undergo a dynamic process of evolution, adaptation, and – in some cases – crisis". Goodship and Cope (2001) argue that: "regulatory agencies, with their different remits, agendas, and styles often compete with each other, resulting in frequent turf war (...)". Regulatory agencies, particularly inspectorate bodies are functionally organised and as presently constituted will run into problems of collaborating in assessing the performance of policies that cut across functionally organised agencies.

Similarly, James (2002) looking at the benefits agency points to the "effects of agency structure in exacerbating the problems of joined up government". There were substantial problems of "vertical" organisation separation between the sections of the UK's former Department of Social Security (DSS) HQ responsible for policy and those in the agency responsible for implementation. The performance system exacerbated problems of horizontal working by encouraging staff to focus on their own work to the substantial exclusion of considering the effects on other organisations' activities.

Thus, the English Audit Commission concludes in relation to crime and disorder partnerships and the role of police authorities: "The focus of many partnership agencies is compliance with national performance indicators. Inevitably, there is a tension between the national performance indicators relating to crime reduction and the broader delivery of community safety."

Accountability

In the new governance of multi-sectoral working, accountabilities become blurred. Joint action and co-funding cloud the responsibilities and obligations of participant organisations in partnership and traditional expressions of accountability become opaque. Accountability to the partnership machinery becomes confused with accountability to the "original" local government, private sector or community interest represented in the partnership structures. Representative responsibilities become confused with executive roles in new, often informal organisational forms. There is an upside, however, if accountability structures "invite and authorise the contributions of social partners, community interests, other levels of government, and other autonomous contributors" (Considine, *op. cit.*).

The accountability of the new partnerships, coalitions and alliances which characterise current local politics and into which the community is increasingly drawn pose complex issues. There are multiple structures of accountability. There are tensions inherent in systems which demand professional accountability (inculcated through training and experience), financial accountability (determined by accounting and audit practice), legal accountability (embodying the obligation to behave within the law), procedural accountability (evident in the extent to which organisational processes conform to statute or rules), and managerial accountability (defined in terms of performance against targets). Nor must we forget or undermine the political accountability exercised through the democratic electoral processes which underpin representative democracy as well as by the political structures which seek to ensure adherence to political position and loyalty to party. Partnerships involve political, financial, and professional accountabilities, many of which are exercised within a new culture of company status. Directors or partnership board members from the community sector carry individual as well as collective responsibility and there is an acknowledged tension between accountability within a specific partnership (*e.g.* as director, trustee or board member) and accountability to the community organisation(s) from which a partner comes. Whilst new forms of priority setting and decision making are emerging, the principles of proper accountability, such as access to information and regular reporting, can be maintained and respected within partnership working.

In established areas of public interest – education, health, policing and so on – there exists in respect of each of these strands of accountability a set of conventions which are reflected in the actual practice of making and receiving "accounts". There remains, therefore, the issue of resolving the appropriate balance both between different forms of accountability (as above) and between the demands of vertical (hierarchical, control-focused) accountabilities and the desire for greater horizontal accountabilities between stakeholders operating at the same level. In the context of a discussion about decentralisation it is important to note that vertical structures tend to dominate with horizontal accountabilities coming second.

Conclusions

Partnerships and employment

It is clear, if only from the UK experience, that in the wider literature of partnerships there is much of relevance to thinking about employment and labour markets. The lessons from Employment Zones throw some light on the attitudes and behaviour of the employment services in relation to area-based working. Neighbourhood initiatives such as those supported by the Single Regeneration Budget offer insights into the role of special programmes; the neighbourhood-based New Deal for Communities has begun to demonstrate the potential for innovation in community-oriented programmes. There is already much evidence from experiments in intermediate labour markets (McGregor et al., 1997). The role of the social economy is increasingly recognised as crucial for local economic development. There is also an expanding literature about the relationships between employment and housing, and between employment and health.

At the same time it is recognised that labour markets are less local than many would wish. There is only limited scope for addressing a number of the inequalities in the labour market at neighbourhood or even city levels. Thus the spatial level at which appropriate partnerships might be constructed is crucial, as is the relationship – hierarchical or otherwise – between regional or sub-regional partnerships, and the more focused but spatially more circumscribed partnerships of local areas. Nor should we forget that for some groups – black and ethnic minorities, people with disabilities, ex-offenders, single parents – area-based initiatives may be less relevant. Employment policies need to address communities of interest as well as of place.

Issues and implications

Are new forms of governance fulfilling their objectives? Do they provide sufficient leeway to the management of public programmes at local level so that public service officers can participate in integrated projects relevant in a local development perspective?

Whilst new forms of governance – area-based initiatives built around networks and partnerships – offer the potential for new forms of cross-sectoral working and policy integration, their performance is often constrained by the demands made upon the partner organisations to meet targets and accountability established on a vertical segmented basis and controlled from central state departments.

Are public accountability requirements satisfied? Do new forms of governance incur a loss of accountability and how can this be surmounted?

New forms of partnership governance pose major issues of accountability but these can be overcome through ensuring transparency of partnership working, providing frequent and clear information about partnership decisions, and requiring partners to make explicit the relative importance of their own organisational accountabilities and their accountability within partnership.

Can new forms of governance support decentralisation, or should they be considered as a substitute for it?

New forms of governance – partnership and area-based initiatives – may themselves be a form of decentralisation and should be pursued with the aim of recognising and supporting both decentralisation and the devolution of responsibility to sub-national stakeholders.

A rethinking of management frameworks and decision-making structures in a local governance perspective could help better achieve the goal of an integrated approach.

Bibliography

ANDERSEN, Helen and MUNCK, Ronnie (1999), *Neighbourhood Images in Liverpool*, JRF Area Regeneration Series, York Publishing Services, York.

CATTELL, Vicki and EVANS, Mel (1999), *Neighbourhood Images in East London*, JRF Area Regeneration Series, York Publishing Services, York.

CONSIDINE, Mark (2002), "The End of the Line? Accountable Governance in the Age of Networks, Partnerships, and Joined-Up Services", *Governance: An International Journal of Policy, Administration, and Institutions*, Vol. 15.1.

DEPARTMENT OF TRANSPORT, LOCAL GOVERNMENT AND THE REGIONS (2002), *Collaboration and Co-ordination in Area-based Initiatives*, DTLR, London.

DIGAETANO, Alan and KLEMANSKI, John S. (1999), *Power and City Governance* Minneapolis, University of Minnesota Press.

GEDDES, Mike(1998), "Local Partnership: A Successful Strategy for Social Cohesion?", European Foundation for the Improvement of Living and Working Conditions, Office for Official Publications of the European Communities, Luxembourg.

GOODSHIP, Jo and COPE, Stephen (2001), "Reforming Public Services by Regulation: A Partnership Approach?", *Public Policy and Administration*, Vol. 16.4.

GRANOVETTER, Mark (1985), "Economic Action and Social Structure: the Problem of Embeddedness", *American Journal of Sociology*, Vol. 91(3).

HAMBLETON, Robin, SWEETING, David and STEWART, Murray (2002), "Leadership and Partnership in Urban Governance", Final report to ESRC, UWE Bristol.

HARDING, Alan (1998), "Public-private Partnerships in the UK", in J. Pierre (ed.), *Partnerships in Urban Governance*, Macmillan, Basingstoke.

HARDY, Cynthia, PHILLIPS, Nelson and LAWRENCE, Tom (1998), "Distinguishing Trust and Power in Interorganisational Relations", in C. Lane and R. Bachman (eds.), *Trust within and between Organisations*, Oxford University Press, Oxford.

HASTINGS, Annette (1996), "Unravelling the process of partnership in urban regeneration policy", *Urban Studies,* Vol. 33.2.

HASTINGS, Annette et al. (1996), *Less than Equal? Community organisations and estate regeneration partnerships*, Policy Press, Bristol.

HOGGETT, Paul (ed.) (1997), *Contested Communities,* Policy Press, Bristol.

HUXHAM, Chris (ed.) (1996), *Creating Collaborative Advantage,* Sage.

HUXHAM, Chris and VANGEN, Siv (2000), "Leadership in the Shaping and Implementation of Collaboration Agendas: How Things Happen in a (Not Quite) Joined-up World", *Academy of Management Journal,* Vol. 43, No. 6.

JAMES, Oliver (2001), "Evaluating Executive Agencies in the UK Government", *Public Policy and Administration,* Vol. 16.3.

JOLDERSMA, Cisca (1997), "Participatory Policy Making: Balancing between Divergence and Convergence European", *Journal of Work and Psychology,* Vol. 6.2.

KANTOR, Rosabeth Moss (1994), "Collaborative Advantage. The Art of Alliances", *Harvard Business Review,* July.

KRAMER, Roderick M. and TYLER, Tom R. (eds.) (1996), *Trust in Organisations Frontiers of Theory and Research,* Sage, London.

LAURIA, Mickey (ed.) (1997), *Reconstructing Urban Regime Theory: Regulating Urban Politics in a Global Economy,* Sage Publications, Thousand Oaks.

LAWTON, Alan, MCKEVITT, David and MILLAR, Michelle (2000), "Coping with Ambiguity: Reconciling External Legitimacy and Organisational Implementation", *Performance Measurement, Public Money and Management,* Vol. 19.3.

LEAT, Diana, SELTZER, Kimberly and STOKER, Gerry (2000), *Governing in the Round; Strategies for Holistic Government,* DEMOS, London.

MACINTOSH, Maureen (1993), "Partnership: Issues of Policy and Negotiation", *Local Economy,* Vol. 7.3.

MCGREGOR, Alan, FERGUSON, Zoe, FITZPATRICK, Iain and MCCONNACHIE, Margaret (1997), "Bridging the Jobs Gap: an Evaluation of the Wise Group and the Intermediate Labour Market", Report for the Joseph Rowntree Foundation, York Publishing Services, York.

OECD (2001), *Local Partnerships for Better Governance,* Paris.

PAGE, David (2000), *Communities in the Balance: the Reality of Social Exclusion on Housing Estates,* Purdue D., York Publishing Services, York.

PARKINSON, Michael (1998), *Combating Social Exclusion; Lessons from Area-based Programmes in Europe,* The Policy Press, Bristol.

PRATT, Julian, PAMPLING, Diane and GORDON, Pat (1999), *Working Whole Systems: Practice and Theory in Network Organisations,* The King's Fund, London.

PROVAN, Keith and MILWARD, H. Brinton (2001), "Do Networks Really Work? A Framework for Evaluating Public-Sector Organisational Networks", *Public Administration Review,* July/August, Vol. 61.4.

PURDUE, Derrick, RAZZAQUE, Konica, HAMBLETON, Robin and STEWART, Murray (2000), *Community Leadership in Area Regeneration*, The Policy Press, Bristol.

REID, Michael (2002), "Rapid Transformations in Post-Socialist Cities: Towards an Uncertain Future", Chapter 6 in R. Hambleton, H. Savitch and M. Stewart (eds.), *Globalism and Local Democracy*, Palgrave, London.

RITTEL, Horst and WEBBER, Mel (1973), "Dilemmas in a General Theory of Planning", *Policy Sciences*, Vol. 4.

SILBURN, Richard, LUCAS, Dan, PAGE, Robert and HANNA, Lynn (1999), *Neighbourhood Images in Nottingham*, JRF Area Regeneration Series.

SKELCHER, Chris and LOWNDES, Vivien (1998), "The Dynamics of Multi-organisational Partnerships: an Analysis of Changing Modes of Governance", *Public Administration*, Vol. 76, Summer.

SKELCHER, Chris et al. (1996), *Community Networks in Urban Regeneration: "It All Depends Who You Know"*, Joseph Rowntree Foundation.

SOCIAL EXCLUSION UNIT (2002), *A New Commitment to Neighbourhood Renewal: National Strategy Action Plan*, Neighbourhood Renewal Unit, London.

STEWART, Murray (1998b), "Partnership, Leadership and Competition in Urban Policy", Chapter 5 in N. Oatley N. (ed.), *Cities, Economic Competition and Urban Policy*, Paul Chapman Publishing, London.

STOKER, Gerry and MOSSBERGER, Karen (1994), "Urban Regime Theory in Comparative Perspective", *Environment and Planning C. Government and Policy*, Vol. 12.

SULLIVAN, Helen and SKELCHER, Chris (2002), *Working Across Boundaries*, Palgrave, London.

TAYLOR, Marilyn (2000), "Communities in the Lead: Organisational Capacity and Social Capital", *Urban Studies*, Vol. 37, pp. 5-6.

WEBB, Adrian (1991), "Co-ordination: a Problem in Public Sector Management", *Policy and Politics*, Vol. 19, No. 4.

WILKINSON, David and APPELBEE, Elaine (1999), *Implementing Holistic Government: Joined-up Action on the Ground*, The Policy Press, London.

WOOD, Martin and VAMPLEW, Clive (1999), *Neighbourhood Images of Teesside*, JRF Area Regeneration Series, York Publishing Services, York.

WOOLCOCK, Michael (1998), "Social Capital and Economic Development; Towards a Theoretical Synthesis and Policy Framework", *Theory and Society*, Vol. 21.

ISBN 92-64-10470-4
Managing Decentralisation
A New Role for Labour Market Policy
© OECD 2003

PART III
Chapter 18

Improving Governance: The Role of the European Union

by
Xavier Prats-Monné
Director, European Commission

Policy orientations of the European Commission on governance

The European Commission identified the reform of European governance as one of its strategic objectives in early 2000. Thus, in July 2001, it adopted a "*White Paper on European Governance*".[1] The White Paper proposes opening up the policy-making process to get more people and organisations involved in shaping and delivering EU policy, and promotes greater openness, accountability and responsibility for all those involved.

Political developments have highlighted that the Union faces a double challenge: there is a need not only for action to adapt governance under the existing European Union (EU) treaties, but also for a broader debate on the future of Europe – as undertaken by the on-going European Convention, in view of the Inter-Governmental Conference. The European Convention in particular has established a Working Group on Economic Governance.[2]

In this context, territorial authorities, as privileged local democracy actors within the countries of the Union, are called upon to play a growing role in the framing and implementation of Community policies.

With this in mind, the Commission's White Paper on European Governance put forward the idea of "target-based tripartite contracts", to be concluded between the member states, the territorial authorities designated by them, and the Commission. In making this proposal, the Commission intended mainly to ensure more flexibility in the means provided for implementing legislation and programmes with a strong territorial impact, while maintaining a level playing field at the heart of the internal market.

There is a general emphasis in the EU Treaties on the need for Community actions to take account of diversity. This is already evident in the very design of the Union's legislative instruments. Community directives are indeed designed to allow the member states a significant degree of flexibility in national transposition; Community regulations also lend themselves to a certain differentiation in the methods of implementation, provided that such differentiation is based on objective assessment criteria.

In addition, in certain areas of action with strong territorial impact, including economic, social, employment or environmental policy, the EU Treaty and policies explicitly provide for local circumstances to be taken into account.

Flexibility is indeed inherent in the very principles of the Union's economic and social cohesion policy. The notion of "partnership" is one of the fundamental principles underlying the programming and implementation of the Union's Structural Funds for the period 2000-2006,[3] although this principle is naturally implemented in full compliance with the respective institutional, legal and financial powers of each of the partners.

The Commission recognises that, with the exception of cohesion policy, Community practice and the intensity of legislative action have not always taken sufficiently into account the growing role of regions and cities in the implementation of national and Community policies. Thus, there is an interest in contractual tools, aimed at developing the possibilities of differentiation between and participation of territories in the realisation of objectives defined at European level or in co-operation between various geographical levels.

However, there are also apprehensions or reservations among some member states, which are rightly concerned that such a contractual approach must not challenge the fundamental principle of the sole responsibility of the member states for carrying out Community policies.

The White Paper's idea of *tripartite contracts* empowering certain sub-national authorities to implement specific actions, aimed at achieving objectives defined in basic Union legislation, gave rise to requests for clarification, both from certain member states and from European networks of regional and local authorities. Thus, in December 2002, the Commission described in broad terms the general conditions for recourse to "tripartite contracts", whether in the context of applying a legislative act or in reference to a Community objective.[4] The Commission proposed to consider using:

- *target-based tripartite contracts*, to describe contracts concluded between the European Community – represented by the Commission – a member state and regional and local authorities in direct application of binding secondary Community law (regulations, directives or decisions); and

- *target-based tripartite agreements*, to describe agreements concluded between the Commission, a member state and regional and local authorities outside a binding Community framework.

The areas in which the pursuit of Community objectives must take into account significant variations in territorial impact, as well as the *a priori* availability of territorial policy management experience, would be prime candidates for the creation of tripartite contracts or agreements.

Since the aim of these contractual tools would be to develop experience and encourage involvement, the clear identification of the regional and local actors to be included in the contract or agreement is an important condition for success. This identification requires the involvement of the member states, not least to ensure that the contract or agreement is compatible with constitutional, legislative and administrative provisions in force in each member state.

The issue of contractual arrangements is currently being discussed in the framework of the preparation of the European Commission's Third Report on Social and Economic Cohesion, due by December, 2003. This report will be the basis for the Commission's proposals for Cohesion policy after 2006.

Decentralisation and the local dimension of the European Employment Strategy

The Commission's White Paper on European Governance stressed the need for a stronger interaction between European institutions, national governments, regional and local authorities and civil society, in line with the principles of openness, participation, accountability, effectiveness and coherence.

It is important to underline that the main responsibility for achieving this rests with EU member states: the European Commission's legal competencies in this area are indeed very limited. However, the Commission, while fully respecting the different national constitutional and administrative arrangements, should ensure that regional and local knowledge and conditions are taken into account when developing policy proposals, including in the field of employment.

Indeed, employment policies are more often than not designed centrally but implemented locally. Local actors from small and medium enterprises to municipalities, can significantly contribute to regional cohesion, innovation and entrepreneurship, and introduce new forms of employment creation; the promotion of social inclusion, equal opportunities and gender equality also requires social support and democratic participation at the local level.

An important local dimension is also implied in areas with severe geographical or natural handicaps, i.e., mountain areas, peripheral areas and those with a very low population density. The Commission's Second Report on Economic and Social Cohesion highlighted the importance of these areas, where a strong local dimension focused on economic development and the promotion of employment must form the basis of cohesion policy.

The local and regional level of the European Employment Strategy

European institutions took note of the potential of local development in the fight against unemployment as early as 1984.[5] However, local employment acquired an increasingly prominent role only after the Commission's White Paper on Growth, Competitiveness and Employment was endorsed by the European Council in 1993.[6] Since the Luxembourg process was initiated in 1997, the development of the local dimension of the EES has appeared as a complex process.

While the EES has so far relied mainly on efforts at European and national level, there is a growing awareness that the objectives that the Union has set itself to improve performance in the area of employment cannot be achieved without greater participation of actors at the regional and local levels.

Title VIII of the EU Treaty lays down the principles and procedures of a co-ordinated European Employment Strategy (EES). Article 128 details the steps leading to the formulation of this strategy, including, on an annual basis: Guidelines for employment and national reports on their implementation; recommendations to the member states; and a Joint Employment Report by Council and Commission to the European Council.[7]

Since their inception, the Luxembourg process and the Employment Guidelines have increasingly incorporated the local dimension, by inviting member states to involve the regional and local levels. Starting with a focus on job creation at local level, the Guidelines underlined first the special role of local authorities and the social partners, and, in the year 2000, the need to support "the special role and responsibility of (...) other partners at the regional and local levels, as well as the social partners".

In March 2000, the Lisbon European Council created a strategy stressing the importance of interaction between economic, employment and social policies, of the mobilisation of all players, and established a reinforced *open method of co-ordination*, described as a "fully decentralised approach, applied in line with the principle of subsidiarity in which the Union, the member states, the regional and local levels, as well as the social partners and civil society will be actively involved, using variable forms of partnership".

Finally, in 2001 a comprehensive approach was included in the Employment Guidelines. All actors at the regional and local levels, including the social partners, must be mobilised to implement the EES by identifying the potential of job creation at local level and strengthening partnerships to this end. Member states will take into account, where appropriate, in their overall employment policy, the regional development dimension. They will encourage local and regional authorities to develop strategies for employment in order to exploit fully the possibilities offered by job creation at local level and promote partnerships to this end with all the actors concerned, including the representatives of civil society.

The European Employment Strategy (EES), and the member states' National Action Plans for employment (NAPs) in particular, can provide a useful framework. However, while there is a general trend in the Union towards a greater consideration for the local dimension of employment, many obstacles identified in the past[8] still persist. Regional and local actors should be better informed and involved in the EES process, and better use should be made of existing policies and instruments at Community, national and sub-national level. To this end, in line with suggestions made by the European Parliament,[9] member states and Community institutions should play a supportive role, notably by: being more accessible to local actors; ensuring better information flow to local actors and a more coherent use of existing policies and instruments; promoting capitalisation, evaluation, and the exchange of best practices and other local experiences.

The role of EU regional and local actors

The institutional and administrative structures of present and future EU member states vary considerably. It would therefore be pointless – and beyond Community competence – to establish common, prescriptive rules for the articulation between different territorial levels.

Depending on the particular legal and administrative framework of different EU member states, responsibility for different aspects of employment and social policy may be allocated to the national, regional or local levels. It is therefore important to facilitate co-ordination between policy-makers at different levels in order to ensure that these policies contribute effectively to local employment strategies.

The development of a local dimension of the EES requires political will at Community, national, regional and local level, as well as awareness-raising, experimentation and exchange of good practices. Local authorities and actors are often confined to implementing measures decided at national or regional level. The EES, National Action Plans, as well as Structural Fund programmes, are not sufficiently well-known at regional and local levels.

Having said that, the implementation of the EES at the national level in recent years, notably through the National Action Plans for Employment (NAPs), underscores the broad trend within EU member states towards decentralisation, as well as an increasing support for the social economy and for the establishment of partnerships.

National employment policies increasingly take into account the role that local and regional actors can play in the EES and national employment plans. member states are continuing to develop the territorial dimension of their employment policies, although NAPs only rarely referred to integrated employment plans promoted by local governments. The NAPs highlight that member states increasingly accept or actively promote closer co-operation of the regional and/or local authorities in the establishment and implementation of their plans. Several member states have allowed their respective regional and local actors to join the EES process and, in some cases, have actively supported this development.

Although the involvement of the regional level is higher than the local, nation-wide programmes tend to be designed in a more flexible way that takes into account the territorial dimension. Programme implementation is being adapted to different circumstances, and increasingly complemented by specific regional or local programmes.

The forms of co-operation of regional and local authorities in the development of the NAPs are quite diverse in the different member states; in some cases, it tends to become institutionalised. Regions themselves are often taking over the task of promoting involvement at the sub-regional level. Some procedural aspects of the open co-ordination method (definition of objectives, implementation, reporting, assessment) are also taken up and used in the relationship – in some cases contractual – between national governments and localities.

EU member states also increasingly address the social economy as an important factor for local development along with enterprises and an appropriate institutional framework. There are widely differing understandings of the meaning of social economy: while all member states include the main components of the social economy (co-operatives, associations, foundations, voluntary and community organisations), the principle of treating these elements as a cohesive group is not common to all.[10]

The concept of partnership at the local level is not well defined in all member states, particularly as concerning the role of local policy-makers and administrations in creating and managing partnerships. However, social partners and public employment services (PES) are increasingly involved in local strategy development and implementation; they have acquired a specific and important role in local and regional labour markets. In some cases, PES now play an active role in implementing and developing regional and local employment strategies and programmes.

Conclusion : the role of the European Commission

The European Employment Strategy introduced a new dimension in the promotion of more and better jobs. At the Community level, through the employment guidelines, annual examination and peer review of member states' performance, and recommendations to individual countries, the EES is providing an integrated framework to meet the Union's objectives in the field of employment and labour market reforms.

At the member states level, through the NAPs and both Community and national financial support, the Employment Guidelines are being translated into a coherent employment strategy.

At the regional and local levels, actors should be given the opportunity to work increasingly together, to interact with national and European institutions and policies, and to develop partnerships in support of the European Employment Strategy. Local actors also have a key role to play in promoting gender equality and developing integrated approaches to social inclusion.

While respecting the existing distribution of competencies within the Community and member states, the European Commission acts mainly in two ways:

- In line with the principles of the White Paper on European Governance, the Commission promotes the information of local actors on the EES and NAPs, as well as the exchange of best practices, benchmarking and peer review in the implementation of NAPs in the area of local development.

- The Commission assists local actors who wish to engage in a more strategic approach to local development, including local employment strategies and Local Action Plans established in the institutional framework of the member states' National Action Plans. It can provide support through the available financial instruments, such as the European Social Fund's programme on innovative actions. Financial support required to implement local programmes for employment, human resources development, and social inclusion, is included in mainstream operational programmes such as the European Social Fund.

The challenge for the future so far as partnership development is concerned is to better include local policy makers and actors so that these instruments and commitments support the development of stronger multi-level institutions.

Notes

1. Reference: document COM(2001)428 final, 25 July 2001.
2. All documents of the Convention can be found at *european-convention.eu.int/*
3. In particular, Article 8 of the EU Council Regulation on the Structural Funds (EC) No. 1260/1999.
4. Commission Communication "A framework for target-based tripartite contracts and agreements between the Community, the member States and regional and local authorities", Document COM(2002)709 final, 11.12.2002.
5. Council Resolution of 7 June 1984 (84/C-161/01).
6. OPOCE, supplement 6/93. For an overview, see the Commission's Report on local development initiatives, 1998 (SEC 98-25).
7. For information and documents on employment policy and the EES, see the following website: *http://europa.eu.int/comm/employment_social/index_en.htm*
8. See for example, Commission communication on local employment COM(2001)629 final, 06.11.2001.
9. EP Resolution C5-0597/2000.
10. See also OECD (2003), *The Non-profit Sector in a Changing Economy*, Paris.

ISBN 92-64-10470-4
Managing Decentralisation
A New Role for Labour Market Policy
© OECD 2003

PART III

Chapter 19

The US: Leveraging Government Capacity through New Forms of Governance

by

Randall Eberts
Executive Director, W.E. Upjohn Institute for Employment Research

The purpose of this chapter is to lay out a set of guidelines that can help policymakers, practitioners, and other stakeholders achieve better integration of labour market, social and economic policies within a decentralised system of employment service delivery. It argues that an evolving form of governance has taken place primarily because of the emergence of local non-government organisations that have become a powerful force and resource within the United States in addressing the needs of the economically disadvantaged and displaced workers. These organisations include social organisations like Goodwill Industries, homeless shelters, free health clinics for low-income persons, neighbourhood housing authorities as well as educational institutions and community foundations.

At the centre of these efforts in the United States, in many cases, is the local Workforce Development Board (WDB). WDBs are entities created under the Workforce Investment Act of 1998 to administer the delivery of employment services at the local level. Much of this volume examines the relationship between the central government and local entities and the efforts to decentralise services and responsibilities to the local level and what this means for accountability and performance. This chapter will focus instead on the Workforce Development Board and discuss its role as the leader and co-ordinator of the breadth of services that are available at the local level. If we think of the vertical integration of services from top to bottom of government relationships, we now need to think about the horizontal relationships across the breadth of service providers at the local level. Many of these horizontal relationships are *informal* ones, since in many cases no formal contract or memorandum of understanding exists between the WDB and these organisations, as there does between the WDB and the service organisations that provide services through the various government-provided workforce programmes.

As underscored in other chapters, the benefits of decentralising the delivery of employment services stem primarily from bringing decision making closer to the individuals who are in need of labour market programmes. Social issues are community problems, and this demands more holistic approaches that encompass multiple issues, multiple stakeholders, and multiple levels of involvement by government, business, and the civil society (Briggs, 2001). By devolving more responsibility of the design and provision of services from central governments to local organisations, service delivery can be more responsive to the needs of these individuals, can better meet the demands of local businesses, and can take into account local economic conditions. Strengthening the role of local organisations also opens the possibility of forming partnerships with other local government agencies as well as with non-government organisations. Well-organised and functioning networks of local organisations can increase the capacity to meet the needs of local communities, not only with respect to employment services but also with respect to broader social and economic needs of local areas.

Yet, the move to decentralising the provision of services may not be sufficient to forge productive partnerships unless there is also a move to shift decision-making truly to the local level. Other aspects and considerations may also need to be implemented before a truly integrated network of providers can be developed, particularly when considering informal relationships. This chapter, therefore, focus on the conditions necessary to form effective partnerships, and it will argue that these conditions in many respects go beyond a decentralised labour market policy. It will enumerate the characteristics of successful partnerships, and summarise these characteristics by proposing a list of guidelines that are important for forging partnerships that go beyond traditional hierarchical relationships typical of US workforce policy.

US perspective on decentralising services

The issue of decentralisation supposes that centralised policy making is the starting point, the norm, and that the movement toward a more decentralised approach is the new model of governance. Given the history of labour policy in many countries, this appears to be a reasonable starting point. Yet, beginning at the top creates a perspective and establishes criteria for effective governance that are different than if one started from the bottom and looked upward.

Straits, in his chapter on the US experience in decentralising employment services, takes a "bottom up" approach. Instead of starting with a centralised policy framework, he begins with a decentralised perspective. At the centre of this governance model is the customer. Accountability, therefore, is to the customer and not to the centralised government agency. Serving the customer well is commensurate with the customer achieving desired outcomes, such as finding and retaining employment that pays a "decent" wage. This may be in contrast to accountability with the central government agency, in which complying with process standards is the basis for accountability.

Such a bottom-up approach is appropriate for describing US employment policy. Throughout its history, grassroots efforts at the local level have shaped the collective response to social programmes and have been the backbone of American society. Since colonial times, there has been a lingering suspicion of the power of the national government. States have retained considerable authority, and the national expansion was built on the strength of local governments. Long before the federal government became a major player in determining social policies, states assumed that role. States offered free labour exchange services and even unemployment insurance. Much changed during the economic crisis of the Great Depression of the 1930s. States could no longer afford to provide such services. Only the superior taxing power of the federal government and its strong leadership could revive and sustain these programmes and expand them to meet the extensive needs of workers across the country during those dire times. Therefore, the role of the federal government emerged as one of providing resources and standardising services for all eligible citizens, more so than one that designs innovative solutions. Since then, many federal workforce development programmes have adopted practices that were first designed by states or other entities. Federal agencies have provided technical assistance to help states implement programmes. They have also sponsored demonstration programmes to test the efficacy of various types of approaches. But many of these efforts came after states and local areas had already attempted some early form of innovative approaches.

Revisiting the principal-agent theory of decentralisation

In the first chapter of this volume, Giguère outlines a principal-agent framework for examining the issues regarding decentralisation. In this top-down view, the principal is the central government agency, and the agent is a local organisation – government entity or otherwise – that works on behalf of the central government agency to perform a set of functions. Presumably these functions are established and prescribed by the central authority to serve a specific purpose, such as assisting displaced workers to find employment. Yet, as principal, the centralised government is the focus. It establishes a set of criteria, either based on process or performance standards, that the agents are expected to follow. In the simplest relationship between principal and agent, the agent dutifully acts on behalf of the principal. The agent may have knowledge, skills, and information that the principal does not, but objectives are established by the principal without significant contribution from the agent. In the case of labour policy, the central government typically has strict objectives and a uniform process that they expect local organisations to follow. Penalties or sanctions are the usual mechanism for aligning the agents' activities with the objectives of the principals. Rarely within this formal structure do innovative ideas and essential information to better serve the customer percolate up from below.

Such a relationship between principal and agent leads to a hierarchical structure with well defined divisions of labour. In this case, the challenge of decentralisation is simply to determine the appropriate division of labour (as well as the silos of programme funding sources) and then to find an effective way of co-ordinating the various service providers at the local level. This governance structure is akin to business alliances in which organisations with clear objectives (*e.g.* profitability) and well-documented operations are combined to optimise profitability. The objectives of all parties involved are aligned and a path to a successful alliance is clearly marked.

The role of Workforce Development Boards in partnerships

The current system in the United States of one-stop career centres, established under the Workforce Investment Act of 1998, is consistent with this type of hierarchical arrangement. Federal programmes, such as labour exchange and job training programmes, are administered locally by local Workforce Development Boards (WDB). These Boards are comprised of business and civic leaders and, to a lesser extent, representatives of social and educational agencies and labour groups. The purpose of the Board is to oversee the administration of labour exchange and job training programmes by local providers. The local providers are under contract with the WDB to provide services that are prescribed by federal programmes and mandates. The local providers may include local government agencies, such as county government agencies or educational institutions, or private organisations such as non profits or in some cases even for-profit organisations.

The WDBs are intended to provide local input into the delivery of employment services and to co-ordinate the efforts of other social service organisations that form a partnership to meet the needs of workers. However, as Straits points out, they function more as agents of the federal government than as autonomous organisations that have the flexibility to tailor programmes to respond to specific needs of local workers affected by unique local economic conditions. Local WDBs are required to meet a myriad of performance standards established by the federal government (17 standards at the present time). In addition, the state government, through which some of the federal funding is funnelled, also imposes various standards, including financial accounting standards, and is subject to micro-managing on the part of state agencies. As a result, the system becomes much more cumbersome and less able to respond to the needs of the customer.

Requisites of effective partnerships at the local level

Social issues, unfortunately, are not as tidy as business objectives. For the most part, programmes to address these issues cannot be packaged in a rigid hierarchical structure, but demand more fluid organisational structures that can cut across boundaries between sectors, types of work, types of service providers, and levels of operation or targeting. For indeed, partnerships among social organisations struggle to define clear purposes and performance measures, since each member may come to the alliance with a different perspective, motivation, and expected outcome. Even the objectives are difficult to agree upon, at times. For instance, finding and retaining a job is a well accepted and desired outcome of employment policy. Yet, the dual objectives become less absolute when one adds to the outcome metric the goal of achieving relatively high wages. Economic principles dictate that the pursuit of high wages can compromise the goal of gaining employment for broad groups of workers. Should finding a job, any job at any wage, be the first priority, or should one wait and remain unemployed until the ideal job comes along? Obviously, a compromise between these two polar cases must be struck. But the appropriate weights placed on these two objectives may vary case by case, being influenced by the workers' skills, current situations, and the local market conditions they face. Even in this decentralised model, the principal (central agency) dictates what most of the outcomes are and how they should be achieved.

To complicate the administration of a hierarchical system even further, we do not know enough about what programmes work and do not work to customise services to address the employment needs of specific individuals, not even among broader subgroups of the population. This ambiguity contrasts sharply with the calculus of business in which the indices of value and competitiveness, such as market share and profitability, and the knowledge and pursuit of established "best practices" are widely understood and quickly adopted.* Therefore, local organisations can contribute more to helping workers than simply dutifully following the directions of the central agency in delivering services. These organisations can offer valuable information about what works and does not work for various groups of workers. But only through the freedom to experiment with different approaches can such information be obtained.

Once obtained and validated, this information must also be shared across partnering organisations, which means that they must speak the same language in terms of purpose and performance outcomes and must trust their partners in accepting their information to be accurate and their experience to be relevant. Establishing a common basis for defining purpose and objectives is not always easy, since different organisations may focus on different aspects of the barriers facing an individual who is pursuing employment options. For instance, one partner may focus on soft skills, another on occupational skills, and a third on behavioural barriers such as substance abuse or mental health. An even more vexing challenge of establishing a common basis of understanding is for alliances that include workforce

* Briggs (2001) and Kanter (1994) offer this contrast between alliances among businesses and partnerships among social organisations.

development organisations and economic development organisations. While each effort is essential for the other organisation's success, there are times in which it may seem that they are operating at cross purposes. For example, economic development efforts typically include a posture of reducing labour costs to attract and retain businesses. At the same time, lower labour costs may mean pursuing labour-saving strategies and opting for jobs with fewer worker benefits. Obviously a region's economic vitality is essential for a stable and healthy labour market, and *vice versa*.

Consequently, there must be strong leadership to help define the common purpose of the partnership and educate partners as to the importance of cutting across the various boundaries that may separate their efforts. The benefit of turning disconnected specialised units into cross-functional teams is to create a system that serves workers (and businesses) holistically, cost effectively, and creatively. It adds value that exceeds the capacity of each partner working alone.

Once a shared vision has been established, the local organisations need to become problem-solvers. Unlike the simple hierarchical structure in which the provider only provides, in this more interactive and flexible system, the provider also helps to decide how to provide services. Thus, the partners find themselves negotiating roles, responsibilities, and resources for carrying out the delivery of services. Considering local organisations not only as service delivery agents but also as problem-solving agents puts a new perspective on the principal-agent relationship. This drastically reduces the principal's role and influence and flattens out the organisational structure by empowering the agents to make more locally based policy decisions. And it poses the question of what is the role of the principal (central government agency) *vis-à-vis* the agent. Perhaps the centralised agency is simply a source of funding, a source of technical assistance, and one that loosely monitors the activities of the local organisations to ensure that services (not necessarily the same services) are available to all workers within the country.

The waiver programme in the United States is a good example of local governments breaking away from the federal procedures and experimenting with innovative programmes of their own. Within broad guidelines, states could change the type and mix of services available to targeted groups and even revise the eligibility criteria to participate in these programmes. In return for this flexibility, the federal government required that states conduct rigorous evaluations of their programmes so that they would know if their programme worked and why and that this information could be shared by others. In this way, a menu of options could be catalogued and pursued by local service delivery organisations to meet the specific needs of individual customers.

Strong leadership is also required to mobilise resources within the community and within the partnering organisations in order to achieve the desired outcomes. Simply following formal procedures or interventions that have been adopted in other areas or that have been prescribed by higher levels of authority may not be sufficient to make for an effective delivery of services. It may take abilities of a leader to motivate workers and other partnering organisations to make it all work. For instance, the Riverside County (CA) Welfare-to-Work programme (GAIN) was far more successful than similar programmes in getting welfare recipients into jobs. Its exceptional performance was attributed in part to the dynamic leadership of the head of the local programme and his ability to motivate staff to inspire welfare recipients to succeed. Therefore, programmes must be able to incorporate the non-formal aspects of successful implementation when replicating and scaling up formal programmes. The need for strong leadership is particularly important for informal partnerships in which the relationship is not based on a contract arrangement or a memorandum of understanding, but only on the shared vision between the organisations.

Partnering organisations must also be advocates for their causes, such as workforce development agencies for workers and economic development agencies for businesses. This advocacy must be on-going. Implementing a programme or set of programmes, which at the time are shown to be effective in serving the needs of workers, does not guarantee that the programme will continue to achieve the same desired outcomes in the same cost-effective manner. The circumstances of workers, the demand for their skills, and general economic conditions affecting the demand for workers with various qualifications all change over time. Unlike for businesses, there is no on-going market test to indicate the benefit-to-cost ratio of these social programmes. Therefore, advocates must continuously monitor the well-being of their respective constituents to assure that the programmes are meeting their needs. The monitoring should include rigorous and independent evaluations. There is a tendency for some service delivery organisations and even advocacy groups to get caught up in their own self-promotion, blindly accepting that the programme is effective without actually evaluating its merits.

Organisations should also be "cheerleaders" for one another, encouraging partnering organisations to pursue sound procedures and to adhere to rigorous performance goals. Each must recognise that the success of their partners enhances their own performance. With each organisation monitoring the performance of the other partners, a system of mutual accountability can be achieved, in which no central organisation is acting as "principal", but rather a community of organisations that hold each other accountable for their actions and progress.

To function effectively, advocacy organisations, which could also be service providers, need to be as unencumbered as possible by regulations so that they can be empowered to promote their cause. In so doing, they become empowered with incentives to work diligently on behalf of the customer. Because there is no one best practice to meet the needs of workers, one needs a more flexible and comprehensive approach to meeting the needs of the customer. Customers with multiple needs and issues cannot be presented with one or two possible interventions. Rather they need a system that offers multiple options from multiple stakeholders at different layers.

Effective problem-solving and advocacy require an engaged set of stakeholders. These stakeholders, regardless of whether they represent business, social organisations, labour groups, or educational institutions, must be given sufficient authority to make "real" decisions. If decision making is only ritualistic and has little significant bearing on the type of services and the manner of delivering them, then the value of these partnerships are drastically diminished and the partnership is in jeopardy of disintegrating. For example, Workforce Development Boards risk losing qualified business leaders that assume active roles as members of boards unless they consider their input to be integral to the decision making process. Organisations must also have competent staff. It is increasingly difficult to attract qualified workers as funding from the federal and state governments are cut and local organisations depend more and more on volunteers and part-time workers.

Guidelines

The requisites listed above pertain to both formal and informal partnerships. However, it should be stressed that these requisites are particularly essential for effective informal partnerships. With a contract or memorandum of understanding to bind their activities, informal relationship depend upon a shared vision, strong leadership, and mutual accountability, among other attributes. I offer the following guidelines of effective partnerships by way of summarising the points made in the previous section.

1. The customer is the central focus.

2. Accountability is primarily to the customer and only secondarily to the funding agencies. "Mutual accountability" among partnering organisations can keep each other on target.

3. Simple hierarchical systems, patterned after business alliances, are not necessarily appropriate for delivering services that address social problems. Social issues are community problems, and this demands more holistic approaches that encompass multiple issues, multiple stakeholders, and multiple levels of involvement by government, business, and civil society.

4. Partnerships must share a common vision and clear purpose.

5. Strong leadership is required to help define the common purpose of the partnership and to educate partners on the importance of cutting across boundaries between their respective organisations.
6. Leadership is also required in order to mobilise resources and encourage workers within organisations to achieve desired outcomes (civic entrepreneurs).
7. Outcomes must be established and agreed upon by all partners and the outcomes must be quantifiable. Partners must "buy-in" to these agreed-upon outcome measures and be held accountable to achieve acceptable levels of performance.
8. Local organisations must become problem solvers and make sure that their insights are shared with all partners.
9. Partners need to trust the accuracy of the information and the relevance of the experience of partnering organisations.
10. Partners must also be advocates for their customers. This motivates and empowers partners to act on behalf of their customers. It also provides the "market test" of the effectiveness of the programmes and continuous monitoring of the outcomes.
11. Stakeholders must be actively engaged in problem solving and advocacy and be assured that their input and deliberations will have direct bearing on the type of service and the manner in which it is delivered. Without active involvement, they will most likely lose interest which diminishes the effectiveness of local organisations.
12. Funding agencies (federal and state) must give local organisations sufficient flexibility to be problem solvers, advocates, and to cut across organisational boundaries.

Conclusions

Reaping the full benefits of decentralisation of employment services requires that informal partnerships be forged between government and non-government organisations. Non-government organisations leverage the capacity of local government entities by deriving much of their resources from private sources, such as private donations, volunteers, and grants from community foundations. In addition to increasing capacity, partnerships among local entities bring together resources in ways that higher levels of governments have not attempted. For instance, in the United States, local partnerships have integrated workforce development activities with economic development efforts. Such partnerships are not found at the state or federal level. Non-government entities are also seen as creative, entrepreneurial and problem solvers in their efforts to meet the needs of their customers.

With respect to employment services, Workforce Development Boards are central to providing the leadership and expertise to foster informal partnerships at the local level. To do so, they must provide the necessary environment and incentives, as described in this paper, to engage, encourage, and hold accountable local non-government organisations, while at the same time they must comply with the rules and regulations of the federal and state employment programmes. An OECD/LEED study tour of the US Midwest as part of the OECD Study on Local Partnerships (2001) revealed that successful partnerships have been established, but it also underscored the challenges they face in balancing the requisites of nurturing and sustaining informal partnerships and maintaining the formal relationships with higher levels of governments.

Bibliography

BRIGGS, Xavier de Souza (2001), "The Will and the Way: Local Partnerships, Political Strategy, and the Well-Being of America's Children and Youth", Working Paper, John F. Kennedy School of Government, Harvard University, November.

EBERTS, Randall W. and ERICKCEK, George A. (2001), "The Role of Partnerships in Economic Development and Labour Markets in the United States", *Local Partnerships for Better Governance*, OECD, Paris.

KANTER, Rossabeth Moss (1994), "Collaborative Advantage: The Art of Alliances", *Harvard Business Review*, July.

OECD (2001), *Local Partnerships for Better Governance*, Paris.

PART III
Chapter 20

Ireland: Linking Public Services and the Local Community

by
Patrick O'Callaghan
Director, Training and Employment Authority (FÁS)

FÁS is a public organisation under the authority of the Ministry of Enterprise, Trade and Employment. It has a budget for 2003 of over eight hundred million euros and provides direct employment and training programmes for over 100 000 people. FÁS operates the public employment service, trains unemployed and redundant persons, supports and encourages training in industry, provides temporary employment programmes for unemployed and other socially excluded groups and encourages community enterprises. It is a national body with regional and local offices to deliver its services on-the-ground.

Traditionally, public services in Ireland have been provided by national organisations. There is a local authority (county and city) structure based on local elected representatives. These are responsible for basic physical environmental matters and a minority portion of the second-level school system. However, since the early 1980s and especially in the late 1980s and early 1990s, they have developed a large number of separate locally-based structures. These have been especially prevalent in relation to social issues including employment and unemployment. FÁS has been very involved in nearly all of these organisations.

Partnership in Ireland

Over the last two decades, Ireland has introduced a range of new governance processes often characterised as "partnerships". These operate at national level, local level and within the firm. The essential impact of all of these is to widen the range of organisations that are involved in decision-making. Put another way, they all involve giving up some of the autonomy traditional held by one organisation. The new forms of governance involve a number of other organisations which, to a greater or lesser degree, influence decision-making.

Ireland's approach to partnership at national level has involved three-year National Agreements between government, employer and union representatives, and other social partners, especially the "Community and Voluntary Pillar". These Agreements have involved an agreed approach to wage increases, taxation, social welfare changes and a range of other social and economic policies. It is widely recognised that one of the contributors (but by no means the only one) to Ireland's success in recent years has been these National Agreements.

Before turning to the issue of local partnership, which is the main topic of this chapter, mention should be made of partnerships within companies. The promotion of employer-worker partnership processes inside companies has been an explicit objective of the last two National Agreements. This primarily reflects a view from the trade union movement that workplace partnership is an essential development of modern, equitable, organisations. However, employer organisations have not necessarily been opposed to such developments, recognising that high performance work organisations require higher levels of work commitment, initiative and co-operation which can be improved in a partnership framework. The most concrete manifestation of this development has been the establishment of the National Centre for Partnership and Performance in 2001. The Centre aims to promote and assist the development of workplace partnership in Ireland in both public and private organisations. FÁS is involved with a number of activities of the Centre.

The local partnership approach

Most of the local partnership approaches evolved out of a dissatisfaction with existing arrangements to tackle social issues such as unemployment. Thus, the Area-based Response to Long-Term Unemployment was started in 1991 under the National Agreement at the time. Twelve Partnership Companies were established with representatives of Government agencies (including FÁS), community groups and social partners. Subsequently, the number of Partnership Companies was expanded to 38. A separate publicly-funded agency, Area Development Management (ADM) LTD, was set up to co-ordinate the approach.

Other local partnership groups have been set up under the Community Development Programme (building local capacity to identify and find solutions to local needs), the Local Employment Service (targeted at the most disadvantaged, long-term unemployed), local drugs task forces (in localities with severe drugs problems), LEADER (for rural, agricultural, areas), City/County Enterprise Boards (to help micro-businesses), Territorial Employment Pacts and RAPID. All of these groups are typically oriented to one type of issue or task.

In recent years, an additional and very important development has been the establishment of City/County Development Boards which have a wider remit to develop strategies across a range of areas on a geographical basis. These Development Boards are constituted in each of the local authority (i.e. democratically-elected) areas and contain elected representatives as well as public agencies, social partners and community/voluntary organisation representatives. These Boards have commenced operation by developing 10-year strategies for their areas and are now moving forward to take actions to progress these strategies. FÁS is represented on all of the Boards.

There have been a number of reviews of local partnerships in Ireland including ones by the OECD (1996, 2001), the National Economic and Social Council (1996) and Combat Poverty (Walsh et al., 1988). This report by Combat Poverty formed part of a wider European study funded by the European Foundation for the Improvement of Living and Working Conditions. The authors of the Combat Poverty report review the experience of local partnerships in Ireland and note eleven issues which are important.

Power and control over resources

Local partnerships, in general are non-statutory bodies and therefore without the power to enforce the implementation of an agreed local action plan. Most local partnerships have an informal say over the resource allocations of partner agencies, which is by necessity a grey area. To compensate for this, local partnerships have relied on access to external funds to undertake their work programmes, a pattern facilitated by the increased provision of such funding by government and the EU. Such funding has important short-term benefits: it gives partnerships their own discretionary finds and it also provides a mechanism to lever additional local resources.

Organisational effectiveness

Much of the initial interest in local partnerships related to their innovative organisational structures. Turning multi-agency structures, involving many participants, into dynamic and effective organisations is influenced by a number of factors: composition, management culture and skills, internal structures, and range of interests.

Operating models for local partnerships

These include *service delivery*, where a partnership designs, funds and delivers services itself, usually on a pilot basis.

A second way of working for local partnerships is an *agency approach*, where local partnerships work with other local organisations (existing or new) to enhance the provision of services. A third approach is referred to as a *brokerage role*, where local partnerships act as support agencies for services providers.

National support structures

The provision of national support and advice is a standard feature of local partnership programmes. This means co-ordination of links between local partnerships on the one hand and central government on the other.

Linkages with local government

Their status in this regard, however, is somewhat ambivalent due to their weak formal linkages with existing local government structures and their anomalous administrative status as quasi-public bodies. A particular focus of concern is the almost complete absence of elected local public representatives on local partnerships. Another issue relates to the multiplicity of local development agencies and cope for duplication of effort and resources.

Good practice in local planning

This task poses considerable difficulties, both technical and political. The first relates to the limited availability and poor quality of local data with many problems being encountered where operational boundaries do not correspond to administrative ones. The second difficulty refers to the capacity of local partnerships to adopt a strategic approach. In particular, how to move from having shopping lists of actions compiled by individual partners to preparing strategies which address, in an innovative and integrated way, key local issues.

Spatial dimension

Local partnership programmes have an implicit spatial dimension. This arises in two main ways; the identification of areas of disadvantage, and the use of local actions as a response to social exclusion and where appropriate the application of approaches that require national lead actions. Recent research has shown that social exclusion is a spatially widespread feature of Irish society.

Involvement of partner agencies

It is important to differentiate between the role played by individual representatives in local partnerships and the contribution of partner agencies. Many representatives are personally committed to the work of local partnerships and bring a lot of goodwill and energy to their role. However, the degree to which such involvement is translated into meaningful support also depends on the willingness and capacity of the parent organisations to engage in joint local planning and decision-making.

Community participation

A key theme in local partnerships is providing a community input into public service policy and provision. Despite significant community involvement at various levels of local partnerships, concerns have been expressed as to the costs of this involvement to participants and community groups and the actual impact of this input on decision-making.

National policy framework for local partnership

A strength of local partnerships is the support they have received at the highest level in the national policy framework. This has facilitated not only the rapid development of these novel structures, but also the piloting of a number of important policy reforms. The other side of this coin is equally important: the capacity of the national framework to transfer local innovation into mainstream policy.

Equal opportunities

Considerable emphasis has been given to the participation of women and, to a lesser extent, of minority groups (*e.g.* travellers, people with disabilities) in local partnerships, reflecting wider public policy concerns about equal opportunities. Various measures, including a government guideline regarding the gender composition of partnership and the publication of a guide to gender equality in local partnerships, have been taken in pursuit of this policy goal.

Competences for successful partnership working

Partnership whether at inter or intra organisational level requires certain attitudes and behaviours if it is to be successful. In order to go beyond vague generalisation on this matter, the National Centre for Partnership and Performance recently published "A Competency Framework for Managing Change through Partnership" (National Centre for Partnership and Performance, 2003). The aim is to more clearly specify the competences required and so assist organisations develop persons in such competences. They identify ten competences as listed below:

- organisational and business awareness;
- leadership;
- championing change through partnership;
- overcoming barriers to change;
- communication;
- building and maintaining relationships;
- influencing;
- data analysis and innovative thinking;
- problem solving and decision making;
- achievement orientation.

The Centre notes that all those involved in a partnership need these competences but the relative important of different ones vary across roles and responsibilities.

Mainstreaming of partnership innovations

A significant objective of the new local partnership approaches in Ireland has been their intention to develop innovative approaches. In many cases, the intention is that successful innovations would then be "mainstreamed" and become part of the normal provision of government organisations.

There are many definitions of mainstreaming and these are based on a range of different understandings. However, common to all of these definitions is the fact that mainstreaming is about changing the way things are done. Common themes emerging from these definitions are the concepts of the transfer of learning; informing (local and national) policy and practise; and focusing mainstream activities or policies on particular areas or target groups. Mainstreaming also involves a transfer or refocusing of resources, whether human, financial or physical. This transfer or refocusing can be within the statutory sector, from the statutory sector to the community or it can operate on a shared basis.

A report by ADM Ltd in 2000 identified four elements of a framework of mainstreaming. The first is innovation where successful or effective innovation is mainstreamed through long-term funding, replication of processes in other areas, or incorporation of innovation into the provisions of the State sector. The second is practise learning, which is extracted from actions carried out or resourced by partnerships in terms of process or practise and is applied within, or recognised and supported by, State agencies, *e.g.* capacity building of groups representing particular communities or target groups. The third is programme bending where mainstream programmes and resources are re-focused into areas of disadvantage *e.g.* the analysis of the local context by partnerships and facilitating the mobilisation of local stakeholders which are then engaged with by State agencies, so that State resources can be re-focused in consultation with local groups into their areas and communities. And the fourth is *policy learning* extracted from local actions in terms of the relevance of their outcomes for setting policy objectives and designing policy responses on the part of state agencies, *e.g.* promoting an inter-cultural approach to education. The learning extracted from local action may also have a broader dimension in terms of the partnership focus on disadvantage, social exclusion and inequality being mainstreamed into the work and remit of the different stakeholders on the boards of local development bodies.

The ADM report examines a number of Irish case studies and draws some conclusions in respect of issues arising. The report finds that the main factors causing difficulties for mainstreaming were: *i)* when the proposed initiative was only presented to state organisations when funding was needed; *ii)* where it was seen as purely a local response to a local need; *iii)* where an initiative did not fit into any "logical" organisational home; *iv)* where the ethos of the initiative was in contradiction to a core ethos of the relevant state body; *v)* changes in key personnel; and *vi)* difficulties in getting groups of state agencies to co-operate rather than compete.

Despite these difficulties, the ADM report gives several examples of positive mainstreaming of local partnership initiatives.

FÁS' particular experiences

FÁS employs about 2 400 staff. A recent count of our participation on "external" committees found 1 000 such participants (this includes people on more than one committee). So, there is a very major involvement by FÁS in such committees. The main committees on which FÁS is involved are set out below:

Table 20.1. **Participation of PES staff in Irish partnerships**

Committee type	FÁS participants
Area partnership companies, incl. subgroups[2]	107
County/city development boards[2]	59
Social economy groups[2]	57
Community training workshops[1]	37
Childcare committees[2]	37
RAPID	35
County enterprise boards	33

1. FÁS programme-related advisory committees.
2. External committees on which FÁS participates.
Source: Author for the OECD.

From FÁS' perspective, there are two kinds of committees/organisations: *i)* where FÁS is the responsible body and we set up the committee to provide an input to our decision-making; and *ii)* where FÁS is one of many (equal) partners and the primary aim is to co-ordinate independent decision-making.

Many of the issues raised in other reports on partnership noted above have been experienced within FÁS. One of the issues that have been less considered in Ireland is the tension between local autonomy in terms of providing a flexible response to local needs. Thus, for example, local offices of the FÁS Employment Service might give more or less attention to certain target groups in different regions.

Another type of problem can arise if one local partnership wants to prioritise certain equity issues (*e.g.* gender, ethnicity) while another wants to target, say, early school leavers. To what extent should such local preferences be respected? These are the kinds of issues facing national organisations like FÁS in dealing with new local forms of governance.

Conclusion and perspectives for good governance in Ireland

In conclusion, and echoing some of the points made earlier in this chapter, some of the main issues that have arisen in FÁS' experience are:

The consultation processes can be very time consuming. At first FÁS tried to only send senior managers to represent the Organisation but this was impossible time wise. We now send a range of staff at different levels.

We have found great benefits from participation on local committees. They can help make much better decisions through better information between actors. They can help prevent misunderstandings. Sharing facilities is facilitated and this can help develop joint ventures. Other groups' priorities are also better understood.

It can take a long time for members of a committee to move away from pursuing purely selfish interests to focusing on client needs. Trust needs to be developed over time.

Good chairing is very helpful and independent facilitation can be useful at first. It is useful for the committee to review its ways of working on a regular basis.

Some partnerships seem to spend too long on consultation and ensuring that no interest is upset. There is a balance to be struck between very extensive consultation and the need for decision-making. The key mistake made by some groups is the confusion between *activity* and *results*.

Problems can arise if a committee is partly playing a consultative role and partly an executive function. The executive function can begin to develop a vested interest in its own survival and growth, and concentrate on establishing new functions rather than working through existing organisations.

There are always temptations for particular interests to try to go outside the committee structure – for example by making their case to the media. This is regrettable but impossible to prevent.

There can be a danger of over-lapping committees being established – for example we have RAPID areas of high disadvantage, we also have Area Partnership Companies for the long-term unemployment and Drugs Task Forces. Obviously, some of the clients in these areas over-lap.

So, while the participation process may result in some stresses and strains, our experience is that it does work in practice. Examples of success include three labour market initiative programmes which are administered by FÁS: Community Employment, the Job Initiative Scheme and the Social Economy Programme.

Community Employment (CE) and Job Initiative Scheme (JIS)

CE and JIS are labour market initiatives, which provides work experience, training and development opportunities for the long term unemployed and other disadvantaged persons through the provision of a range of Community Services which otherwise, would not be available. CE provides part-time work while JIS is full-time.

A Framework Agreement policy has been agreed centrally to ensure that these initiatives have real relevance to their localities. Each region within FÁS is required to work within this framework with the local partnership groups in each area. These groups have representation from Community, Trade Unions, Local Government and Employers. In practice, local FÁS management meet with the partnership group's employment related sub-committee on a regular basis to decide which schemes and which community sponsoring groups will be prioritised.

In the prioritisation of project proposals being put forward statistical data is supplied by FÁS. This data relates to levels of unemployment in the areas being considered, degrees of disadvantage *versus* available opportunities and analysis of earlier initiatives.

Agreement is reached by way of general discussion in the spirit of partnership where the basic criteria is primarily aimed towards the progression of the unemployed and disadvantaged and sponsoring committees are prioritised based on social need. Once agreed, projects are given annual contracts by FÁS and all administration relating to eligibility of the participants (workers) and programmes are administered by FÁS.

Social Economy Programme (SEP)

The Social Economy Programme got its impetus from "Partnership 2000 for inclusion employment and competitiveness", a three-year national programme which was concluded between the Irish government and the Social Partners (Trade Unions, employers associations, farming associations and also the organisations of unemployed people, women's groups and others working to counter social exclusion).

The Social Economy Programme seeks to: i) maximise the role of social economy enterprises in the regeneration of local economies within local disadvantaged areas, communities and communities of interest; and ii) maximise employment opportunities for the long-term unemployed or other disadvantaged persons.

A National Monitoring Committee (comprising the Social Partners) under the chair of the Department of Enterprise and Employment oversees the development and implementation of the Social Economy programme as agreed in a "Framework Document". The National Monitoring Committee monitors and evaluates the achievement of the objectives of the programme and also provides policy advice to Government organisations on the development of the Social Economy Programme.

While the funding and administration of the SEP is carried out by FÁS in consultation with partnership, companies have the responsibility to develop an agreed local strategy for the operation of the SEP. The Local Working Group meets quarterly. The Local Working Group gives advice and makes recommendations on projects seeking funding. The projects must meet the objectives set out in the "Framework Document" guidelines and criteria and must have been assessed by FÁS. Projects funded are awarded in the context of locally agreed priorities and funding available.

So, in conclusion, FÁS has been very involved in new forms of local governance involving partnerships. This fits within the overall partnership ethos of the country. We have improved our services through such partnership processes. However, there are a variety of issues that arise and which must be overcome if a partnership approach is to be successful.

Bibliography

NATIONAL CENTRE FOR PARTNERSHIP AND PERFORMANCE (2003), "A Competency Framework for Managing Change through Partnership", Dublin.

NESC – National Economic and Social Council (1996), *Strategy into the 21st Century*, Dublin.

OECD (2001), *Local Partnerships for Better Governance*, Paris.

OECD (1996), *Ireland: Local Partnership and Social Innovation*, Paris.

WALSH, J., CRAIG, S. and McCAFFERTY, D. (1988), *Local Partnerships for Social Inclusion*, Dublin.

ISBN 92-64-10470-4
Managing Decentralisation
A New Role for Labour Market Policy
© OECD 2003

PART III
Chapter 21

Austria: Bridging Economic Development and Labour Market Policy

by
Michael Förschner
Director, Ministry of Economy and Labour

The beginning

Almost 20 years ago Austria started to deliver labour market policy with the support of locally-based institutions, mainly non-profit organisations (NPOs). They were considered closer to the problem and its solution respectively, not bound by bureaucratic restrictions and not identified as being part of the official administration, therefore often more successful in approaching certain target groups with their specific problems. Although the number of private-run partner organisations increased steadily and results were positive it became obvious in the first half of the 1990s that the overall challenge had changed. A more territorially-based approach was defined where the linkages and interdependencies of labour market performance with other institutions and actors of the respective area became visible.

The idea was to form regional agreements of co-operation between the "major players", *i.e.* the regional government, the regional labour market service, and the social partners in order to combine resources and focus on special regional needs. A first such agreement was signed as early as 1993 between the Austrian government and the regional government of Styria and labour market policy was considered to have an important role.

Two years later when Austria joined the European Union regional agreements were signed within the overall concept of European Structural Funds (objectives 1, 2 and 5b). They were mainly focused on entrepreneurial issues. Labour market policy, although defined as an integral part in each single programme, was never at the core of the attention. Labour market policy was concentrated in horizontal programmes 3 and 4, though they were delivered regionally through the branch offices of the Labour Market Service (LMS or AMS in German – the public employment service). It had become a tripartite organisation at the very same time as Austria joined the Union. While the strong involvement of the social partners within this new organisation proved to be a big step forward in service delivery, regional involvement remained weak.

The regional dimension of labour market policy is reflected in a strongly decentralised structure of this federal organisation giving weight and decision power (including funding decisions of up to € 3.64 million) to regional boards. On these boards sit the regional director and representatives of the social partners. The reason for this arrangement is the basic funding structure of labour market policy in Austria. Its funds are provided by contributions of employers and employees. In addition, the Labour Market Service Act explicitly states that the representation of regional governments on LMS boards is subject to them making a certain contribution to labour market programmes of the LMS, a criterion that has not been met until now. Until a few years ago, the co-operation between regional governments and the LMS remained weak and unsystematic.

In 1997, a time of frustrating high unemployment rates throughout Europe, the concept of Territorial Employment Pact (TEP) was designed by the European Commission as a new experimental form of a more regionalised employment policy, taking aboard local actors in a partnership agreement. It was considered to be more flexible, providing wider acceptance, more resources and therefore better and different solutions. At about the same time the Austrian federal government was trying to sign agreements with regional governments in certain fields to combat rising unemployment more effectively, but also to raise additional funds. A series of agreements on youth employment were signed.

A more general discussion was started on how regional governments could be approached to contribute to the federal employment policy in a more systematic way. One main topic of interest was the large employment potential of social services, where in Austria the regions are the biggest providers, hence employers, but also demanders of services. An increase in activities by regional governments in this field would have enormous effects on the labour market. Another concern was to intensify the co-operation with local initiatives to assist people most in need and to help develop local communities. Certain fields were identified where such initiatives could be of special interest. A third element of the discussion was how to better combine policy interventions. It was agreed that policy decisions should in general be more employment-orientated, and should reflect employment effects more closely. Resources of different funds should also be combined so that strategic interventions could be made and synergies created, without additional budgetary cost.

Based on experience from other OECD countries (mainly Ireland and Finland) and the TEP programme of the European Commission, a concept was framed. As no additional budget was available, the agreement would focus on how to combine existing budgets within a certain region to achieve better results and to create agreements about mechanisms for information flow, common decision making etc. Data about target groups, local initiatives, measures and instruments were of mutual interest and it was felt that these should be identified and financial agreements reached on how to co-fund them. The agreement itself was to be signed between main regional partners. These are the LMS on regional level, the regional government of the area and the social partners. Additional partners also became involved in some regions. The Ministry was not among the organisations signing the agreements as it has no part in the regional setting framework. The idea is that the partners should form a common strategy based on a shared analysis of the regional situation and then combine resources in a common approach to combat unemployment. The Ministry offered to fund the local organisational structures of this partnership or Territorial Employment Pact. This includes the cost of personal needed to run the office and keep the partnership going. No additional budget was promised. In other words, all of the operating budget had to come from the regional LMS, the regional government, communities or other local institutions.

Soon it became apparent that situations, expectations and therefore possibilities differed from region to region. A first round of agreements was reached on a rather weak overall strategy, with their main goal being to get co-operation started. Although criticised by some for what seemed to be a lack of clear aims, this open approach did secure the participation of rather different actors with very different expectations. And once the first basic agreement was reached, it was then possible for the Ministry to influence the design and content of the TEP by showing best practice and offering advice.

Reasons for success

Whenever one tries to identify with certainty the reasons why this programme became a European example of best practice it becomes difficult to name the key factors. Since this is not an evaluation report (for this see Campbell, 2001, and the oncoming Austrian TEP evaluation) but rather a summary of personal experience at the ministerial level, the following arguments are necessarily more sketchy than exhaustive. But nonetheless, they do provide insight into the Ministry's approach to partnerships. The following elements certainly played their part in the later success of the Austrian TEPs:

- funding of operating structures by the Ministry;
- creation and funding by the Ministry of an independent TEP co-ordination unit;
- guidance instead of guidelines;
- long-term planning process secured by budget provisions from the European Social Fund;
- execution of new and separate tasks through the TEPs.

As stated above, the Ministry limited its funding contribution mainly to the necessary operating structures of the Pacts. In addition, the costs of some evaluations, public relations activities and a limited number of local projects were also borne centrally. With this small contributions of an average € 2 million annually altogether, partnership agreements on the regional level were signed that now amount to between € 250 and € 300 million each year. This does not mean that no co-funding on the regional level would have existed without this concept. But it surely suggests that the Pacts contributed effectively to the structure and co-ordination of labour market policy and social policy at the regional level.

A big difference between the Austrian Pacts and those of other counties' is the creation of the TEP co-ordination unit. The Ministry found it impossible to cope with the many different regional and local requirements and the enormous number of actors involved. In addition, experience has shown that a neutral form of communication often facilitates co-operation between the central level, the regions and the projects respectively. So it was decided to set up an independent unit to co-ordinate TEPs throughout Austria. This unit co-ordinates the network of partnerships in Austria, supports the ministry in delivering its ideas but also assists the activities of the partnerships on the ground. It facilitates national and international know how transfer, provides a common public relations design for the Pacts and co-operates work with the evaluation unit. Again the cost of this unit is considered comparatively low compared to its output.

When it became clear that the concept seemed worthwhile retaining, the Ministry included TEPs in the new Structural Fund programme (Objective 3, Austria 2000-2006, Priority 6), thereby securing funding of their local operational structures until 2006. This provided them with a stable budget situation which made it easy to develop go into a more long time planning process. Contracts between the Ministry and the regions for funding of these operational structures are now running on a two to three year time span. The new series of contracts start on 1st January 2004 and will run for a period of three years.

For a period of perhaps two years, the supported regional co-ordination offices' main task was the co-ordination of other bodies' activities. This changed with the European Union initiative EQUAL. EQUAL is an experimental Community Programme introduced to combat inequalities and disadvantages on the labour market in a very wide sense. To reach this goal, a pre-condition is that development partnerships (DP) be formed by all relevant actors to find new approaches and solutions. It was obvious on first glance that this initiative was going in more or less the same direction as the TEPs. Although there are some differences, the Ministry invited TEPs to take a role in the creation of the EQUAL development partnerships. In doing so, the role of the Pacts changed from mere co-ordination towards a creative unit with its own budget (about € 20 million are spent by DPs annually). This provided them with a new identity. The same happened when the Special Programme for the Disabled made use of this Pact structure. Again, competencies for disabled people are split between the federal and the regional level. So increased co-operation was needed and the framework to do so was hence provided.

This accumulation process gained such momentum that some people started warning not to exaggerate and overload the partnerships with all those impossible tasks, many of which had never been successfully delivered in the past. The Pact framework was considered not to be strong enough to take on board too many new initiatives. It might be important to watch this development carefully. But as has been outlined in the context of EQUAL, the structural innovation process is at least as important as the content innovation process. In other words, by seeking to use the Pact structure to deliver other new initiatives, the government is signalling that it holds these arrangements in high regard as forms of organisational innovation.

The future – New design, new relationships?

Current discussions among policy makers point towards two rather different possible future scenarios, both of which seem reasonable. The first scenario underlines the necessity of TEPs becoming more independent from central intervention. According to this view, if the partnership model is truly accepted by the regions, there is no reason for a central government to continue funding the operational structures and thereby shaping the regional process. The advantage of such a development would be to confront the TEPs with the key question of whether these actors can see the advantages of the partnership for their region. And if the advantages are seen by the partners, surely they will continue to co-operate and work together within the framework created and probably shape it further to their own future needs.

The second scenario concentrates on the valuable contribution TEPs have made to totally different aspects of labour market policy. Over the last seven years, they succeeded in finding a new co-operative model of labour market and social policy, in making more efficient use of local initiatives, in supporting gender mainstreaming, and in supporting the community initiative EQUAL and the Special Programme for Disabled ("*Behindertenmiliarde*"). They created an enormous local potential for future tasks to tap into. With their open and non-formal method of co-operation and agreement, it is possible to integrate new partners and to work on rather different tasks. Formal structures always have their limits according to their juridical duties and their official boards. On the contrary the equal basis of discussion created within the Austrian TEPs includes a number of non-official partners, mainly non-profit, whose contribution is of high value for the design and delivery of labour market policy in general.

According to this scenario, a framework has been created that enables local institutions and people to find solutions to their local needs within the overall concept of a national and regional policy. As outlined earlier, initiatives from the central government have been successfully transferred to the partnerships and they have been given – but have also actively taken – a key role in the delivery of these new approaches. This role would be highly different with totally independent partnerships. A strong linkage between Pacts and national policy is therefore assumed by most to be valuable.

The contemporary process of development of the Pacts now goes in the direction of a continuation of this linked model but under different circumstances:

Part A of a future central funding would still involve the central support of the local organisational structure of the Pacts. Part B could involve an increase of support to true bottom-up ideas that need additional budgets to develop. Such an approach was outlined in programmes of the European Commission such as "Local Capital for Employment", designed to give relatively small amounts of money to local initiatives via local intermediary structures. The advantage of such a model lies with the easy approach to budgets for units that usually are in no position to receive assistance or for ideas not covered by any official programme. Its disadvantage might be that the assistance given is not substantial enough to really cover basic needs. Another disadvantage lies in the additional bureaucracy such a programme might create as public spending requirements of course have to be met also in small funding cases. First experience in Austria has shown disappointing results for the latter.

Part C of a new design would be for optional state programmes to be made open to TEPs. This was been tried successfully for the first time when additional budgets were made available for inserting gender mainstreaming into Austrian partnerships. Under this kind of relationship it would be necessary to make a clearer distinction between those parts of the agreement that are based on agreed local needs and those based on central government incentives. This "three-pillar model" could be a solution to the desire to combine both development models: to give the TEPs more independence from the central government in order to define their own identity and to secure their important role in delivering labour market policy for the state as a whole.

It should not be overlooked that Austrian partnerships do have one crucial weakness, namely their relatively weak co-operation with economic departments and entrepreneurs. Although this seams understandable given that the first main approach was to create of a stronger link between labour market and social policy, it hinders development in the economic context. The Irish partnership model is seen as one of the best OECD examples because it has shown very clearly that the participation of entrepreneurs and perhaps even more important of entrepreneurial thinking, can be crucial for the success of partnerships. This weakness was stated and widely accepted at a meeting of Austrian TEPs in October 2002 and intensified efforts to better integrate the more business-orientated partners were agreed upon.

Partnerships are one aspect of a modern system of governance. They create co-operation between different levels of public administration and privately run and non-profit organisations. As in many other countries, the Austrian partnerships have been shown to contribute positively to this new form of regionally-based co-operative model of employment policy (in its wider meaning). They have been highly flexible regarding different regional settings and conditions and provided a framework for rather different political demands. The central funding of their organisation is a very cost effective way of supporting this development and thereby combining central tasks with regional needs. Within the next few years and with the enlargement of the Union, partnerships will become transnational, crossing borders and strengthening their forms of co-operation across administrations and alongside new needs. There are a lot of future possibilities open to them. We will see if they can fulfil the expectations.

ISBN 92-64-10470-4
Managing Decentralisation
A New Role for Labour Market Policy
© OECD 2003

PART III

Chapter 22

The UK: Co-ordinating Public Services through Local Partnerships

by
Michael Geddes
Warwick Business School

While there are many differences between the experiences of OECD member countries in local governance, there are also some important underlying similarities among most if not all of them:

- The relationship between the three spheres of state, market and civil society is subject to change, and in particular to an erosion of the previous domain of the state and the public sector by pressure from the market sector, and from civil society.
- This pressure results partly from the challenges to the legitimacy of the state and the efficiency of the public sector. Representative democracy is challenged by more direct forms of political participation and activism; while the services provided by the public sector struggle to meet the needs of a more educated, critical and affluent population.
- As a result of the challenge to the state and public provision, the ideology of the market is hegemonic; but at the same time there is widespread recognition of the inequalities which the market produces.
- The enhanced demands on civil society organisations to both play a governance role and to deliver public services is producing serious challenges to the capacity of the "third sector".

In this context, which is one of a shifting and contested policy environment, there is a tendency to look to partnerships which bring together actors from all three spheres, in order to: i) enhance the legitimacy of governance; ii) share risks and costs, in the context of a "risk environment" and pressures on resources; and iii) enhance the problem solving capacity of the governance system, and especially its ability to deliver "joined up" solutions to so-called cross-cutting, "wicked" issues (Geddes and Benington, 2001).

Local strategic partnerships

English local strategic partnerships (LSPs) are an important example of this tendency. They represent a major recent innovation in the pattern of local governance in England. An LSP is a body which: i) brings together at a local level the different parts of the public sector as well as the private, business, community and voluntary sectors so that different initiatives and services support each other and work together; ii) is a non-statutory, non-executive organisation; and iii) operates at a level which enables strategic decisions to be taken yet is close enough to the grassroots to allow direct community engagement.

Initial guidance on the establishment of LSPs was issued by the national government in early 2001. Currently, LSPs have been set up in the vast majority of localities in England. Progress has been faster in those 88 localities containing the most deprived neighbourhoods in England which are eligible for government funding from the Neighbourhood Renewal Fund (NRF). This is conditional on the existence of an LSP. However, many other localities have reacted enthusiastically to the government's proposals.

A number of recent government initiatives relate closely to the core tasks of LSPs:

- The introduction of statutory Community Strategies. These are intended to improve the economic, environmental, and social well-being of each area, and contribute to the achievement of sustainable development across the country. Local authorities have many of the responsibilities and powers needed to bring about improvements in their communities, but other public services, local people, business and the voluntary and community sectors also need to be able to contribute. It is therefore the task of the LSP to prepare and implement the community strategy for the area.

- Steps to rationalise and simplify existing partnerships. It is recognised that there is an urgent need to rationalise the confusing proliferation of partnerships, plans and initiatives at local level, to reduce duplication and unnecessary bureaucracy and to make it easier for partners, including those outside the statutory sector, to get involved. LSPs have been tasked with the "rationalisation" of local partnerships within their area.

- The launch of a national strategy to renew the country's most deprived neighbourhoods. The objective of the National Strategy for Neighbourhood Renewal is to narrow the gap between the most deprived neighbourhoods and the rest of the country, with common goals of lower unemployment and crime, and better health, education, housing and physical environment. Effective neighbourhood renewal is seen to depend on services working together to plan and deliver concerted improvements in public services. Local people, business and the voluntary sector all need to be able to contribute. It is a task of the LSP to develop and deliver a local neighbourhood renewal strategy.

- The development of local public service agreements (LPSAs) between central and local government to tackle key national and local priorities (on health, education, employment, crime, and housing), with agreed flexibilities, pump-priming and financial rewards if improvements are delivered. Local authorities need to show that their proposals are supported by local people, and need to work with other partners to deliver LPSA targets, through the agency of the LSP.

This challenging set of tasks require LSPs to: *i)* develop a variety of means to consult with local people; *ii)* build common purpose and shared commitment among partners, avoiding the domination of any one partner or set of partners; *iii)* develop and publicise common aims and priorities; *iv)* share local information and good practice; *v)* identify, encourage and support effective local initiatives; and *vi)* develop a common performance management system.

For those LSPs in receipt of Neighbourhood Renewal Fund (but not others), an annual accreditation process managed by government regional offices has sought to ensure that LSPs are both strategic and inclusive, are effectively action focused and performance managed, with a capacity to learn and develop.

Local public service agreements

Within the new context for local governance provided by the LSP, local public service agreements are seen by government as a means of delivering public services better on the ground, in ways which both encourage local authorities to meet and exceed national targets, and which at the same time reflect local needs and priorities.

A LPSA is an agreement between an individual local authority and the national government. It sets out the local authority's commitment to deliver specific improvements in performance and the government's commitment to reward those improvements. The scheme was developed from proposals from the Local Government Association and the government's Public Service Agreements for individual central departments. It was piloted with 20 authorities in 2001-2002 and over the next two years all local authorities (with the exception of second tier districts) which wish to do so can negotiate an LPSA. Government wishes local authorities to involve other organisations in the development of the LPSA.

The essence of an LPSA is that:

- the authority commits itself to achieving a dozen or so specific targets that will require performance beyond what could otherwise be expected;
- government offers to reward success achieved;
- government also offers to help achieve success by a pump-priming grant; scope for extra borrowing; and possible relaxations in statutory and administrative requirements;
- the targets chosen should reflect both national and local priorities, with the majority relating to the national PSA targets related to local government services.

LPSAs are intended to complement other policies seeking to improve service delivery outcomes, including the local authority's Best Value

Performance Plan (which may suggest potential targets) and Neighbourhood Renewal floor targets. In areas eligible for the Neighbourhood Renewal Fund, LPSAs must include targets related to neighbourhood renewal.

Challenges facing the partnership model of local governance

The environment within which LSPs and LPSAs are emerging is one of major change in the contemporary forms of governance, with new forms emerging in response to the deficiencies of traditional, large bureaucratic "silos", a more fragmented and fluid set of institutional structures and relationships, and changing relationships between the state, the market and civil society. Many of these tendencies are closely related to the government's key policy drivers such as the modernisation of government and local government, continuous improvement in the performance of public services, and joined up working to tackle cross-cutting issues such as social inclusion and neighbourhood renewal.

The assumption behind the establishment of LSPs is that a framework of strategic partnership at the local level will create more efficient, inclusive and pluralist local governance, bringing together key organisations and actors (from the three spheres of state, market and civil society) to identify communities' top priorities and needs, and work with local people to provide them. This is consistent with the widely-shared perception in the policy community of the advantages of partnership working as the way of achieving effective outcomes, and solutions to so-called "wicked issues", by building trust, sharing knowledge and resources, and working collaboratively across boundaries. LPSAs add a dimension of "vertical partnership" between central and local government to the "horizontal" partnership relationships of LSPs. However, if LSPs and LPSAs are to deliver on the challenging agenda to which they are committed, they will have to find ways to manage a number of tensions.

Local and strategic?

For an LSP to be both strategic and local, it needs to tailor its role and function to the opportunities and constraints in its area. The initial capacity of emerging LSPs will be conditioned by the history of past partnership working and the character and capacities of key partners, bringing "to the table" a set of vested interests, knowledge, aspirations, hopes and fears. But places vary. Achieving a common vision will have a different meaning in areas where the task is to overcome deprivation compared to those where it is more to manage the spin-offs of economic success without jeopardising the existing quality of life. In a large city, it may be difficult to reconcile city-wide strategic priorities with the diversity of local communities and their needs, while in a smaller locality the LSP may struggle to engage key strategic players. Local history, identity, political culture matter and being strategic requires vertical and horizontal integration in terms of policy and governance across agencies, and with sub-regional and regional bodies.

Being strategic also demands specific qualities in the partnership. LSP members must be able to take an overview rather than be driven by sectional interests. They must have the authority to represent their own organisations and carry through its commitment. Experience to date indicates that the formative and developmental stages of partnership are vital but take time. This is the case where the LSP is set up on the foundations of a previous partnership, which will require partners to adapt to changed goals, structures and membership; but also when the LSP is a new creation, requiring the establishment of new relationships and trust.

Leadership is seen to be crucial. Whilst the local authority may be expected to take the lead, there is a fine line between leadership and domination. But other partners may be reluctant to invest the time and resources to counterbalance the danger of one player becoming over-dominant. It is important to establish clear mutual expectations about roles and responsibilities, to get the pace of development right, and to accommodate and exploit difference, maximising the synergy from the combination of perspectives, roles and expertise. In some of those areas where the LSP has been set up quickly to access NRF resources, there seems to have been insufficient time and space for these processes – but in others the "carrot" of NRF funds has been a spur for the LSP partners to "get their act together".

Inclusive, effective and accountable?

The potential membership of LSPs is very wide. The evidence shows that there is substantial difference in both the size of membership of LSPs, and the structures through which members are accommodated and involved. Many LSPs have between 20 and 40 members, but some are much smaller than this while others are much larger. In a significant number of cases the nature of "membership" is less than clear – for example whether individuals are members in a personal capacity or as representatives of their organisation. There is normally a common core of members from local government and other public agencies, but more diversity in business and voluntary and community sector membership. The involvement of local councillors also varies widely.

Achieving effective community participation has proved particularly testing for LSPs dealing with a large population and wide range of interests and policy issues. Many LSPs are finding that it requires new knowledge and skills to:

- map local groups and umbrella organisations;

- identify and work with hard-to-reach groups that may have been excluded from decision making in the past (young people, BME groups);
- create structures that work for neighbourhoods and communities of interest;
- provide long term support and capacity building for the community sector.

LSPs with access to NRF funding can draw on dedicated funding to support community engagement, but in other localities these special funds are not available.

The emergence of LSPs has also raised politically sensitive issues about representativeness and democratic accountability. For many local councillors, these new bodies and arrangements are being put in place without apparent consideration of their implications for local democracy. Government guidance gives attention to the accountability of partner organisations to the LSP, but does not address LSPs' own accountability. It remains unclear where LSPs sit alongside electoral democracy or how local people hold the LSP to account.

LSPs are exploring different ways of developing the capacity for effective action whilst also opening up their decision making and delivery processes to a wide range of organisations. This can be done through wider partnership structures, for example, cross-representation on other partnerships, tiered arrangements or sub-groups that undertake detailed work on specific objectives or issues. Thus in some places the LSP is not so much a single partnership as a nest or network of local partnerships, including as many as several hundred people.

There is also substantial variation in the extent to which LSPs have acquired dedicated staff and resources to support the work of the LSP. In a few cases, LSPs now have significant staff teams which are independent of any one partner, but the majority still depend on a minimal support team, which is often still provided by a lead partner such as the local authority.

While developing their own (sometimes complicated) structures and processes, LSPs are also beginning to explore ways to streamline and reduce the overall numbers of local partnerships. But current experience is often that the complex network of local partnerships engages with a wide range of very different interests and is not easy to disentangle or dismantle. The capacity of LSPs to reduce the "partnership overload" also depends upon willingness by central government to desist from creating further partnerships and facilitate the rationalisation of existing ones.

The evidence is that there is still a tension in many LSPs between the imperative to be inclusive and accountable, and the imperative towards effective action. memberships and working practices are still evolving in most cases. LSPs with large memberships with widely disparate access to resources and influence, and those which prioritise inclusiveness in their working processes, may find it harder to agree upon action. However, those which have relatively small and tight memberships may find that they are open to accusations of governance by a local elite.

From strategy to action to outcomes

Key initial tasks of LSPs are the development of Community Strategies and local Neighbourhood Renewal Strategies. Emerging evidence suggests that LSPs are making good progress in agreeing the broad vision of such strategies, but that difficulties increase as delivery requires moving from generalities to specific commitments. Translating strategy into action can expose weaknesses, tensions and unresolved conflicts between partners. In order to achieve real change, LSPs must address the delivery of mainstream services, the quality and effectiveness of these and the bending of local policy and practice in line with partnership priorities. This can cause tensions not only within the partnership, but particularly if local priorities are seen to clash with vertical drivers from parent departments at national level. The mainstreaming of LPSAs and the principles they embody will be crucial in this respect. The initial response to the pilot LPSA programme appears to have been broadly positive on the part of both local and central government. Local authorities have welcomed the impetus to innovative thinking which has been offered, while sometimes finding that the additional resources and flexibilities have been less than anticipated. However, the transition from a limited pilot programme to a mainstream process will test the capacity of both central and local partners.

Performance management

An increasingly important issue for LSPs is that of performance management and measurement. This applies both to the activity of the LSP itself, and to the perceived need to hold partners to account for delivery of agreed actions and outcomes – and if necessary deal with non-performance. Government is now piloting a performance management framework for LSPs. This may prove attractive to LSPs which recognise the importance of strong horizontal performance management drivers to counter-balance the strong vertical accountabilities to which most partners are subject. This is especially true for those that have been able to build up a strong enough staff team to undertake a performance management role.

However, some LSPs currently take the view that the approach to performance management which is appropriate to a traditional organisation is much less appropriate for an LSP. Partnerships such as LSPs are essentially voluntary institutions, not formal organisations, and performance management and measurement arrangements need to reflect this context. It is also widely recognised that there are increasing levels of difficulty associated with the movement from measuring inputs and outputs to measuring outcomes, and in measuring performance on so-called "cross-cutting" issues requiring joined up working between service providers. In a similar way, it is recognised that measuring the performance of partnerships poses greater difficulties than in the context of single services or organisations. A key issue for LSPs is how to measure the value added to the activities of individual partners by the partnership (while recognising that partnership working involves costs as well as potential benefits).

For some LSPs, issues of learning and development may be more important than the introduction of formalised performance management systems. The need for LSPs to have a systematic approach to building skills and knowledge (and at the same time to avoid information overload) has been recognised, and local learning plans have been piloted in a number of LSPs, with specific reference to the neighbourhood renewal function. More widely, some LSPs are beginning to explore the possibilities of working together to share knowledge and experience, and to benchmark their own performance against their peers within learning networks.

Conclusions

It is, as yet, too early to say whether the new forms of governance represented by LSPs and LPSAs are fulfilling their objectives of joining up the fragmented system of local governance in England to deliver better and more integrated local services. While partnership is seen as a means of enhancing problem solving capacity under conditions of complexity and uncertainty, there is a risk that partnership working may add to the complexity and impenetrability of the governance process.

The emphasis of LSPs on the inclusive representation of stakeholder interests, including those of community interests, needs to be aligned with, rather than counterposed to, local democratic accountabilities. LPSAs represent a potentially valuable model of central-local partnership, but the principle of central government flexibility needs to be applied in a more thoroughgoing way. The value added by partnership remains hard to measure, and moves such as the introduction of performance management systems may contribute to the bureaucratisation of local governance which LSPs are intended to short-circuit.

Bibliography

DEPARTMENT OF THE ENVIRONMENT, TRANSPORT AND THE REGIONS (2001), "Local Strategic Partnerships, Government Guidance", London. *www.neighbourhood.gov.uk/publications*

GEDDES, Mike and BENINGTON, John (eds.) (2001), *Local Partnerships and Social Exclusion in the European Union*, Routledge, London.

OFFICE OF THE DEPUTY PRIME MINISTER (2000) (updated 2003), "Local Public Service Agreements", London. *www.local-regions.odpm.gov.uk/lpsa/*

UNIVERSITY OF WARWICK, UNIVERSITY OF THE WEST OF ENGLAND, OFFICE FOR PUBLIC MANAGEMENT and LIVERPOOL JOHN MOORES UNIVERSITY (2003), "Evaluation of Local Strategic Partnerships: Report of a Survey of All English LSPs", for the Office of the Deputy Prime Minister and Department of Transport, London.

ISBN 92-64-10470-4
Managing Decentralisation
A New Role for Labour Market Policy
© OECD 2003

PART III

Chapter 23

Norway: Developing an Integrated Approach in the Regions

by
Petter Knutzen
Deputy Director-General, Ministry of Regional Development
and Local Government

Regional policy and regional reform

To start with the end of a long process: from 1 January 2003, the government's special measures for regional development are being decentralised as a "lump sum" to politically elected bodies at regional level. With this reform, the issues of regional priorities, partnerships, accountability and cross-sector co-ordination are put to the forefront of the regional debate in Norway.

The reform has actually been named an "accountability reform". As will be argued in this chapter, this means that the political leadership at regional level will have full responsibility for the results that are being achieved through the measures involved.

In response to this new framework, it is expected that a new generation of partnerships will emerge involving national government agencies, regional government actors and the social partners at regional level.

The background picture

To a large extent, regional development in Norway has been a question of economic growth and social welfare in the peripheral and predominantly rural regions, mostly in the northern parts of the country. Historically, centralisation of the population to the larger cities has been regarded as a challenge to national welfare goals. Consequently, preservation of the basic features of the settlement pattern has been an important national value and political objective for the last fifty years.

In accordance with this tradition, public policies on education, communication and transport, social security, labour market, health and general welfare have been conducted with rather strong emphasis on the national "obligations" towards the peripheral parts of the country. This started long before oil resources made Norway a rich industrialised nation, and is mainly concerned with regional distribution of goods and services in the *public sector*. In this category, one should also include parts of the agricultural subsidies and some specifically reduced duties and taxes.

On top of this so-called "broad" and general regional policy, there exists a more "narrow" regional policy, consisting of special programmes aimed mostly at small business investment and innovation, industrial sites and local mobilisation efforts. These measures are especially aimed at local and regional economic development in the *private sector* in peripheral parts of the country.

Scale and scope of the regional policies

In the year 2000, the Ministry of Local Government and Regional Development made an assessment of the size of regional allocations in the nation's annual budget. The results can be summed up as follows:

1. The already mentioned special programmes for regional development (the "narrow" regional policy) amounted to 1.7 billion NOK which is approx. 0.3% of the annual budget.
2. Special measures within the sectoral policies with explicit goals of equalising regional imbalances amounted to 14 billion NOK. That was 2.5% of the annual budget.
3. Sector policy measures of vital importance to regional development, but without explicit and inherent regional goals were summed up to 100 billion NOK, which was 18% of the annual budget.

The basic features of policy organisation at regional level produce a split picture. The sectoral policies (points two and three above) corresponds to the so-called "broad" regional policy are mostly run through a set of state agencies at regional level, but mostly at the premises of the national sectors themselves. The specific, or extra, measures for regional development (the 1.7 billion in the first point) are for the most part delegated to the politically elected county councils, which are the representative bodies at regional level.

For several years, there has been an intense debate about the allocation of these tasks and responsibilities for sectoral policy at the regional level. Two different governments have presented White Papers to the Parliament on the issues involved, and the current Centre-Conservative government got Parliamentary support for its new position in June 2002. The outcome of these political processes can be summed up as follows:

- the politically elected *county councils* will have the role of leading developmental actor at regional level, and will conduct their policies through a partnership including state agencies, municipalities and private sector;
- the municipalities will be the prime providers of social services to their inhabitants;
- the state agencies at regional level will be implementers of national sector policies, among them labour market policy, in collaboration with the other members of the partnerships.

The reform is accompanied by a large change in how the specific funds for regional development (the 1.7 billion) are to be transferred to the county councils. From 2003, on the funds will be provided as *a lump sum* with a large *flexibility in usage*, instead of through eight different streams of funds with different rules and formal frameworks. The funds for regional development are now completely *decentralised*, compared to a regime of *delegation* up to this year.

However, the reform did not transfer any new tasks to the county councils from the state agencies, which was a strong wish from the politicians at regional level. Neither has it so far provided the state agencies at regional level with more leeway for regional adjustments within the national sector based policies. The White Paper simply stated that this latter issue will be under continuous consideration in the time to come.

Accountability and partnerships

This outcome provides two challenges for the regional politicians. The first question is whether this spilt structure with its co-ordinating mechanism of partnerships will work. The second, and closely connected question, is how the regional politicians will use their enlarged freedom in handling the specific development funds to promote "joint ventures" and closer collaboration with the state agencies and at the same time be fully responsible for results achieved through the development measures.

The issue of accountability

The old, fragmented regime of delegation of the development funds at regional level contained different measures for a variety of objectives, each with differing formal frameworks. The main measures were aimed at business loans and grants for investment, grants to entrepreneurs, grants to municipality's industrial infrastructure (sites, waterworks and harbours), and local mobilisation efforts. In addition, state programmes concerning large industrial lay-offs and local employment crises and water supply improvements were run in close collaboration with the county councils.

Under the new, decentralised regime for the development funds, all these different measures are put together into one large general development measure transferred to the county councils as a "lump sum". The regional politicians from this year on have the power to set priorities among these – or other – objectives at their own discretion. The new, common framework makes no guidelines for the priorities at regional level, except that the use of the funds directly or indirectly, shall improve innovation and productivity of the regional industrial production and hence promote regional economic growth.

The goals and strategies to attain this general national objective are to be decided upon through the political processes at regional level. As a basis for the regional priorities lies a comprehensive county (regional) plan with a four year time horizon. It is expected that the objectives and strategies, programmes and development projects will be made on an annual basis within the framework of a regional development programme or action plan brought forward through discussions within the partnership.

Will the participation of the partnership in the decision regarding regional strategies blur the question of accountability? This remains to be seen, but from the point of view of the central government there is no doubt: the Minister in charge has made it perfectly clear that the county councils are accountable for the results achieved by means of the decentralised development funds. In consequence, the decentralisation of funds is not followed up by any kind of agreements or contracts between central and regional government, as for example the EU structural programmes or the French system of planning-contracts. Another example of this strict division of roles lies in the fact that each region, or county, has an obligation to make a system of goal-related indicators for result measurement. The Ministry at central level takes no part in the building of the measurement-systems, its only part is to see to that such systems are being shaped.

Why make such fuss about a reform covering so small an amount of the funds which impact upon regional development? The answer lies in the new character of the funding arrangements themselves, and in the way they are supposed to fuel the functioning of the partnerships.

Partnerships and regional co-ordination

Regional development is in essence a cross-sectoral effort. The combined effort of the regional state agencies, not to mention the even wider national "per capita" transfers are believed to have a greater impact on regional imbalances and regional development than do the specific (narrow) development funds. Nonetheless, the importance of the latter type of funds lies partially in the fact that they come as regional surplus money on top of the sectoral funds, following national priorities favouring the scarcely inhabited periphery.

The new, decentralised regime offers enhanced opportunities for the county council to stimulate the other actors to make stronger efforts to back up regional political priorities through common strategies, programmes and projects. State agencies for agriculture, fisheries, the labour market, and post-graduate education, all perform important functions in both the shaping and implementation of national policies. When the specific development funds are freed of their national priorities, the county council has in principle a larger opportunity to involve the state agencies in the regional development strategies, especially if these strategies are agreed upon in the partnership. This opportunity is seen as an important prerequisite for the county councils to take a leading developmental role.

These are the intentions behind the "Accountability Reform". Its success depends on the ability of regional politicians to shape their new, leading role, but also on the extent to which national co-ordination supports the work in the regional partnerships. A third, and equally important factor, is the development of the economy in general. In the final paragraphs of this chapter, elements of the three issues will be briefly sketched.

New role for regional politicians

The regional actors have some partnership experience. For the last four years, under the old, fragmented regional development regime, the county council and the state agencies have formed partnerships together with the social partners. As pointed out by the OECD Study on Local Partnerships, the Norwegian partnership experience so far has been more information-based than strategically oriented. The "silos" prevailed, and common action took place only at project level at best.

A basic question is whether the political bodies in the regions is able to pave the way for constructive co-ordination based of equal partners. Leadership in this context must obviously put large emphasis on the creation of common views on the situation at hand to prepare the grounds for common goals and strategies. Such goals and strategies must pay respect to the state agencies' obligation to their sectoral and national interests. Far too many debates on regional co-ordination have ended up in a power-struggle over the ownership of tasks. Co-ordination has too often been seen as a matter of hierarchical subordination.

Partnerships are by principle an opposite method of co-ordination. The efforts of partnerships must be based on trust, co-operation and consensus at least around common denominators. In view of the heated debate in Norway on this matter in the later years, there are probably a lot of barriers that have to be broken down. How the county councils, and their administrations, as the leading actor in the partnerships handle this situation will be a vital success criterion for the regional reform.

New role for the ministry and central government

The reform described above also produces new challenges for central government. Two features of such challenges are already evident.

The Accountability Reform rests heavily on budgetary changes, which in turn changes the relations between the ministry responsible for regional development and the regions. The Ministry has to adapt to a new "hands-off" situation following the intentions of extended regional independence, in contradiction to a strong "hands-on" attitude in the old regime. The Ministry now puts strong emphasis on developing a new role more like a facilitator for the regions.

The other aspect of new central government position towards the regions lies in the way territorial elements are included in the sectoral policymaking at national level. OECD work on partnerships frequently states that the lack of co-ordinated national policy strongly hampers cross-sectoral policy making at regional level. This issue is taken seriously in ongoing policy making concerning innovation policy, administrative structures for business support and re-localisation of governmental offices. In all three processes, regional agencies play a more dominant role compared to previous efforts on the same issues.

Economic forecasts provide threats and possibilities

Changes in the general economic environment might put strain on the newly established regional independence. During the winter of 2003, unemployment has been rising, and we have seen lay-offs in urban service sectors and manufacturing industries, the latter often located in the more peripheral parts of the country. This will sharpen the focus on collaboration between labour market policy and regional development policy. Regional labour market state agencies play an important role in the partnerships, emphasising both demand-sided job training regionally, and market driven restructuring of the labour force nationally. If unemployment continues to rise, the ability of partnerships to encompass both labour market efforts and regional development objectives will be tested.

Other macroeconomic events might create different challenges for the Accountability Reform. For different reasons primary sectors like fisheries and agriculture might face restructuring challenges in the years to come, due to new technologies, logistics and global institutional frameworks. Both industries are of vital importance for the remote areas, and it is most unlikely that the regions alone can deal with the consequences. The policy debate concerning these resource-based industries has just begun, but the forthcoming structural changes will most likely involve both national and regional authorities. The degree of unanimity and the strategic approach of regional partnerships can in such a situation give a clear picture of the strength of the new roles for regional actors placed between market forces and national political pressures for action.

ISBN 92-64-10470-4
Managing Decentralisation
A New Role for Labour Market Policy
© OECD 2003

PART III
Chapter 24

Sweden: New Pathways for Labour Market Policy

by
Leni Svenningsson
Director, National Labour Market Board (AMS)

New forms of governance are flourishing in many countries, including Sweden, promoting policy co-ordination and the adaptation of labour market policy to regional and local needs.

In Sweden, regional development policy underwent great changes during the 1990s. The government launched a new development policy, which is now being implemented. The characteristic feature of the new policy is that it takes the form of Regional Growth Agreements and programmes, drawn up in regional partnerships.

These growth programmes and partnership models are well in line with the very strong Swedish tradition of tripartite agreements and collaboration between social partners. Sometimes it has been said that Sweden has managed to combine the best of two systems; capitalism and socialism, private ownership and public welfare.

This has been called "the Swedish model". The model succeeded in bringing together the employers' associations and the trade unions allowing them to reach common agreements. This constituted the basis for the development of strong union and employer associations in Sweden for many years.

The "Saltsjöbaden Agreement" of 1938, which introduced centralised wage negotiations, came to symbolise the co-operative spirit between these social partners and through tripartite agreements and close co-operation between the government and the social partners, Sweden became known as a country of social peace.

The rise of the Swedish model

In a purely economic sense, the Swedish model was a means for avoiding inflation in a full-employment economy, developed by two union economists – Rudolf Meidner and Gösta Rehn.

Their analysis asserted the compatibility of full employment and economic stability if the government followed a restrictive fiscal and monetary policy, keeping profits and demand for labour low enough to limit wage increases, but, at the same time, avoiding unemployment by active labour market policy measures. By the end of the 1950s and through to the 1960s and the 1970s, this model became almost a permanent feature for Swedish governments and an integral part of the government's role.

During these three decades, the role of the social partners in policy formation was very important, especially in economic and labour market policy. Together with strong administrative bodies like AMS (the National Labour Market Board), the unions and the employers set priorities for labour market policies. AMS was headed by a 15-member directorate, nine of whom represented the unions and the employer associations, and provided a perfect forum for establishing consensus; full employment, economic growth, social security and industrial peace.

So, the administration of labour market policy was based on very active tripartite co-operation within the AMS directorate and in other parts of the Labour Market Authority, at the regional and local levels. The social partners became jointly responsible for ensuring the development and implementation of the necessary labour market programmes which generate a long-term commitment to solving employment problems and keeping the employment issue at the centre of economic policy debate. These were "the Golden Years" of the Swedish model.

The fall of the Swedish model

There were, however, some weaknesses in the Swedish economic policy that eventually became a serious threat to the model as a whole and brought about its downfall during the 1980s and 1990s. The most significant weakness was the government's inability to prevent overheating in the form of excess profits and wage demands, which would later lead to cost inflation.

Meidner and Rehn had made it very clear that the goal was full employment without inflation. The governments followed the model in times of recession (i.e. they used supply-side labour market policy instead of expansive measures), but they were politically unable to pursue restrictive policies in boom times. This resulted in cost inflation and the deterioration of international competitiveness. The governments tried to neutralise cost inflation by repeated devaluations and their attempts to control the wage formation process by income policy measures and interventions reflected the disintegration of the Swedish model, which had the autonomy of the social partners as a central component.

It could perhaps be said that the Swedish model collapsed because of the failure of the social partners to accept their full responsibility for policy outcomes. The 1980s were characterised by exceptionally high profits, an overheated labour market, high wage drift, cost inflation, industrial conflict and not least the employers' decision to pursue a new strategy for decentralising wage policies. The employers' decision to refrain from central wage negotiations in 1990 constituted what seemed to be the final blow to the Swedish model.

In a consistent manner, the employers also withdrew from all formal tripartite co-operation. They decided to leave most of the institutions based on social partnership, such as the National Labour Market Board.

A shift in favour of bipartite decision-making and negotiations

The principal goals of the Swedish model have never changed – to make full employment compatible with price stability, and to increase growth and employment. But the methods used for reaching the goals have changed. In some areas, the process of renewal has already begun.

There has been a shift from the tripartite central model in employer-employee relations in favour of bipartite decisions-making at the work-place level, and the centralised Swedish wage negotiation system has given way to more industry-level and local (often individual) bargaining.

The Swedish employers are against re-entering central tripartite negotiations or formal tripartite institutions, finding it more beneficial to stay outside such arrangements, based on the opinion that the old universal solutions do not fit the new flexible labour market, due to the effects of globalisation on national economies.

The refusal of the employers to act as a full negotiating partner in the 1990s was not only a notable frustration for the central trade unions but also for the social democratic government. The tripartite administration of national labour market policy was also broken. Inside AMS, this was seen as a great drawback for achieving active labour market policy.

While the inclusion of social partners in the shaping of labour market policies is still a cornerstone of Danish labour market administration, the social partners are now almost non-existent in the Swedish labour market administration.

Responsibility for labour market policy taken over by the government

Today, AMS is headed by a directorate appointed by the government and includes people with great experience of labour market policy. However, these senior decision-makers do not represent any external organisation. Similarly, the county labour market boards are appointed by the government according to the same principles as to the AMS directorate.

In order to increase the local influence, there are local employment service committees, where representatives for the local business sector and social partners take part, but where the majority of the members are local politicians appointed by the municipalities.

It is said that the local co-operation between the partners is working well, but they do not have the necessary funding needed to implement their own policy. The reason is obvious.

While the government acknowledges that the prerequisites for an efficient and flexible labour market are different in different parts of the country, labour market policy in Sweden is being expressed in terms of a national policy and a national responsibility in order to avoid locking-in effects in the local labour market and to grant equal rights and obligations to citizens in different parts of the country.

As an answer to the economic crisis and the steady rise in the unemployment rate and the drastic fall in employment level in the 1990s, in the last few years the Swedish government has pursued a strong national top-down labour market policy and established a very strict management by objectives strategy.

There is strong emphasis on national goals for labour market policy, such as lowering the unemployment rate to less than 4% and raising the employment level to 80%. In addition, operational targets and results are used throughout the organisation down to the local employment offices, in order to reach these goals.

Partial revival of tripartite co-operation in regional growth agreements

As a national policy, labour market policy also has a regional dimension. This dimension has developed considerably during the last five years in Sweden, much in line with the European Employment Strategy (EES).

A collaborative structure has been built up where the main instruments are known as Regional Growth Agreements. These Agreements are drawn-up in a broad partnership led by county administrative boards or regional self-governing bodies and involving *inter alia* the municipalities, county councils, the business sector and local business associations, trade unions, the county labour board, universities, the regional skills councils, etc.

The participation of the business community is considered to be a prerequisite for the success of the programmes or as the government has emphasised: "The regional public actors are encouraged to enter into discussions with representatives of local and regional business communities to ensure that their views and needs are integrated into the action programmes". The emphasis on business involvement and the belief in public-private partnerships as a strategy for arranging development can to some extent be seen as a partial revival of the traditional tripartite co-operation between the social partners.

A long-term, nationwide model for overall national growth policy

The first round of regional growth agreements was drawn up in all counties during 1998-1999, to be implemented during the period 2000-2002. They will be extended up to and including 2003.

The government has expressed the opinion that the agreements that should be developed and improved through experience and evaluation: "The government's aim is for the growth agreements to reflect Swedish regional perspective on how growth and employment should be promoted. This is a long-term, nation-wide model and therefore constitutes an important cornerstone of overall national growth policy".

In its recent bill on regional policy, the Government proposed that the term "regional growth agreement" be changed to "regional growth programme", at the start of new programme period 2004-2007, reflecting the more comprehensive nature of the policy.

In reports that have been compiled on how the growth agreements have developed so far, there are a lot of interesting observations and criticisms.

As was said before, prior to its accession to the European Union in 1995, regional governance had not been strongly developed in Sweden. Sweden lacked, for example, the sort of regional structure needed to effectively implement the EU's structural fund programmes. The growth agreements and the partnership model were introduced by the government as a measure to address this situation. But no detailed study was made as to whether the model has been effective, and, if so, in which situations. Obviously, development cannot be ordered into existence through political decisions. The task of policies is primarily to create good general preconditions – including basic structures – for regional development. In Sweden, this involves an effective municipal equalisation system in which local taxation resources are transferred from the more densely-populated regions to the more sparsely-populated regions, an active labour market policy, a wide access to knowledge and skills for the workforce and an extension of higher education, contributing to a cluster-based innovation policy etc. The EU's structural funds are part of this general policy.

By introducing the growth programmes and the partnership model, the government is signalling that it regards the issue to be important and that it is willing to act unconventionally and non-bureaucratically to achieve its goal.

However, there is sometimes a gap between words and actions. Regulations as well as goals for various policy areas and authorities must still be complied with. Neither are any extra funds provided for the process.

One observation is that it has been difficult to involve central government authorities in the work on growth agreements at the regional level, which makes cross-sector co-operation and co-ordination difficult. The sectorisation of public administration is also a problem in Sweden. The use of central government funds for work on growth agreements is strictly regulated. There are, for example, still very few opportunities for AMS to engage in innovative package deals with the regional partnerships.

Of course, the significance of the Growth Agreements is reduced by the fact that partnerships lack any real funding resources and there is a belief that most of the measures implemented would have been implemented anyway. In some cases, Growth Agreements can even complicate regional development policy since they force regional players to adapt their planned measures to a model that has been determined at a central level. In this sense, Growth Agreements entail a centralisation of regional development policy.

A compromise between market and democracy

In its new bill, called "A Policy for Growth and Viability throughout Sweden", the government answers these criticisms and proposes some important shifts in the approach to regional development policy. While regional equalisation remains the overall goal for regional policy, this goal has to be supplemented with a more optimistic growth objective.

The government has stated that key policy areas which have a significant impact on regional development should be better integrated in order to fulfil the goal of regional development policy. A co-ordination programme between several policy areas has already been launched which is designed to take practical steps towards achieving more effective co-ordination. The sectorisation of the public administration has to be broken, according to the government.

Furthermore, the government now provides the option for all municipalities to form a co-operative body in each county, which would take over regional economic development from the county administrative boards. Almost half of the 21 counties have now formed such a body. This is in line with a policy that future organisations of regional government should be structured with the state and the municipalities as the main partners. The regional partnerships will have greater democratic legitimacy if the work is led by elected representatives with strong backing in the municipalities and not by a central administrative authority.

This development corresponds with the Swedish experience that a market economy is a sensitive organism that requires a firm, stable democratic system in order to thrive and achieve its potential. Local self-government creates a link between the central government and the civil society, which in Sweden has provided the basis for the effective building of democracy and the most strategic use of the society's resources. Consequently, a well-established local democracy has been a prerequisite for building a stable productive society.

The fundamental requirement is to find the compromise between market and democracy.

A process of learning has started

As we can see, the partnership models and regional growth programmes are well in line with the Swedish tradition of co-operation. Swedes possess a substantial degree of "participative skills". We prefer consensus of opinion.

And we realise that there is a need for a decentralised employment policy.

As was indicated above, Sweden has always developed a national employment policy. In a homogenous and well integrated labour market this has worked well, but in many cases it has ignored significant local and regional deviations and has contributed to increasing performance differences between regions.

With the effects of globalisation on national economies and the introduction of information based new technologies, the notion of a distinctly national economy is becoming even more problematic.

Several assumptions can be made. Perhaps, it is no longer true to say that a state needs *one* homogenous employment policy. Perhaps, it is just as rational to have a combination of different regional strategies. Perhaps, in the future, a national employment policy will have to be much more sophisticated and differentiated so as to be able to take account of significant regional and local variations.

There are, for example, localities and regions where employment is dominated by one single or a few large employers that are part of the national or international economy. When these key companies are closed down or relocated, dramatic difficulties often ensue for the local labour market which they leave.

To make labour market policy implementation more appropriate with regard to the local conditions and needs, to contribute to long-term employment outcomes, and to reconcile the objective of efficiency in labour market policy with those of social inclusion, regional development and the quality of life – this is the great challenge for the future.

The current experiments with Regional Growth Agreements and partnership models could be a much needed impulse to national rethinking in this field. Sweden still has to address the issue of the balance between regional and national labour market policies. Perhaps, like Norway, Sweden will have to give more autonomy to regional policy-makers.

Sweden is in a process of learning. The more we learn, the better we will be at achieving our goals. The work done by the OECD and by the Co-operative Action Programme on Local Economic and Employment Development gives us a better understanding of what we still have to learn with regard to implementing effective regional employment policies.

PART III

Chapter 25

Russia: Experimenting with Local Partnerships

by

Valery Popov
Head of the Federal Employment Service, Perm Region

A need for a cross-sector approach

The Perm region, situated in the west Ural Mountains, numbers about three million inhabitants, half of whom are active in the labour market. The history of the region has defined its employment structure and labour flows. Perm is a typical example of an industrial region where the problems brought about by rapid industrial restructuring are predominant in the labour market. During the last few years, the demand for skilled workers has increased in the industrial centres of the region, while the supply of skilled labour has remained insufficient. At the moment, this mismatch in the demand and supply of labour is the most predominant feature of the labour market in the Perm region.

A right diagnosis and understanding of the causes of the regional labour market mismatch was obviously essential for the right choice of policy measures. It is important to stress that the regional employment services (RES) already had the facilities and data to survey the regional labour market – since 1994 the collection of regional labour market information has been carried out on a regular basis by the RES. Together with experts of Tacis (an EU programme), the RES carried out an in-depth analysis of the regional labour supply and demand to identify the roots of the labour market mismatch. The survey showed that the sectoral structure of industries and their dynamics directly influence employment in different sectors and the flow of labour across sectors. It became clear that labour market problems could only be solved if all stakeholders were involved. Their co-operation was needed in order to remove the existing intersectoral barriers to labour flows.

Introducing new ways to tackle labour market problems

The transition to a market economy in Russia has stimulated various actors to seek new ways of satisfying their needs. Over the past two years in the framework of the Tacis programme, a project was developed to redesign both the regional and local labour market in the Perm region. In the beginning of the project the experts had identified three key factors that could help to alleviate the mismatch between labour supply and demand in the Perm region: *i)* co-ordination of the labour supply and the companies' needs; *ii)* skills upgrading; and *iii)* small business development for people with low employability.

To tackle the labour market imbalance, a local partnership organisation based on the tested European experience was needed. The Perm region together with Tacis experts developed a pilot project aiming to remove the existing labour supply and demand mismatch and to provide skilled labour for industry by retraining and raising qualifications. A small town – Krasnokamsk – has been selected as a "testing ground" for this project.

The town has 75 000 inhabitants and there are about 30 large and medium sized enterprises which are the key to the city's economy. They employ about 70% of the labour force and generate about 96% of the gross earnings of this area. There are also five agricultural enterprises. The economic transformations of the 1990s negatively affected the enterprises of the city that were oriented at the internal market. However, at the time of the start of the project there was a positive upturn in the economy due to the depreciation of the rouble and import substitution. Yet, growth in the industry boosted labour force turnover in the sectors with low wages, which depleted their socio-economic situation even further. The regional employment service calculated that unemployment was at 12.5%, slightly higher than the regional average.

Applying the partnership concept

The implementation of the partnership project required a lot of work to change the approaches of managers at all levels of the small community. Dozens of meetings have been held, the project has been supported by the mayor of the city as well as by key industrialists who saw a valuable seed in this project.

As a result, a non-commercial partnership, Perspektiva, was founded by the biggest industrial companies of Krasnokamsk, together with training institutions, city administration, the regional employment service and the Municipal Enterprise Support Fund. The partnership has the status of an independent legal entity. The executive body of the partnership consists of four full-time staff – a manager, a credit officer, an accountant and an expert in staff monitoring. Perspektiva is to a large extent a self-financing project – its budget consists of the contributions made by partners and to a lesser extent of funds provided by Tacis.

In the framework of Tacis, Perspektiva has benefited from training seminars and assistance from Irish partnership organisations, *e.g.* a short-term visit by an expert from the Galway city partnership introduced a new partnership methodology and provided a lot of energy and optimism to the project. The project was completed almost a year ago and, even though the experts of the EC have left, the project is due to renewed.

The budget for the following year is now financed entirely by the partners. The activities of Perspektiva focus on the following four areas:

1. Identifying the needs of enterprises in human resources in the region (not necessarily those of partners).

2. Improving the flexibility of education and training services according to labour market needs. Perspektiva seeks to rally partners' efforts in this field, involving higher training institutions, and financing their assistance through public and private funds.
3. Supporting small business development. The objective is to create an entire system of small business support in order to generate employment for disadvantaged groups such as women, war veterans, and the disabled. For this purpose a micro-loan fund has been created and is now financed by the partners. This new mechanism is very important: the community supervises how its money is spent.
4. Supporting local initiatives – a new focus for Perspektiva. In the EU countries this activity is widely spread and the Perspektiva partners believe that supporting local initiatives is very important in order to link up with people in the community and also to identify the most important issues of community groups, such as young people, lone parents, immigrants, disabled, etc. They also believe that this area opens good prospects for the future of the partnership.

Conclusions and perspectives

To summarise, this is a good example of federal institutions linking their efforts with grassroots initiatives. We believe that this pilot project has given a good insight as to how we can improve governance. The experience of Krasnokamsk has not shown any conflicting interests among the partners but perhaps problems would emerge in a different scenario. However, we hope that with a more active approach from our Labour Ministry and with the national employment policy, which envisages co-financing of active labour policies, to be financed mainly from regional budgets as well as from employers' funds, the Perspektiva project will be a rich source of experiences for the employment services throughout the country.

This is the first time in Russia where a federal organisation has devolved its responsibility for labour market policy to a grassroots organisation that was formed very much on a voluntary basis. Also, membership in such a voluntary organisation obviously encourages the local labour market actors to gradually take a more efficient and active approach to solving community problems. This was a useful exercise to pool financial resources and to learn how to use these funds efficiently because all of the partners were stakeholders.

It is planned to disseminate the experience of this project to other regions, and six regions have already shown interest. They have visited Krasnokamsk and joint seminars have been organised. It is hoped that throughout this year, the experience from the pilot project will be further disseminated and that other policy initiatives in the region will help to balance the supply and demand of labour.

ISBN 92-64-10470-4
Managing Decentralisation
A New Role for Labour Market Policy
© OECD 2003

PART III

Chapter 26

The Impact of Partnerships on Public Governance

by
Paul Cullen
Counsellor, Irish Representation to the European Union

The previous chapters have provided us with a rich tapestry that captures the wide range of activities promoted over the years by the LEED Programme of the OECD. The picture contains some very marked differences of pattern and colour that reflect how broadly similar approaches have been translated in different ways across countries, regions and localities.

This chapter picks out a number of the strands in this tapestry by focussing upon three particular aspects – primarily based upon my own experience of the development of the Irish experience of local partnerships – before proceeding to identify some important themes that warrant in my view continued attention by the LEED Programme.

Life cycle issues in partnership organisations

Stewart and other contributors have rightly suggested that it can be useful to consider local partnership experiments in terms of the life cycle of the organisational forms involved. Organisations normally go through phases of development which run the full gamut of experience from their founding, through youthful and mature stages with possibly, after some crisis or other, a welcome phase of rejuvenation.

Adopting this approach can be helpful in the context of some of the questions raised about the Irish experience. This is important because the origins of the Irish area-based partnerships stem from a particular set of circumstances encountered in Ireland in the early 1990s – elements of which bear some resemblance to current problems in Poland depicted by Boni (Chapter 8 in this volume).

Ireland's industrial and employment policy systems have been relatively centralised and hierarchical reflecting the absence in Ireland of regional government structures found in other European countries. The state-led economic development in Ireland since the mid 1960s has been implemented through strong national agencies. Decision-making, at regional and local level, tends to be concerned with delivery rather than policy. Policy formulation is concentrated almost exclusively at national level since local government in Ireland has exercised an unusually limited range of functions – with few statutory powers or tax raising competences to address poverty and unemployment. The weakness of local government was a factor prompting the establishment of the new local area Partnerships as independent legal entities. Local partnerships were seen as a way of renewing the culture of governance by making public organisations more dynamic and responsive to the needs of civil society.

The territorial base for the Irish area-based partnerships did not reflect established electoral or geographical units but were specifically targeted at pockets of cumulative disadvantage in urban and rural areas where long-term unemployment, poor educational performance and out-migration were particularly serious problems. The primary objective was to apply, in a labour market context, an approach that had been applied at national level, namely to have a problem solving approach, to mobilise the resources of those who had a potential contribution to make and to be flexible in devising remedies, including a willingness to experiment. The process of national concertation and its focus on solidarity with those disadvantaged sections of the community likely to miss out on the benefits of economic development, gave the Irish local employment initiatives a different character to earlier decentralisation moves in other more industrialised states. There was a consensus between the political leadership at national level of the day and the social partners at national level about the need to sidestep the inefficiency and the inadequacy of the traditional administrative structures.

There were both "push" and "pull" factors at work in the effort to engage with local communities as key drivers of change in the culture of governance. A key "push" factor was the fact that the Taoiseach's (Prime Minister's) Office was the promoter of the partnership approach at national level and was intent upon linking this process to strategic management reform within public administration. The experiments in local partnership were another means of encouraging alertness to stakeholder interests and customer service ideas and increasing managerial autonomy for middle level administrators.

There was a parallel "pull" factor also in the growing demand from community development bodies for a participatory approach to local development to counteract what was seen as the ineffective reach and responsiveness of powerful centralised agencies.

A conscious effort to make a break from the clientalist traditions of national political culture was part of the rationale for the Irish experiments. That evoked a predictable reaction. Local politicians resented the idea that strategies were being framed without their involvement. They were even more resentful of the fact that those strategies were resourced by the EU structural funds and that they did not have a role in the allocation of these resources. While there is still an on-going debate and a continuing tension between direct forms of participation and representative democracy, the local partnership experiments in Ireland have nonetheless contributed positively to renewal of the local government. Ironically this has been achieved through the proliferation of additional structures without, so far, a radical re-evaluation of the continuing effectiveness of the 38 area-based partnerships.

It seems natural in the context of developments in the US to discuss initiatives in terms of the experience of their founding, subsequent stabilisation and the factors that influence either their decline or a re-orientation of their mission. In contrast, there is an amazing tolerance in Ireland for the co-existence of a proliferation of potentially over-lapping initiatives. The political climate does not seem to be conducive to identifying either the conditions or the timescale within which such initiatives can be considered to have discharged their mission – whether through success or failure.

Changes in the funding allocation process over the course of their life cycle are another key factor influencing the development of the Irish partnerships. There have been very significant shifts in the strategies of the authorities providing funding and in the accountability routines they require. The Irish partnerships have passed through at least four different stages of development reflecting variations in the funding allocation process. First, when originally established, and at the stage when they were embarking upon preparation of strategic plans for their areas, the Irish partnerships received only limited funding from the exchequer to cover core administrative costs. Secondly, the Irish government successfully negotiated the provision by the EU of a Global Grant for Local Development to fund the implementation of these plans. This represented a new departure in supporting local development in Ireland and an interesting mechanism for effecting synergies across the separate silos represented by the European Regional Development Fund and the European Social Fund. Thirdly, the Global Grant was succeeded by a new operational programme – the Local Urban and Rural Development – which featured as one of nine such programmes under the EU-funded Community Support Framework for Ireland over the period 1994 to 1999. Finally, since 1999 the partnerships have reverted to their original funding arrangements and are no longer directly supported by the EU structural funds and rely instead on the national exchequer for their core funding.

The EU Employment Strategy and the local development dimension

Ireland's employment policies fit well with the European Employment Strategy framed in 1997 and generally known as the "Luxembourg Process", procedures dealing with employment issues which were laid down in the amended Treaty establishing the European Community. The "open method of co-operation" (OMOC) entails exchanging good practice, assessing national policy, setting targets and responding to Commission recommendations. In Ireland, the framework of social partnership agreements at national level has facilitated a smooth adaptation to the OMOC's process of annually generated national action plans: the process of scrutinising national policy against annual guidelines and the recommendations overseen by the Commission and the Council. The experience of the Irish authorities in adjusting to the monitoring and evaluation routines required by the European Commission as part of the management of the European social fund also helped to accustom them to the "peer review" discipline of the open method of co-ordination. OMOC involves *non-binding co-ordination* and is wholly compatible with the principle of subsidiarity – a point which has been made by Prats-Monné in his chapter. It does not undermine the competencies of the member states – rather it reflects the reality whereby labour markets will continue to be characterised by strongly national characteristics.

Dr. Rory O'Donnell, Director of Ireland's National Social Economic and Social Council, has argued convincingly that the deepening of European integration was a major factor in Ireland's economic transformation. The doubling and reform of the structural funds in the 1990s had a significant impact on the Irish economy. From 1989 to 2000 Ireland's annual receipts from the structural funds averaged about 2.6% of GNP. Dr O'Donnell has traced what he calls "*a European dimension to several of the innovative and experimental policy approaches adopted by Irish government and public agencies in the past decade*" and identifies "*the local development partnerships involving the social partners, the community and voluntary sector and state agencies*" as a relevant example. It is hardly surprising that he acknowledges that, whether at national or European level, "*the success of these new approaches to governance is, of course, far from complete*" (O'Donnell, 2002).

The European Commission's recent review of the European Employment Strategy (EES) also raises questions, which have also been pressed by the European Parliament, about how the "top-down" character of the EES process might be ameliorated through improving the involvement of national parliaments, the social partners, and civil society, as well as local and regional bodies. We will have to await the outcome of the Convention on the Future of Europe and the subsequent Inter-governmental Conference to see how these issues are resolved.

At a practical level, many of the countries which are poised to join the European Union in the current process of enlargement recognise the particularly valuable role of the OECD, not least because the OECD's own historic mode of engagement is a very real precursor of what we now term "the open method of co-ordination" within the EU. The OECD had pioneered this particular mode of extended, open conversation and peer review. Moreover, given the new status of the accession of member states as potential beneficiaries of the structural funds, I believe that administrators and politicians from those countries will soon find that the OECD offers a "safe place" in which potentially sensitive issues around governance and accountability can be explored.

The positive contribution of central co-ordination and technical assistance to partnership models at national level

It is as well to remember that partnership organisations remain small bodies. The duties associated with the management, co-ordination and secretariat of the board of directors have usually been carried out by a very small team. Staff, office rent, materials and equipment represent the core operation costs which have often been financed by grants received mainly from the exchequer or the EU for fixed-term periods. Their programme budgets are also relatively modest when compared to the overall level of public expenditure committed to related areas, i.e. labour market and social affairs. For instance, a recent OECD study revealed that the estimates for total partnerships expenditures on programmes and projects in both Austria and Ireland correspond to around 3% of labour market programmes (OECD, 2001).

The OECD Study on Local Partnerships highlighted the positive contribution to vertical as well as horizontal co-ordination of a central support unit offering technical assistance to local initiatives. This issue has been touched upon in a number of chapters in this book including those by Eberts (Chapter 19) and Straits (Chapter 4). We have seen examples located within government administrations, such as the National Labour Market Agency or the Tripartite Boards in Austria and the Association of Municipalities (as in Finland), or intermediary organisations such as Area Development Management Ltd (ADM) which was established in 1992 by the Irish government, in agreement with the European Commission, as an autonomous body responsible for helping to set up and co-ordinate the local partnership companies and to allocate and monitor their funding. In Ireland, ADM plays a crucial role in capturing the lessons of experience from the 38 area-based partnerships and filtering them through to government while also acting as a guarantor of accountability for the overall local development programme.

The formal co-ordination role discharged by ADM Ltd in Ireland has in turn been complemented in recent years by the establishment of a network of partnerships, known as PLANET, which serves as the representative voice of the 38 area-based partnerships in Ireland. A registered co-operative, PLANET was established in 1997 as an independent network, financed entirely by its members. It plays an important representative and advocacy or lobbying role as well as facilitating the exchange of information and good practice between the 38 partnerships.

Such entities enable the exchange of information between the central level and local level partnerships and assist in promoting the governance objectives of partnerships. They have also pioneered education and training initiatives for the participants in partnership efforts. Such support programmes are needed to boost the capacity to participate of organisations representing the main social inclusion target groups – as well as the managers, staff and partner representatives on partnership boards.

Lessons for the OECD and its LEED Programme

The LEED Programme is beginning to frame a new mandate and to devise the priorities which should determine its programme of activities for 2006 and beyond. The dichotomy between the alternative models of decentralisation aimed at securing collaboration between agencies and economic actors focused primarily on employability and economic development on the one hand, and the explicit focus, as in Ireland – in the case of the area-based partnerships at any rate – on multi-dimensional approaches at local level to tackling problems of unemployment and exclusion, is one issue that has surfaced in the debates of the Warsaw conference and the chapters of this publication. This is an interesting dichotomy and it is something that LEED might continue to look at in terms of this relationship between labour market policy and local governance.

The relationship between labour market policy and local governance is a theme which, in the light of the current debate, we might urge LEED to explore further. The OECD is well placed to view the relationship between labour market policy and local governance against an awareness of a wider whole government reform context, in which governance *per se* sits alongside policy making and public management as three interrelated aspects of a whole government reform package. The engagement of LEED with this theme fits well with the triangular paradigm which the General Secretary of the OECD, Donald Johnson, had identified as a framework within which a balance can be sought between economic growth, social cohesion and governance *per se*.

So while we may not have reached a stage at which sun-setting deadlines has yet been fixed for particular partnership experiments, it is equally clear that they have not yet begun to wither away! The participants in these experiments still struggle within separate policy frameworks, networks and service structures which undoubtedly detract from their ability to share methods and skills, to co-ordinate actions and to pursue objectives in partnership using common resources. It is hardly surprising that such successes as partnerships have recorded have been neither linear nor cumulative in character. At best, their continued existence is a case of constant and shifting negotiation. It would hence be fair to say that partnerships are still undergoing a fluid and open process of change.

Bibliography

O'DONNELL, Rory (2002), *Ireland in Europe – The Economic Dimension*, Institute of European Affairs.

OECD (2001), *Local Partnerships for Better Governance*, Paris.

OECD PUBLICATIONS, 2, rue André-Pascal, 75775 PARIS CEDEX 16
PRINTED IN FRANCE
(84 2003 04 1 P) ISBN 92-64-10470-4 – No. 53233 2003